P9-DTV-297

NOV

ŀ

Personality Disorders in Older Adults

Emerging Issues in Diagnosis and Treatment

The LEA Series in Personality and Clinical Psychology
Irving B. Weiner, Editor

Exner (Ed.) • Issues and Methods in Rorschach Research

Frederick/McNeal • Inner Strengths: Contemporary Psychotherapy and Hypnosis for Ego-Strengthening

Gacono/Meloy • The Rorschach Assessment of Aggressive and Psychopathic Personalities

Ganellen • Integrating the Rorschach and the MMPI-2 in Personality Assessment

Handler/Hilsenroth • Teaching and Learning Personality Assessment

Hy/Loevinger • Measuring Ego Development, Second Edition

Kelly • The Assessment of Object Relations Phenomena in Adolescents: TAT and Rorschach Measures

Kelly • The Psychological Assessment of Abused and Traumatized Children

Kohnstamm/Halverson/Mervielde/Havill (Eds.) • Parental Descriptions of Child Personality: Development Antecedents of the Big Five?

Loevinger (Ed.) • Technical Foundations for Measuring Ego Development: The Washington University Sentence Completion Test

McCallum/Piper (Eds.) • Psychological Mindedness: A Contemporary Understanding

Meloy/Acklin/Gacono/Murray/Peterson (Eds.) • Contemporary Rorschach Interpretation

Nolen-Hoeksema/Larson • Coping With Loss

Rosowsky/Abrams/Zweig • Personality Disorders in Older Adults: Emerging Issues in Diagnosis and Treatment

Sarason/Pierce/Sarason (Eds.) • Cognitive Interference: Theories, Methods, and Findings

Tedeschi/Park/Calhoun (Eds.) • Handbook of Psychological Treatment Protocols for Children and Adolescents

Weiner • Principles of Rorschach Interpretation

Wong/Fry (Eds.) • The Human Quest for Meaning: A Handbook of Psychological Research and Clinical Applications

Zillmer/Harrower/Ritzler/Archer (Eds.) • The Quest for the Nazi Personality: A Psychological Investigation of Nazi War Criminals

Personality Disorders in Older Adults

Emerging Issues in Diagnosis and Treatment

Edited by

Erlene Rosowsky, PsyD
Department of Psychiatry, Harvard Medical School

Robert C. Abrams, MD
Joan and Sanford I. Weill Medical College of Cornell University

Richard A. Zweig, PhD
Hillside Hospital—Long Island Jewish Medical Center

LAWRENCE ERLBAUM ASSOCIATES, PUBLISHERS
1999   Mahwah, New Jersey   London

Lawrence Erlbaum Associates, Inc., Publishers
10 Industrial Avenue
Mahwah, NJ 07430

Cover design by Lisa Rosowsky

Library of Congress Cataloging-in-Publication Data

Personality disorders in older adults: emerging issues in
    diagnosis and treatment / edited by Erlene Rosowsky,
    Robert C. Abrams, Richard A. Zweig.
    p. cm.—(LEA series in personality and clinical psychology)
Includes bibliographical references and index.
ISBN 0-8058-2683-1
1. Personality disorders in old age. I. Rosowsky, Erlene. II.
    Abrams, Robert C. III. Zweig, Richard A. IV. Series.
RC554.P483   1999
    618.97′68582—dc21   98-49371
                                                              CIP

Printed in the United States of America
10 9 8 7 6 5 4 3 2 1

Contents

Contributors   **ix**

Preface   **xi**

Foreword   **xv**
Larry Siever

I. Conceptual Background

1   Conceptual Overview of Personality Disorders   **3**
in the Elderly
John F. Clarkin, Lisa A. Spielman, and Ellen Klausner

2   Personality and Aging: A Psychotherapist Reflects Late in His   **17**
Own Life
Leston Havens

II. Research and Assessment: Overview and Outcome Measures

3   Personality Disorders in Adults: A Review   **31**
Richard A. Zweig and Jennifer Hillman

4   Personality Disorders After Age 50: A Meta-Analytic Review   **55**
of the Literature
Robert C. Abrams and Sandra V. Horowitz

5   Personality Disorders and Treatment Outcome   **69**
*Theodore J. Gradman, Larry W. Thompson, and Dolores
Gallagher-Thompson*

6 Dimensional Measures and the Five-Factor Model: Clinical 95
Implications and Research Directions
Paul R. Duberstein, Larry Seidlitz, Jeffrey M. Lyness, and
Yeates Conwell

7 Determining Personality Disorders in Older Adults Through 119
Self-Identification and Clinician Assessment
Linda M. Dougherty

8 Conceptual and Methodological Issues in the Assessment 135
of Personality Disorders in Older Adults
Daniel K. Mroczek, Stephen W. Hurt, and William H.
Berman

III. Clinical Issues: Diagnosis and Treatment

9 The Patient–Therapist Relationship and the Psychotherapy 153
of the Older Adult With Personality Disorder
Erlene Rosowsky

10 The Influence of Personality on Reactions of Older Adults 175
to Physical Illness
Milton Viederman

11 Neuropsychological Contributions to Differential Diagnosis 189
of Personality Disorder in Old Age
John H. Miner

12 Personality Disorders in Older Adults: Some Issues 205
in Psychodynamic Treatment
Wayne A. Myers

13 Cognitive-Behavioral Therapy, Personality Disorders, 215
and the Elderly: Clinical and Theoretical Considerations
Robert M. Goisman

14 Pharmacologic Treatment of Personality Disorders in Late Life 229
Marc Agronin

IV. Systems and Social Issues

15 Personality Disorders and the Difficult Nursing Home   **257**
Resident
Erlene Rosowsky and Michael A. Smyer

16 Ethical Issues in the Clinical Management of Older Adults   **275**
With Personality Disorder
Victor Molinari

Afterword: Personality Disorders in Late Life and Public   **289**
Policy: Implications of the Contextual, Cohort-Based,
Maturity, Specific Challenge Model
Bob G. Knight

Author Index   **295**

Subject Index   **309**

Contributors

Robert C. Abrams, MD
*Joan and Sanford I. Weill Medical
    College of Cornell University*

Marc Agronin, MD
*Miami Jewish Home and Hospital for
    the Aged
University of Miami School of
    Medicine*

William H. Berman, PhD
Fordham University

John F. Clarkin, PhD
*Joan and Sanford I. Weill Medical
    College of Cornell University*

Yeates Conwell, MD
*University of Rochester Medical
    Center*

Linda M. Dougherty, PhD
Piedmont Geriatric Hospital

Paul R. Duberstein, PhD
*University of Rochester Medical
    Center*

Dolores Gallagher-Thompson,
    PhD
*VA Medical Center / Stanford
    University*

Robert M. Goisman, MD
Harvard Medical School

Theodore J. Gradman, PhD
*VA Medical Center / Stanford
    University*

Leston Havens, MD
Harvard Medical School

Jennifer Hillman, PhD
Penn State Berks

Sandra V. Horowitz, PhD
*Columbia University Teachers'
    College*

Stephen W. Hurt, PhD
*Joan and Sanford I. Weill Medical
    College of Cornell University*

Ellen Klausner, PhD
*Joan and Sanford I. Weill Medical
    College of Cornell University*

Bob G. Knight, PhD
University of Southern California

Jeffrey M. Lyness, MD
*University of Rochester Medical
    Center*

John H. Miner, PsyD
Harvard Medical School

Victor Molinari, PhD
*Houston Veterans Affairs Medical
    Center*

Daniel K. Mroczek, PhD
Fordham University

Wayne A. Myers, MD
*Joan and Sanford I. Weill Medical
    College of Cornell University*

ix

Erlene Rosowsky, PsyD
Harvard Medical School

Larry Seidlitz, PhD
*University of Rochester Medical
    Center*

Larry Siever, MD
Mount Sinai School of Medicine

Michael A. Smyer, PhD
Boston College

Lisa A. Spielman, PhD
*Joan and Sanford I. Weill Medical
    College of Cornell University*

Larry W. Thompson, PhD
*VA Medical Center / Stanford
    University*

Milton Viederman, MD
*Joan and Sanford I. Weill Medical
    College of Cornell University*

Richard A. Zweig, PhD
*Hillside Hospital—Long Island Jewish
    Medical Center*

Preface

As geriatric mental health clinicians we know that certain of our older adult patients are difficult to treat. We know, too, that their being "difficult" is often a byproduct of their personality functioning—who they are as people—and not exclusively a result of the Axis I disorder or medical condition for which they originally sought treatment. The interpersonal difficulties, affective instability, distortions of the clinician–patient relationship, and unpredictable responses to clinical interventions for which personality disorder patients are notorious are all to be found in older adults as well as in younger patients.

Yet we have discovered that neither the behavioral science nor the clinical literatures offer much guidance to the clinician or researcher seeking to understand the phenomenon of personality disorders in the second half of life. The data base on personality disorders in older adults is remarkably thin, providing only preliminary empirical research and descriptive clinical or theoretical articles. At a time when notions of "successful aging" and of successfully treating behavioral disorders of the elderly have begun to capture the imagination of both the scientific community and the broader public, this scarcity of research regarding geriatric personality disorder seemed striking and disproportionate to its relevance for geriatric mental health clinicians.

The catalyst for this volume was a symposium entitled "Personality Disorders in the Elderly: Research Problems and Clinical Implications," presented at the annual meeting of the American Psychological Association in 1995, at which two of the editors (Erlene Rosowsky and Richard Zweig) were organizers and participants and the other editor (Robert Abrams) served as discussant. We brought differing scientific perspectives and clinical backgrounds to the effort, but we found that we shared a seemingly eccentric interest in an under-researched but exciting area of psychological inquiry. It was this discovery, and our surprise at the large attendance and high level of interest shown at the symposium, that inspired this effort to bring together such work as now exists into a single volume, in the hopes of inspiring more.

The book has been designed in four parts. The first presents a conceptual overview of personality disorders and the aging personality. The second is a review of the research on personality disorder in adulthood and late life. The third and fourth parts are focused on clinical applications—diagnosis and treatment in the third, and the care of personality-disordered elderly patients in the institutional setting or nursing home, in the fourth. The final section also addresses ethical concerns raised by this specific population as well as public policy implications.

A broad range of leading scientists and clinicians were asked to contribute, each being given the difficult assignment of integrating the disparate topics of personality disorders, gerontology or geriatric psychology/psychiatry, and their own area of expertise. Consequently we have come to appreciate each chapter, each essay, as comprising a "three-legged stool." Considering the paucity of data from which most contributors were compelled to begin, we anticipated that the chapters would essentially become provocative starting points from which dialog and further research might emerge. The increasing inclusion of personality as a variable worth considering in geriatric mental health research and practice will be the most valid indication of our success in this endeavor.

Indeed, this collection of reports and essays arrives at few conclusions and raises many questions. Do we need a new nosology for personality disorders in older adults? What is the best way to study the disordered personality in old age—clinical categories or dimensions emerging from factor analyses? What are the core considerations for clinical management of these patients, and the implications for established forms of psychotherapy? What is the effect of older personality disorder patients on individual health care settings or larger systems of care? These questions only serve to raise further questions. Yet it is our hope that by having compiled some of the best thinking and writing currently available to address these issues, we will have forged a helpful beginning.

ACKNOWLEDGMENTS

We want to thank those who have made this book possible. Over the years, our older adult patients have helped us come to know the unique phenomenology of personality in later life. Our mentors—including George Alexopoulos, Bennett Gurian, David Guttman, Gregory Hinrichsen, and Charles Peterson—inspired and encouraged us to attempt to chart unmapped areas of geriatrics and gerontology. Our colleagues, a number of whom have contributed to this volume, urged us on with their enthusiastic and creative thinking as part of this initiative. We appreciate the institutional support of the Department of Psychiatry, Harvard Medical School, the Joan and Sanford I. Weill Medical College of Cornell University, and the Hillside Hospital—Long Island Jewish Medical Center, our respective affiliations.

We acknowledge as well support from the National Institute of Mental Health (Dr. Abrams; Grants K07 MH01025-5 and P20-MH49762) and from a fund established in the New York Community Trust by DeWitt Wallace (Dr. Abrams).

Thank you to Susan Milmoe, senior consulting editor at LEA, and to Tracy Welch, who has tirelessly helped bring this project to light.

Our special thanks to our families and friends, whose support and patience make all challenges possible.

—Erlene Rosowsky
—Robert C. Abrams
—Richard A. Zweig

Foreword

Larry Siever, MD
Mount Sinai School of Medicine

In attempting to consider the interaction between aging and personality disorder, one inevitably confronts the major questions facing investigators and clinicians dealing with personality disorders. Are personality disorders constant over time? If they were entirely constant, then changes would not be anticipated with aging. The physical and psychological changes that accompany aging offer a naturalistic opportunity to evaluate how personality changes over time. With aging comes an increased likelihood of a variety of illnesses, including dementing illnesses like Alzheimer's disease. Many of these may be associated with discrete brain changes that may induce "organic" personality disorders. However, other more subtle changes may come in the absence of a specific disease process. Some neurotransmitters decrease their activity throughout the aging process so that, for example, activity of the catecholamines may be reduced in their functional effectiveness because of changes presynaptically and in the sensitivity of postsynaptic receptors. Other changes associated with aging include waning cognitive capacities, loss of sensory activity, and decreased body strength.

These changes may contribute to the changes in behavior that clinicians observe in the personality disorders. For example, Abrams and Horowitz (chap. 4) allude to the "muting" or dampening of impulsivity and dramatic internalization in borderline and other "dramatic cluster" personality disorders. Could this be related in part to the natural tuning down, or "down regulation," of receptors or decreased availability of neuromodulaters related to arousal or activation? Other personality disorders such as obsessive-compulsive personality disorder or anxiety-related personality disorder may worsen during the aging process. Could this worsening have to do with increasing need for structure and rules in the face of declining sensory and cognitive capacities? Could increased paranoid traits be related to decreasing sensory capacity and ambiguity of incoming information?

If personality and its disorders are viewed as a set of coping strategies, defenses, and behaviors designed to adapt to the surrounding environment, then the success or failure of a person's adaptation will depend both on changes in environmental circumstances and/or the capacity of his or her internal resources including the integrity of central nervous system function. Depending on these changes and this capacity, the personality may drift in and out of a realm of what might be considered normalcy. In this way, the personality changes that are observed with aging represent an opportunity to broadly understand change in personality. The editors have done a commendable job in assembling chapters that address this fascinating topic from a number of vantage points.

Clarkin, Spielman, and Klausner (chap. 1), in the context of their historical overview of personality disorders, raise a number of critical issues that are echoed throughout the other chapters. They emphasize the distinction between personality, character, or temperament. They highlight the issue of change in personality throughout the life cycle and how the changes of old age interact with personality. The critical question that is raised is whether, because of the changes of aging including declining cognitive and sensory capacities, the boundary for what is normal and what is abnormal may need to shift as the individual ages. They wonder what degree of inflexibility would be sufficient to be considered abnormal in this age range. A corollary, of course, is whether there is any discontinuity between personality and personality disorder. Another area of interest is the stability and onset of personality disorders in childhood and adolescence, the other end of the spectrum, which is not the focus of this book but raises equally important issues regarding stability of personality.

Havens (chap. 2) provides a more personal perspective on the issue of aging and personality disorders drawn from his experience as a psychotherapist. He writes of the importance of intention in people's relations to the world. Whereas the patients he writes about were relatively intact in their cognitive and sensory capacities, it is precisely that sense of intentionality that may be challenged for many older adults who have to cope with declining capacities that interfere with their effectiveness and the demoralization that accompanies these declines. Working with such patients poses a particular challenge for therapists who must refine their intentionality in the context of a "self" that may feel compromised and ineffective.

The next section of the book covers research and assessment, particularly in relation to outcome measures. Zweig and Hillman (chap. 3) comprehensively review assessment issues in personality disorder in adults, emphasizing the problems inherent in objectively characterizing personality disorder traits. They introduce the dimensional concept, one that reemerges again and again throughout this volume. They address the most commonly presented hypotheses regarding the overlap between Axis I and

Axis II disorders and review longitudinal studies of the course of personality disorders. Particularly useful is the summary of the measures of DSM personality disorders. Abrams and Horowitz (chap. 4) provide a review of the prevalence of personality disorders in the second half of life and conclude that the literature may in fact lead to an underestimation of the clinical importance of personality disorders in the aging. They also emphasize the usefulness of a dimensional approach. The dimensional approaches utilized in academic psychology are reviewed in detail by Duberstein and colleagues (chap. 6), and a number of other conceptual and methodologic issues are covered by Mroczek, Hurt, and Berman (chap. 8).

Rosowsky (chap. 9) presents actual case studies of patients who have been in psychotherapy treatment that help to illuminate the issues of transference and countertransference in older adults. Miner (chap. 11) makes a valuable contribution in dealing with neuropsychologic issues that become critical when they are compromised by a variety of dementing processes that often occur in elderly patients. Myers (chap. 12) provides case histories of patients that seem more amenable to dynamically oriented psychotherapeutic treatments in their elderly years than they might have been in their youth, perhaps because of the decreased intensity of temperamental drives and the muting effect of life experience. Goisman (chap. 13) provides a perspective on cognitive behavioral therapy in the elderly, an approach gaining increasing empirical support for severe personality disorder patients in the general population, but that has not been examined so specifically in elderly personality disorder patients. Agronin (chap. 14) tackled some of the dynamic issues that often play out in the context to pharmacologic treatment of these patients and provides some useful guidelines for clinicians in how to approach the elderly patient with a personality disorder that may require pharmacotherapy. Molinari (chap. 16) addresses some of the ethical issues in clinical management of adult patients, including how to deal with the "difficult" patients that strain available support systems and, through clinical vignettes, confronts the dilemmas raised in determining competence of particular patients regarding the use of scarce health resources.

Other chapters deal with the relationship between comorbid personality disorder and outcome of Axis I disorders (Gradman, Thompson, & Gallagher-Thompson, chap. 5); differences between older patients' and clinicians' identification and assessment of personality disorders (Dougherty, chap. 7); the relationship of personality factors to the hospital experiences of older adults with medical illness (Viederman, chap. 10); and the implications of personality disorders for adaptation to life in nursing homes (Rosowsky & Smyer, chap. 15). The volume closes with a commentary on personality disorders in late life and public policy (Knight, Afterword).

All the chapters raise thought-provoking questions and highlight the scarcity of empirical data, as well as the limitations of clinical literature dealing with elderly patients with personality disorders. The editors are to be commended for collecting a wide range of perspectives and reviews addressing this important neglected area.

PART I

Conceptual Background

Conceptual Overview of Personality Disorders in the Elderly

JOHN F. CLARKIN, PhD
LISA A. SPIELMAN, PhD
ELLEN KLAUSNER, PhD
Joan and Sanford I. Weill Medical College of Cornell University

Time is central to the concept of personality and personality disorders. Personality implies continuity of the individual across time such that each individual has a distinctive way of acting, thinking and feeling. It is what enables people to know friends, to count on them, and to predict what they will do (even though sometimes they are wrong). But life throws slings and arrows, and people are not totally consistent. This enables people to say that a person is "not himself (or herself) today." The issue of personality implies consistency, but there is always the issue of change within consistency.

Although stability is the hallmark of the individual, change is most likely to occur at certain points in the life span or the life trajectory of an individual. It is expected, for example, that adolescents will change as they leave the structured environment of high school and proceed to the less structured environment of college and work. Certainly changes in behavior and attitudes are anticipated when individuals marry and "settle down." And when considering aging and continuity and change in personality, it might be expected that some new balance between these two poles as an individual ages, retires from a lifetime of work, and the network of friends gets smaller or changes. This chapter considers both personality and personality disorders with a specific focus on how these constructs relate to older people.

EARLY CONCEPTUALIZATION OF PERSONALITY
AND PERSONALITY TRAITS

The origin of the word "personality" comes from the setting of the Greek and the Roman amphitheaters. Due to the size of the amphitheater the actors wore masks that acted as a small megaphone through which the actor's voice was amplified. This was the "persona," and personality therefore represents the individual characteristics of the character being portrayed (Stone, 1993). "Persona," the Latin word for mask, emphasizes the outward, or surface, aspects of the individual. In contemporary personality research and personality psychology, the term usually connotes the individual's crystallization of typical ways of relating to other people and dealing with the environment (Millon, 1981). Personality researchers have attempted to capture personality in a limited number of traits that are defined as typical or characteristic ways that the individual has of relating to the environment. There seems to be a general agreement about the definition of traits and the emphasis on the measurement of traits, but, in contrast, there is much disagreement about which particular traits are most salient in large samples of individuals.

In addition to the traits of personality psychology, there has also been a focus on *temperament* and *character*. Interestingly, the word "temperament" comes from the Latin word for weather, suggesting the variable moods or dispositions of the individual. Every student of psychology and philosophy knows about the Greek temperaments that supposedly arise from the four elements of earth, air, fire, and water representing, respectively, temperaments characterized by sadness (melancholic), irritability (choleric), cheerfulness (sanguine), or sluggishness (phlegmatic). "Character" comes from the ancient Greek word indicating engraving, or to dig in, and thus refers to the individual qualities that have been etched into individuals in their developmental years. Early psychoanalytic theoreticians used the term *character* almost synonymously with the term *personality*. Freudian developmental stages were associated with oral, anal, and genital character. Character type also referred to the particular defense mechanisms and constellation of these mechanisms in the individual.

PERSONALITY DISORDERS AS CONCEPTUALIZED
SINCE *DSM-III*

The creation of the "personality disorders" on Axis II in the *DSM–III* in 1980 was an initiative that has stimulated clinical and research attention to personality pathology as distinguished from symptomatic conditions (e.g., anxiety and depression). This initiative was preceded by an impressive history in psychology of describing and measuring personality traits and their consequences on quality of life, and an extensive history in clinical psychiatry on the diagnosis of abnormalities of personality. The field is now faced with the daunting task of integrating the best from these traditions, and deriving descriptions of the personality disorders that provide reliable assessment and construct validity.

DSM–IV (American Psychiatric Association, 1994) describes a personality disorder as having four key elements: It has a pattern of inner experience and behavior (i.e., cognition, affectivity, interpersonal functioning, and impulse control) that deviates markedly from the cultures' expectations, it develops in adolescence or early adulthood and remains stable across the adult life span, it is inflexible and pervades a broad range of personal and social situations, and it leads to significant distress or impairment in functioning. The *International Classification of Diseases* (ICD) system is even more explicit about operational criteria for diagnosing a personality disorder in a yes–no manner before proceeding to assigning a specific personality disorder.

As outlined in *DSM-IV*, the first decision of the clinician is whether or not the patient meets these criteria for a personality disorder, and the second order decision is the type of personality disorder manifested. The patterns and types of inner experience and behavior that define specific personality disorders are described in 10 disorders, which in turn are grouped by heuristic and content reasons into three clusters of personality disorders. Cluster A includes paranoid, schizoid, and schizotypal personality disorders. Cluster B is composed of the antisocial, borderline, histrionic, and narcissistic personality disorders. Cluster C includes avoidant, dependent, and obsessive-compulsive personality disorders.

Difficulties with the *DSM* Approach

The intersection of advancing age and personality disorders brings to light difficulties and issues hidden in the whole personality disorder concept as conceptualized in *DSM*. Consider the issue of personality disorders and time, including aging. The *DSM* makes clear that a personality disorder diagnosis cannot be made on an individual younger than age 18, because that individual has not had time to consolidate a personality/disorder. In addition, there is the specification in the criteria that they must be enduring behaviors/traits that demonstrate consistency across time. But, there is little concern in the discussion about the other end of the life course. It is noted that in late life a diagnosis of Personality Change Due to a General Medical Condition is appropriate when enduring changes in personality occur as a result of physiological effects of a medical condition, such as a brain tumor (APA, 1994, pp. 631–632).

Thus, a consideration of the nature of personality disorders in the elderly provides a wonderful opportunity to consider all of the issues thus far ignored by the Axis II committee. These issues are: How does adult personality disorder change/remain the same across the adult life span, including old age; how do cognitive changes that are common in old age affect personality/disorders; how does temperament, the biological component of personality and its disorders, change with age?

There is a strong, current conception that personality, and therefore personality disorders, remain stable in the adult years. There is research that substantiates the primacy of stability (Costa & McCrae, 1988). However, as is discussed in this chapter, the meaning of stability is heterogeneous, and the type of stability, and the nature of the measures of personality traits/disorders may lead to differing conclusions. Furthermore, empirical knowledge about how this complexity about change and stability intersects with advancing age in the human is quite meager indeed.

The 1980 creation of Axis II (i.e., the personality disorders) in *DSM–III* prompted a large group of empirical work on the personality disorders. It is argued here that whereas that initial burst of research activity has been quite informative, it is now time to access what has been accomplished and make adjustments so that the result is not simply more of the same. To date, much descriptive and phenomenological work at a cross-sectional level has been done. Relatively little of this work has been done with elderly populations. It is time to examine the theoretical conceptualization of personality disorders and to go beyond the nonvalidated checklists of *DSM–IV* Axis II. It is also time to utilize these theoretical conceptualizations in order to articulate longitudinal studies that could potentially explicate the mediating and moderating variables in the story of continuity and change in personality and personality disorders.

CURRENT RESEARCH DIRECTIONS IN THE FIELD
OF PERSONALITY DISORDERS

The picture of personality and personality disorders in the elderly should be viewed in the overall context of research development in the field as a whole. The issues of concern for scientific theories of personality disorder have been noted elsewhere (Lenzenweger & Clarkin, 1996); normal personality and personality disorder, the state-trait issue, study populations and the epidemiology of the personality disorders, longitudinal course and life-span issues, genetic and biological underpinnings, and the validity of the personality disorders.

Whereas information is not extensive, personality disorder researchers suggest a general population prevalence for personality pathology in the range of 10% to 15% (Weissman, 1993). For example, a recently completed case identification study in a college student population confirmed a prevalence figure of approximately 10% (Lenzenweger, Loranger, Korfine, & Neff, 1997). Clearly, personality pathology is ubiquitous, but the prevalence is less well-estimated for the elderly population.

Normal and Abnormal Personality

The boundary between normal personality and personality disorder can be conceived of as a dimensional change or as a somewhat abrupt, clearly differentiated categorical one (Widiger, 1992). A related debate is whether or not normal personality traits, when exaggerated, become personality disorder symptoms. To put the issue somewhat differently, research to date has not addressed the comparability between the *DSM–IV* personality disorder classification, and the empirically based dimensional structures that define personality (Costa & Mc-Crae, 1990).

Consistency Versus Change

A cardinal feature and basic assumption is that the personality disorders are enduring conditions that are traits rather than simply ephemeral states. The existing literature contains little longitudinal data, so this cardinal tenet is basically an assumption; the available empirical information consists of some data on the life course of antisocial personality disorder (Robins, 1966, 1978). Longitudinal studies do support the stability of normal personality traits in a number of age groups, including young adults (Finn, 1986) and even the elderly (Costa & Mc-Crae, 1988).

The issue of change within a context of consistency is complicated by the fact that there are numerous ways to measure personality (i.e., self-report, observer data, test behavior) and there are numerous statistical definitions of change itself (Caspi & Bem, 1990). These concepts are important in order to appreciate the current research opinion that consistency in personality is greater than the amount of change. It is only with these concepts that it can be realized that this general statement has important exceptions.

Absolute stability refers to the constancy in the amount of an attribute over time. The most relevant example of this in the elderly literature is the work by Costa and McCrae (McCrae & Costa, 1990). They found evidence for consistency in personality traits as measured by the NEO–Personality Inventory in aging individuals. They noted little change in the amount or degree of traits over time. *Differential stability,* on the other hand, refers to stability of an individual within a group over time. For example, if person A ranks as 5 out of 100 people in amount of altruism, consistency is present if they keep that relative ranking over time whether or not the amount of altruism goes up and down over time in the group as a whole. *Structural stability* refers to the consistency of correlational patterns among traits across time. Thus, researchers may show that the factor structure of traits within a group of people remains the same across time. *Ipsative stability* refers to the continuity of the individual across time. The researcher can examine each individual for continuity or change across time and then group individuals who have the same or similar patterns. Block (1971) found five male and six female types or typologies longitudinally.

In addition to describing the phenomena of continuity and change, scientists are interested in the factors that mediate and moderate continuity and change. Age, individual differences, developmental stages may all be mediators of continuity and change for the individual. Moderating variables—that is, variables that influence the change in time—could include genetic factors, environment factors, and person–environment interactions. This chapter emphasizes only several of the myriad of mediating and moderating variables of change on the personality and personality disorders in the elderly.

Biological Foundations

A promising area of research is the exploration of the genetic and biological underpinnings of personality and personality pathology. Genetic factors play an influential role in determining personality (Plomin et al., 1990). In contrast, research documenting the relation of genetic factors to personality disorders is more sparse. Another area of current speculation and research is the role of central nervous system neurotransmitters and personality traits and pathology. This material is reviewed later in reference to temperament and its potential change in the aging individual.

Validity

And finally, the issue of the validity of the personality disorders as currently defined in *DSM–IV* must be emphasized. Whereas the field is progressing in the reliable assessment of the personality disorders as defined on Axis II, this in no way guarantees the validity of these disorders as defined. There is, in fact, no clear benchmark or gold standard for validity in the personality disorder realm. Spitzer (1983) proposed a so-called LEAD standard (longitudinal data expert raters and the use of all available diagnostic information) in which the longitudinal study of personality disorders using expert raters could establish the validity of these conditions. Such a study does not exist at the present time in adults, let alone extend to the years of aging.

RESEARCH IN AGING AND PERSONALITY

The first issue of relevance to those interested in the elderly is the phenomenological, cross-sectional description of elderly who would be considered by clinicians to suffer from a personality disorder. Because the criteria for the presence of personality disorder were articulated without the elderly in mind, they must be examined for application to this age population. As noted earlier, *DSM–IV* (APA, 1994) described a personality disorder as a pattern of inner experience and behavior that deviates markedly from the cultures' expectations, which develops in adolescence or early adulthood and remains stable across the adult life span. This pattern is inflexible and pervades a broad range of personal and social situations, and leads to significant distress or impairment in functioning.

This loose definition of the boundary between normal and abnormal personality raises issues as applied to the elderly. Notice the assumption that what has jelled by the end of adolescence remains stable across the entire adult life span. What are the cultural expectations about the personality of the elderly? Aging brings with it a certain amount of inflexibility, especially when the individual is hampered by medical illness or cognitive changes. What degree of inflexibility would be "inflexible" in this age range?

A major issue in the field concerns the nature of the border between personality and personality disorders. Some argue for the continuity between personality and personality disorders, others argue for a clear boundary between the two based on various notions of the difference. This is yet again another debate in the personality area that does not directly consider the elderly. It may be that the border between normal and abnormal personality is different, or should be defined differently at various points in the life span.

A second issue is, given the presence of a personality disorder in the elderly, what particular kind of personality disorder(s) does the individual have? The current criteria are based on data from young adult samples and may not relate to the way that geriatric patients express the symptoms related to personality disorders. Further, the taxonomy established by the *DSM* may not be as relevant for geriatric patients as for young adults. Symptoms may cluster together in different constellations as people age, and may be more or less predominant at different stages of life. Therefore, does the taxonomy of the current 10 personality disorders in *DSM–IV* map onto the types of personality disordered behavior that is observed in the elderly? There are reasons to think not. For one thing, many of the criteria in Axis II are behaviors (e.g., impulsive behaviors) that tend to dampen with age. The individual may no longer have those behaviors, and so would not meet the behavioral criteria for the disorder. Consider borderline personality disorder (BPD). The elderly individual may have had a history of impulsive behavior and suicidal behavior, but at this later age may only show the cognitive stigmata of BPD (i.e., identity diffusion). Thus, the individual would no longer meet the criteria for BPD. In contrast to the behavioral criteria, some of the cognitive criteria may become more prominent in the elderly. For example, some elderly become more obsessive and cautious. Another reason to doubt the applicability of the Axis II criteria to the elderly is the frequency of "not otherwise specified" (NOS) diagnoses in this population. This suggests that the disorder is present, but the typology is not rich enough to capture the individuals. For these reasons, there is enough concern to lead to research on the particular taxonomy of personality disorders with criteria that are more representative of elderly individuals.

There is a lack of epidemiological studies on personality disorders in older adults. The rates of illness cited in the literature, which average around 20%, are based solely on clinical samples. Most researchers agree that these rates are higher than what would be found in the general population, but, as yet, there are few educated guesses about what that rate would be.

Abrams and Horowitz (1996), in a study of personality disorders in elderly patients with comorbid Major Depression, found a rate of 18%. By far the most populous classification for patients with personality disorder diagnoses was NOS (36%), with the next highest category being Dependent (12%). This underscores the possibility that the taxonomy developed for *DSM* based on younger adults may not be the most accurate reflection of how personality disorders are expressed in geriatric patients.

Issues of Temperament

Another issue concerning the elderly and personality/personality disorders is the role of contributing variables to personality such as temperament and cognition. Personality researchers have appropriately emphasized the role of temperament in personality. Buss and Plomin (1975, 1984) suggested three fundamental temperaments: activity, emotionality, and sociability. Activity indicates the total energy output of the individual (i.e., busy, fast-moving vs. passive or lethargic). *Emotionality* refers to both the repetition and extent of emotional arousal. *Sociability* indicates the extent to which the individual craves the presence of others ranging from very gregarious individuals to those who are detached and loners.

Siever and colleagues (Siever & Davis, 1991; Siever, Klar, & Coccaro, 1985) articulated a dimensional model of temperament that involves four major areas: cognitive/perceptual organization, impulsivity/aggression, affective instability, and anxiety/inhibition. These dimensions are utilized to help understand various Axis I and Axis II disorders. Schizophrenia and schizotypal personality disorder, for example, are seen as disturbances in the cognitive/perceptual organization. The dimension of impulsivity/aggression would be manifested in explosive disorders, pathological gambling, and antisocial and borderline personality disorders. Siever and colleagues made speculations about these dimensions and their relation to biological systems.

Cloninger and colleagues (Cloninger, Svrakic, & Przybeck, 1993) hypothesized the presence of heritable dimensions of novelty seeking, harm avoidance, and reward dependence, each associated with neurobiological systems. *Novelty seeking* is the disposition toward the active seeking of novel stimuli and excitement. *Harm avoidance* is a disposition to avoid aversive stimuli, the avoidance of any form of punishment or novelty. *Reward dependence* is a proclivity to seek social approval.

Probably the most developed and sophisticated theoretical articulation of biological systems and personality is that by Depue (1996). Depue outlined an underlying neurobiological system to understand three personality superfactors of positive emotionality, constraint, and negative emotionality. For example, Depue argued that the behavioral facilitation system (BFS) is a central component in positive emotionality, which involves incentive reward motivation, forward locomotion that supports goal acquisition, and cognitive processes related to active goal seeking. It is hypothesized that the four processes are mediated by two major ascending dopamine projection systems. Constraint relates to a core construct of affective and cognitive impulsivity and this system is hypothesized to be derived from the functional activity in central nervous system serotonin projections. Finally, negative emotionality highly related to Eysenck's trait of neuroticism is composed of traits that evoke a subjective experience of negative emotions such as anger, hostility, depression, anxiety, alienation, and proclivity to distress in response to life circumstances. Suggestions about underlying neurobiology of this negative emotionality are quite premature, but the locus ceruleus may modulate this affective system. Given the biological changes with aging, it is quite plausible that changes in temperament can lead to changes in the personality with age.

In each of these somewhat speculative but creative conceptualizations, it is quite plausible that with aging at least some of the temperamental substrates change enough to produce noticeable changes in behavior related to personality and the personality disorders. Activity, impulsivity/aggression, and novelty seeking are likely areas of temperamental change.

Cognitive Changes

A second variable that contributes to personality is cognition, and it too may change with age, manifesting concomitant changes in personality and personality disorders. Dementia and changes in personality and emotional expression is the extreme case of changes in cognition with aging and concomitant changes in personality traits and personality disorders. For example Lebert, Pasquier, and Petit (1995) examined the relation between affective change in frontal lobe dementia (FLD) and premorbid personality traits. Outpatients seen in a memory disorders unit were assessed with biological tests, and all fulfilled the *DSM–III–R* criteria for primary degenerative dementia. Moods assessed by patient interview and questionnaire included elation, flat affect, and emotionalism. Premorbid personality traits were assessed by a caregiver questionnaire assessing four personality traits clusters: paranoia, conscientiousness, obsession-compulsion, and extraversion. There was no correlation between premorbid personality traits with the affective state in FLD. Lebert et al. concluded that the affective states of elation, flat affect, and emotionalism were unrelated to the premorbid personality traits reported by the caregiver or relative. They assumed, therefore, that mood change in FLD is organically based. It is noted that personality change in the patient is cited by the families of these demented elderly as the most troubling aspect of the disease.

It is more difficult and challenging to study less extreme and more subtle changes in cognition and the way these might impact on personality. It is known that over the life span, impulsive aspects of the personality disorders, such as antisocial personality disorder, decrease, whereas dependent and obsessive-compulsive increase (Loranger, 1996). It could be speculated that doubts about people's cognitive abilities may lead to more dependency and more obsessive attempts at control.

Changes in Bodily Integrity

Aging brings with it both the issue of facing the finiteness of life and bodily changes, some of which are debilitating and eventually life threatening. How individuals, with their idiosyncratic crystallization of personality and personality disorders, cope with these changes is crucial for optimal adjustment in old age. The individual must cope with changes in physical appearance, changes in motor agility and speed, changes in cognitive speed, and various degrees of disability directly related to physical decline and illness. Is this process conceptualized as individuals with their personality coping with these changes, or do the changes bring about traitlike changes in the personality?

The term *disability* can refer to what the person can do (i.e., functional capacity) or to what a person actually does (i.e., behavioral disability). It is interesting and most relevant to the issue of personality that the correspondence between physical capacity and actual functioning is incomplete (Guralnik, Seeman, & Gill, 1994; Judge, Schechtman, Cress, & FICSIT Group, 1996). The temporal and causal relations between disability in the elderly, depressive symptoms, and comorbid conditions are not well-understood (Gurland, 1991).

The issues of change and stability in personality and personality disorders with aging is not just one of academic interest. There are serious practical family and clinical aspects to this issue. For example, irritability and hopelessness, more related to personality and to depression as a clinical syndrome, may be more important in the long-term adjustment of the elderly individual than just the resolution of acute depression itself. These and similar traits may shape the life satisfaction of both the elderly individual and the people in the environment. Social support, found to be so important to the life satisfaction and health of the elderly, may be heavily influenced for good or ill by such personality traits and their trajectory of change.

CONCLUSIONS

Despite major advances in the personality disorders since the field agreed on criteria for their diagnosis with the subsequent empirical research, there are major problems and potential areas of development in this area. Some of these difficulties are general and beyond the realm of geriatric psychiatry, and others are highlighted by the consideration of aging and personality/personality disorders. A general issue is the empirical research without a general theoretical conceptualization to guide data collection and interpretation (Lenzenweger & Clarkin, 1996). A related issue is the general reliance on the *DSM* criteria, which are arbitrary and lacking in empirical validity, to guide the assessment process. Geriatric psychiatry would do well to avoid this limited approach that is prominent in adult psychiatry today. A third issue is the relevance of personality traits that relate to temperamental and biological mechanisms that can be articulated and examined. This approach should be encouraged in geriatric psychiatry. It is predicted that this dimensional approach will bear more fruit than a categorical approach based on an arbitrary diagnostic system on Axis II. What consistency is there if the realm of interpersonal behavior after the organism has developed beyond puberty? There is little information concerning what happens to this consistency as changes occur in old age related to memory and executive functions, temperamental variables, and dramatically changing life roles. As long as there is an almost exclusive emphasis on stability of personality disorders and traits, and ignorance of change and the mechanisms of change, the elderly and personality will be ignored.

The concept of personality disorder indicates a long-standing pattern of cognition, affectivity, and interpersonal functioning that is inflexible and leads to significant distress. The specific traits that describe the variety of ways this personality dysfunction can be manifested are currently captured in the 10 personality disorders of *DSM–IV*. Controversy remains over the differentiation, construct validity, and stability of these 10 disorders as currently conceptualized (Livesley, 1991). There is evidence that the personality disorders are a significant clinical issue with a prevalence rate of approximately 11% in nonclinical populations, and a higher prevalence of certain disorders in clinical populations. Most of the existing information is cross-sectional, and longitudinal studies are needed to describe both the long-term stability of these disorders and the mechanism of their impact on psychosocial adjustment and symptom disorders. Treatment approaches have been articulated for the personality disorders themselves, but this effort is in its infancy, and little has been done with the elderly. It has become clear in nonelderly adult samples that the treatment of Axis I conditions in the presence of personality disorders is slower and less beneficial than treatment for those without personality disorders.

REFERENCES

Abrams, R. C., & Horowitz, S. V. (1996). Personality disorders after age 50: A meta-analysis. *Journal of Personality Disorders, 10,* 271–281.

American Psychiatric Association. (1994). *Diagnostic and statistical manual of mental disorders* (4th ed.). Washington, DC: Author.

Block, J. (1971). *Lives through time*. Berkeley, CA: Bancroft Books.

Buss, A. J., & Plomin, R. (1975). *A temperament theory of personality development*. New York: Wiley.

Buss, A. J., & Plomin, R. (1984). *Temperament: Early developing personality traits*. Hillsdale, NJ: Lawrence Erlbaum Associates.

Caspi, A., & Bem, D. J. (1990). Personality continuity and change across the life course. In L. A. Pervin (Ed.), *Handbook of personality: Theory and research* (pp. 549–575). New York: Guilford.

Cloninger, C., Svrakic, D., & Przybeck, T. (1993). A psychobiological model of temperament and character. *Archives of General Psychiatry, 50*, 975–990.

Costa, P., & McCrae, R. (1988). Personality in adulthood: A 6-year longitudinal study of self-reports and spouse ratings on the NEO personality inventory. *Journal of Personality and Social Psychology, 54*, 853–863.

Costa P., & McCrae, R. (1990). Personality disorder and the five-factor model of personality. *Journal of Personality Disorders, 4*, 362–371.

Depue, R. A. (1996). A neurobiological framework for the structure of personality and emotion: Implications for personality disorder. In J. F. Clarkin & M. F. Lenzenweger (Eds.), *Major theories of personality disorder* (pp. 347–390). New York: Guilford.

Finn, S. (1986). Stability of personality self-ratings over 30 years: Evidence for an age/cohort interaction. *Journal of Personality and Social Psychology, 50*, 813–818.

Guralnik, J., Seeman, T., & Gill, T. (1994, January 19–20). *Physical performance and functional disability: Data from the EPESE, MacArthur and Safety studies*. Paper presented at NIA Workshop on "Physical Functional Independence in Older Persons," Washington, DC.

Gurland, B. J. (1991). The range of quality of life: Relevance to the treatment of depression in elderly patients. In L. S. Schneider (Ed.), *Diagnosis and treatment of depression in late life* (pp. 61–80). Washington, DC: American Psychiatric Press.

Judge, J. O., Schechtman, K., Cress, E., & FICSIT Group. (1996). The relationship between physical performance measures and independence in instrumental activities of daily living. *Journal of the American Geriatric Society, 44*, 1332–1341.

Lebert, F., Pasquier, F., & Petit, H. (1995). Personality traits and frontal lobe dementia. *International Journal of Geriatric Psychiatry, 10*, 1047–1049.

Lenzenweger, M. F., & Clarkin, J. F. (1996). The personality disorders: History, classification, and research issues. In J. F. Clarkin & M. F. Lenzenweger (Eds.), *Major theories of personality disorder* (pp. 1–35). New York: Guilford.

Lenzenweger, M. F., Loranger, A. W., Korfine, L., & Neff, C. (1997). Detecting personality disorders in a nonclinical population: Application for a two-stage procedure for case identification. *Archives of General Psychiatry, 54*, 345–351.

Livesley, W. J. (1991). Classifying personality disorders: Ideal types, prototypes, or dimensions? *Journal of Personality Disorders, 5*, 52–59.

Loranger, A. W. (1996). Dependent personality disorder. *Journal of Nervous and Mental Disorders, 184*(1), 17–21.

McCrae, R. R., & Costa, P. T., Jr. (1990). *Personality in adulthood*. New York: Guilford.

Millon, T. (1981). *Disorders of personality: DSM–III, Axis II*. New York: Wiley-Interscience.

Plomin, R., Chipuer, H., & Loehlin, J. (1990). Behavioral genetics and personality. In L. Pervin (Ed.), *Handbook of personality: Theory and research* (pp. 225–243). New York: Guilford.

Robins, L. (1966). *Deviant children grown up*. Baltimore: Williams & Wilkins.

Robins, L. (1978). Sturdy childhood predictors of adult antisocial behaviors: Replications from longitudinal studies. *Psychological Medicine, 8*, 611–622.

Siever, L. J., & Davis, K. L. (1991). A psychobiological perspective on the personality disorders. *American Journal of Psychiatry, 148*, 1647–1658.

Siever, L. J., Klar, H., & Coccaro, E. (1985). Biological response styles: Clinic implications. In L. J. Siever & H. Klar (Eds.), *Psychobiological substrates personality* (pp. 38–66). Washington, DC: American Psychiatric Press.

Spitzer, R. (1983). Psychiatric diagnosis: Are clinicians still necessary? *Comprehensive Psychiatry, 24,* 399–411.

Stone, M. H. (1993). *Abnormalities of personality: Within and beyond the realm of treatment.* New York: Norton.

Weissman, M. (1993). The epidemiology of personality disorders: A 1990 update. *Journal of Personality Disorders, 7*(Suppl. Spring), 44–62.

Widiger, T. (1992). Categorical versus dimensional classification. *Journal of Personality Disorders, 6,* 287–300.

CHAPTER 2

Personality and Aging: A Psychotherapist Reflects Late in His Own Life

Leston Havens, MD
Harvard Medical School

Today the term *personality disorders* seems a blur of ideas—symptom pictures, various self-concepts, ego or defense patterns, temperamental factors, and the "host," that is, the ground of disease rather than the disease itself.

Symptom pictures dominate contemporary diagnosis, although two centuries' experience shows that they have a shifting, often transitory life. Self-concepts gained prestige, in part from Winnicott's (1965) true self, false self, and false personality distinctions and Kohut's (1977) revision of psychoanalysis. Defense pattern analysis continues, its hierarchy of defenses being one of the few approaches to a normative psychology. The scientific study of temperament, although only beginning, gains from the new genetic technology. Separation of host from disease factors has been more difficult for psychological than for physical medicine. Psychological work remains in the position of mid-19th century physical medicine. Then medicine awaited the appearance of routine tests of normal function such as reflex and pinprick procedures, which separated health from sickness, with doctors speaking adjectivally, that is, calling patients febrile and chlorotic—much as patients are still termed bipolar or phobic—as if that is all they were. A meaningful grasp of the normal was gained for physical medicine but has yet to appear psychologically, with its capacity to set limits on the pathological.

The study of older people does not resolve the blur of personality disorders, but it shifts perspective in at least two important ways. It changes the relation between patient and helper and it throws into relief certain aspects of normal functioning. This chapter describes the ways that professional relationships tend to be changed, toward a more informal, less hierarchical relationship and toward one more tentative, hypothetical, even bewildered, as the number of possible impinging factors increases. The study of older people also directs attention to aspects of normal functioning. Most of this chapter is devoted to four: reflectiveness, the relation between willing and depending, the relation between connecting and disconnecting, and the final project of dying well. As is true of much psychological writing, I will be writing at least a little about myself, especially myself as an older person.

I believe the consideration of old age has a leveling effect. Because old age brings forward reflections on death, both patient and helper confront that ineluctable fact of the great universal. Death is discussed at the end of these remarks, but note its effect on helper and patient. Both must be awed, both are partly helpless, and both face perhaps the principal phenomenon each confronts. The two are united and humbled by their equal helplessness.

And at last the older person, as patient, gains an advantage, being closer to death. Professional superiority, which like patriotism is often the last refuge of scoundrels, falls away. It is a wonderful gain for psychotherapy. The two parties come together, each hoping to learn from the other: the old hope to regain the lust for life of the young, and the young hope to gain the wisdom of many old people. Then it is easier to learn about each other. Younger people, when not too much envied, are incentives for the old to be revived and to remember. The young may watch with a mixture of fear and admiration the ability of many old people to get so close to death and be still alive. I have seen again and again a revival of liveliness in the old and a deepening grasp of life in the young. Little serves the grasping of life—which is surely a central goal of psychotherapy—so well as this intermixing of deep feelings and mutual admiration. We touch each other and are enlarged. I believe the central challenge of psychotherapeutic work is to be both as professional *and* as human as we can be. Treatment of the old makes that easier.

Treatment of the old offers another opportunity. The old are often at least a little infirm, so biological factors intrude. The old also offer knowledge, although it may at first seem hidden, of what their unconscious mind has over time delivered to their consciousness; they have met partly hidden motives and memories too often not to make them part of themselves. And they have seen a great deal of the various contexts of life, so the interpersonal is no distant idea. These three phenomena—biological, unconscious, and contextual—represent a pluralization of the work. With the old we cannot afford to be simple-minded Freudians or interpersonalists, or narrow biologists of the mind. Psychiatry's and clinical psychology's Tower of Babel has to find a common voice.

What does it mean to find a common voice? I would not have it be a busy voice crowded with ideas pressing toward conclusions. The difficult task of education is to make the rich heritage of our ideas familiar to students so that they become second nature, that is, so familiar they recede into the background of their minds, operating automatically, with the result that therapists do not reach nervously for this idea or that. The complexity of the work is such that we cannot depend on a conscious, ratiocinative process to provide answers to the problems one life presents to another. Free minds, offering their own unique solutions, are required to meet the unique individualities before us, minds that are the products of a full, careful training, time, and gradually secured confidence. Such was the goal of my *Approaches to the Mind,* my own education (1973). A broad training also preserves the dignity of our tradition, preparing therapists for patients.

Both the leveling of the professional field and the opening of informed minds to the receipt of encounters with older patients offer another challenge, sometimes with singular clarity, to the work: How can what is strong and productive be located and supported? Dealing with crises, searching for pathology, therapists often let the good news slip by. I do not mean what existential workers too often suggest, that everything pathological be dismissed by a sentimental, overly normalizing critique of human problems. I mean an alertness to what is effective in the other. Even in those who have lived long and perhaps learned much, effective function may not be easy to identify and celebrate. Here are four challenges.

REFLECTIVENESS

This human capacity may well be the most distinctive one we have, the capacity to double back on ourselves, and to throw up memories and symbolic forms for perusal and reflection. There is a famous account, from T. S. Eliot's old age (1943):

> And last, the rending pain of re-enactment
> Of all that you have done, and been; the shame
> Of motives late revealed, and the awareness
> Of things ill done and done to others' harm
> Which once you took for exercise of virtue,
> Then fools' approval stings, and honour stains.

The old are often described as having lost not only new, living futures, but recent memory as well, as they are consumed by rememberings and regrets. The sturdiest temperament, the luckiest life, cannot be without second thoughts. Hence the pertinence of Eliot's words.

A 70-year-old man insisted he would rather have died than think hard about his past mistakes, an insistence that kept him from seeking professional help for 15 years. Then a daughter told him he was a good man and should not suffer more. He told her some of his mistakes. She said that everyone makes mistakes. Did he think he was so different? His may not have been the worst mistakes. She spoke in an offhand way that made his self-pity feel trivial.

I said something about the insouciance of youth. He had just arrived in my office, so I did not presume his self-concern had been much allayed. Also, I was his age, shared some of his concerns, and sensed how hard it might be to speak. First, I thought, I must honor his reflectiveness—that painful capacity to remember, think about, and often judge his past—before we exposed the contents of that reflectiveness. When we were comfortable with one another, when we had exchanged the badges of experience and courage, then we could make such an exposure a perspective giving, even an acceptance giving, and a renewal.

It is a rare individual who has lived 70 years without giving some evidence of courage and endurance. It was easy to spot those he kept behind his modesty; the reflectiveness itself disclosed them. The very ability to keep touch with one's behavior, to feel the pain it may have caused others, to regret and wish to correct, means the easiest ways out—the denial or distortion of the past—have been avoided. These are no small evidences of courage. Klein (1960) was perhaps the first to note the "depressive position" in development, the move away from megalomania and denial, toward a sense of responsibility, however much that responsibility may be exaggerated. It is a beginning of the social compact, the willingness to remain part of what has happened. And the sense of responsibility is also a virtue as the beginning of self-knowledge: As individuals live with their regrets, they may gain knowledge of what in fact they have contributed to events, what they may need to watch in themselves, lest the same parts of themselves once again damage what they love.

My patient proved only too eager to expose the "mistakes" he had made. He described an "arrogant ambition" that made his family responsibilities a poor second to the attention he gave career and money. He had told himself he needed money to support the large family. He had wanted to distinguish himself so that he would have not only money but a fatherhood of which everyone could be proud. His wife was also ambitious for him; she knew little of her own abilities, with a result common in those days, that her enabling function served him better than it did herself. There was no strong voice calling him back to the urgencies of family and children. He went blithely on. He could remember angry moments when the others' needs fell away before his anxious seeking. All this he recounted straightforwardly. It was only much later, when the wife left him and the children suffered the split, that he awoke to what he had done. He felt he could never forgive himself.

I could share his regrets because I had experienced some of that too. I also winced when he called himself a narcissistic character, which was at least partly right. I suspected he did not need as much help as I had found, just because he already regretted and had begun both his reparations and a more sensible new life. What I thought he wanted and deserved was an ear to hear and another's heart to bespeak his pain and hopes. The pain he had already begun to address, the hope I approached indirectly, through admiration for his reflectiveness and the implicit belief I had in his resources of character. Too often reflectiveness is itself reflected on solely in terms of its self-abnegating content, with resulting shame and further self-blame. The reflectiveness is not then admired for itself, for what it says of thoughtfulness and courage. The latter were easy to hear with this man who had already used his reflectiveness to initiate reparations and the new life.

I also did not want him to forgive himself. We all need to keep our characteristic mistakes in mind as we can be sure there will be fresh opportunities to demonstrate them again. At the same time, there is little value in trashing ourselves forever, if only so as not to alienate what friends we have. The space between is smaller than people hope. To keep alive to who we really are is a cold shower for the much vaunted optimisms and complacencies of popular character. In my experience, the wisest and most enviable often seem a bit wary, as if they were watching carefully both the world and themselves. So much for easy judgments of the healthy personality.

I could remind him he had been young once and that the young need some measure of arrogance and incaution if they are to venture out into the world on their own, propelled by the intoxicating thrust of youth. And no one gets it right. Everyone errs at least a little between the great dilemmas of "how to be," that is, trying to decide between being bold or careful, optimistic or pessimistic, caring most for self or others, society or solitude (Gustafson, 1995). Or consider therapists' dilemmas of whether to be empathic or skeptical, warm or objective, feeling or thinking, and so on. The possibilities of error and rigidity in any particular situation are endless. Probably the most people can do is to note their inclinations and try to lean against them now and then. He had been bold and self-concerned, but not so much as many others. Is there any path but "live and learn"? Certainly the teaching books do not agree.

I went on like this to his evident relief. He did not need me to pound home any moral lessons; he had been doing that by himself for many years. He needed to get on with his life. No doubt there would be less blind ambition, more wariness without any guidance from me.

I am suggesting reflectiveness is a sign of health, not to be dismissed by diagnostic nomenclatures of affective disorder, as a sign of depression. We can term psychotherapy itself *supported reflection,* in this case celebrating the patient's thoughtfulness while the ground of judgment is extended beyond "mistakes" and "arrogance" to include youthfulness, the universal need to learn, and his own already evident capacity to "do better." These would only have been happier thoughts if they were not also part of something felt and real between us. I had to like him and he had to like me, which in part was to share a "likeness" of feelings between us. Then the new experience had a chance to override the older regretting one. It became as real, and in the course of time, more real than what had preceded it.

My patient perked up. He went on to make a life many could admire and one he could enjoy. It was also a joy for the psychotherapist.

WILLING

A woman of 60 had made a "perfect family" and 10 years ago had struck out on her own. It had not worked. She asked me to help her find a "new direction" and "not make mistakes."

She told me her family thought she was "crazy." A psychiatrist that her husband took her to agreed. She half-agreed. All through her youth her parents had not known what to do with her. A loner, a very able student, she was at once both her father's "favorite" and "impossible." She completed college, married young, and started that perfect family with a "perfect husband." He was certainly a great performer both financially and sexually, as well as handsome and loyal. All her friends envied her. They had two beautiful children. The son went through Harvard and both children married and had children of their own.

During a brief hospitalization prescribed by the psychiatrist who thought she was sick, she met a "soulmate," another patient who loved to talk with her. She loved it too. She also realized she had never enjoyed talking with her husband. They had exchanged information, almost never fought, relied on each other, but never "really talked." Such are the occasional benefits of hospitalization.

When I first met her, she was still talking with her once fellow patient. He, however, had become demanding and intrusive and was back in the hospital. That relationship was one of the mistakes she said she did not want to repeat. But it gradually emerged that she did not want to return to her husband either. There was this problem of talk. In time she persuaded the husband to accept a divorce and an adequate financial settlement for herself. I was beginning to sense her considerable power.

This matter of patients' power, or strength of willing, is a much neglected topic. Surely it is an important measure of persons. There are times in reading Kraepelin (1904) that he seems to suggest loss of will is the most important defect in schizophrenia. On the other hand, too much will, in the form of willfulness, may appear almost equally pathological, as in the discussions of borderline patients. I have observed that if the patient has more power then the helper, the helper may feel threatened and try to control that power by pathologizing it. (I believe I have also seen this occur when the patient is of greater intelligence.) One of the harshest lessons of life is the frequent danger of superiority, especially in institutions. People of weak mind or will, unless the weakness very much obstructs the institution, can be appreciated. They may "get along by going along," as the saying is. Most important, they do not threaten anyone; in fact, they help others to feel sympathetic and superior. But woe to those strong in mind and will who do not know their strength or do not conceal it. The envy and fear aroused can have malignant results. I began to wonder if a similar process had not been at work in my patient's life.

She had made a perfect family in part by making it a beautiful one. I could verify this possibility by the way she dressed and carried herself as she gradually gained self-assurance with me. She took pride in the homes she had made, their gardens, and the ambiance. Nor was this a conventional beauty. She had often had to fight for her plans, to the eventual astonishment of those who had resisted her. She could carry the day in part because of her style, which I perceived to be charismatic. That could protect her power, I thought, but there was a problem. She did not seem aware of either her power or her charisma.

This was welcome news for me. It gave me something relatively easy to do: bring her knowledge of the power and charisma. There is only one predictable danger, besides the danger of my being wrong. Many patients hearing a therapist speak of those qualities suspect the therapist is either using a technical trick or trying to seduce them. They may feel distanced or inflamed, the victim of a trick or drawn into acting out the inflammation. I dealt with the danger of distancing her, as well as of my being wrong, by saying this: "Of course I may be wrong, but it is not because I'm using a technique or trick. *I want you to know who I think you are.* It is just what physicians and surgeons do when they announce the patient's heart and lungs are sound, which allows the patient to exercise or survive an operation. You have as much right to know what I think is strong about you as what I think is weak."

Note that in speaking of her power I was also approaching a weakness. She did not know her power. This may explain the many years she had spent in a largely conventional existence with conventional relationships. She had depended on these relationships to shape her life, and only later in life did she begin to reshape it. Her unconsciousness of power also may explain much that was difficult and surprising in that life. For example, her powerful convictions had been disturbing to her husband and later to the first psychiatrist; in fact, they found her mad. A familiarity with her power and awareness of its effect on more timid spirits might have modified her presentations of herself and avoided trouble. There were many less serious, often ludicrous examples. People were forever responding to her as if she were both a movie star and a close friend. One day the senior person in her church, seeing her come through the door, gave out a surprising yelp of pleasure, spread his arms wide, and rushing toward her, threw them around her. He had forgotten he had canapés in both hands, which were smeared across her back. This was the kind of enthusiasm she often provoked. Her dentist, always a bit flirtatious with her, more recently when she was looking and feeling better, began the examination of a tooth. She was lying before him, in one of those long dentists' recliners. Suddenly he blushed, stammered something, and ran out of the office. His staff was puzzled and embarrassed. The dentist himself called later to apologize. He said he was afraid he was going to have an asthmatic attack! Perhaps most telling of all were the responses of children. More than once, daughters told their parents, who were friends of the patient, how much they wanted to grow up and be just like her. These are the feelings inspired by movie stars or world-class athletes.

We do not think enough about the effects of great personal power, even though the world has suffered terribly from its Hitlers and Stalins. The effects of benign personages can also be remarkable. Sometimes a child is born into a family who, from birth, seems an extraordinary blessing; a source of solutions rather than problems, of kindness, responsibility, even radiance. Such a child, perhaps like my patient, may also seem a stranger, because he or she is so different from the other family members. Family myths grow up quickly about such children—for example, that the father could not have produced such a child.

The reader must wonder if I, too, may not have fallen victim to her charms. Was my praise simply the ravings of a besotted therapist? She did remind me of my mother, as my mother might have become. So much for medical objectivity! I wrote that the danger of positive appraisals was not only of distancing through what is perceived as "technique" but inflammation of the relationship. What was I to say, and mean, if she responded to my appraisal by proclaiming that she loved me and I must love her, if I meant what I said. That would be the acid test of objectivity. Perhaps it is easier for me now that I am old and the fires banked lower. I know what I have long said and what I have suggested the young people in training say, to whom it happens more often. "Thank you very much. I am flattered because it is a beautiful thought, although I cannot be what you may want. The work excludes it. But the work does not exclude something related, which is better news. You can love, perhaps the greatest human capacity. My job is to move that supreme attribute to someone with whom you can make a life. I must insure that."

My patient did not fall in love with me. She had too strong a head. What she did was what I hoped. She went in search of others to love and carried her unusual abilities into a creative life that is still unfolding.

CONNECTING AND DISCONNECTING

A central human capacity is to connect with others, to make with others a meaningful life, but also to disconnect, to leave behind what is gone and establish fresh meanings. We want to be able to say of both past and future, it meant and means something to us. The difficulty of disconnecting has many forms. Some have to attend to everything they hear or think, are imprisoned in attention, and therefore cannot think for themselves. Others return to events over and over again checking and rechecking, as in compulsive states. It is a central property of nervous tissue, this continuity, and is indispensable to such acts as remembering. It can also be a tyrant.

A woman who was almost 70 came to me when her famous husband died and she felt lonely and uncertain. She was also aware of a different life she had long postponed. But she felt she was too old to begin again. She also did not see what she had already done, what she had completed. Because, I believe, what she had done was not at the heart of her wishes, she felt as if she had stood in for someone else. I thought that someone else was her mother whom she adored and emulated, perhaps at the sacrifice of her own gifts. This obscured a sense of her real accomplishments. She had given the famous husband a secure setting for his work, calmed his nervous fears, and took their children through difficult times, to independence. Then she was face-to-face with both opportunity and despair.

She had put others first, including her mother and her husband. The opportunity was to put herself first and the life she had postponed. How was I to help her past the despair, the sense of her age, the conviction that she must remain connected to what she had done and half-regretted, not free to strike out afresh?

Wasn't it time to let the old dreams go? Shouldn't I reconcile her to the accomplishments, prepare for a quiet retirement, help her muse on what she had done? Even the freshness I felt in her spirit might be only a last flicker.

But I was moved by that spirit, and by a remark she recalled making as a young woman, a remark she almost dismissed: "I can write better than Eudora Welty." It was like a flash of lightning. This was a serious and critical person. She had already shown me some interesting pages. I thought, she just might be right.

I have come to believe that no one does anything significant alone. Psychotherapy gains its importance not only from being able to bring solitary and despairing people into relationships but also from what springs up in luckier circumstances without it: the gaining of fresh perspectives on past, present, and future; seeing ourselves as others see us; support; encouragement; the recovery or discovery of ideals and values. It also can do something not often gained even in the luckiest circumstances, finding a balance between the dilemmas of life I mentioned earlier. How much should one connect *and* disconnect?

A great deal is made today of connecting, forming, and deepening relationships. But disconnection is as necessary. I like to tell people listening to lectures that they do not have to listen. If they check back every 5 or 10 minutes, then they are likely to find the speaker saying much of what they have already heard. And every listener harbors important problems needing frequent attention: If you do not attend to them during the day, then they will wake you at night. Therefore, few external occasions should command one's complete attention. Most people know this. They learned early in life, especially in school, to put on their faces expressions of interest and attention while their minds go elsewhere. Happily, only a few are imprisoned in attention, afraid not to attend lest they be thought independent or rebellious. I suspect some people go mad because their minds cannot be sent away freely but must escape by "losing it."

My patient was not one of those supremely sad souls, but she was a little captured by her regrets and self-doubts. They held her to the same past I wanted her to celebrate and then be done with. I have found you cannot free people from the past by its investigation alone, or even its celebration. One needs to light up the future.

"But I'm 70," she said. Perhaps it was necessary for our work that I be even older, because I wasn't ready to give up on my future either. I don't mean I can't go gently into that dark night. Despite my regrets, I am a lucky man who has received much more from life than I thought likely. Still, I have always been a possessive person, someone eager to collect and hold on. So I could welcome her to my not-always-pleasant tribe. I wanted her to hold on, to own a future.

Much of psychotherapy is about holding on, surviving the onrush and persuasiveness of despair, while standing quietly for something better. It is so tempting to look for quick solutions, advise or set to work, when the greater gift can be to listen, receive, and still hope. Happily she was kind. That was a gift she all too easily gave, in this instance to my hope. And giving me my hope, she could begin to hear it. At first, I think, she only rekindled her own hope so as not to disappoint mine; it was not yet hers. But working at her gift, holding on to my hope, she came to see the gift, first in my eyes, then gradually in her own. It was a real coming to life. She began to extend the hope, take it in new directions, surprise both herself and to a lesser extent me, with what she could do.

The reward she provided was not only her kindness, but the new life she was making for herself. She could then make the gift to me, that she had always been so good at giving, a great gift to herself, a gift that included a new belief in herself.

DYING WELL

I have written elsewhere about someone I watched die (Havens, 1993). He came to me with a clear project. "How can I say goodbye to those I love?" It was a task I had never faced before, though in this man's generous fashion he made it as easy for me as he could. He was reticent to ask; he said he thought it was more than he had asked of anyone. I would have been wrong to contradict him. So I said what I felt. "I'll do my best. I feel privileged to be asked. I'm sure you will do as much for me as I ever do for you."

We can think of psychotherapy as the play of intentions. He wanted to say goodbye to those he loved. I intended to help him do it. I was also in the position of perhaps saying goodbye to the man himself. The result was, my intention toward him had a form very similar to his toward the others. I like to repeat Gandhi's statement about social action. "*You* must be the change you wish to see in the world." I thought, I must be the change I wish to see in his world. How can I help him die unless I can do it myself? But I had not been thinking much of dying at all.

He was a medical man himself and a distinguished student of scientific medicine. He was likely to have done what he could to live. I could therefore be of little help to his medical care. What I needed to change was not only the way I thought about dying but the very way I could carry it out myself. I said to my-self, it's about time.

He did not intend to die. He did intend to die well. Now here I was, beginning to harbor the same intention for myself. Was I any more ready than he was? On the other hand, I was suddenly thankful to him. I already had something I should tell him before he died. The stage was gradually filling with intentions pushing for expression.

I could therefore say, "I would want to tell them how much I loved them." Note that I had not been quite faithful to Gandhi's principle. I might have done better right then and there, to express what I already owed him. That way I would have modeled carrying out intentions rather than trying to shape his. In-stead I had told him, without quite knowing it, what I had begun to wonder about doing myself. Fortunately we were enough alike so he could say, with a di-rectness that made the statement believable, "That is what I have wanted to do."

Intentions are said to be the basic form of human relations to the world (Searle, 1996). He had just said his intention was to tell the loved ones how much he loved them. That was at least part of his intention to say goodbye. But he was not sure he could do it. He had given me the same intention. Could I give him back the requisite means?

Intentions are a better description than actions of our relations with the world for just the reason my patient illustrated. So many of our relations are silent. We only pray or hope or, as we say, intend, and our good intentions are said to pave the road to hell. This he feared, which is another, often dominating relation to the world, an affect, not an intention, but accompanying intention. He had dealt with his fear partly by attempting to please and placate the world. This had inhibited the direct expression of his intentions and left him with the task he gave me.

Intentions may be a better name for our basic relation to the world than the more familiar ones, like drives or connections, just because it implies both drive and connection, and because it can cover such a range of nuances, like dream of, plan, desire, pursue. And, of course, intentions can be unconscious and, even if conscious, seemingly cut off from possibilities of action, for example, as in the woman of 70 or this dying man, because the intentions do not seem part of the person they have been. I could help the woman of 70 realize a once remote in-tention, by being able to recognize convincingly who she really was. I wanted her to meet herself, we might say, wanted her to feel *seen*. My presence was im-portant in affecting this introduction on account of who I was, not only a doctor supposedly expert in recognizing sickness and health, but also someone changed by what I saw. In this I was faithful to Gandhi. She had to deal with this changed person. Already the dying man had changed me. How did that help me to change him?

I think it was because we were both thinking of our children. Children have a great way of both appearing and disappearing. They appear when they are born, disappear into their own lives and most of all when we or they die. Perhaps it is these sometimes surprising appearances and disappearances that help secure children both the extraordinary love they elicit and the extraordinary neglect and abuse they sometimes receive. Often we just do not know what to do with them. I think this was part of what confounded my dying patient. How do you say goodbye to these so intimate strangers?

First of all, we confronted the mystery together. We puzzled and remembered together. My rememberings prompted some of his, and his some of mine. For example, he remembered one afternoon playing in the snow with his oldest daughter. They romped and tumbled, sledding and colliding, laughing and loving one another. It was a description no one could hear without delight. He told the now-grown daughter. She could hardly remember the scene but she could feel his love, a love this modest man had not felt worthy to impose when well and was still more hesitant to reveal in the face of his dying. What they felt in the half-remembered scene was a great gift he gave them both, reconciling him and to some extent her as well, to the fact of his going. He remembered other scenes with other loved ones, so they could relive the best they had together. The dying man went out on a wave of what they meant to one another, not erasing death, but making it bearable and living.

I suspect it was the joining of intentions that precipitated these events; neither of us had to go it alone. We could combine our limited courages into something that worked. The joining of felt intentions, not empathy alone, emboldens us all, to the results we seek.

Character pathology is the inevitable lot of life. None of us get ourselves right. What we can do is discover felicity, what Joseph Conrad called the jewel set in the iron of failures and shortcomings.

REFERENCES

Eliot, T. S. (1943). *Four quartets.* New York: Harcourt Brace.

Gustafson, J. P. (1995). *Brief vs. long psychotherapy.* Northvale, NJ: Aronson.

Havens, L. (1973). *Approaches to the mind.* Cambridge, MA: Harvard University Press.

Havens, L. (1993). *Coming to life.* Cambridge, MA: Harvard University Press.

Klein, M. (1960). *The psychoanalysis of children.* New York: Grove Press.

Kohut, H. (1977). *The restoration of the self.* New York: International Universities Press.

Kraepelin, E. (1904). *Lectures on clinical psychiatry* (T. Johnstone, Ed.). London: Baillière, Tindall and Cox.

Searle, J. R. (1996). *The philosophy of mind.* Springfield, VA: The Teaching Company.

Winnicott, D. W. (1965). *The maturational processes and the facilitating environment.* New York: International Universities Press.

PART II

Research and Assessment: Overview and Outcome Measures

CHAPTER 3

Personality Disorders in Adults: A Review

RICHARD A. ZWEIG, PhD
Hillside Hospital—Long Island Jewish Medical Center

JENNIFER HILLMAN, PhD
Penn State Berks

Personality disorders may be among the most prevalent, yet ill-defined, of mental disorders. Individuals manifesting personality disorders have been described by mental health practitioners as "difficult," "hateful," and "help-rejecting," or at best, "infantile," "demanding," "resistant," and given to "snatching defeat from the jaws of victory." They are known to be chronically more prone to distorted perceptions of others, more vulnerable to their own affective storms, and more predisposed to impulsive and self-destructive acts than individuals affected by other psychiatric syndromes. In general, these patients manifest a "generalized failure of adaptation" characterized by "persistent dysfunctional relationships and chronic impairments in the ability to love, to work, or both" (Pilkonis, 1997, p. 379). Although diagnostic systems such as the *Diagnostic and Statistical Manual of Mental Disorders* (*DSM;* American Psychiatric Association) have attempted to classify personality disorder types according to specified criteria sets, in clinical settings these patients are more often stigmatized as having a global "Axis II problem." Such patients are widely viewed as more likely to form a tenuous therapeutic alliance, to be noncompliant, or to refuse mental health treatment. These characteristics, in turn, contribute to the unique sense of therapeutic nihilism and aversion that these patients engender in their care providers. Finally, as these individuals with personality disorder age, they are conventionally assumed to "burn out" or "become more like themselves," as if to fulfill the prophesy that they are not treatable.

In an effort to further clarify the nature of personality disorder, the fourth edition of the *DSM* (American Psychiatric Association, 1994) provides a definition and generic set of criteria for personality disorder: "An enduring pattern of inner experience and behavior that deviates markedly from the expectations of an individual's culture, manifested by disturbance in two of the following areas: (1) Cognition; (2) Affectivity; (3) Interpersonal functioning; and (4) Impulse control" (p. 633). The generic criteria also specify several characteristics that qualify these deviant experience/behavior patterns as a disorder. The individual's behavior must be shown to be inflexible, or to manifest across a range of clinical states or environmental situations. Aspects of their behavior must be maladaptive, in that they are associated with impaired social or occupational functioning and subjective distress. Finally, their maladaptive behavior must be pervasive, or stable and of long duration. However, and of importance to gerontologic clinicians, the *DSM–IV* qualifies the latter criterion by adding that whereas personality disorders have their onset in young adulthood, they may not come to clinical attention until late in life due to the loss of stabilizing environmental situations or supportive relationships. These generic criteria help, but the diagnostic assessment of personality disorders remains complicated.

In practice, it may be difficult to differentiate an individual's maladaptive traits from clinical symptom states, cultural roles, and situation-specific behaviors. Judgments as to what constitutes a maladaptive behavior or impaired functioning are necessarily value laden and subjective, and especially so when the impairment is not evident to the individual. The duration and pervasiveness of maladaptive behavior can be difficult to determine. Clinicians may have difficulty reliably assessing the possibility that an underlying personality disorder was previously buffered by a stabilizing environment. Perhaps it is these complexities that prompt many clinicians to consistently defer from making a specific *DSM* Axis II diagnosis, or to view it only as a "diagnosis of exclusion" to be given primarily to treatment nonresponders or otherwise unlikable patients.

Although research on personality disorders in adults has not fully resolved the diagnostic dilemmas already described, it has led to advances in the understanding of methods to sharpen diagnostic tools, and of the extent to which these disorders are indeed inflexible, maladaptive, and pervasive. This chapter reviews issues and research related to the diagnostic assessment, epidemiology, and longitudinal course of personality disorders in adults, as well as what is known about the impact of these disorders on the treatment outcome of Axis I disorders. Because relatively little empirical research regarding personality disorders in older adults exists, this chapter is intended to provide geriatric mental health specialists with an overview of research on the diagnosis and treatment of adults with personality disorder. This perspective may then be used to evaluate the emerging literature regarding personality disordered elderly as presented in the chapters that follow.

ISSUES IN THE DIAGNOSTIC ASSESSMENT
OF PERSONALITY DISORDERS

An understanding of the current state of diagnostic assessment of personality disorders must be based on an overview of general measurement issues complicating diagnosis, diagnostic models for classification, and the relative advantages of different assessment approaches. A review of hypotheses regarding the relation between personality disorders and Axis I mental disorders is also presented.

Measurement Issues

The diagnostic assessment of personality disorders in adults is hampered by the relativism (or "fuzziness") of the construct. Of course, any definition of mental health is relativistic, and in the absence of a clear gold standard, current empirical models of outcome assessment ideally incorporate the perspectives of the patient, clinician, and society (Strupp, 1996). However, in the diagnosis of personality disorder, this may be difficult to achieve. The *DSM–IV* appears to follow such a model, as personality disorder is defined not only as a maladaptive pattern of experience and behavior but also as deviant relative to culture-specific expectations or norms. However, this may raise a profound dilemma for practicing clinicians who may be ill-equipped to evaluate whether a given personality style "deviates markedly" from the individual's culture, ethnic group, or age cohort. Further, judgments of the maladaptiveness of a trait are supposed to be based on the presence of social or occupational dysfunction. Such dysfunction is in itself relative to a given context (Widiger, 1994) and rarely systematically assessed (Pilkonis, 1997), thus adding to the continued subjectivity of this judgment. Additional proof of the relative nature of the current diagnostic system is suggested by the fact that the threshold at which point a maladaptive trait becomes a disorder appears to be arbitrary (Cloninger, 1987). One might hope that the five-factor model of personality dimensions, derived from research on nonclinical populations, might assist in making diagnostic judgments more objective. Recent research efforts are underway to bridge the gap between these personality dimensions and the *DSM–IV* personality disorder constructs (Costa & Widiger, 1994).

The empirical measurement of personality disorders faces several other practical challenges that impact on diagnostic accuracy to a degree not encountered with other mental disorders. Personality disorders, for example, tend to be apparent in the context of close interpersonal relationships, but are rarely assessed by direct observation of an interpersonal dyad. Behaviors chosen as criterion variables for most personality disorders often have pejorative connotations, and because many afflicted individuals are unaware of the maladaptive nature of their traits, reporting biases are common. Further, personality disorders (by definition) are lifelong, and provide no benefit of a premorbid baseline to be used as a reference point in diagnosis. As noted, clinical state and situational context may strongly influence the presentation of personality traits, and may be difficult to control empirically (Jacobsberg, Goldsmith, Widiger, & Frances, 1989; Weissman, 1993). Current diagnostic criteria sets lack behavioral anchors for most personality disorders, lack a mechanism for specifying severity within a given categorical diagnosis, and contain criteria that overlap between categories. These problems may account for the high comorbidity among personality disorders, the poor correspondence of self- and interviewer-rated measures, and the prevalence of "mixed" or "not otherwise specified" (NOS) diagnoses of personality disorders (Farmer & Nelson-Grey, 1990; Klein, 1993; Pilkonis, 1997; Shea, 1993). Given these formidable measurement problems, it seems unsurprising that diagnostic reliability for personality disorder assessment is notoriously unsatisfactory.

Models of Personality Disorder Diagnosis

The conceptual models employed in each successive edition of the *DSM* have played a large role in the accuracy and usefulness of a diagnosis of personality disorder. The classic "categorical model" of personality disorders, on which judgments relied prior to *DSM–III,* held that personality disorders were homogeneous, mutually exclusive categories. The advantages of this model were apparent in its simplicity and its consistency with clinical convention. However, because criteria were ill-defined and "pure" personality types were rarely observed, diagnostic judgments were very unreliable.

The third and fourth editions of the *DSM* turned to a "prototypal model" in which consensually or empirically derived criteria sets were devised for each personality disorder, and assignment was based on a probabilistic approximation of an ideal or prototype. Because it also permitted the diagnosis of "mixed" personality disorder, this model had the added advantages of capturing more of the heterogeneity of individuals' personalities, enhancing diagnostic reliability, and promoting empirical research through the use of specified criteria. Still, as mentioned earlier, this diagnostic model has been criticized for its lack of quantitative detail (e.g., difficulty specifying disorder severity; loss of information regarding subclinical traits), inclusion of overlapping criteria sets, and sponsorship of a proliferation of NOS diagnoses that lack clinical usefulness.

More recently, "dimensional models" of personality disorder have gained favor (Klein, 1993). In their purest form, these models have individuals rated on several broad dimensions of personality or temperament, and account for variation in both normal and abnormal personality. For example, Costa and McCrae (1990) amassed considerable evidence for a five-factor model encompassing all personality traits: neuroticism, extraversion, openness, agreeableness, and conscientiousness. Cloninger (1987) proposed a biosocial model based on three ge-netically based dimensions of personality defined by their stimulus–response characteristics: novelty seeking, harm avoidance, and reward dependence. These dimensional models generally seek to capture the true heterogeneity of person-ality, facilitate research and diagnostic reliability, and eliminate artificial bound-aries within diagnostic categories. Yet, integrating unfamiliar personality dimen-sions into clinical practice could be complex. Further, even the use of a multi-dimensional personality disorder description would lack information regarding the motivational meaning of a given trait for a given individual (e.g., low "open-ness" might have a differential meaning and benefit to a holocaust survivor than to a retired executive) (Frances & Widiger, 1987; Klein, 1993; Pilkonis, 1997).

Measures of Personality Disorders

Decades of research on normal and abnormal personality has resulted in several methods of measuring personality disorders and their constituent traits. These measures can be collapsed into four general categories: multiscale self-report in-ventories, structured clinical interviews, single trait measures, and functional impairment measures (see Table 3.1). Each has advantages and limitations.

Multiscale self-report inventories represent the most traditional approach, and have the advantages of being easy to administer, derived from empirical meth-ods, capable of controlling for patient response styles, and unaffected by exam-iner biases. However, the reliability of these self-reports may be compromised by their sensitivity to state effects (e.g., anxiety, depression) on trait scores, and their scale items may not parallel the criteria sets for personality disorder listed in *DSM–IV* (Widiger & Frances, 1987).

Structured clinical interviews represent a more recent advance in personality disorder measurement, and have enhanced the reliability of clinician diagnosis, with Kappa coefficients ranging from .41 to .89. Structured interviews also ad-here more closely to *DSM* criteria sets, allow informant data to be incorporated, and permit an evaluation of the pervasiveness and duration of a given trait. However, they are time-consuming, rely on clinician inference for certain items (e.g., lack of empathy), are influenced by clinician attentiveness to state and situ-ational effects, and may not adequately control for response bias (Frances & Wid-iger, 1987; Jacobsberg et al., 1989; Pilkonis, 1997).

Among the newer approaches to personality disorder assessment are self-report inventories that more closely adhere to *DSM* personality disorder con-structs such as the Schedule for Nonadaptive and Adaptive Personality (SNAP; Clark, 1993) and the Wisconsin Personality Disorders Inventory (Klein, 1993). Other newer measures assess either single traits (e.g., hostility, impulsiveness) or the functional impairment (e.g., social role adjustment) that is associated with personality disorders. Single trait approaches have been particularly useful in testing psychobiological hypotheses such as the association of serotonin dys-

TABLE 3.1
Selected Measures of *DSM* Personality Disorders

Multiscale Self-Report Inventories
  Millon Clinical Multiaxial Inventory (MCMI–III; Millon, 1983)
  Personality Diagnostic Questionnaire (PDQ–R; Hyler & Reider 1987)
  Personality Assessment Inventory (PAI; Morey, 1991)
  NEO Personality Inventory (NEO–PI–R; Costa & McCrae, 1992a)
  Schedule for Nonadaptive and Adaptive Personality (SNAP; Clark, 1993)
  Wisconsin Personality Disorders Inventory (Klein, Benjamin, & Rosenfelt, 1993)

Structured Clinical Interviews
  Personality Disorders Examination (PDE; Loranger, Susman, Oldham, & Russakoff, 1987)
  Structured Interview for Disorders of Personality (SIDP; Stangl et al., 1985)
  Structured Clinical Interview for *DSM–III* Personality Disorders (SCID–II; Pfohl, Stangl,
    & Zimmerman, 1983)

Single Trait Measures
  Buss–Durkee Hostility Inventory (Buss & Durkee, 1957)
  Barratt Impulsiveness Scale (Barratt & Patton, 1983)

Functional Impairment Measures
  Inventory of Interpersonal Problems (IIP; Horowitz et al., 1988)
  Social Adjustment Scale–Self-Report (Weissman & Bothwell, 1976)

---

function and impulsive aggression in patients with borderline and antisocial personality disorders (Shea, Widiger, & Klein, 1992).

Despite the advent of newer, more reliable methods of diagnosing personality disorder, these methods are not in widespread use in clinical practice. In an empirical study of diagnostic decision making, Westen (1997) reported that clinicians were more likely to base an Axis II diagnosis on a patient's report and clinician observations than objective ratings of interpersonal functioning. It is probable that structured or objective measures are even more rarely used in conventional practice with older adults.

Hypothesized Relations Between Axis I and Axis II Disorders

By virtue of their placement on a separate diagnostic axis, personality disorders are defined as distinct from other mental disorders. However, personality disorders coexist with Axis I disorders at rates estimated from 25% to 75% (Frances & Widiger, 1987), a fact that has led to speculation regarding possible etiologic relations between these two diagnostic axes. Presented next are the most commonly cited hypotheses regarding possible relations between Axes I and II (Klein, 1993). Of note, these hypotheses seek to explain findings of comorbidity between personality disorders and mood or anxiety disorders. (For a broader discussion of possible interactions between personality and other disorders, see Duberstein, chap. 6 in this volume).

The *Predisposition Hypothesis,* which is often associated with psychodynamic models of mental illness, suggests that one condition (i.e., a personality disorder) creates a diathesis or risk for developing another condition (i.e., an Axis I disorder). Many researchers have found an association between personality variables and various psychiatric disorders (Hirshfeld & Cross, 1987). Most persuasive are those findings evidencing that recovered depressives show elevations on measures of maladaptive traits such as emotional instability and interpersonal dependency. However, in the absence of prospective or longitudinal studies linking the presence of personality disorder to the initial onset of an Axis I illness, the validity of this hypothesis remains uncertain.

The *Subclinical/Prodrome Hypothesis,* closely associated with biological psychiatric models, holds that personality disorders are subclinical or prodromal forms of related Axis I disorders that represent forms of neurobiologic dysregulation and share a common biogenetic substrate. Proponents such as Siever and Davis (1991) argued, for example, that four basic domains may underlie all mental disorders: cognitive-perceptual disorganization, impulsivity-aggression, affective instability, and anxiety-inhibition. Thus, the comorbidity of borderline personality and mood disorders, for example, is presumed to reflect a common basis in "affective instability." Several studies have found support for a common biological etiology for some Axis I and Axis II disorders (e.g., Depressed and borderline personality samples both have abnormalities of REM latency during sleep). Although there is also some suggestive data from genetic studies linking Axes I and II disorders, the actual mode of inheritance remains unclear (Weissman, 1993).

A related model, the *Life Event/Trauma Hypothesis,* also proposes a common substrate to personality and Axis I disorders. However, its proponents claim that it is severe, enduring psychological stressors, particularly in early childhood, that result in both mood and personality disorders rather than biogenetic factors. Various research studies have identified a link between early childhood trauma, depression, and borderline personality disorder (e.g., Ellason, Ross, Sainton, & Mayran, 1996; Fonagy, Leigh, M. Steele, & H. Steele, 1996).

The *Complication/Scarring Hypothesis* posits that some severe or recurrent Axis I disorders, such as Major Depression, may result in a scarring of the personality that later appears as a personality disorder. For example, clinicians have noted that some recurrently depressed individuals develop an enduring loss of initiative. However, this hypothesis would seem at odds with the *DSM* notion that personality disorder has its onset in early adulthood. One recent prospective study partially addressed this hypothesis by assessing personality before and after treatment for Major Depression in first-episode patients, and failed to find significant effects (Shea, Mueller, Solomon, Warshaw, & Keller, 1996).

The *Modifier/Pathoplasty Hypothesis* probably garners the most empirical support of all of these hypotheses. The underlying supposition here is that Axis I and Axis II syndromes coexist, but that one modifies the expression of the other.

For example, a comorbid personality disorder may modify the symptom presentation, course, or outcome of a depressive disorder. Most persuasive are studies (e.g., Beardon et al., 1996; Frank, Kupfer, Jacob, & Jarrett, 1987; Thompson et al., 1988) confirming that the comorbid presence of a personality disorder in depressives impedes their treatment responsiveness. The mechanisms by which this may occur have yet to be specified.

The *Orthogonal Hypothesis* suggests that personality disorders and Axis I disorders arise independently and coexist by chance. However, the fact that a high degree of comorbidity is observed (e.g., between mood and personality disorders) would seem to argue against this.

In sum, several hypotheses have been proposed to explain the observed high rates of comorbidity between personality disorders and Axis I disorders. Because the etiology of many mental disorders appears multifaceted and determined by biogenetic, psychological, and social factors, it seems likely that more than one of these hypotheses will prove correct, and the relation of Axis II to Axis I will be revealed as bidirectional (Klein, 1993).

Implications for Diagnosis of Personality Disorders

Although the measurement and diagnosis of personality disorders is made difficult by the "fuzzy" nature of the construct, flaws in diagnostic classification schemas, imperfect measures, and the uncertain etiologic relation between personality disorders and other mental disorders, advances in these areas have contributed to enhanced methodological rigor and improved reliability and validity of diagnosis. Drawing on the sum of current research findings, the following recommendations may be offered regarding assessment of personality disorders (Abrams, 1990; Klein, 1993; Pilkonis, 1997): (a) Self-report and structured interview measures of personality disorder should be combined to enhance diagnostic reliability and validity. (b) Informant measures/interviews may be quite valuable in order to assess the longitudinal course of the disorder and degree of social/occupational impairment, as well as whether the behavior is normative within a given culture or age cohort. (c) A clinical state measure or Axis I evaluation is recommended to reduce possible state/trait confounding effects and to assess for response bias. (d) A dimensional approach utilizing both dimensional measures of personality and of personality disorders is suggested.

EPIDEMIOLOGY OF PERSONALITY DISORDER IN ADULTS

The advent of more rigorous assessment techniques for *DSM* personality disorders has led to preliminary studies estimating the prevalence rates of personality disorder in community and clinical samples of adults (for a review of findings among older adults, see Abrams, chap. 4 in this volume). However, these findings are not definitive as they are subject to the general methodological problems inherent in diagnosing personality disorders (Weissman, 1993). Several other caveats regarding interpreting this data must be mentioned. Few prevalence studies of personality disorder in nonclinical populations exist, whereas surveys of clinical populations are more common. Studies of nonclinical populations are often community-based and may include disproportionate sampling of relatives of clinical probands. Prevalence rates within a given study may vary depending on the assessment method used. Finally, because most studies permit the diagnosis of personality disorder even when a comorbid Axis I condition is present, the accuracy of the prevalence rate is dependent on the validity of the measure used. With these cautions in mind, the following represents a brief review of preliminary findings regarding the prevalence of personality disorders in adults, and of the association of personality disorders with demographic factors and adverse life events.

Prevalence of Personality Disorders in Adult Nonclinical and Clinical Samples

Findings regarding prevalence rates of personality disorders in community (non-referred) samples have been reported by Weissman (1993) and are reported in the *DSM–IV* (1994). Notably, most of the data on prevalence of personality disorders (except for antisocial personality disorder) are derived from three community-based studies (Maier et al., 1992; Reich, Yates, & Nduaguba, 1989; Zimmerman & Coryell, 1990) which utilized either structured interview (SIDP, SCID) or self-report (PDQ) methods. Prevalence rates for antisocial personality disorder are based on results obtained from the national Epidemiologic Catchment Area (ECA) study.

The overall prevalence rate for any personality disorder is estimated to be 10% to 13.5% based on community surveys of adults (Weissman, 1993). Personality disorder is defined as a "lifetime" diagnosis, and so this finding suggests that at least one tenth of community-dwelling adults manifest this problem throughout the course of their lives. The markedly high prevalence of these disorders is underscored when comparing these rates to the ECA lifetime prevalence rates of Axis I disorders such as schizophrenia (1.5%) and more common conditions such as clinical depression (6.4%) and alcohol abuse / dependence (13.8%; Robins & Regier, 1991). Although personality disorder may be masked by an Axis I condition, it seems surprising that the prevalence of this condition is not more widely acknowledged. Further, because these estimates are based largely on community surveys of willing participants and personality-disordered adults may have higher refusal rates, actual prevalence rates in a representative population sample may be even higher.

Estimated prevalence rates for specific personality disorders based on community surveys may be summarized (see Table 3.2). The highly variable rates for certain disorders appear to depend on the method of assessment used. For

example, individuals manifesting dependent and obsessive-compulsive personality disorders show higher rates when self-report measures are used instead of
interview methods (Weissman, 1993). In addition, it seems noteworthy that
some personality disorders (e.g., Narcissistic and Avoidant) occur rarely in community surveys but are rather common in clinical settings. Whether this represents a methodological artifact or the high degree to which these individuals utilize clinical services is unclear.

In clinical settings, the overall prevalence rate of personality disorder tends to
be considerably higher (see Table 3.2), and this finding appears to hold across diagnostic categories. For example, comorbid personality disorder is estimated to
affect 35% to 48% of clinically depressed outpatients (Pilkonis & Frank, 1988;
Shea et al., 1987). For inpatients with depression or mixed affective disorder,
rates of 43% to 52% are reported (Mellman et al., 1992; Pfohl, Coryell, Zimmerman, & Stangl, 1987). Bipolar inpatients and outpatients may exhibit rates ranging from 23% to 62% (Shea et al., 1992). Anxiety-disordered outpatients and inpatients evidence rates of 35% and 43%, respectively (Maier et al., 1992; Mellman et al., 1992). Among medical outpatients, when patients with any psychiatric morbidity are surveyed, 28% also manifest a personality disorder (Casey &
Tyrer, 1990). Hence, across varied clinical settings about 30% to 40% of mood or
anxiety-disordered adults receiving psychiatric treatment display a comorbid
personality disorder.

TABLE 3.2
Estimated Prevalence Rates for Personality Disorders

Personality Disorder	General Population Rate (%)		Clinical Setting Rate (%)
	DSM–IV (1994)	Weissman (1993)	DSM–IV (1994)
Cluster A			
Paranoid	0.5–2.5	0.4–1.8	2.0–30.0
Schizoid	N/A	0.5–0.9	N/A
Schizotypal	3.0	0.6–5.6	N/A
Cluster B			
Antisocial	3.0/1.0*	2.4	3.0–30.0
Borderline	2.0	1.1–4.6	10.0–20.0
Histrionic	2.0–3.0	1.3–3.0	10.0–15.0
Narcissistic	< 1.0	0.0–0.4	2.0–16.0
Cluster C			
Avoidant	0.5–1.0	0.0–1.3	10.0
Dependent	N/A	1.6–6.7	N/A
Obsessive-Compulsive	1.0	1.7–6.4	3.0–10.0

*Rates for males/females
Note: Unless otherwise noted, prevalence rates denoted are combined for males/
females.
N/A indicates that data are not available.

Association of Personality Disorder with Demographic Factors and Adverse Life Events

Recent prevalence studies in large nonclinical samples have permitted examination of the relation between personality disorder and demographic factors such as age, gender, and marital status, as well as reports of adverse life events. For example, rates of personality disorder are often inversely correlated with age (Maier et al., 1992; Weissman, 1993; Zimmerman & Coryell, 1989). The most striking example of this age effect is provided in the ECA data on antisocial personality disorder, in which the 1-year prevalence rates sharply decline from 2.1% in the < 30 age group to 0.2% in the 45 to 64 age group (Robins & Regier, 1991). However, some have argued that this finding is due to the fact that younger people more commonly act out the pathological behaviors that define antisocial personality disorder, and that current diagnostic criteria may underestimate the lifetime prevalence of this disorder (Zimmerman & Coryell, 1989).

Other cross-sectional studies (e.g., Reich, Nduaguba, & Yates, 1988) point to a modest decline in Cluster B personality disorder traits with age, but this association may not be linear and could represent an age or cohort effect. Longitudinal studies, to be discussed later in this chapter, may assist in clarifying this issue.

Findings regarding the relation between personality disorder and gender are less clear. For example, some researchers report a higher overall personality disorder prevalence rate in males (Zimmerman & Coryell, 1989), whereas others report a female predominance (Maier et al., 1992). Other, more recent findings suggest that prevalence rates vary by gender but only for certain personality disorder types (e.g., antisocial personality disorder has been reported more commonly in males; Golumb, Fava, Abraham, & Rosenbaum, 1995; Robins & Regier, 1991).

In contrast, prevalence appears directly related to marital status, as higher rates of personality disorder are found in unmarried, separated, and divorced individuals (Zimmerman & Coryell, 1989). This supports the notion that dysfunctional interpersonal relationships often are a hallmark of this disorder (for further discussion of this issue, see Rosowsky, chap. 9 in this volume).

A growing body of research also suggests that personality disordered individuals experience higher rates of adverse life events. For example, the presence of personality disorder has been associated with higher reported rates of marital problems, a poorer employment history, higher rates of alcohol use, and a seven times higher lifetime incidence of suicide attempt compared to individuals without this disorder (Reich et al., 1989; Zimmerman & Coryell, 1989). Again, some specific types of personality disorder (e.g., borderline personality disorder) may place individuals at particularly high risk for these adverse events, and even lead to a higher risk of physical disability (Weissman, 1993) and mortality.

In sum, data from community studies suggest that personality disorders occur at relatively high rates, are extremely prevalent in clinical settings, and are frequently comorbid with other mental disorders. Given the limitations of current methodologies for assessing personality disorders mentioned earlier, these findings are somewhat tentative. Still, results indicating a link to adverse life events lend support to the argument that personality disorder is associated with serious functional impairment, and that affected individuals are not merely the "worried well." In fact, these individuals are not only functionally impaired but also appear more prone to experience major psychiatric illness.

EFFECTS OF PERSONALITY DISORDER ON MOOD DISORDER

The negative impact of personality disorder on the symptoms and treatment of a major psychiatric disorder has been most widely documented in studies of mood disorder, although a similar impact is found in studies of panic disorder and substance abuse / dependence (for excellent reviews of the effect of personality disorder on Axis I disorders, see Shea et al., 1992 and Reich & Vasile, 1993). Most of the mood disorder studies have examined Major Depression with or without comorbid personality disorder in order to assess for differences in depressive syndrome onset, symptom intensity, and outcome following somatic and psychotherapeutic treatments.

Personality Disorder and Clinical Presentation of Mood Disorder

Personality disorder does appear to adversely affect the onset of Major Depression. Studies of depressed inpatients and outpatients find that those with comorbid PD report earlier onset depression (Charney, Nelson, & Quinlan, 1981; Mellman et al., 1992; Pfohl, Stangl, & Zimmerman, 1984), although this may be most significant for Cluster B personality disorders (Shea et al., 1987). For example, in the Mellman et al. study (1992), depressives with PD experienced mood disorder onset at a mean age of 16 years, compared with a mean of 28 years for the group without personality disorder. Whether this represents the adverse impact of depression on personality development, or a vulnerability to depression in the personality disorder group is unclear, and awaits prospective studies.

The relation between personality disorder and other clinical variables such as depressive symptom intensity, duration, and frequency of recurrent episodes is less clear. In studies of depressed inpatients and outpatients, comorbid personality disorder has been associated with increased depressive symptom severity, longer duration of episode, and a higher rate of recurrent episodes (Pfohl et al., 1987; Shea et al., 1987). Others researchers have not found an association between personality disorder and these clinical variables (Charney et al., 1981; Mellman et al., 1992). One possible explanation is that this association occurs in individuals with Cluster B (histrionic, narcissistic, borderline, antisocial) personality disorders (Shea et al., 1987) but not in other types.

Personality Disorder and Treatment Outcome for Mood Disorder

Research examining treatment effects has documented the adverse impact of comorbid personality disorder on the outcome of pharmacologic and psychosocial treatments for Major Depression. This negative effect has been observed repeatedly in mixed-adult samples, and in initial samples of older adults (for a review of mood disorder outcome studies in older adults, see Gradman and colleagues, chap. 5 in this volume).

In regard to somatic treatments, depressed individuals with comorbid personality disorder typically are found to have slower or poorer responses to tricyclic antidepressants (Black, Bell, Hulbert, & Nasrallah, 1988; Pfohl et al., 1987; Reich, 1990; Shea et al., 1990). Once in remission, they may be more vulnerable to relapse following a positive response to tricyclics (Faravelli, Ambonetti, Pallanti, & Pazzagli, 1986) or ECT (Zimmerman et al., 1986). Because the duration of treatment was limited to less than 6 months in many of these studies, it also is unclear whether more extended pharmacologic intervention would have enhanced outcome.

Controlled studies of brief psychotherapeutic treatment for depressives with comorbid personality disorder parallel the previous disappointing findings for somatic treatments. For example, in the NIMH Treatment of Depression Collaborative Research Program study, outpatients with Major Depression and comorbid PD who were treated with psychotherapy for 16 weeks displayed more residual symptoms and less improvement in social functioning than those patients without personality disorder (Shea et al., 1990). Similarly, in a study of interpersonal psychotherapy, depressed outpatients with higher ratings of personality disturbance exhibited slower time to remission (29 weeks) than those with lower disturbance ratings (19 weeks; Beardon et al., 1996). Thus, even when targeted treatments that address interpersonal dysfunction are utilized, these patients do more poorly and appear to require longer treatment duration to improve.

Preliminary studies of combined antidepressant plus psychotherapeutic treatment for Recurrent Major Depression also found that personality disorder significantly affects outcome. Frank et al. (1987) treated depressed outpatients to recovery utilizing combined imipramine and interpersonal psychotherapy. Slower responders were more likely to evidence comorbid personality disorder (63%) than normal responders (33%). In fact, trait variables such as personality disorder and "ego resilience" correctly classified 65% of all treatment responders (Pilkonis & Frank, 1988). Frank et al. speculated that because rapid onset of response is often found with pharmacotherapy, the slow responders may have been responding primarily to psychotherapeutic treatment.

Initial long-term follow-up studies also suggest a less than favorable prognosis for depressives with personality pathology. In a 15-year prospective study of depressives who were treated naturalistically, personality pathology predicted greater symptom chronicity and accounted for 20% of the variance in outcome (Andrews et al., 1990). In a similar 18-year follow-up study in which depressives with personality disturbance were assessed using the Eysenck Personality Inventory, "neuroticism" was associated with greater social impairment and poorer global outcome at follow-up (Duggan, Lee, & Murray, 1990). Extrapolating from these follow-up studies, it might be posited that some individuals with personality disorder likely reach older adulthood without having ever fully recovered from prior depressive episodes and with chronic deficits in social functioning.

So why does personality disorder so adversely affect treatment outcome of depression? Shea et al. (1992) speculated that a variety of mechanisms may be operative. First, depression with comorbid PD may differ biologically from a typical major depressive disorder, rendering classic pharmacologic and psychotherapeutic approaches less effective. Second, comorbid personality disorder may both engender negative life events and erode needed interpersonal supports to a degree that militates against recovery from depression. Finally, individuals with personality disorder tend to be less compliant with treatment, have more difficulty developing a treatment alliance, and compromise therapists' attempts to implement effective interventions. These proposed mechanisms would appear to apply to older as well as to younger adults.

To summarize, current data suggest that personality disorder affects the onset of depression and impacts negatively on both short- and long-term outcome following standard treatment approaches. Given the degree to which personality disorder exacerbates personal distress, heightens risk for adverse life events, impairs social and occupational functioning, and impedes accessibility to treatment, it seems surprising that any individuals with this disorder would respond (even slowly) to standard approaches. Further, it might be expected that as these individuals age, the malignant nature of their clinical condition would only worsen. However, as is discussed in the next section, the prognosis for personality disorder in older adulthood appears less uniformly pessimistic and more complicated.

AGING AND PERSONALITY DISORDER

The question of what happens to personality disordered adults as they age is a complex one, and would require several methodologically sophisticated longitudinal studies to answer definitively. Still, some trends may be noted by exploring findings regarding normal personality development and aging. In addition, theories and existing longitudinal research regarding the fate of personality disordered middle and older adults lend vital insight (for an excellent review of these issues, see Agronin, 1994).

Aging and Normal Personality Development

Reviews of the literature regarding normal personality and aging generally conclude that major personality dimensions remain relatively stable throughout the life course (Bengston, Reedy, & Gordon, 1985; Shaie & Willis, 1986). These conclusions are drawn from longitudinal studies spanning as many as 30 years that use self-report measures of personality dimensions such as neuroticism and extraversion. Costa and McCrae (1992b) also estimated that as much as three fifths of the variance in personality traits is stable throughout the life course. Such notions about normal personality are in accord with the conventional wisdom that "a zebra does not change its stripes." It might be assumed that personality disorder, which by definition has its onset in young adulthood and persists throughout life, exhibits a similar longitudinal stability.

Does this mean that personality does not develop or change during the life course? Does the zebra ever "change its stripes"? Developmental psychologists have argued that whereas major dimensions may not change, specific traits such as interiority (Neugarten, 1979) and androgeny (Helson & Wink, 1992; Gutmann, 1987) may be augmented with age. With respect to traits bearing on personality pathology, others have noted that affective control increases (LaBouvie-Vief, DeVoe, & Bulka, 1989) whereas sociopathy decreases with age (Woodruff Guze, & Clayton, 1971). Because these findings are based on cross-sectional data, it is not clear whether age or cohort (i.e., generational) differences explain these changes. Costa and McCrae (1992) admitted that there are other exceptions to the stability rule, such as changes seen between adolescence and adulthood, changes in specific traits such as activity level, and changes in response to psychiatric disorders, catastrophic stressors, or psychotherapy. In sum, whereas large-scale personality dimensions are relatively constant with age, the possibility of trait changes (particularly on the individual level) as a function of age, life experience, or other factors does exist. This caveat would seem to imply that the traits underlying disorders of personality are also relatively invariant, yet accessible to change through such experiences as psychotherapy.

Theories Regarding the Impact of Aging on Personality Disorder

Mental health practitioners who work with older adults have added their perspective to more directly address the question of the course of personality disorders as individuals age. One of the more popular theories is a modification of the aforementioned "predisposition hypothesis." This psychodynamic model (Sadavoy & Leszcz, 1987) holds that personality-disordered middle-age and older adults are more vulnerable to age-related stressors such as loss, physical illness, and forced dependency. When confronted with such events, they adapt poorly, and experience increased psychopathology with age. This model is consistent with clinical experience and therefore is rather appealing, but such a generic cumulative effect would seem to predict a higher prevalence of major psychiatric illness in later life than is actually observed.

Other theories propose age-related changes in specific personality disorders. For example, the "Maturation Hypothesis" suggests that "immature" Cluster B personality types (histrionic, narcissistic, antisocial, borderline) improve or become more treatable with age, whereas the "mature" personality disorder types (obsessive, schizoid, and paranoid) worsen with age (Kernberg, 1984; Solomon, 1981; Tyrer, 1988). Part of this hypothesis is consistent with research already cited suggesting a normative maturation effect during the transition from late adolescence to adulthood, as well as possible age-related increases in affective control. Others (Abrams, 1990; Rosowsky & Gurian, 1991) suggest that older adults with Cluster B personality disorders may only appear to have improved with age. For example, an institutionalized, frail elderly patient may simply not have the same ability to engage in behaviors diagnostic of borderline personality disorder such as promiscuous sex or reckless driving (Abrams, 1990). These personality disordered elderly adults may engage in more subtle symptom displays that may be overlooked by many clinicians (Hillman, Striker, & Zweig, 1997).

Still other theories, such as the "Adaptive Context" hypothesis (Bergmann, 1991), claim that certain personality disorders (e.g., dependent and paranoid) improve with age owing to their adaptability to common age-related stressors such as physical illness. Although empirical support for such a specific theory is scant, others have affirmed that personality disorder may emerge or attenuate in later adulthood in relation to a stabilizing or destabilizing social niche (Sadavoy & Fogel, 1992).

Most notable is that despite the diversity of all of these theories, they each reflect clinicians' perspectives that personality disorder continues to play a vital role in mediating an older adult's adaptation to later life. In addition, they may represent a growing consensus that personality disorder may fluctuate in phenomenology, if not in basic structure, across the life span.

Longitudinal Studies of the Course of Personality Disorder

Longitudinal studies would appear key to establishing whether personality disorder remains invariant or changes as people age. Although some long-term follow-up studies exist, Perry (1993) noted that the majority are specific to individuals with borderline personality disorder who were treated naturalistically. These studies include varying lengths of follow-up (2–16 years) and relatively few assessments over the follow-up interval. Further, because many subjects in these studies were young adults at index assessment who typically were middle-age at the time of follow-up, these results cannot be generalized to an elderly population.

Still, some preliminary substantive findings emerge. From index hospitalization to follow-up, individuals with borderline personality disorder continue to experience high levels of comorbid Axis I conditions and increased suicide risk.

Most notable, however, is the apparent time effect found when studies examine the percentage of subjects who continue to meet diagnostic criteria for borderline personality disorder at follow-up. When subjects from such studies are grouped collectively, Perry (1993) found that rates of borderline personality disorder decline in proportion to the length of the follow-up interval, and presumably to the age of the subject. For patients with borderline personality disorder, only 52% and 33% still met borderline personality disorder criteria at 10- and 15-year follow-ups, respectively. A similar result was obtained for male patients with antisocial personality disorder, of whom 87% and 72% still met criteria at 3- and 9-year follow-up intervals, respectively. In regard to social functioning, individuals with borderline personality disorder again improved, although most patients still displayed impairment in this area and a high percentage continued to utilize psychiatric treatment. Perry (1993) noted that it is unclear whether these improvements are suggestive of an age or treatment effect, although it would seem unlikely that treatment effects fully account for these longitudinal changes. Of course, methodological weaknesses of the previous studies limit inferences regarding their generalization to older adults. Features such as a cross-sequential design to reduce cohort effects, efforts to control for differential attrition, and greater use of dimensional personality measures would clarify future findings. Yet, these longitudinal studies provide an initial mapping of the course of some personality disorders over time.

What conclusions regarding aging and personality disorder can be derived from empirical findings regarding normal personality development and the longitudinal course of personality disorder in adults? First, whereas adaptive and maladaptive personality dimensions are likely to be stable over time, maturation effects and changes at the specific trait level are likely to occur. For example, if increased "affective control" or decreased "activity" is common with aging, some natural masking of features of borderline personality disorder (e.g., affective instability and impulsiveness) might be expected with age. Other core features of borderline personality disorder, such as unstable interpersonal relationships and impaired social adjustment, would be expected to persist into late adulthood and to manifest themselves in a manner similar to that seen among younger personality disordered adults (e.g., treatment drop-out; Zweig & Hinrichsen, 1992). Further, if subsequent studies do find this maturation effect to be common among individuals with personality disorder, guidelines for determining age of onset for a diagnosis of personality disorder may warrant revision. A second conclusion is that proof of a general worsening or amelioration of personality disorder severity with age is lacking. In fact, just as in youth, older individuals with personality disorder seem to remain at higher risk for Axis I disorders. The severity of personality disorder in later life seems less determined by age alone than by factors such as prior adaptation, life experience, and the buffering effects of the individual's psychosocial niche (Gutmann, 1988).

CONCLUSIONS AND IMPLICATIONS FOR THE STUDY
OF PERSONALITY DISORDER IN LATER LIFE

A review of the research regarding personality disorder in adults yields several conclusions that are relevant to understanding personality disorder in older adults. Preliminary epidemiologic findings in nonclinical and clinical populations suggest that personality disorders as a group are rather prevalent, are often comorbid with Axis I disorders, and are associated with serious adverse life events. Whereas diagnostic assessment is impeded by the complexity of the construct, limitations of current assessment tools, and the need for an agreed-on dimensional model, diagnostic reliability and validity have been enhanced by the broader array of methods and measures employed in research. Of note, personality disorders in adults appear to exert a marked negative impact on the onset and treatment outcome of mood disorders; affected individuals respond more slowly or less fully to standard treatments such as psychotherapy and psychotropic medication. Finally, whereas these disorders generally persist over time, their severity may be multidetermined and their manifestations may shift in response to age-related fluctuations in constituent traits or other maturation effects. It would therefore seem that the rule that "A zebra does not change its stripes" is valid, but that a corollary allowing for subtle shadings into "a horse of a different color" would be heuristically useful.

Findings derived from research on personality disorder in adults become most significant for geriatric mental health clinicians when considering the ubiquity of this condition and the degree to which it affects emotional functioning. Weissman (1993) noted that "personality disorders constitute one of the most important sources of long-term impairment in both treated and untreated populations" (p. 60). There is reason to suspect that the same is true for populations of older adults; Abrams, Spielman, Alexopoulos, and Klausner (1998) suggested that personality disorder traits predict posttreatment functional deficits. More data is needed to draw firm conclusions. Based on findings in young and middle-age adults, several predictions regarding personality disorder in older adulthood can be made: (a) Personality disorder is highly comorbid in depressed elderly, and adversely impacts on social adjustment and overall treatment outcome. (b) Personality disorder in later life is associated with a higher incidence of adverse life events, as seen in younger adults, ranging from poorly controlled medical problems to suicide attempts. (c) Elderly adults with personality disorder are at increased risk for other syndromes such as anxiety, somatization, and substance dependence disorders. (d) Some manifestations of personality disorder, such as degree of affective control, change in later life, whereas core features remain.

Noted less often, but of significance, are the "social costs" of personality disorder borne by an older adult's family and social environment (for a review of social and ethical issues and personality disorder, see Molinari, chap. 16 in this volume). Regarding these social costs of untreated disorders in adults, Strupp (1996) pondered:

> Why should a society care about a person's sense of well-being? The answer, it seems to me, lies in the hidden costs that intrapsychic and interpersonal conflicts exact from families whose children become delinquents, drug addicts, adolescent single mothers, and so forth. Conversely, a parent's sense of well-being may translate to comparable feelings in a child. (p. 1023)

In older adults with personality disorder, the social costs are probably felt most directly by spouses, children, and other relatives, all of whom may experience a form of "caregiver burden." Yet, remarkably little is known about these interpersonal and transgenerational effects, as well as about the indirect economic costs attributable to personality disorders (Pilkonis, 1997). Given the costs that individuals with personality disorders exact from others in their interpersonal environment, it is understandable that older adults suffering from personality disorders remain stigmatized and shunned by their families, and even by their health care providers (Hillman, Striker, & Zweig, 1997). Newer methods of understanding and treating these individuals, however, will hopefully lessen the costs and increase the gains, not only to affected older adults but to the families and societies in which they reside.

REFERENCES

Abrams, R. (1990). Personality disorders in the elderly. In D. Binenfeld (Ed.), *Verwoerdt's clinical geropsychiatry* (pp. 151–163). Baltimore: Williams & Wilkins.

Abrams, R., Spielman, L., Alexopoulos, G., & Klausner, E. (1998). Personality disorder symptoms and functioning in elderly depressed patients. *American Journal of Geriatric Psychiatry, 6,* 24–36.

Agronin, M. E. (1994). Personality disorders in the elderly: An overview. *Journal of Geriatric Psychiatry, 27,* 151–191.

American Psychiatric Association. (1994). *Diagnostic and statistical manual of mental disorders* (4th ed.). Washington, DC: Author.

Andrews, G., Neilson, M., Hunt, C., Stewart, G., & Kiloh, L. (1990). Diagnosis, personality, and the long-term outcome of depression. *British Journal of Psychiatry, 157,* 13–18.

Barratt, E. S., & Patton, J. H. (1983). Impulsivity: Cognitive, behavioral, and psychophysiological correlates. In M. Zuckerman (Ed.), *Biological basis of sensation-seeking* (pp. 77–116). Hillsdale, NJ: Lawrence Erlbaum Associates.

Beardon, C., Lavelle, N., Buysse, D., Karp, J. F., & Frank, E. (1996). Personality pathology and time to remission in depressed outpatients treated with interpersonal psychotherapy. *Journal of Personality Disorders, 10,* 164–173.

Bengtson, V., Reedy, M., & Gordon, C. (1985). Aging and self-conceptions: Personality processes and social contexts. In J. E. Birren & K. W. Schaie (Eds.), *Handbook of the psychology of aging* (pp. 544–593). New York: Van Nostrand Reinhold.

Bergmann, K. (1991). Psychiatric aspects of personality in older patients. In R. Jacoby & C. Oppenheimer (Eds.), *Psychiatry in the elderly* (pp. 852–871). Oxford, England: Oxford University Press.

Black, D., Bell, S., Hulbert, J., & Nasrallah, A. (1988). The importance of Axis II in patients with major depression. *Journal of Affective Disorders, 14,* 115–122.

Buss, A. H., & Durkee, A. (1957). An inventory for assessing different kinds of hostility. *Journal of Consulting Psychology, 21,* 343–348.

Casey, P. R., & Tyrer, P. (1990). Personality disorder and psychiatric illness in general practice. *British Journal of Psychiatry, 156,* 261–265.

Charney, D., Nelson, J., & Quinlan D. (1981). Personality traits and disorders in depression. *American Journal of Psychiatry, 138,* 1601–1604.

Clark, L. A. (1993). *Manual for the schedule for nonadaptive and adaptive personality (SNAP).* Minneapolis: University of Minnesota Press.

Cloninger, C. R. (1987). A systematic method for clinical description and classification of personality variants. *Archives of General Psychiatry, 44,* 573–588.

Costa, P., & Widiger, T. (1994). *Personality disorders and the five-factor model of personality.* Washington, DC: American Psychological Association.

Costa, P., & McCrae, R. (1990). Personality disorders and the five-factor model of personality. *Journal of Personality Disorders, 4,* 362–371.

Costa, P., & McCrae, R. (1992a). *NEO-PI-R professional manual.* Odessa FL: Psychological Assessment Resources.

Costa, P., & McCrae, R. (1992b). Trait psychology comes of age. In T. Sonderegger (Ed.), *Nebraska symposium on motivation 1991* (pp. 169–204). Lincoln, NE: University of Nebraska Press.

Duggan, C., Lee, A., & Murray, R. (1990). Does personality predict long-term outcome in depression? *British Journal of Psychiatry, 157,* 19–24.

Ellason, J., Ross, C., Sainton, K., & Mayran, L. (1996). Axis I and II co-morbidity and childhood trauma history in chemical dependency. *Bulletin of the Menninger Clinic, 60,* 39–51.

Faravelli, C., Ambonetti, A., Pallanti, S., & Pazzagli, A. (1986). Depressive relapses and incomplete recovery from index episode. *American Journal of Psychiatry, 143,* 888–891.

Farmer, R., & Nelson-Grey, R. O. (1990). Personality disorders and depression: Hypothetical relations, empirical findings, and methodological considerations. *Clinical Psychology Review, 10,* 453–476.

Fonagy, P., Leigh, T., Steele, M., & Steele, H. (1996). The relation of attachment status, psychiatric classification, and response to psychotherapy. *Journal of Consulting and Clinical Psychology, 64,* 22–31.

Frances, A. J., & Widiger, T. A. (1987). Personality disorders. In A. E. Skodol & R. L. Spitzer (Eds.), *An annotated bibliography of DSM-III* (pp. 125–133). Washington, DC: American Psychiatric Association.

Frank, E., Kupfer, D. J., Jacob, M., & Jarrett, D. (1987). Personality features and response to acute treatment in recurrent depression. *Journal of Personality Disorders, 1,* 14–26.

Golumb, M., Fava M., Abraham, M., & Rosenbaum, J. (1995). Gender differences in personality disorders. *American Journal of Psychiatry, 152,* 579–582.

Gutmann, D. (1987). *Reclaimed powers: Toward a new psychology of men and women in later life.* New York: Basic Books.

Gutmann, D. (1988). Late onset pathogenesis: Dynamic models. *Topics in Geriatric Rehabilitation, 3,* 1–8.

Helson, R., & Wink, P. (1992). Personality change in women from the early forties to the early fifties. *Psychology and Aging, 7,* 46–55.

Hillman, J., Striker, G., & Zweig, R. (1997). Clinical psychologists' judgments of older adult patients with character pathology: Implications for practice. *Professional Psychology: Research and Practice, 28,* 179–183.

Hirschfeld, R. M., & Cross, C. K. (1987). The measurement of personality in depression. In A. J. Marsella, R. Hirshfeld, & M. Katz (Eds.), *The measurement of depression* (pp. 319–343). New York: Guilford.

Horowitz, L. M., Rosenberg, S. E., Baer, B. A., Ureno, G., & Villasenor, V. S. (1988). Inventory of Interpersonal Problems: Psychometric properties and clinical applications. *Journal of Consulting and Clinical Psychology, 56,* 885–892.

Hyler, S. E., & Reider, R. O. (1987). *PDQ–R: Personality Diagnostic Questionnaire–Revised.* New York: New York State Psychiatric Institute.

Jacobsberg, L., Goldsmith, S., Widiger, T., & Frances, A. (1989). Assessment of *DSM–III* personality disorders. In S. Wetzler (Ed.), *Measuring mental illness: Psychometric assessment for clinicians* (pp. 141–159). Washington, DC: American Psychiatric Association.

Kernberg, O. (1984). *Severe personality disorders: Psychotherapeutic strategies.* New Haven, CT: Yale University Press.

Klein, M. H. (1993). Issues in the assessment of personality disorders. *Journal of Personality Disorders, 7,* (Suppl.), 18–33.

Klein, M. H., Benjamin, L., & Rosenfelt R. (1993). The Wisconsin Personality Disorder Inventory. *Journal of Personality Disorders, 7,* 285–303.

LaBouvie-Vief, G., DeVoe, M., & Bulka, D. (1989). Speaking about feelings: Conceptions of emotion across the life span. *Psychology and Aging, 4,* 425–437.

Loranger, A., Susman, V., Oldham, J., & Russakoff, L. (1987). The Personality Disorders Examination: A preliminary report. *Journal of Personality Disorders, 1,* 1–13.

Maier, W., Lichtermann, D., Klingler, T., Heun, R., & Hallmeyer, J. (1992). Prevalences of personality disorders (*DSM–III–R*) in the community. *Journal of Personality Disorders, 6,* 187–196.

Mellman, T. A., Leverich, G. S., Hauser, P., Kramlinger, K., Post, R. M., & Uhde, T. W. (1992). Axis II pathology in panic and affective disorders: Relationship to diagnosis, course of illness, and treatment response. *Journal of Personality Disorders, 6,* 53–63.

Millon, T. (1983). *Millon Clinical Multiaxial Inventory manual* (3rd ed.). Minneapolis: Interpretive Scoring Systems.

Morey, L. C. (1991). *Personality Assessment Inventory (PAI) professional manual.* Odessa FL: Psychological Assessment Resources.

Neugarten, B. (1979). Time, age, and the life cycle. *American Journal of Psychiatry, 136,* 887–894.

Perry, J. C. (1993). Longitudinal studies of personality disorders. *Journal of Personality Disorders, 7*(Suppl.), 63–85.

Pfohl, B., Stangl, D., & Zimmerman, M. (1984). The implications of *DSM–III* personality disorders for patients with major depression. *Journal of Affective Disorders, 7,* 309–318.

Pfohl, B., Coryell, W., Zimmerman, M., & Stangl, D. (1987). Prognostic validity of self-report and interview measures of personality disorder in depressed inpatients. *Journal of Clinical Psychiatry, 48,* 468–472.

Pfohl, B., Stangl, D., & Zimmerman, M. (1983). *Structured Interview for the DSM–III Personality Disorders, SIDP.* Unpublished manuscript, University of Iowa College of Medicine, Iowa City.

Pilkonis, P. A. (1997). Measurement issues relevant to personality disorders. In H. H. Strupp, L. M. Horowitz, & M. J. Lambert (Eds.), *Measuring patient changes in mood, anxiety, and personality disorders* (pp. 371–388). Washington, DC: American Psychological Association.

Pilkonis, P., & Frank, E. (1988). Personality pathology in recurrent depression: Nature, prevalence, and relationship to treatment response. *American Journal of Psychiatry, 145,* 435–441.

Reich, J. (1990). Effect of *DSM–III* personality disorders on outcome of tricyclic antidepressant-treated nonpsychotic outpatients with major or minor depressive disorder. *Psychiatry Research, 32,* 175–181.

Reich, J. H., & Vasile, R. G. (1993). Effect of personality disorders on the treatment outcome of Axis I conditions: An update. *Journal of Nervous and Mental Disease, 181,* 475–484.

Reich, J., Nduaguba, M., & Yates, W. (1988). Age and sex distribution of *DSM–III* personality cluster traits in a community population. *Comprehensive Psychiatry, 29,* 298–303.

Reich, J., Yates, W., & Nduaguba, M. (1989). Prevalence of *DSM–III* personality disorders in the community. *Social Psychiatry and Psychiatric Epidemiology, 24,* 12–16.

Robins, L., & Regier, D. (1991). *Psychiatric disorders in America: The epidemiologic catchment area Study.* New York: The Free Press.

Rosowsky, E., & Gurian, B. (1991). Borderline personality disorder in late life. *International Psychogeriatrics, 3,* 39–52.

Sadavoy, J., & Fogel, B. (1992). Personality disorder in old age. In J. E. Birren, R. B. Sloane, & G. D. Cohen (Eds.), *Handbook of mental health and aging* (2nd ed., pp. 433–462). San Diago: Academic Press.

Sadavoy, J., & Leszcz, M. (1987). *Treating the elderly with psychotherapy: The scope for change in late life.* Madison: International Universities Press.

Schaie, K. W., & Willis, S. (1986). *Adult development and aging* (2nd ed.). Boston: Little, Brown.

Shea, M. (1993). Psychosocial treatment of personality disorders. *Journal of Personality Disorders, 7,* Supplement, 167–180.

Shea, M. T., Glass, D. R., Pilkonis, P., Watkins, J., & Docherty, J. P. (1987). Frequency and implications of personality disorders in a sample of depressed outpatients. *Journal of Personality Disorders, 1,* 27–42.

Shea, M. T., Leon, A. C., Mueller T. I., Solomon, D. A., Warshaw, M. G., & Keller, M. B. (1996). Can major depression result in lasting personality change? *American Journal of Psychiatry, 153,* 1404–1410.

Shea, M. T., Pilkonis, P. A., Beckham, E., Collins, J. F., Elkin, I., Sotsky, S. M., & Docherty, J. P. (1990). Personality disorders and treatment outcome in the NIMH Treatment of Depression Collaborative Research Program. *American Journal of Psychiatry, 147,* 711–718.

Shea, M. T., Widiger, T. A., & Klein, M. H. (1992). Comorbidity of personality disorders and depression: Implications for treatment. *Journal of Consulting and Clinical Psychology, 60,* 857–868.

Siever, L. J., & Davis, K. L. (1991). A psychobiological perspective on the personality disorders. *American Journal of Psychiatry, 148,* 1647–1658.

Solomon, K. (1981). Personality disorder in the elderly. In J. R. Lion (Ed.), *Personalty disorders: Diagnosis and management* (2nd ed., pp. 310–338). Baltimore: Williams & Wilkins.

Stangl, D., Pfohl., B., Zimmerman, M., Bowers, W., & Corenthal, C. (1985). A structured interview for the *DSM–III* personality disorders: A preliminary report. *Archives of General Psychiatry, 42,* 591–596.

Strupp, H. (1996). The tripartite model and the *Consumer Reports* study. *American Psychologist, 51,* 1017–1024.

Thompson, L., Gallagher, D., & Czirr, R. (1988). Personality disorder and the outcome of the treatment of late life depression. *Journal of Geriatric Psychiatry, 21,* 133–153.

Tyrer, P. (Ed.). (1988). *Personality disorder: Diagnosis, management, and course.* London: Wright.

Weissman, M. (1993). The epidemiology of personality disorders: A 1990 update. *Journal of Personality Disorders, 7*(Suppl.), 44–62.

Weissman M., & Bothwell, S. (1976). Assessment of social adjustment by patient self-report. *Archives of General Psychiatry, 33,* 1111–1115.

Westen, D. (1997). Divergences between clinical and research methods for assessing personality disorders: Implications for research and the evolution of Axis II. *American Journal of Psychiatry, 154,* 895–903.

Widiger, T. (1994). Conceptualizing a disorder of personality from the five-factor model. In P. T. Costa & T. A. Widiger (Eds.), *Personality disorder and the five-factor model of personality* (pp. 311–318). Washington, DC: American Psychological Association.

Widiger, T., & Frances, A. (1987). Interviews and inventories for the measurement of personality disorders. *Clinical Psychology Review, 7,* 49–75.

Woodruff, D., Guze, S., & Clayton, P. (1971). The medical and psychiatric implications of antisocial personality (sociopathy). *Diseases of the Nervous System, 32,* 712–714.

Zimmerman, M., & Coryell, W. (1989). *DSM–III* personality disorder diagnoses in a nonpatient sample: Demographic correlates and comorbidity. *Archives of General Psychiatry, 46,* 682–689.

Zimmerman, M., & Coryell, W. (1990). Diagnosing personality disorders in the community: A comparison of self-report and interview measures. *Archives of General Psychiatry, 47,* 527–531.

Zimmerman, M., Coryell, W., Pfohl B., Corenthal, C., & Stangl, M. A. (1986). ECT response in depressed patients with and without a *DSM–III* personality disorder. *American Journal of Psychiatry, 143,* 1030–1032.

Zweig, R., & Hinrichsen, G. (1992, November). *Impact of personality disorder on affective illness in older adults.* Paper presented at the 45th Annual Scientific Meeting of the Gerontological Society of America, Washington DC.

CHAPTER 4

Personality Disorders After Age 50: A Meta-Analytic Review of the Literature

ROBERT C. ABRAMS, MD
Joan and Sanford I. Weill Medical College of Cornell University

SANDRA V. HOROWITZ, PhD
Columbia University Teachers' College

The literature on personality disorders in late life is sparse and inconclusive, not surprisingly so given the long-standing uncertainty about whether Axis II represents an appropriate nosology for the elderly (Fogel & Westlake, 1990). Various authors have suggested a lower prevalence of personality disorders in old, as opposed to young, adults in clinical and epidemiological samples (Casey, 1988; Kroessler, 1990); no differences between elderly males and females (Ames & Molinari, 1994); and fewer personality disorders overall, particularly in Cluster B (Abrams, Rosendahl, Card, & Alexopoulos, 1994; Kunik, Mulsant, Rifai, Sweet, Pasternak, Rosen, & Zubenko, 1994). However, the prevalence of personality disorders in the second half of life essentially remains unknown. A review of pre-*DSM–III* European field studies uncovered prevalences ranging from 2.8% to 11% among community-dwelling elderly (Gurland & Cross, 1982), but these and subsequent reports have been so methodologically diverse that simple prevalence estimates were precluded. This chapter describes efforts to systematically review the literature on personality disorders after age 50. The principal aim is to discover any trends in the frequency and distribution of personality disorder symptomatology in this age group, and to consider the implications for future research.

METHOD

Selection of Studies

A literature search was undertaken with the purpose of finding all studies of personality disorders that included subjects over age 50. Age 50 was ultimately chosen as a floor after it appeared unlikely that an exclusively geriatric sample would yield sufficient data for the kind of analysis envisioned; this decision had the effect of broadening the focus of inquiry to personality disorder after mid-adulthood. Criteria for inclusion in the meta-analysis procedure also specified use of the diagnostic criteria of *DSM–III, DSM–III–R*, or *DSM–IV*, encompassing historically all of the nosological frameworks that have considered personality disorders on a separate diagnostic axis; the latter stipulation limited the chronological focus to 1980 or later. Also, case reports or series of fewer than 10 patients were excluded at this stage.

A total of 30 studies published between 1980 and 1997 (inclusive) that examined personality disorders in older adults were located in January 1998 by searching Medline and PsyLit databases and by requesting referrals of articles from personality disorder researchers. The search reported here represents an update of an earlier effort using the same method (Abrams & Horowitz, 1996). A total of 14 (46.66%) of these articles failed to meet inclusion criteria for the meta-analysis. Among those omitted were five articles focusing on a single personality disorder, including the Epidemiological Catchment Area studies assessing exclusively for antisocial personality disorder (Bland, Newman & Orn, 1988; Kramer, German, Anthony, Von Korff, & Skinner, 1985; Robins et al., 1984; Rosowsky & Gurian, 1991; Weissman et al., 1985); two studies describing material already covered in another article being used in the analysis pool (Abrams, Young, Alexopoulos, & Holt, 1991; Kunik et al., 1993); two studies failing to use *DSM* criteria (Gurland & Cross, 1982; Kastrup, 1985), of which the first also reported non-original data; two studies including elderly subjects but not presenting data according to age breakdowns (Frank, Kupfer, Jacob, & Jarrett, 1987; Pilkonis & Frank, 1988); and three articles reporting only or relying mainly on dimensional scores for personality disorders or clusters (Cohen, Nestadt, Samuels, Romanowski, McHugh, & Rabins, 1994; Coolidge, Burns, Nathan, & Mull, 1992; Reich, Nduaguba, & Yates, 1988).

The remaining 16 articles (Table 4.1) published original data and had sufficient information concerning the prevalence of personality disorders in older adults to permit an exploratory meta-analysis procedure. Because of the small number of publications available, those studies are included that reportedly assessed the full spectrum of personality disorders but failed to specify frequencies for some or all of the individual disorders, as well as those studies that provided data on all personality disorders. As in earlier meta-analysis, investigations were

TABLE 4.1
Prevalence of Personality Disorders in Adults
Older and Younger than 50

	Over Age 50		Under Age 50	
	Sample		*Sample*	
	N	%	N	%
Abrams, Alexopoulos, & Young (1987)	36	6	—	—
Abrams et al. (1994)	30	7	—	—
Ames & Molinari (1994)	100	26	—	—
Casey & Schrodt (1989)	100	7	100	23
Schneider et al. (1992)	50	22	—	—
Devanand et al. (1994)	40	10	—	—
Fogel & Westlake (1990)	544	11	1,778	17
Thompson, Gallagher, & Czirr (1988)	120	33	—	—
Kunik et al. (1994)	547	13	—	—
Mezzich et al. (1987)	494	6	4,357	22
Speer & Bates (1992)	128	30	—	—
Golomb et al. (1995)	136	57	180	55
Silberman et al. (1997)	30	80	—	—
Coolidge, Janitell, & Griego (1994)	83	18	—	—
Molinari & Marmion (1995)	76	63	—	—
Molinari, Ames, & Essa (1994)	200	56	131	51
Overall Prevalence Rate (Based on studies listed)	20%		22%	

characterized according to sample size; sample composition (i.e., gender and age); comparison groups; study setting; method of assessing subjects for personality disorder criteria (i.e., structured interview, retrospective chart review, or consensus of clinicians and researchers); source of information for the personality disorder assessment (i.e., subject, informant, clinical observation); Axis I psychiatric comorbidity; and specific structured interviews, if any, used to measure the presence of Axis II disorders.

Coding and Interrater Agreement

Coding sheets were used to extract pertinent information from the separate studies measuring personality disorders in older adults. Two coders independently recorded the dependent variable, the percentage of subjects over age 50 diagnosed with one or more personality disorders, as well as the major inclusion criteria. Five randomly selected studies were coded by both coders. Coder agreement was 97% on both the dependent variable and the inclusion criteria. Such high agreement may have resulted from the relatively small number of studies available for the meta-analysis as well as the straightforward, objective nature of the data extracted.

Prevalence Rates and p Values

The literature search uncovered 16 published papers meeting inclusion criteria for a meta-analysis of personality disorders occurring in adults over age 50. The existence of three prevalence rates has been judged adequate to calculate an overall prevalence rate in a meta-analysis (Christensen, Hadzi-Pavlovic, & Jacomb, 1991); however, such small numbers can only be considered a preliminary step, a useful method of organizing a review of the current state of measurement of personality disorders in the age group of interest. Pursuing this approach, the following prevalence rates were calculated from the existing data: The overall prevalence of personality disorders in adults both older and younger than age 50, and the prevalence of individual personality disorders in both age groups. The prevalence of personality disorders between adults older and younger than age 50 and between males and females older than age 50 were then compared. Finally, there was a comparison of prevalences of personality disorder according to setting (psychiatric inpatient vs. psychiatric outpatient and nonpatient community), assessment method (structured interview vs. consensus of researchers and clinicians or chart review) and source of information (clinical observation vs. other sources).

The DerSimonian and Laird (D & L) modified Cochran method was selected for combining event rates (Berlin, Laird, Sacks, & Chalmers, 1989). This method treats each study as a separate stratum, using a weighted average of prevalence rate differences that allows for among-study variability. A conservative testing procedure, the D & L method weights prevalence rates using both the variance of data within the individual studies as well as the variance between groups, or among the studies being compared. Thus, it provides a more precise estimate of the overall prevalence rate than would otherwise be possible (Hedges & Olkin, 1985).

Finally, we used Z tests to compare different frequencies of personality disorder between groups, calculating the standard error in each case with weighted least squares estimates.

RESULTS

The sample for the meta-analysis included 16 studies investigating the frequency of personality disorders in older adults. The range of total sample size for individual studies varied from 30 to 4,851; however, the number of adults age 50 or older investigated in these studies ranged from 30 to 547, with a mean of 356.79 ($SD = 207.99$) subjects. The number of younger adults investigated in these studies ranged from 100 to 4,357, with a mean sample size of 2,157.58 ($SD = 1,697.55$). The mean proportion of females/males represented by these studies was 55/46 ($SD = 10.87$), regardless of age.

The overall prevalence rate for any diagnosis of personality disorder in the over 50 group, calculated using a weighted average, was 20%. Individual studies showed considerable variation, reporting frequencies of personality disorders from 6%, in a sample of elderly recovered depressives and nonpatient elderly residing in the community (Abrams, Alexopoulos, & Young, 1987), to 80% in a mixed-diagnosis sample of chronic mental patients (Silberman, Roth, Segal, & Burns, 1997). The comparable prevalence rates for the under 50 group, based on the five studies reporting this data, was 22% overall, with a range from 17% to 55% (Table 4.1).

The individual personality disorders that occurred most frequently in the older adults were the Paranoid (19.8%), Self-defeating (a pre-*DSM–III–R* experimental category; 12.3%), and Schizoid (10.8%). The rate of occurrence for all other personality disorders in older adults was between 2% and 7.8% (Table 4.2). Based on the studies presenting this data, the individual personality disorders that occurred most frequently in adults under age 50 were Paranoid (31.4%) and Narcissistic (12.6%). The rate of occurence for all other personality disorders in younger adults was between 1.2% and 6.6%.

Because the minimum number of data points required to calculate an overall prevalence rate is three, meta-analytic techniques could be applied to five between-group comparisons across studies. These comparisons included adults older than age 50 versus adults younger than age 50; males versus females within the over 50 age group; psychiatric inpatient versus outpatient and nonpatient community settings; structured interview assessment versus consensus of clini-

TABLE 4.2
Prevalence of Individual Personality Disorders
in Adults Older and Younger than 50

	Over Age 50		Under Age 50	
	Rate (%)	# of Studies	Rate (%)	# of Studies
Paranoid	19.8	5	31.4	2
Antisocial	2.6	6	4.8	3
Dependent	5.4	8	4.5	5
Obsessive Compulsive	7.8	12	6.6	5
Narcissistic	4.6	7	12.6	3
Histrionic	4.9	7	3.4	5
Passive Aggressive	6.2	7	1.8	3
Borderline	7.1	7	3.4	3
Avoidant	7.7	8	3.2	3
Schizoid	10.8	6	2.3	2
Schizotypal	4.9	5	1.2	3
Self-Defeating	12.3	2	—	—
Mixed	2.0	4	5.9	2
NOS	6.5	3	—	—

cians and researchers or chart review; and clinical observation versus other sources of information. In the first two comparisons, the likelihood of receiving any personality disorder diagnosis did not significantly differ according to age, or, within the older group, according to gender. Failure to uncover significant differences in these comparisons may have reflected the large variability in sample size (Table 4.1) as well as the small number of studies available for the comparison.

Settings varied across the 16 studies in the analysis. Nine of the studies (55%) drew either the full sample or part of the sample from among psychiatric inpatients. In four studies, subjects were recruited exclusively from psychiatric outpatient clinics. Two studies were conducted using community samples, and a senior citizen center was chosen for the remaining study. The setting had a significant effect on the frequency of personality disorders diagnosed in the over 50 age group; investigators conducting studies with psychiatric outpatients or subjects living in the community were more likely to diagnose personality disorders than were those working with psychiatric inpatients, $Z = 2.61, p < .005$ (Table 4.3).

Four methods of personality disorder assessment were used for the 16 studies: structured interviews (7 studies), questionnaire (5 studies), a consensus of clinicians and researchers (2 studies), and retrospective chart review (2 studies). The method of assessing subjects for personality disorder criteria made a significant difference in the frequency of diagnosis: Questionnaire, consensus methodology, and chart review grouped together resulted in a higher rate of personality disorders than did the use of a structured interview ($Z = 4.44, p < .0001$) (Table 4.3).

The origin of the information used for diagnosis was also reviewed. Clinical observation of behavior was used as the source of information for deciding whether or not subjects met personality disorder criteria in six (37.5%) of the

TABLE 4.3
Comparative Prevalences of Personality Disorder
in Adults Over 50

	M	SE	Z	95% C.I.
Setting				
Psychiatric inpatient	.11	.001*	2.61	(.06, .57)
All others combined	.23	.020		
Assessment Method				
Structured interview	.13	.001**	4.44	(.29, .84)
All others combined	.15	.004		
Source of Information				
Clinical observation	.12	.001*	2.61	(.06, .57)
All others combined	.22	.020		

*$p < .005$.
**$p < .0001$.

studies. This source resulted in lower frequency of personality disorder diagnoses than did the use of material from informants or from patient self-report given in questionnaires or in clinical or structured interviews, $Z = 2.61$, $p < .005$ (Table 4.3).

DISCUSSION

The study of personality disorders in the elderly has been clouded by conceptual and methodological difficulties to the extent that opportunities for clinically relevant investigation have been neglected. There has even been some uncertainty about whether older adults can legitimately have personality disorders. The introduction to Axis II in *DSM–III* noted that personality disorders are present for most of adult life but become "attenuated" by middle age (American Psychiatric Association, 1980); yet, in order to make the diagnosis, symptoms were required to be present currently. Taken together, these statements and stipulations suggest that personality disorders were intended by the framers of *DSM–III* to be assigned infrequently to older patients, because even if these individuals had relevant symptoms in young adulthood, the diagnostic threshold for severity or number of criteria would be likely to be lost over time through "attenuation." Only in the "Organic Personality Syndrome" of *DSM–III* and *DSM–III–R* (American Psychiatric Association, 1987) were there no explicit concerns about age or duration of symptoms in the assessment of personality dysfunction. However, both "Organic Personality Syndrome" and its *DSM–IV* successor, "Personality Change Due to a General Medical Syndrome," have been classified apart from personality disorders largely because symptoms need not be evident since young adulthood, and also because a specific organic etiology is required. The "Organic Personality Disorder" of *ICD–10* (World Health Organization, 1992) covers much the same ground as the "Personality Change Due to a General Medical Condition" of *DSM–IV*. However, these syndromes are all somewhat peripheral to the core Axis II personality disorders. Also note that none of the studies included in this meta-analysis, each of which used *DSM–III* or *DSM–III–R* criteria, specified a diagnosis of "Organic Personality Syndrome."

Thus, it seems possible that the general instructions and time-frame guidelines for Axis II of *DSM–III*, *DSM–III–R*, and *DSM–IV* have served to discourage clinicians from making personality disorder diagnoses in the second half of life. Concern about the validity of clinical information given by an acutely depressed elderly patient, or one with impairments in memory and judgment, is another factor that may have inhibited clinicians from making personality disorder diagnoses in elderly patients (Abrams, 1995). Reflecting what probably occurs widely in clinical practice because of these difficulties, most of the studies used in this meta-analysis did not document in detail how the presence or absence of personality disorder symptoms since young adulthood was determined; it is suspected that some of this data may have been more influenced by cross-sectional clinical presentation than by a meticulous tracking of symptoms since adolescence.

Moreover, none of the authors commented on the possibility of nonorganic late-onset personality disorders (syndromes either absent or subthreshold in young adulthood that then present as meeting criteria for a personality disorder in middle or old age) or *past* personality disorders (those personality disorders that do, in fact, attenuate so that they fail to meet diagnostic threshold by middle or old age). Although unrecognized by *DSM–IV*, late onset and past personality disorders would be of considerable theoretical interest. If, as has been suggested, criteria for various personality disorders are age biased (Fogel & Westlake, 1990), then more detail on the longitudinal presentation of these symptoms would be a helpful contribution of future research. Nevertheless, the overall rate of 20% culled from this meta-analysis is larger than the frequency of 10% reported in pre-*DSM–III* field studies (Gurland & Cross, 1982), arguing against the existence of a powerful age bias in the *DSM* criteria.

In recent years there has been speculation about a true age effect with respect to personality disorders, beyond that related to clinicians' diagnosing practices, whereby both the overall frequency and the range of disorders are reduced in the later decades of life (Kroessler, 1990; Reich, Nduaguba, & Yates, 1988). Cluster B disorders, conceptualized as disorders of impulse control and viewed on the basis of young adult follow-up data as conditions of immaturity (Tyrer, 1988) have been thought to be especially infrequent in the elderly (Abrams et al., 1994; Kunik et al., 1994). This phenomenon is consistent with age-regression data using the Eysenck Personality Inventory, which shows reductions in Neuroticism and Extraversion with age, implying progressively greater stability and impulse control (Eysenck, 1987). The publication of small case series of reports of elderly Borderline patients (Rosowsky & Gurian, 1991) has, if anything, reinforced the impression of this occurrence as a rarity.

Not all authors have been in agreement with the existence of the putative age effect, however. At least one study considered here found a personality disorder rate of 33% in a sample of treated elderly depressives (Thompson, Gallagher, & Czirr, 1988). Another report (Kunik et al., 1994) argued that rates of personality disorders in an impatient geriatric psychiatry unit would be comparable to those of younger adults in a similar setting if dementia cases were excluded. On the level of trait dimensions underlying personality disorders, there is now substantial evidence from the NEO Personality Inventory for long-term stability of individuals as they age (Costa & McCrae, 1990).

To cull the existing personality disorder literature for evidence of age-related effects has always appeared to require a meta-analytic approach. Differences among studies in sample composition, diagnostic methods, and design would have burdened a descriptive review, even of this relatively small literature. Initial efforts to review the literature using meta-analytic techniques yielded only 11 studies up to 1995 that met inclusion criteria (Abrams & Horowitz, 1996). Therefore the next step was to repeat the analysis to determine whether or how additional data might affect the preliminary results we reported. Although 16 studies were now found, the heterogeneity of the studies and the small number of subjects included have continued to limit the conclusions that could be drawn from the meta-analysis.

Thus, the literature at this time still appears to be inconclusive on the question of an age effect in personality disorder diagnosis. Specifically, among the five studies that included cells of young and over 50 adults, there was no significant difference in the rate of personality disorders between the young and older subjects. Although the combined rate of 20% for personality disorders in persons age 50 and older is relatively low compared to groups of younger patients with depressive disorders (Pilkonis & Frank, 1988), the small number of studies involved, the considerable range in rates of personality disorders reported, and the overall instability of findings again suggest that this finding should not be interpreted as evidence of an age effect. The instability of findings is underscored by the fact that the addition of six more studies to the meta-analytic pool resulted in a doubling of the overall frequency of personality disorder diagnosis in the under age 50 subjects to 20%, from the 10% previously reported (Abrams & Horowitz, 1996).

Nor can the lack of significant difference with younger adult prevalences found here be given very much weight, because even with the additional publications added from the initial meta-analytic efforts undertaken in 1995, the number of studies and subjects involved was still relatively small, and direct comparisons by age were not the prinicpal focus of the meta-analysis. Once again, it must be concluded that the literature in its present state neither supports nor contradicts previous suggestions of an age effect.

Other findings from the meta-analysis, such as the absence of gender differences in the overall rate of personality disorder diagnosis in the over 50 population, were also limited by the variability within comparison groups. Although this failure to find gender differences in the meta-analysis is consistent with a previous report (Ames & Molinari, 1994), the same methodological issues involving discrepant settings, methods of personality disorder diagnosis, and sources of clinical information suggest that this question will also require further study.

The findings of greater prevalence of personality disorders in outpatient, or community, rather than inpatient settings and using consensus methods and chart reviews versus structured interviews were both contrary to initial expectation before examination of the literature meta-analytically, yet they were similar to findings from the 1995 meta-analysis (Abrams & Horowitz, 1996): The outpatient and nonpatient samples were not predicted to have rates of personality disorder greater than that of psychiatric inpatients; and Gunderson (1992) cited studies in which systematic assessment of clinical samples for several personality disorders resulted in higher rates of diagnosis than is usual in clinical practice. However, the impression, as in the earlier meta-analysis, is that false positives accounted for some of the large number of personality disorders in the nonpatient or community surveys and in the clinical studies using consensus or chart review, owing to the less rigorous approach sometimes involved in these methods (Hurt, Hyler, Frances, Clarkin, & Brent, 1984). For example, both the nonpatient surveys and clinical studies using consensus or chart review may have reflected a diagnostic process focusing more on current presentation than on pervasiveness since young adulthood, a criterion that is given greater emphasis by some structured interviews (Loranger, Susman, Oldham, & Russakoff, 1987); establishing pervasiveness since young adulthood may be more difficult in older subjects because of the longer time frames involved.

That clinical observation produced fewer personality disorder diagnoses than self-report or informant data was less surprising, and also replicated the finding in the earlier meta-analysis. It has been observed previously by psychotherapists working in this area that elderly patients sometimes rate themselves as more symptomatic on Axis II than do clinicians (Personal communication, E. Rosowsky, 1995). However, further study in these areas will still be required. Another issue relevant to the validity of clinical data used to make personality disorder diagnoses, either from self-report or informants, is the effect of Axis I comorbidity on personality disorder diagnosis. Because few subjects in the meta-analysis pool were assessed for personality disorders before treatment for Axis I conditions, the influence of acute Axis I symptomatology on the rate of personality disorder diagnosis in this age group could not be considered.

One outstanding difference in this survey compared to that performed in 1995 was the distribution of frequencies of the individual personality disorders. In the earlier study (Abrams & Horowitz, 1996) it was reported that the highest rates of personality disorder diagnosis in the Obsessive Compulsive and Dependent categories were among the older subjects in the meta-analysis subject pool. This finding of a predominance of Cluster C disorders among elderly subjects, particularly elderly depressives, had been consistent with earlier data (Abrams, 1991); the predominance of Cluster C diagnoses in populations of elderly depressives had been thought to reflect possible contamination from residual depression; it was also speculated that unfamiliarity of young clinicians with elders' realistically greater reliance on assistance from caregivers might also contribute to spuriously high rates of Dependent personality disorder (Abrams et al., 1987; Abrams et al., 1994). In contrast, the present study found a predominance of personality disorders in the over 50 group in Cluster A, the "schizophrenia spectrum" cluster, with Paranoid and Schizoid the first and third most frequently diagnosed personality disorders in the overall sample. The presence of mild paranoid symptomatology, or chronic subdelusional suspiciousness, as found here has been observed previously in epidemiologic samples of elderly adults (Christenson & Blazer, 1984). However, findings taken from a meta-analytic survey relying on small numbers of studies and subjects are likely to remain unstable, possibly reflecting the peculiarities of a particular study's sample (e.g., a chronically mentally ill group might be expected to have more subjects within the schizophrenia spectrum). Instability of findings is likely to persist until there is a greater critical mass of data.

The discouraging state of this literature may lead some to underestimate the clinical importance of personality disorders in the aging population. However, several authors (Abrams et al., 1994; Kunik et al., 1993) have commented on the relatively high proportion of Personality Disorder not Otherwise Specified in their samples, suggesting that personality dysfunction may be more frequent in this age group than would be indicated by the number of subjects meeting full criteria for specific disorders. The prominence in the present sample of Self-defeating personality disorder, never a formally recognized entity, could be used to make the same argument, namely much useful information is missed unless personality dysfunction in older adults is studied at a "subcategorical," or dimensional level. For this reason, the use of assessment instruments that provide dimensional as well as categorical data, such as the Personality Disorder Examination (Loranger et al., 1987), can be helpful in capturing the contributions of personality dysfunction to the overall clinical picture presented by older patients.

Further, older individuals with personality disorder may be more vulnerable to the development of Major Depression (Abrams et al., 1987), and when personality disorder is present, the first episode of depression may occur earlier in life (Abrams et al., 1994; Kunik et al., 1993). Personality disorder has been associated with negative outcomes of brief psychotherapy with elderly depressives (Thompson et al., 1988), although conclusions about the effects of personality disorder on the course of geriatric depression should await investigations controlling for the disparities in somatic treatment seen in naturalistic studies. In the interim, however, some have suggested that personality disorder may be related to specific aspects of depression in older age groups. For example, there have been reports linking Axis II symptomatology to suicide, chronicity, excess functional disability, and decreased quality of life in geriatric Major Depression (Abrams, Horowitz, & Alexopoulos, 1995; Loebel, 1990; Lyness, Caine, Conwell, King, & Cox, 1993; Moore, 1985).

Others reviewing the difficulties in this line of research have suggested that a new nosology, more attuned to the life experiences of individuals as they age and partly analogous to the separate scheme for children and adolescents, would be helpful in creating new knowledge in this area (Abrams, 1991; Fogel & Westlake, 1990). In the short term, however, there is a need for investigations using standardized personality disorder assessments in relatively homogeneous groups of older adults.

ACKNOWLEDGMENT

This research was supported by NIMH grant K07-MH01025-05.

REFERENCES

Abrams, R. C. (1991). The aging personality (editorial). *International Journal of Geriatric Psychiatry, 6,* 1–3.

Abrams, R. C. (1995). Personality disorders and aging. In J. Lindesay (Ed.), *Neurotic disorders in the elderly* (pp. 155–171). New York: Oxford University Press.

Abrams, R. C., Alexopoulos, G. S., & Young, R. C. (1987). Geriatric depression and *DSM–III–R* personality disorder criteria. *Journal of the American Geriatric Society, 35,* 383–386.

Abrams, R. C., & Horowitz, V. (1996). Personality disorders after age 50: A meta-analysis. *Journal of Personality Disorders, 10,* 271–281.

Abrams, R. C., Horowitz, S. V., & Alexopoulos, G. S. (1995, May). *Personality and quality of life in old depressives.* New Research Abstracts presented at the annual meeting of the American Psychiatric Association, Miami, FL.

Abrams, R. C., Rosendahl, E., Card, C., & Alexopoulos, G. S. (1994). Personality correlates of late and early onset depression. *Journal of American Geriatric Society, 42,* 727–731.

Abrams, R. C., Young, R. C., Alexopoulos, G. S., & Holt, J. H. (1991). Neuroticism may be associated with history of depression in the elderly. *International Journal of Geriatric Psychiatry, 6,* 483–488.

American Psychiatric Association. (1980). *Diagnostic and statistical manual of mental disorders* (3rd ed.). Washington, DC: Author.

American Psychiatric Association. (1987). *Diagnostic and statistical manual of mental disorders* (3rd ed., rev.). Washington, DC: Author.

American Psychiatric Association. (1994). *Diagnostic and statistical manual of mental disorders* (4th ed.). Washington, DC: Author.

Ames, A., & Molinari, V. (1994). Prevalence of personality disorders in community-living elderly. *Journal of Geriatric Psychiatry Neurologist, 7,* 189–194.

Berlin, J. A., Laird, N. M., Sacks, H. S., & Chalmers, T. C. (1989). A comparison of statistical methods for combining event rates from clinical trials. *Statistics in Medicine, 8,* 141–151.

Bland, R. C., Newman, S. C., & Orn, H. (1988). Prevalence of psychiatric disorders in the elderly in Edmonton. *Acta Psychiatrica Scandinavica, 77* (Suppl. 338), 57–63.

Casey, D. A., & Schrodt, C. J. (1989). Axis II diagnoses in geriatric inpatients. *Journal of Geriatric Psychiatry Neurologists, 2,* 87–88.

Casey, P. (1988). The epidemiology of personality disorder. In P. Tyrer (Ed.), *Personality disorders: Diagnosis, management and course* (pp. 74–81). London: Wright.

Christensen, H., Hadzi-Pavlovic, D., & Jacomb, P. (1991). The psychometric differentiation of dementia from normal aging: A meta-analysis. *Psychological Assessment, 3,* 147–155.

Christenson, R., & Blazer, D. (1984). Epidemiology of persecutory ideation in an elderly population in the community. *American Journal of Psychiatry, 141,* 1088–1091.

Cohen, B. J., Nestadt, G., Samuels, J. F., Romanowski, A. J., McHugh, P. R., & Rabins, P. V. (1994). Personality disorder in later life: A community study. *British Journal of Psychiatry, 165,* 493–499.

Coolidge, F. L., Burns, E. M., Nathan, J. H., & Mull, C. E. (1992). Personality disorders in the elderly. *Clinical Gerontologist, 12,* 41–55.

Coolidge, F. L., Janitell, P. M., & Griego, J. A. (1994). Personality disorders, depression and anxiety in the elderly. *Clinical Gerontologist, 15,* 80–83.

Costa, P. T., & McCrae, R. R. (1990). The five-factor model and its relevance to personality disorders. *Journal of Personality Disorders, 6,* 343–359.

Devanand, D. P., Nobler, M. S., Singer, T., Kiersky, J. E., Turret, N., Roose, S. P., & Sackeim, H. A. (1994). Is dysthymia a different disorder in the elderly? *American Journal of Psychiatry, 151,* 1592–1599.

Eysenck, H. J. (1987). Personality and aging: An introductory analysis. *Journal of Social Behavior and Personality, 3,* 11–21.

Fogel, B. S., & Westlake, R. (1990). Personality disorder diagnoses and age in inpatients with major depression. *Journal of Clinical Psychiatry, 51,* 232–235.

Frank, E., Kupfer, D. J., Jacob, M., & Jarrett, D. (1987). Personality features and response to acute treatment in recurrent depression. *Journal of Personality Disorders, 1,* 14–26.

Gunderson, J. G. (1992). Severe personality disorders: Diagnostic controversies. In A. Tasman & M. B. Riba (Eds.), *American Psychiatric Press review of psychiatry* (Vol. II, pp. 9–24). Washington, DC: American Psychiatric Press.

Golomb, M., Fava, M., Abraham, M., & Rosenbaum, J. F. (1995). The relationship between age and personality disorders in depressed outpatients. *Journal of Nervous and Mental Disease, 183,* 43–44.

Gurland, B. J., & Cross, P. S. (1982). Epidemiology of psychopathology in old age. *Psychiatric Clinics of North America, 5,* 11–26.

Hedges, L. V., & Olkin, I. (1985). *Statistical methods for meta-analysis.* San Diego, CA: Academic Press.

Hurt, S. W., Hyler, S. E., Frances, A., Clarkin, J. F., & Brent, R. (1984). Assessing borderline personality disorder with self-report, clinical interview, or semi-structured interview. *American Journal of Psychiatry, 141,* 1228–1236.

Kastrup, M. (1985). Characteristics of a nationwide cohort of psychiatric patients—with special reference to the elderly and the chronically admitted. *Acta Psychiatrica Scandinavica, 319* (Suppl. 71), 107–115.

Kramer, M., German, P. S., Anthony, J. C., Von Korff, M., & Skinner, E. A. (1985). Patterns of mental disorders among the elderly residents of eastern Baltimore. *Journal of the American Geriatrics Society, 33,* 236–245.

Kroessler, D. (1990). Personality disorders in the elderly. *Hospital Community Psychiatry, 41,* 1325–1329.

Kunik, M. E., Mulsant, B. H., Rifai, A. H., Sweet, R. A., Pasternak, R., Rosen, J., & Zubenko, G. S. (1993). Personality disorders in elderly inpatients with major depression. *American Journal of Geriatric Psychiatry, 1,* 38–45.

Kunik, M. E., Mulsant, B. H., Rifai, A. H., Sweet, R. A., Pasternak, R., & Zubenko, G. S. (1994). Diagnostic rate of comorbid personality disorders in elderly psychiatric inpatients. *American Journal of Psychiatry, 151,* 603–605.

Loebel, J. P. (1990). Completed suicide in the elderly. In *Abstracts of the Third Annual Meeting and Symposium,* American Association for Geriatric Psychiatry, San Diego, CA.

Loranger, A. W., Susman, V. L., Oldham, J. M., & Russakoff, L. M. (1987). The personality disorder examination: A preliminary report. *Journal of Personality Disorders, 1,* 1–13.

Lyness, J. M., Caine, E. D., Conwell, Y., King, D. A., & Cox, C. (1993). Depressive symptoms, medical illness, and functional status in depressed psychiatric patients. *American Journal of Psychiatry, 150,* 910–915.

Mezzich, T. E., Fabrega, Jr., H., Coffman, G. A., & Glavin, Y.F.W. (1987). Comprehensively diagnosing geriatric patients. *Comprehensive Psychiatry, 28,* 68–76.

Molinari, V., Ames, A., & Essa, M. (1994). Prevalence of personality disorders in two psychiatric inpatient units. *Journal of Geriatric Psychiatry and Neurology, 7,* 209–215.

Molinari, V., & Marmion, J. (1995). Relationship between affective disorders and axis II diagnoses in geropsychiatric patients. *Journal of Geriatric Psychiatry and Neurology, 7,* 61–64.

Moore, J. T. (1985). Dysthymia in the elderly. *Journal of Affective Disorders* (Suppl.), 515–521.

Pilkonis, P., & Frank, E. (1988). Personality pathology in recurrent depression: Nature, prevalence, and relationship to treatment response. *American Journal of Psychiatry, 145,* 435–441.

Reich, J., Nduaguba, M., Yates, W. (1988). Age and sex distribution of *DSM-III* personality cluster traits in a community population. *Comprehensive Psychiatry, 29,* 298–303.

Robins, L. N., Helzer, J. E., Weissman, M. M., Orvaschel, H., Gruenberg, E., Burke, J. D., Jr., & Regier, D. A. (1984). Lifetime prevalence of specific psychiatric disorders in three sites. *Archives of General Psychiatry, 41,* 949–958.

Rosowsky, E., & Gurian, B. (1991). Borderline personality disorder in late life. *International Psychogeriatrics, 3,* 39–52.

Schneider, L. S., Zemansky, M. F., Bender, M., & Sloane, B. R. (1992). Personality in recovered depressed elderly. *International Psychogeriatrics, 4,* 177–185.

Silberman, C. S., Roth, L., Degal, D. L., & Burns, W. (1997). Relationship between the Millon Clinical Multiaxial Inventory–II and Coolidge Axis II Inventory in chronically mentally ill older adults: A pilot study. *Journal of Clinical Psychology, 53,* 559–566.

Speer, D. C., & Bates, K. (1992). Comorbid mental and substance disorders among older psychiatric patients. *Journal of the American Geriatric Society, 40,* 886–890.

Thompson, L. W., Gallagher, D., & Czirr, R. (1988). Personality disorder and outcome in the treatment of late-life depression. *Journal of Geriatric Psychiatry, 21,* 133–146.

Tyrer, P. (1988). *Personality disorders: Diagnoses, management and course.* London: Wright.

Weissman, M. M., Myers, J. K., Tischler, G. L., Holzer, III, C. E., Leaf, P. J., Orvaschel, H., & Brody, J. A. (1985). Psychiatric disorders (*DSM–III*) and cognitive impairment among the elderly in a U.S. urban community. *Acta Psychiatrica Scandinavica, 71,* 366–379.

World Health Organization. (1992). *The* ICD–10 *classification of mental and behavioral disorders: Clinical descriptions and diagnostic guidelines.* Geneva, Switzerland: Author.

CHAPTER 5

Personality Disorders and Treatment Outcome

THEODORE J. GRADMAN, PhD
LARRY W. THOMPSON, PhD
DOLORES GALLAGHER-THOMPSON, PhD
VA Medical Center/Stanford University

In the last 15 years, a number of studies have found that personality disorders complicate, delay, or obstruct somatic or psychological treatment of Axis I affective and anxiety disorders in adults (Pfohl, Stangl, & Zimmerman, 1984; Pilkonis & Frank, 1988; Shea et al., 1990). Reviewing the *DSM–IV* definition of personality disorder sheds light on probable reasons (American Psychiatric Association, 1994). Long-term maladaptive interpersonal strategies, misinterpretation of situations and people, disturbed emotional reactions, and poor impulse control clearly complicate treatment of more circumscribed conditions such as Major Depression or Panic Disorder. Earlier onset of depressive and anxious symptoms, as well as greater symptom severity, duration, and relapse, have been found for these personality disordered individuals (Abrams, Rosendahl, Card, & Alexopoulos, 1994; Black, Bell, Hulbert, & Nasrallah, 1988; Devanand et al., 1994; Fava et al., 1996; Loebel, 1990). Personality disordered patients report more social discomfort, loneliness, reticence, friction, and fewer social contacts, as measured on the Social Adjustment Scale (Shea et al., 1990). Psychotherapy and pharmacotherapy rely on interpersonal collaboration and persuasion to achieve results. It is no wonder that personality disordered individuals have difficulty developing a good working therapy alliance, and exhibit greater attrition and poorer compliance with both somatic and psychological treatments (Krupnick et al., 1996; Zweig & Hinrichsen, 1992). When they do stay in therapy, a longer treatment period has generally been required (Shea, Widiger, & Klein, 1992).

Few studies have examined the treatment of elderly personality disordered individuals. Thompson, Gallagher, and Czirr (1988) found that depressed older adults with a concurrent personality disorder were much less likely to reach remission during a 20-session cognitive, behavioral, or dynamic psychotherapy treatment protocol for major depression. Two other studies (Zweig & Hinrichsen, 1992; Vine & Steingart, 1994) found similar negative associations between the presence of a personality disorder and treatment outcome, but three other studies (Abrams et al., 1994; Kunik et al., 1993; Molinari & Marmion, 1995) found no such association. Each of these studies is discussed in greater depth later.

The literature review that follows begins with an overview of studies of prevalence of personality disorders in the elderly. A detailed discussion of the treatment outcome studies of personality disordered older adults mentioned earlier follows. Outcome studies of a wider age range of adults with personality disorders concludes the literature review. This includes studies of somatic and psychological treatment of major depression, other affective disorders and anxiety disorders, as well as direct treatment of personality disorders. Finally, preliminary data is presented from a separate treatment outcome study of 95 older outpatients with Major Depression (Thompson, Gallagher-Thompson, Hanser, & Gantz, 1991). These patients were treated for 20 weeks with either the antidepressant medication desipramine alone, or cognitive-behavioral therapy (CBT) alone, or both in combination; their personality patterns were measured with the Millon Clinical Multiaxial Inventory (MCMI–I, Millon, 1983; and MCMI–II, Millon, 1987).

PREVALENCE AND AGE OF ONSET: ADULTS AND OLDER ADULTS

Abrams and Horowitz (1996) reviewed 23 studies of personality disorder prevalence in the elderly (11 meeting their criteria of thorough, *DSM*-based diagnoses of all personality disorders) conducted between 1980 and 1994. Their meta-analysis revealed an overall prevalence rate of about 10% for personality disorders in adults over age 50, with higher prevalence among depressed older adults compared to other groups studied. An earlier study by Abrams, Alexopoulos, and Young (1987) suggested that older adults with personality disorders appeared to be more vulnerable to the development of major depression. Beyond these studies, however, there is a paucity of epidemiological data on the incidence and prevalence of personality disorders among older adults. Some have suggested that personality disorders may be underdiagnosed and/or their symptoms underreported in older persons (Kroessler, 1990; Rosowsky & Gurian, 1991); others suggest that because the concept of personality disorders is relatively new, with the addition of Axis II diagnoses to *DSM–III* (APA, 1980), there may be more difficulty developing reliable and valid assessment methods for older persons (Segal, Hersen, Van Hasselt, Silberman, & Roth, 1996).

Personality disorders are placed in three clusters in the *DSM–III, DSM–III–R,* and *DSM–IV* systems of nomenclature (APA, 1980, 1987, and 1994). The most common personality disorders in the elderly samples reviewed by Abrams and Horowitz (1996) were in the Personality Disorder Cluster C, widely known as the anxious/fearful cluster. Within this, obsessive-compulsive personality disorder occurred in 3% of the elderly examined, dependent personality in 2%, avoidant personality in 1%, and passive-aggressive personality in 1%. The Cluster B (dramatic/erratic) personality disorders include narcissistic, histrionic, and borderline and each had approximately a 1% prevalence rate in the samples of older adults, whereas antisocial personality disorder had a .3% rate. The Cluster A (odd/eccentric) personality disorders include paranoid with a .8% prevalence rate, schizoid with a .5% rate, and schizotypal with a .3% rate. A "not otherwise specified" (NOS) diagnosis was made in 2% of the elderly samples studied. Within the studies reviewed, age and gender did not seem to alter the likelihood of personality disorder diagnosis.

Among inpatient or outpatient elderly persons with affective disorders, the prevalence of personality disorders is thought to be between 6% and 72%, generally in the 30% to 40% range (Fogel & Westlake, 1990; Kunik et al., 1993; Thompson, Gallagher-Thompson, & Klein, 1988; Vine & Steingart, 1994). The Cluster C (fearful) disorders were the most common in a variety of studies of the elderly (Agbayewa, 1996; Fiorot, Boswell, & Murray, 1990; Vine & Steingart, 1994) and of outpatients of all ages. Younger individuals, especially inpatients, were sometimes found to be more likely to suffer from Cluster B (dramatic) personality disorders (narcissistic, histrionic, borderline and antisocial; Shea et al., 1992). Agbayewa (1996), in a study of 89 elderly inpatients and 119 matched younger inpatients in a University Hospital in Vancouver, found that personality disorders were diagnosed more frequently in the young (40.3%) than in the elderly (27%), with Cluster C disorders the most common in the elderly (especially dependent and obsessive-compulsive) and Cluster B disorders the most common in the young. Personality disorder was associated with more severe episodes in the elderly, compared to longer episodes and poorer family relations in the younger patients. Depressed older adults with personality disorders may show greater somatic preoccupation and anxiety-proneness than younger adults (Zweig & Hinrichsen, 1992). More studies are needed to replicate these findings and elucidate the differences in prevalence and expression between younger and older adults with personality disorders.

Overall, the incidence of personality disorders in both the general elderly population and depressed elderly appears to be as high as in younger individuals, contrary to the notion that personality disorders "burn out" with age (*DSM–III–R;* APA, 1987). The earlier burn out theory has been moderated to the current view that some disorders tend to "remit with age, whereas this appears to be less true for some other types" (*DSM–IV,* APA, 1994, p. 632). Data indicate, overall, that personality traits appear to be relatively stable over time (McCrae & Costa,

1990), and personality disorders may or may not be as well (Abrams, 1996). The current state of knowledge and repeated clinical observation leads toward an overall postulation that personality disorders, although somewhat different in expression in older adults, are relatively prevalent and just as potentially obstructive in somatic or psychological treatment of depression.

Several studies have found that for both older and younger adults, personality disorder is associated with an earlier age of onset of depression, greater severity of symptoms, and greater chronicity. For example, Abrams and his colleagues (1994) found that in their study of 30 recovered elderly depressives, personality disorders were observed more frequently in those who had a history of depression before age 60 than those with a late onset. The personality disorders more frequent in the early onset group included avoidant, dependent, and NOS. Early onset individuals also scored higher on the antisocial, schizoid, schizotypal, borderline, obsessive-compulsive, and self-defeating scales on the Personality Disorder Examination (PDE; Loranger et al., 1991; Loranger, Susman, Oldham, & Russakoff, 1987). These findings confirm clinical observation that there are many elderly patients who present with a first episode of severe major depression in old age, having led lives relatively free of personality psychopathology (Kunik et al., 1993). Other research has found an association between the presence of a personality disorder and chronic affective symptoms (Devanand et al., 1994), increased suicide rate (Loebel, 1990), and greater severity of depressive symptoms (Agbayewa, 1996). Greater severity and chronicity of depressive symptomatology may be present in personality disordered elderly individuals compared to younger individuals (Agbayewa, 1996). All of these factors—earlier time of onset, greater symptom severity (including suicidality), and greater chronicity—help explain the increased difficulty in treating depressed persons who also present with personality disorders. The ongoing behavioral, emotional, and cognitive difficulties experienced by personality disordered individuals may in fact create a greater, earlier, and more persistent vulnerability to depression.

DEPRESSION TREATMENT OUTCOME: OLDER ADULTS

Seven treatment outcome studies specifically addressing the treatment of older adults with personality disorders were located; all have focused on the treatment of depression and are briefly summarized in Table 5.1.

The Thompson et al. (1988) study was a randomized clinical trial comparing the outcome of different forms of psychotherapeutic treatment for depressed individuals with and without a personality disorder (see also Thompson, Gallagher, & Breckenridge, 1987). It examined the comparative effectiveness of relatively short-term cognitive therapy (as described in Beck, Rush, Shaw, & Emery, 1979), behavioral therapy (as described in Lewinsohn, 1974), and psychodynamic therapy (as descibed in Horowitz & Kaltreider, 1979) for the treatment

TABLE 5.1
Outcome Studies of Depressed, Personality Disordered Elders

Citation	Study Design	Study Findings
Thompson, Gallagher, & Czirr (1988)	Comparison of depressed elders with & without PDs (N = 75) treated with psychotherapy vs. control (delayed Tx)	Treatment failure was four times more likely among subjects with personality disorders, particularly passive-aggressive and compulsive
Fiorot, Boswell, & Murray (1990)	Comparison of dependent (N = 18) vs. compulsive (N = 20) elders treated with psychotherapy	Higher success with dependent subjects than compulsive subjects using eclectic psychotherapy for depression
Vine & Steingart (1994)	Comparison of day hospital treated elders (N = 64) with and without PD	Personality disordered (esp. Cluster B) subjects show more chronic depression and impaired social support
Zweig & Hinrichsen (1992)	Comparison of depressed elders (N = 125) with and without PD, treated naturalistically	Personality disordered subjects show more complex depressive symptoms and earlier dropout
Kunik et al. (1993)	Comparison of depressed older inpatients (N = 154) with and without PD	Personality disordered subjects show same outcome to somatic/psychosocial therapy mix (4-week treatment)
Molinari & Marmion (1994)	Comparison of relapse of 52 recovered affective disorder elders with and without PD	Relapse rates after 1 year were the same with or without personality disorder
Abrams et al. (1994)	Comparison of 30 recovered depressed early vs. late onset elders	Both groups had positive response to either inpatient or outpatient treatment, more personality dysfunction in early onset

of major depressive disorder in a sample of 75 outpatients age 60 or older. The measures utilized included the Beck Depression Inventory (BDI; Beck, Ward, Mendelson, Mock, & Erbaugh, 1961); Hamilton Rating Scale for Depression (HRSD; Hamilton, 1960, 1967); and the Schedule for Affective Disorders and Schizophrenia (SADS; Spitzer & Endicott, 1977), which was used to make a Research Diagnostic Criteria (RDC; Spitzer, Endicott, & Robins, 1978) diagnosis for the various depressive disorders. In that study, personality disorders were assessed using the Structured Interview for *DSM–III* Personality Disorders (SIDP; Stangl, Pfohl, Zimmerman, Bowers, & Corenthal, 1985). Findings were as follows: First, patients without personality disorders fared better than the 72% with personality disorders on several of the outcome measures noted (as determined by independent evaluators both at the immediate end of treatment and at later follow-ups). In fact, at treatment termination (following 16 to 20 sessions of individual therapy), only 2 of the 21 patients without a diagnosable Axis II disorder were treatment failures (i.e., still met criteria for a diagnosis of definite or probable major depression), compared to 20 of the 54 personality disordered individuals. Thus, the likelihood of treatment failure was about four times greater for the individuals with a personality disorder (37%) than for those without (9.5%). The second major finding was that personality disorders of the fearful cluster (C) were predominant, and there were significant differences in response to therapy within this group. Passive-aggressive or compulsive personality disordered individuals had fewer successes than failures (1:2), whereas dependent or avoidant personality disordered individuals had more successes than failures (2.5:1), suggesting that dependent or avoidant features may be part of the depressive syndrome, and other more stable personality features may be more predictive of negative response to treatment.

Follow-up interviews conducted at 6 months, 1 year and 2 years after treatment termination found essentially the same pattern of much better maintenance of gains for patients without personality disorders, although at 1 year it was no longer statistically significant. At 2 years a smaller group was available for follow-up (N = 59); again the same pattern was observed, but without statistical significance. A more detailed analysis of these data suggested that the avoidant and mixed personality disordered patients specifically were at higher risk for relapse at the 2-year follow-up point (Rose, Schwartz, Steffen, & Gallagher-Thompson, 1991).

It should be noted that the Thompson et al. (1988) study had several shortcomings. First, although the measures of depression were completed before, during, and after treatment, the SIDP was completed by all participants only after the acute phase of therapy was over. At that time they were asked to respond to questions about the symptoms of various Axis II disorders in two different ways: First, was the symptom part of their "usual self"? and, was it present during their depression? Those who responded affirmatively to having personality disorder features during their depressive episode were included in the personality disordered group. However, over half (58%) of those persons reported having fewer features of a personality disorder as part of their "usual self." This discrepancy may be due to the fact that bias in memory can affect responses about one's "usual self" or it may reflect a tendency to overreport symptoms as part of the depressive episode. Corroborative information from families was sought but not obtained in most cases, due to concerns about confidentiality on the part of the patients. A second factor that may have influenced these results relates to the composition of the sample: Most of the patients were well educated and self-referred, and so may have been reluctant to describe their "usual self" in an accurate manner if doing so would not present themselves in a positive light to the interviewer. Unfortunately, the impact of these sources of bias on the results obtained could not be evaluated specifically.

Fiorot et al. (1990) compared treatment outcome between depressed older women (age 55 or older) with concomitant compulsive versus dependent personality disorders. Outcome was measured by ratings derived from the MCMI depression scale (Millon, 1987) and the Global Assessment Scale (Endicott, Spitzer, Fleiss, & Cohen, 1976). MCMI ratings were obtained before treatment was begun, and only those who stringently fit criteria for a pure compulsive ($N = 20$) or dependent personality disorder ($N = 18$) were included in the research. Findings indicated that dependent patients responded somewhat better to eclectic psychotherapy of about 1 year's length; so, despite the difference in duration of treatment, this is essentially similar to what Thompson et al. found (1988). Dependent individuals saw themselves as weak and needing to be cared for by another; compulsive individuals were self-critical and guilt-ridden, chronically anxious about criticism and generally created distance from others to avoid criticism. Both groups had an affiliative (vs. achievement) orientation, but dependent persons were more initially anxious and dysthymic, and were less likely to drop out of therapy. Despite the fact that the sample size was small, and was comprised only of Jewish individuals, this study represented an important first step in more detailed comparisons of response to treatment among different personality disorder types.

Vine and Steingart (1994) grouped 64 older adults receiving treatment-as-usual in a psychiatric day hospital according to presence or absence of a personality disorder. The patients were followed by a psychiatrist for 13 months or more. Like other studies of personality disorders among depressed individuals, the authors found a high number (33%) fulfilling criteria for personality disorder on admission, as measured by the SCID–II (Spitzer, Williams, Gibbons, & First, 1990), which is a semistructured interview closely following *DSM–III–R* criteria. Outcome for all personality disordered patients, and in particular Cluster B personality disordered individuals (histrionic, narcissistic, borderline, antisocial), was significantly worse than for those without a personality disorder, both in terms of continuing depressive symptomatology and impaired social support after treatment ended. In this study no cases had Cluster A (paranoid, schizoid, schizotypal) personality disorders, and the largest number of personality disorders were among the Cluster C group—similar to the studies of Thompson et al. (1988) and Zimmerman, Pfohl, Coryell, and Corenthal (1988). In the Vine and Steingart study, none of the patients with Cluster B disorders recovered, whereas 8 of 13 with Cluster C disorders did. They also found strong agreement between informant and patient interview data, although Cluster B patients tended to underreport symptoms on the SCID–II. Some limitations of that study included the variable length and type of treatment received by the participants, and the lack of a control group for comparison purposes.

Zweig and Hinrichsen (1992) followed 125 depressed older adult (age 60 or older) outpatients treated in a hospital-based mental health clinic. Unfortunately, type and duration of treatment(s) were unspecified. Of these 125 patients, only 26% had a concurrent personality disorder, with compulsive, borderline, dependent, and mixed being the most frequent. Patients with any of these personality disorders tended to be younger and male, and expressed more depressive symptoms and higher subjective distress at intake, as well as more somatic complaints, anxiety, sexual dysfunction, and suspiciousness. Zweig and Hinrichson reported that presence of a personality disorder (regardless of type) was associated with more complicated depressive syndromes and early dropout from treatment. Some limitations of this study include the fact that no standardized measures of personality disorder were used, and no other outcome measures were reported.

Kunik and associates (1993) studied 154 older individuals (age 50 or older) who had major depression and were inpatients on a geropsychiatric unit. Only 25% of their patients met criteria for a personality disorder—mainly NOS (32%) or dependent (27%)—with only rare diagnoses of other disorders. Contrary to expectation, they found that personality disordered patients had inpatient stays of similar lengths (averaging 4 weeks), received similar therapies (ECT, tricyclic antidepressant medications, psychotherapy, and/or recreation therapy), and improved to a similar and significant extent as those patients who did not have a personality disorder diagnosis. However, those with a personality disorder tended to have had recurrent bouts of depression, an earlier age at first episode, a concurrent anxiety disorder, history of suicide attempts, and a history of poor interpersonal relationships. Limitations of this study include lack of follow-up after discharge to determine whether improvements were maintained, lack of use of a standardized instrument to measure personality disorders, and a relatively short duration of treatment, so that only about 51% were reported to have achieved remission of their major depression by the time of discharge from the hospital.

Molinari and Marmion (1995) studied 52 male VA geropsychiatry inpatients. Using the SIDP, they found a prevalence of 61.5% of personality disorders in this sample, all of whom were significantly depressed as well. Treatment type and duration were not described in detail, but it was noted that most received a combination of antidepressant medication and supportive psychotherapy. The 52 patients had attained at least partial remission of their depression at the time of discharge, and were followed up 1 year later to determine relapse rates between those with or without a personality disorder. Relapse was determined by readmission to the same inpatient facility. It was found that there were no significant differences in relapse rates between the two groups. Comparison of differences between patients in the different clusters was not conducted, but it appeared that the odd Cluster A personality disorders were more common in this study than in most others, with 8 patients meeting one of those diagnoses. Limitations of this study include the fact that most of the patients were from a low socioeconomic background, treatments were not fully described, and no other measures of outcome besides relapse were used.

Abrams and his colleagues (1994) studied 30 recovered elderly depressives (age 60 or older) who had received either inpatient or outpatient psychiatric treatment for their depression. Personality disorders were measured using the PDE (Loranger et al., 1987); however, actual diagnoses were not used as the dependent variable but rather the extent to which patients had elements of each diagnostic category. Several interesting findings were reported. First, personality dysfunction was observed more frequently in those patients with a history of depression before age 60 compared to those with late onset; next, early onset patients had more elements of avoidant, dependent, and NOS personality disorders; finally, positive outcomes were reported on the HRSD and the Cornell Scale for Depression in Dementia (Alexopoulos, Abrams, Young, & Shamoian, 1988), regardless of the extent of personality dysfunction. Limitations of this study include the fact that treatments were not specified in terms of type or duration and diagnostic formulations were not made (making results difficult to compare to other studies). Patients were assessed after they recovered from their depression; so their memories of symptoms present during the depression could have been subject to bias—in addition to the possible bias of wanting to present themselves well.

In summary, then, review of these studies indicates that poor treatment outcome tends to correlate with the presence of personality disorders in older adults, although that has not always been the case. Firm conclusions are hampered at present due to methodological problems such as small and unrepresentative samples, lack of consensus as to the best assessment procedure and measure to use with older adults, and lack of attention to additional problems of aging (e.g., compromised cognitive function) that could complicate the treatment picture. Nonetheless, it appears that the literature on older adults does not contradict the existing literature on mixed age adults. Personality disorders (particularly those in Cluster B, which are found in the elderly as well as in younger persons) present obstacles to treatment success. Dependent and avoidant individuals (Cluster C) may respond better to treatment because they tend to be more collaborative and may therefore comply more readily with therapeutic procedures than those with other types of disorders. Still, they seem to require longer time in treatment than nonpersonality-disordered older adults to achieve the same positive benefits.

DEPRESSION TREATMENT OUTCOME: ALL ADULTS

The literature indicates greater agreement on the negative impact of personality disorders on treatment for Axis I problems when adults are studied as a group, and older adults are not singled out. Review of the larger number of studies in this category suggests that treatment outcomes tend to be poorer, treatment effects tend to be delayed, and relapse tends to be more frequent among personality disordered adults than among those without a concurrent personality disorder (see reviews by Shea, Widger, & Klein, 1992, and Goldstein,

Gruenberg, & Bruss, 1996). These general findings also have emerged in European studies as well (Patience, McGuire, Scott, & Freeman, 1995). Even treatments like light therapy for seasonal affective disorder were found to be more effective with nonpersonality disordered individuals (Reichborn-Kjennerud & Lingjaerde, 1996). In the carefully executed, prospective National Institute of Mental Health (NIMH) collaborative study (Shea et al., 1990), personality disordered patients showed significantly less improvement on social functioning and were more likely to have residual symptoms of depression, although mean depression scores and work functioning scores at termination were not significantly different between adults with and without personality disorders. Four types of treatment for major depression were studied, including cognitive therapy, interpersonal therapy, imipramine plus clinical management, and pill–placebo plus clinical management. The only treatment type where the presence of a personality disorder was not associated with poorer outcomes was in the cognitive therapy, where personality disordered patients did as well or better than those with no personality disorder diagnosis. There is some evidence that cognitive therapy is particularly helpful with depressed individuals of all ages with personality disorders (Shea, 1993; Shea et al., 1990), but that finding could also reflect the fact that cognitive therapy has been one of the most frequent modes of therapy used in many recent empirical studies. Results of selected treatment outcome studies with depressed adults (not exclusively elderly) are summarized here, and appear in brief form in Table 5.2.

Ilardi and Craighead (1995) reviewed somatically oriented treatment studies for major depression with personality disorder comorbidity, and found that the presence of a personality disorder decreased the acute recovery rate from 50% to 76% of patients with major depression alone to 16% to 52% of those with comorbidity. This effect was strong for tricyclic antidepressants in particular (used in the majority of studies), but was questionable with MAO inhibitors and electroconvulsive therapy (ECT; Goldstein et al., 1996). Studies with SSRIs were less frequent, but suggestive of a good response to treatment regardless of personality disorder status, at least for fluoxetine (Fava et al., 1994).

Diguer, Barber, & Luborsky (1993) found that the presence of a personality disorder correlated with increased depressive symptom severity; however, personality disordered patients showed a similar rate of change after dynamic psychotherapy compared to depressed clients without a personality disorder. However, there were still severity differences at termination of treatment that persisted at the time of 6-month follow-up. These findings were interpreted to mean that personality disorders may lead to greater severity of depression, and that psychological treatment works to about the same degree and therefore leaves the personality disordered patient with residual symptoms. Bearden, Lavelle, Buysse, Karp, & Frank (1996) found similar results using interpersonal psychotherapy (as described by Klerman, DiMascio, Weissman, Prusoff, & Paykel, 1974. Other studies (e.g., Shea et al., 1990) investigating the impact of cog-

TABLE 5.2
Selected Outcome Studies of Depressed, Personality Disordered Adults

Citation	Study Design	Study Findings
Shea, Widger, & Klein (1992)	Comprehensive review of outcome studies of depressed adults with or without PD	Personality disorders associated with poorer response to treatment for depression both somatic and psychosocial approaches
Goldstein, Gruenberg, & Bruss (1996)	Review and individual studies of somatic Tx of MDD	Somatic treatment of personality disordered depressed individuals yields poor outcome compared non-PD subjects Effect for tricyclics, less ECT, MAOIs
Ilardi & Craighead (1995)	Review of many, mostly naturalistic somatic outcome studies of MDD	Poorer outcome with somatic intervention of individuals with personality disorders comorbid with MDD
Patience, McGuire, Scott, & Freeman (1995)	Multisite Edinburgh study of 113 MDD patients randomly treated with 4 different treatments	Patients with PD were younger and showed greater symptom severity. Outcome was greater depression and poorer social functioning for comorbid PD patients
Reichborn-Kjennerud & Lingjaerde (1996)	Norwegian study of light therapy with 42 adults with and without PDs	Patients with Seasonal Affective Disorder with a diagnosis of any PD less likely to respond to light therapy
Shea et al. (1990)	NIMH collaborative multisite depression Rx of 239 outpatients 3 Tx plus control group	Patients with PDs (74% of sample) had more residual symptoms and poorer social functioning; no post Tx difference for mean depression or work functioning. Cognitive therapy condition—no differences
Fava et al. (1994)	Fluoxetine Tx of 83 outpatients with MDD treated with fixed dose	No differences between PD and non-PD subjects; clusters show differential response—B predicts better outcome
Diguer et al. (1993)	Dynamic psychotherapy with 25 MDD outpatients 16 sessions dynamic Rx	PD patients show same rate of change with greater initial symptom severity and therefore greater residual symptoms
Hardy et al. (1993)	Dynamic or cognitive therapy for MDD $N = 114$, 8–16 sessions; 37 had Cluster C personality disorders	Cluster C PD patients show higher initial severity and same change rate-dynamic therapy; cognitive-no post Tx differences with or without Cluster C PD
Sato et al. (1994)	Outpatients ($N = 96$) treated with various antidepressants for 5+ months (Japan)	Cluster A PD patients show particularly poor response to Tx, all clusters worse outcome than non-PD patients

nitive therapy on treatment for depression found that presence of a personality disorder did not show the expected negative effect in terms of reaching recovery criteria. Shea et al. (1992) suggested that interpersonal and psychodynamic methods of psychotherapy may be more treacherous with personality disordered individuals. They rely heavily on the patient's ability to form a therapeutic relationship, compared to the more structured approach of cognitive therapy.

Several studies have focused more narrowly on particular personality disorder clusters. Hardy et al. (1995) found that 37 of 114 depressed clients with Cluster C personality disorders also began treatment with more severe symptomatology. Furthermore, personality disordered clients with higher severity showed less improvement than those beginning with lower severity. Those who were given brief (8 or 16 sessions) psychodynamic or interpersonal psychotherapy showed improvement but maintained the same difference in symptom severity posttreatment. In contrast, patients given cognitive-behavioral therapy show no posttreatment differences between personality disordered and nondisordered. The dramatic Cluster B individuals also fared more poorly than nonpersonality disordered individuals in most studies (Goldstein et al., 1996). Finally, in one of the few studies available regarding Cluster A (odd, eccentric) personality disorders, their presence was associated with a poorer response to antidepressant therapy, in contrast to the more positive response to treatment seen in patients with Cluster B or C disorders (T. Sato, Sakado, S. Sato, & Morikawa, 1994). That study was conducted in Japan and included over 100 psychiatric outpatients ranging from age 21 to 70. It was also true that patients with any personality disorder responded more poorly overall than those without that additional diagnosis in the Sato et al. study, which is consistent with other findings reported in this review.

ANXIETY TREATMENT OUTCOME: ALL ADULTS

No studies of the impact of personality disorders on the treatment of anxiety disorders in the elderly were found, although a few treatment outcome studies for a wider age range have been done. One study of social phobia and personality disorder in 34 adults showed that those with or without personality disorders benefited from cognitive or behavioral therapies equally, although personality disordered individuals were more symptomatic, both before and after treatment (Mersch, Jansen, & Arntz, 1995).

Treatment of patients with other types of anxiety disorders appears to yield similar results. For example, panic disorder patients with comorbid personality disorders had a less favorable response to pharmacological treatments (Green & Curtis, 1988) and to combined pharmacological treatment with self-directed exposure (Mavissakalian & Hamann, 1987), although they did improve to some degree. In a study done by Feske, Perry, Chambless, Renneberg, and Goldstein

(1996), patients with avoidant personality disorder were more severely impaired on all self-report measures of social phobia, but responded well to exposure treatment. Despite that fact, they continued to report more severe impairment on all outcome measures at posttest and 3-month follow-up. Taken together, these results tend to corroborate results for personality disordered adults with depression: Namely, anxious patients with personality disorders had generally poorer outcomes than those with no Axis II pathology.

PERSONALITY DISORDER TREATMENT OUTCOME: ALL ADULTS

Treatment of personality disorder itself is a relatively new area of study. No outcome studies have been found focusing on treating personality disorders in the elderly besides single case studies. Shea's (1993) review of psychosocial treatments of personality disorders found that behavioral treatments have been used with some success with borderline and avoidant personality disorders. Linehan's (1993) cognitive-behavioral treatment of borderline personality disorder patients with parasuicidal behaviors is reported to reduce frequency of these behaviors (and of hospitalization) as compared to the treatment as usual condition. Dynamically oriented treatments have been successful with a mixed group of mostly Cluster C (anxious-fearful) personality disordered patients (Winston et al., 1991). A cognitive-behavioral case formulation study of a variety of personality disorders (Turkat & Maisto, 1985) found about a 25% positive outcome, with many dropouts and no formulation possible in a few patients. Controlled studies with avoidant personality disorder point to social skills training or other behavioral components as the key to success (Alden, 1989; Cappe & Alden, 1986; Marzillier, Lambert, & Kellett, 1976). Rathus, Sanderson, Millers, and Wetzler (1995) found that MCMI–II personality disorder scale elevations were lowered from pre- to posttreatment in panic disorder patients treated with cognitive-behavioral treatment of panic. The MCMI–II includes a high depression/anxiety adjustment to minimize state effects on the evaluation of personality functioning (Rathus et al., 1995, p. 61). Rathus interpreted this finding to mean either that experiencing panic symptoms may have a markedly adverse effect on personality, or that cognitive-behavioral therapy fostered some shifts in personality functioning. A randomized, controlled study of fluvoxamine, cognitive therapy, or placebo with 44 panic disorder adults with personality disorders (Black, Monahan, Wesner, Gael, & Bowers, 1996) found that cognitive therapy had the potential to reduce abnormal personality traits in an 8-week treatment protocol. Abnormal personality traits were unchanged in the fluvoxamine group and increased in the placebo group.

Other studies of pharmacological interventions with personality disorders have been somewhat more positive. Psychopharmalogical interventions with borderline and schizotypal patients have demonstrated that neuroleptics had some positive impact; specifically, fluoxetine, lithium, and carbamazepine were beneficial with impulsive, aggressive behavior, whereas tricyclic antidepressants seemed to have little or negative impact on these disorders (Fava et al., 1994; Shea et al., 1992). Overall, these data indicated modest changes were possible with some types of treatment, but treatment of Axis I disorders is much more promising without a comorbid personality disorder being present.

SUMMARY OF LITERATURE REVIEW

Few randomized, controlled treatment outcome studies have been conducted with personality disordered individuals of any age; only seven outcome studies focusing on older adults were found. There were no controlled studies available focusing on other Axis I disorders besides Major Depression, Dysthymic Disorder, Panic Disorder, or Social Phobia. Direct treatment of personality disorders is only beginning to receive attention. There are a number of new theories and suggested treatment approaches from several theoretical vantage points (e.g., Beck, Freeman, & Associates, 1990; Benjamin, 1996; Clarkin & Lenzenweger, 1996; Livesley, 1995; Millon, Davis, & Associates, 1996). Shea (1993) described four major theoretical orientations: psychodynamic, interpersonal, cognitive, and behavioral (although the first two and last two are closely related). Interpersonal theorists draw heavily on dynamic models, but tend to emphasize more specific interpersonal patterns that can be addressed in therapy. Therapy largely focuses on interpreting the client's behavior, uncovering maladaptive types of early attachment, differentiating from parental figures, and use of behaviorally oriented strategies to modify relationship patterns. In contrast, cognitive theorists emphasize an individual's underlying beliefs (called schemas), which are activated over different situations, and tend to be relatively rigid (Beck, Freeman, & Associates, 1990). They begin with a conceptualization of the case, including defining and understanding the development and manifestation of the primary schema(s). Therapy proceeds by presenting patients with tools to expand their perception of the distressing situations and of the schema(s) themselves. It includes numerous behavioral experiments to encourage experimentation with new behaviors and beliefs. Therapy is structured with agendas, written and behavioral homework, and incremental skill building procedures. Relatively specific approaches to most of the personality disorders are presented in Beck et al. (1990). Note that the authors of this chapter have used structured cognitive procedures, with encouraging results, with a wide range of personality disordered older adults. In particular, avoidant, borderline, dependent, antisocial, and narcissistic personality disorders respond well to these methods; older adults with paranoid, obsessive-compulsive, or passive-aggressive personality disorders do not respond as well, according to collective clinical experience.

Nevertheless, an attempt should be made to provide effective treatment whenever possible. For example, in work with paranoid individuals, it has been found that focusing on specific maladaptive beliefs concerning vulnerability and decreased self-efficacy (which seem to reflect a diminished ability to cope without a high degree of vigilance) have enabled some entry into their generally tightly closed belief system. This is consistent with Beck et al.'s (1990) approach. The use of positive data logs to enable construction of new schemas has also proved moderately successful with many different kinds of personality disorders, along with frequent use of behavioral experiments to create curiosity about other possible ways to behave in distressing situations.

Much more information is likely to become available as this field of study expands, but given the present state of the art, a few tentative conclusions can be repeated here. First, personality disorders appear to play a major role in undermining treatment of Axis I conditions, especially among younger patients, but perhaps among the elderly as well. Second, regardless of age at the time of treatment, individuals with personality disorders tend to develop Axis I conditions earlier in their lives, exhibit frequent and severe forms of social isolation, often show greater severity of depressive symptoms, and require greater time, effort, and allowance for setbacks and relapse than nonpersonality disordered individuals exhibiting similar Axis I difficulties. Third, among older adults, the same general trend has been found in most (but not all) of the studies that have been conducted, with much more research needed to clarify the relationships and to suggest effective treatment methods.

PRELIMINARY DATA FROM A SECOND CONTROLLED OUTCOME STUDY

A second randomized clinical trial has recently been completed in which different forms of treatment for major depression were provided to 102 older adults (age 60 and older) who were community-dwelling outpatients volunteering to participate in the research at no charge to them (the first clinical trial is described in Thompson et al. (1988), discussed earlier in this chapter). Treatments consisted of 16 to 20 sessions of individual care, based on random assignment to one of three conditions: the antidepressant medication desipramine alone, cognitive-behavioral therapy (CBT) alone, or both in combination (Thompson, Gallagher-Thompson, Hanser, & Gantz, 1991). Desipramine treatment was based on the NIMH collaborative study protocol and was performed by experienced geriatric psychiatrists. In this condition, patients were seen for approximately 30 minutes per session. They were started on very low doses of desipramine, which was gradually increased depending on the magnitude of side effects and the patients' willingness to tolerate these. Psychiatrists maintained a supportive attitude in talking with patients about problems, and emphasized the importance of medication in diminishing their level of distress. Plasma levels were obtained at 1 month following the onset of medication and at other points if deemed useful. Blood pressure was monitored at every session and a symptoms and side effects checklist was completed during every session. CBT was based on the cognitive model of Beck et al. (1979), emphasizing monitoring and modification of unhelpful negative thinking patterns. It also included behavioral components from Lewinsohn (1974), focusing primarily on increasing pleasant events in everyday life. Methods were modified for older adults and conducted by psychologists specializing in gerontology with at least 1 year experience specifically with CBT. The combination treatment included a somewhat shortened session with the psychiatrist focusing on symptom review and medication usage, and the standard session with the psychologist. Patients were seen for a total of 16 to 20 sessions, of whichever form of treatment they had been assigned to, over a 4-month period. Those assigned to the combined condition met for that number of sessions separately with the psychiatrist (for medication) and the psychologist (for CBT). In brief, the overall findings of this trial were that combined treatment was significantly better than the drug alone condition, whereas CBT was no different from the combined treatment condition in its effects on standard depression indices. Outcomes were assessed using change scores on the BDI and the HRSD, along with change in RDC diagnoses.

In addition to these measures, the MCMI was administered at intake to assess the presence of personality disorders. This self-report scale is based on his comprehensive clinical theory that is the foundation for the *DSM–III, DSM–III–R*, and *DSM–IV* diagnostic criteria systems. Empirical support for this theory includes Blais, McCann, Benedict, and Norman (1997) and Choca, Retzlaff, Strack, Mouton, and Van Denburg (1996). Millon's theories derive from Freud's three fundamental polarities: subject–object, active–passive, and pleasure–pain (Millon et al., 1996). The *self–other dimension* refers to the source of one's reinforcements, and is also called individuation versus nurturance. The *active–passive dimension* refers to the instrumental behaviors an individual uses to obtain reinforcement—initiating activities or reacting to them. Millon described this in evolutionary terms as self-accommodation or environmental modification. The *pleasure–pain dimension* refers to the nature of reinforcements—toward the positively reinforcing or away from the aversive or negatively reinforcing events. Millon called this life enhancement versus life preservation. He also postulated a *severity dimension,* in which increased severity denotes great deficits in social competence and periodic, reversible psychotic episodes. From these basic dimensions, Millon et al. (1996) classified all of the personality disorders. The presence or absence of a personality disorder in this study was determined by using his recommended cutoff score of base rate 85, which should yield high sensitivity and specificity for these diagnoses.

The older adults who participated in this clinical trial were recruited through referrals from physicians and/or mental health workers, or were self-referred based on response to news media announcements indicating free treatment for depression if specific criteria were met. Over 700 phone interviews were conducted with elderly persons who felt they were experiencing clinical depression. From these interviews, 344 of these were invited to the clinic for a more detailed clinical evaluation, including psychiatric history, SADS, MCMI, BDI, and HRSD. Patients who were diagnosed as being in a current episode of Major Depressive Disorder were then seen by a staff psychiatrist to confirm the diagnosis and determine if immediate hospitalization was needed. Patients passing this screening were given a complete physical examination, including detailed medical history and various laboratory tests (including an EKG) to determine if there were any contraindications for using desipramine. Those qualifying ($N = 102$) for the study were age 60 or older, diagnosed with MDD, had an HRSD greater than 14, BDI greater than 16, no medical or psychiatric contraindications, no evidence of serious alcohol abuse, no evidence of a psychotic disorder, no evidence of bipolar disorder, no immediate suicide risk, and had adequate transportation to reach the clinic.

Demographically, these outpatients were predominantly in their middle to late sixties. They were reasonably well educated for their age cohort. The female to male ratio was two to one. Most were White and about one third were still in some form of employment. The duration of the current episode was greater than 2 years. A total of 35 patients dropped from the study—12 from the desipramine condition, 15 from the combination condition, and 8 from CBT alone. Dropouts were similar in age, education, duration of episode, initial level of depression and marital and employment status. More females than males than dropped (chi-square = 3.92, $p < .05$). The dropouts tended ($p = .059$, Fisher exact probability) more often to be from the conditions that included drug treatment, mostly because of dissatisfaction with that treatment or intolerance of the drug. Note that the following analyses are based on a sample size of 95 because that is the total number (of the 102) for whom complete MCMIs were available. Tables 5.3, 5.5, and 5.6 describe the demographic characteristics of these individuals, grouped in different ways. Table 5.3 contains information for the full sample; Table 5.5 contains demographic information for the patients in each of the three clusters (A, B, and C) into which the personality disorders were grouped; and Table 5.6 contains similar information by level of severity of the personality disorder.

Table 5.3 provides sociodemographic data for the 95 patients with valid MCMI scale scores, along with initial depression levels as reflected in the BDI and the HRSD. Note that the pretreatment levels of depression in the self-report and behavioral rating scales depicted in that table indicated a mean level of moderate to severe depression. Patients ranged from age 60 to 84; their education ranged from the eighth grade to graduate school, with the mean falling above 2 years of college. Occupation ranged from skilled laborer to professional, but the majority of patients had occupations higher than the clerical/sales level. Thus, this study involved mostly patients in the young–old age range who were well-educated with higher level managerial/executive-type occupations.

Table 5.4 presents the means and standard deviations of the Base Rate scores for the MCMI scales indicating a Clinical Personality Pattern and those reflecting Severe Personality Pathology. The first set reflect general personality style features, whereas persons who score high on the severe scales are more vulnerable to the experience of transient psychotic episodes and decompensation. The

TABLE 5.3
Sociodemographic Variables and Initial Level of Depression
for Patients with Valid MCMI–II Scales (N = 95)

	Age	Gender (F/M)	Education	Occupation	BDI[1]	HSRD[2]
M	66.74	63/32	14.66[3]	3.14[4]	24.18	18.61
SD	5.83		2.30	1.19	6.82	3.98

[1]Beck Depression Inventory
[2]Hamilton Rating Scale for Depression
[3]Years Completed
[4]Occupation is rated on a 7-point scale where 1 = Professional and 7 = Unskilled Labor.

TABLE 5.4
MCMI Base Rate Scale Scores for Patients Grouped
According to Personality Patterns

	Patient Groups													
	Total N = 95		No PD N = 21		Type A N = 11		Type B N = 8		Type C N = 55		Mild N = 62		Severe N = 12	
Clinical Personality Pattern	M	SD	M	SD	M	SD	M	SD	M	SD	M	SD	M	SD
Schizoid	72	22	60	19	107	14	57	18	72	17	76	21	74	26
Avoidant	75	20	59	18	95	10	70	19	79	17	79	17	88	19
Dependent	75	26	57	21	75	30	60	15	83	25	80	26	78	21
Histrionic	45	28	55	21	16	19	84	16	42	25	41	28	54	33
Narcissistic	41	30	49	17	29	29	86	17	33	28	34	31	61	28
Antisocial	49	23	57	10	45	28	75	15	42	24	42	24	71	17
Compulsive	64	21	59	16	80	13	58	21	64	22	67	21	61	27
Passive-Agg.	64	28	58	20	52	34	83	18	67	30	61	29	94	20
Severe Personality Pathology														
Schizotypal	61	14	50	11	78	20	60	12	62	12	61	9	79	24
Borderline	63	15	60	10	56	19	78	16	63	14	59	11	86	17
Paranoid	55	16	51	16	57	19	76	16	53	14	53	14	73	19

table includes the total sample along with patient groups reflecting type of personality disorder. For purposes of this analysis, patients with Base Rate scores below 85 on all of the scales ($N = 21$) were classified as having no personality disorder. Patients with one or more of the Base Rate scale scores greater than 84 ($N = 74$) were grouped according to membership in personality clusters (Type A, B, and C) as specified in *DSM–IV* (APA, 1994). If patients had Base Rate scale scores greater than 84 in more than one cluster, then they were assigned membership in the cluster with the highest scale score. Patients were also classified according to severity of personality disorder as reflected in the MCMI classification system. Patients with no Base Rate scores above 84 on the Severe Personality Pathology Scales were classified as mild, and patients with one or more scores greater than 84 on these scales were classified as severe. These data are included for informational purposes, because no other comparative data could be found in the literature.

As expected, Type A (odd/eccentric) had the highest Base Rate score on the Schizoid scale, but were also marginally high (i.e., greater than 74) on the Avoidant, Compulsive Schizotypal, and Dependent scales. Type B (dramatic/erratic) were highest on the Histrionic and Narcissistic scales, and marginally high on the Borderline and Paranoid scales. Type C (anxious/fearful) were highest on the Dependent and Avoidant scales and the means for all other scales were below the marginally high cutoff. When patients were classified according to severity using the MCMI breakdown, the highest mean scores for the mild group occurred on the Dependent, Avoidant, and Schizoid scales in that order. No other scores were above 74. For the severe group, the highest mean score occurred on the Passive-Aggressive scale, followed by Borderline and Avoidant. Other scores in the marginally high range include the Dependent and Schizotypal scales.

Table 5.5 shows the demographic breakdown for patients with no personality disorder along with patients grouped according to membership in personality clusters (Type A, B, and C) as specified earlier. Approximately 78% of the 95 patients in this study were classified as having a personality disorder. Of these, 74% were assigned membership to the anxiety/fearful cluster, 11% to the dramatic/erratic cluster, and 15% to the odd/eccentric cluster. There were no significant differences among the four groups for any of the sociodemographic measures. The odd/eccentric cluster (Type A) appeared to have a higher male to female ratio, but this was not statistically significant. Pretreatment level of depression was also comparable for all four groups. This picture is consistent with the findings of others who report similar depression levels prior to treatment for older individuals with and without personality disorders (Abrams & Horowitz, 1996; Agbayewa, 1996; Fiorot et al., 1990; Vine & Steingart, 1994).

Regression analyses were completed to determine if mean Base Rate scores would predict level of depression at outcome of treatment. Initial exploratory analyses indicated that one subject had large leverage due to extremely high scores on the BDI and the HRSD, and this subject was deleted for subsequent analyses. In the first analysis, posttreatment BDI was entered as the dependent variable. Independent variables entered included the pretreatment BDI level followed by the mean Base Rate score for each personality cluster. The multiple R was .405 ($p < .003$), but this was due primarily to the contribution of pretreatment level of depression ($t = 3.372$; $p = .001$). None of the three personality types significantly accounted for any of the nonshared variance. Treatment condition was then entered in the regression. The multiple R increased to .476 ($p < .001$), due primarily to the effect of pretreatment level ($t = 4.034$; $p = .000$) and treatment condition ($t = 2.654$; $p = .009$). None of the personality types contributed significantly, though the dramatic/erratic cluster was marginal ($t = 1.890$; $p = .062$). A similar analysis was completed for the HRSD. Again, only pretreatment level contributed significantly ($t = 4.220$; $p = .000$) to the posttreatment level of depression. When treatment condition was entered, both pretreatment HRSD (4.378; $p = .000$) and treatment condition ($t = 2.007$; $p = .048$) contributed to posttreatment HRSD scores. There was no treatment condition by personality-type interaction effect. Thus, personality cluster as defined in this study did not predict level of depression at outcome of treatment, although there was some suggestion that dramatic/erratic might be related.

Table 5.6 shows the sociodemographic and level of depression data for patients grouped according to the severity of personality disorder as determined

TABLE 5.5

Sociodemographic and Depression Data for Personality Clusters A, B, and C

	Age	Gender (F/M)	Education	Occupation	BDI[1]	HSRD[2]
Patients With no Clinical Personality Scale Score ≥ 85: $N = 21$ (22.1%)						
M	67.24	15/6	15.33[3]	2.71	22.76	19.19
SD	6.61		2.03	1.19	5.38	5.33
Patients in Type A Cluster: $N = 11$ (11.6%)						
M	68.36	4/7	14.73	2.82	23.09	19.09
SD	6.87		2.80	1.25	9.45	4.53
Patients in Type B Cluster: $N = 8$ (8.4%)						
M	67.12	6/2	14.62	3.00	20.38	16.50
SD	5.79		2.13	1.20	4.31	1.41
Patients in Type C Cluster: $N = 55$ (57.9%)						
M	68.36	38/17	14.73	3.38	23.09	19.09
SD	6.87		2.80	1.15	9.45	4.53

[1]Beck Depression Inventory
[2]Hamilton Rating Scale for Depression
[3]Years Completed
[4]Occupation is rated on a 7-point scale where 1 = Professional and 7 = Unskilled Labor.

Note: For all group comparisons, $p > .05$ for all variables.

TABLE 5.6

Sociodemographic and Depression Data

According to Level of Severity of Personality Disorder

	Age	Gender (F/M)	Education	Occupation	BDI[1]	HSRD[2]
Patients With no Clinical Personality Scale Score ≥ 85: N = 21 (22%)						
M	67.24	15/6	15.33[3]	2.71	22.76	19.19
SD	6.61		2.03	1.19	5.38	5.33
Patients With One or More Clinical Personality Pattern Scales ≥ 85: N = 62 (65%)						
M	66.84	41/21	14.32	3.24	24.31	18.27
SD	5.88		2.41	1.20	6.92	3.54
Patients With One or More Severe Personality Pathology Scales ≥ 85: N = 12 (13%)						
M	65.33	7/5	15.25	3.33	26.00	19.33
SD	4.12		1.96	1.07	8.48	3.52

[1]Beck Depression Inventory

[2]Hamilton Rating Scale for Depression

[3]Years Completed

[4]Occupation is rated on a 7-point scale where 1 = Professional and 7 = Unskilled Labor.

Note: For all group comparisons, $p > .10$ for all variables.

by the MCMI. Of the 74 patients with evidence of a personality disorder, approximately 84% had one or more of the Clinical Personality Pattern Scales on the MCMI above a Base Rate score of 84, whereas 16% had a Base Rate score greater than 84 on one or more of the Severe Personality Pathology Scales. Again, as seen with the APA personality classification system in Table 5.5, there were no significant differences among the three groups for demographic measures or pretreatment level of depression. Absence of pretreatment differences in level of depression is inconsistent with prior literature showing higher pretreatment depression levels in young adult patients with personality disorder than in those without (Diguer et al., 1993; Patience et al., 1995; Shea et al., 1992), but agrees with other studies evaluating older depressed patients as noted earlier.

Regression analyses were also completed using this severity classification to determine if mean Base Rate scores would predict level of depression at outcome of treatment. Again, initial exploratory analyses indicated that one subject had large leverage due to extremely high scores on the BDI and the HRSD, and this subject was deleted. In the first analysis, posttreatment BDI was entered as the dependent variable. Independent variables entered included the pretreatment BDI level followed by the mean Base Rate score for the Severe Personality Pathology scales. The multiple R was .430 ($p < .000$). In this analysis, both pretreatment level of depression ($t = 3.323$; $p = .001$) and mean Base Rate severity score ($t = 2.670$; $p = .009$) contributed significantly to posttreatment BDI scores. Treatment condition was then entered in the regression. The multiple R increased to .478 ($p < .000$). All three independent variables contributed significantly to outcome level of depression. The significance level for pretreatment BDI was $t = 3.741$ ($p = .000$); for treatment condition, $t = 2.271$ ($p = .026$); and for mean Base Rate severity score, $t = 2.608$ ($p = .011$). Finally, the mean Base Rate score for the Clinical Personality Pattern was entered to determine if the remaining nonshared variance for the severity score still contributed to outcome depression. As expected, pretreatment BDI was significant ($t = 3.338$; $p = -.001$), but the mean Base Rate severity score still contributed significantly to outcome BDI scores ($t = 2.312$; $p = .023$). Analysis for the HRSD showed an identical pattern. Mean Base Rate severity score accounted for a significant proportion of outcome depression HRSD scores when pretreatment HRSD scores were entered ($t = 2.586$; $p = .011$). The multiple R for this analysis was .456 ($p < .000$). Mean Base Rate Severity still accounted for a significant proportion of the variance when treatment condition ($t = 2.560$; $p = .012$; $R = 488$) and Clinical Personality Pattern scores ($t = 2.479$; $p = .015$; $R = .463$) were entered into the regression. As with analysis of personality type, there was no treatment condition by severity interaction effect. Thus, these data strongly suggest that the severity of personality disorder as defined by MCMI scores are associated with outcome, irrespective of whether the treatment is medication, CBT, or a combination of both. These data are in agreement with most of the prior studies reviewed earlier in this chapter, and should encourage continued work to evaluate the importance of personality disorder in the elderly.

This study suffers from limitations that makes generalization to other clinical situations somewhat problematic. The study recruited volunteers from the community, and a number of them were not actually seeking treatment at that time. The sample also generally reflected a high socioeconomic, high functioning segment of the elderly, which may respond differently to treatment than other elderly groups. Attempts were made to select subjects with a minimum of other possible Axis I diagnoses or problems, and the relation between severity of personality disorder and outcome may be less evident in patients with dual diagnoses or multiple disorders.

Thus, in summary, it is clear from this description of recent work that older, significantly depressed outpatients with a concurrent personality disorder are less likely to respond well to treatments compared to those with similar depressive diagnoses but no concurrent Axis II pathology. It is also clear that patients with the more severe personality disorders responded more poorly to all treatments. Although a different methodology was used to determine the presence of a personality disorder than in an earlier study (Thompson et al., 1988), the proportion of patients in the two studies with a personality disorder was similar (74% vs. 72%). Finally, the number of patients in each of the three DSM–IV clusters was also consistent with prior studies, with Cluster C being the most predominant.

CONCLUSIONS

This chapter aimed to provide a comprehensive, critical review of the existing literature on how older adults with personality disorders of various kinds respond to treatments, and to present previously unpublished data from the most recent study comparing differential response to treatment among older adults both with and without Axis II pathology. Much more remains to be studied, particularly about the interaction between personality disorders and relapse, for those with major affective disorders. Future research should more directly address the needs of minority older adults, who may be more difficult to diagnose and to treat because of differing cultural expectations and norms. Finally, research needs to be done on the optimal length of treatment needed (as well as the preferred modality of therapy) so that personality disorders can actually be treated more effectively in their own right. Although this research can be difficult to implement, its rewards can also be great in terms of increased happiness and better qualilty of life for the nation's older adults.

REFERENCES

Abrams, R. C. (1996). Editorial review: Personality disorders in the elderly. *International Journal of Geriatric Psychiatry, 11,* 759–763.

Abrams, R. C., Alexopoulos, G. S., & Young, R. C. (1987). Geriatric depression and *DSM–III–R* personality disorder criteria. *Journal of the American Geriatrics Society, 35(5),* 383–386.

Abrams, R. C., & Horowitz, SV (1996). Personality disorders after age 50: A meta-analysis. *Journal of Personality Disorders, 10(3),* 271–281.

Abrams, R. C., Rosendahl, E., Card, C., & Alexopoulos, G. S. (1994). Personality disorder correlates of late and early onset depression. *Journal of the American Geriatric Society, 42,* 727–731.

Agbayewa, M. O. (1996). Occurrence and effects of personality disorders in depression: Are they the same in the old and young? *Canadian Journal of Psychiatry, 41,* 223–226.

Alden, L. (1989). Short-term structure treatment for avoidant personality disorder. *Journal of Consulting and Clinical Psychology, 56(6),* 756–764.

Alexopoulos, G. S., Abrams, R. C., Young R. C., & Shamoian, C. A. (1988). Cornell scale for depression in dementia. *Biological Psychiatry, 23,* 271–284.

American Psychiatric Association. (1980). *Diagnostic and statistical manual of mental disorders* (3rd ed.). Washington, DC: Author.

American Psychiatric Association. (1987). *Diagnostic and statistical manual of mental disorders* (3rd ed., rev). Washington, DC: Author.

American Psychiatric Association. (1994). *Diagnostic and statistical manual of mental disorders* (4th ed.). Washington, DC: Author.

Bearden, C., Lavelle N., Buysse, D., Karp, J. F., & Frank, E. (1996). Personality pathology and time to remission in depressed outpatients treated with interpersonal psychotherapy. *Journal of Personality Disorders, 10(2),* 164–173.

Beck, A., Rush, J., Shaw, B., & Emery, G. (1979). *Cognitive therapy of depression.* New York: Guilford.

Beck, A., Freeman, A., & Associates. (1990). *Cognitive therapy of personality disorders.* New York: Guilford.

Beck, A., Ward, C., Mendelson, M., Mock, J., & Erbaugh, J. (1961). An inventory for measuring depression. *Archives of General Psychiatry, 4,* 561–571.

Benjamin, L. S. (1996). *Interpersonal diagnosis and treatment of personality disorders* (2nd ed.). New York: Guilford.

Black, D. W., Bell, S., Hulbert, J., & Nasrallah, A. (1988). The importance of axis II in patients with major depression. *Journal of Affective Disorders, 14,* 115–122.

Black, D. W., Monahan, P., Wesner, R., Gabel, J., & Bowers, W. (1996). The effect of fluvoxamine, cognitive therapy, and placebo on abnormal personality traits in 44 patients with panic disorder. *Journal of Personality Disorders, 10*(2), 185–194.

Blais, M., McCann, J., Benedict, K., & Norman, D. (1997). Toward an empirical/theoretical grouping of the *DSM–III–R* personality disorders. *Journal of Personality Disorders, 11,* 191–198.

Cappe, R. F., & Alden, L. E. (1986). A comparison of treatment strategies for clients functionally impaired by extreme shyness and social avoidance. *Journal of Consulting and Clinical Psychology, 54*(6), 796–801.

Choca, J., Retzlaff, P., Strack, S., Mouton, A. & Van Denburg, E. (1996). Factorial elements in Millon's personality theory. *Journal of Personality Disorders, 10*(4), 377–383.

Clarkin, J. F., & Lenzenweger, M. F. (Eds.). (1996). *Major theories of personality disorder.* New York: Guilford.

Devanand, D. P., Nobler, M. S., Singer, T., Kiersky, J. E., Turret, N., Roose, S. P., Sackeim, H. A. (1994). Is dysthymia a different disorder in the elderly? *American Journal of Psychiatry, 151*(11), 1592–1599.

Diguer, L., Barber, J. P., & Luborsky, L. (1993). Three concomitants: Personality disorders, psychiatric severity, and outcome of dynamic psychotherapy of major depression. *American Journal of Psychiatry, 150,* 1246–1248.

Endicott, J., Spitzer, R., Fleiss, J., & Cohen, J. (1976). The global assessment scale: A procedure for measuring the overall severity of psychiatric disturbance. *Archives of General Psychiatry, 33,* 766–771.

Fava, M., Alpert, J. E., Borus, J. S., Nierenberg, A. A., Pava, J. A., & Rosenbaum, J. F. (1996). Patterns of personality disorder comorbidity in early-onset versus late-onset major depression. *American Journal of Psychiatry, 153 (10),* 1308–1312.

Fava, M., Bouffides, E., Pava, J. A., McCarthy, M. K., Steingard, R. J., & Rosenbaum, J. F. (1994). Personality disorder comorbidity with major depression and response to fluoxetine treatment. *Psychotherapy and Psychosomatics, 62,* 160–167.

Feske, U., Perry, K. J., Chambless, D. L., Renneberg, B., & Goldstein, A. J. (1996). Avoidant personality disorder as a predictor for treatment outcome among generalized social phobics. *Journal of Personality Disorders, 10*(2), 174–184.

Fiorot, M., Boswell, P., & Murray, E. J. (1990). Personality and response to psychotherapy in depressed elderly women. *Behavior, Health and Aging, 1*(1), 51–63.

Fogel, B. S., & Westlake, R. (1990). Personality disorder diagnoses and age in inpatients with major depression. *Journal of Clinical Psychiatry, 51*(6), 232–235.

Goldstein, R. D., Gruenberg, A. M., & Bruss, G. S. (1996). Co-occurrence of major depressive disorder and personality disorder: Treatment implications. *Directions in Psychiatry, 16*(18), 1–8.

Green, M. A., & Curtis, G. C. (1988). Personality disorders in panic patients: Response to termination of medication. *Journal of Personality Disorders, 2,* 303–314.

Hamilton, M. (1960). A rating scale for depression. *Journal of Neurology, Neurosurgery and Psychiatry, 23,* 56–62.

Hamilton, M. (1967). Development of a rating scale for primary depressive illness. *British Journal of Social and Clinical Psychology, 6,* 278–296.

Hardy, G. E., Barkham, M., Shapiro, D. A., Stiles, W. B., Rees, A., Reynolds, S. (1995). Impact of cluster C personality disorders on outcomes of contrasting brief psychotherapies for depression. *Journal of Consulting and Clinical Psychology, 63*(6), 997–1004.

Horowitz, M., & Kaltreider, N. (1979). Brief therapy of the stress response syndrome. *Psychiatric Clinics of North America, 2,* 365–377.

Ilardi, S. S., & Craighead, W. E. (1995). Personality pathology and response to somatic treatments for major depression: A critical review. *Depression, 2 ,* 200–217.

Klerman, G. L., DiMascio, A., Weissman, M. M., Prusoff, B., & Paykel, E. S. (1974). Treatment of depression by drugs and psychotherapy. *American Journal of Psychiatry, 131,* 186–191.

Kroessler, D. (1990). Personality disorder in the elderly. *Hospital and Community Psychiatry, 41*(12), 1325–1329.

Krupnick, J. L., Sotsky, S. M., Simmons, S., Moyer, J., Watkins, J., Elkin, I., & Pilkonis, P. A. (1996). The role of therapeutic alliance in psychotherapy and pharmacotherapy outcome: Findings in the National Institute of Mental Health treatment of depression collaborative research program. *Journal of Consulting and Clinical Psychology, 64,* 532–539.

Kunik, M. E., Mulsant, B. H., Rifai, A. H., Sweet, R., Pasternak, R., Rosen, J., & Zubenko, G. S. (1993). Personality disorders in elderly inpatients with major depression. *American Journal of Geriatric Psychiatry, 1*(1), 38–45.

Lewinsohn, P. (1974). A behavioral approach to depression. In R. Friedman & M. Katz (Eds.), *The psychology of depression: Contemporary theory and research* (pp. 157–176). New York: Wiley.

Linehan, M. M. (1993). *Cognitive-behavioral therapy of borderline personality disorder.* New York: Guilford.

Livesley, W. J. (Ed.). (1995). *The DSM–IV personality disorders.* New York: Guilford.

Loebel, J. P. (1990). Completed suicide in the elderly. In *Abstracts of the Third Annual Meeting and Symposium. American Association for Geriatric Psychiatry. San Diego, California* (p. 2). Bethesda, Maryland: AAGP

Loranger, A. W., Susman, V. L., Oldham, J. M., & Russakoff, L. M. (1987). The personality disorder examination: A preliminary report. *Journal of Personality Disorders, 1,* 1–13.

Loranger, A. W., Lenzenweger, M. F., Gartner A. F., Susman, V. L., Herzig, J., Zammit, G. K., Gartner, J. D., Abrams, R. C., & Young, R. C. (1991). State-trait artifacts and the diagnosis of personality disorders. *Archives of General Psychiatry, 48,* 720–728.

Marzillier, J. S., Lambert, C., & Kellett, J. (1976). A controlled evaluation of systematic desensitization and social skills training for socially inadequate psychiatric patients. *Behavior Research and Therapy, 14,* 225–238.

Mavissakalian, M., & Hamann, M. S. (1987). DSM–III personality disorder in agoraphobia: II. Changes with treatment. *Comprehensive Psychiatry, 28,* 356–361.

McCrae, R. R., & Costa, P. T. (1990). *Personality in adulthood.* New York: Guilford.

Mersch, P., Jansen, M., & Arntz, A. (1995). Social phobia and personality disorder: Severity of complaint and treatment effectiveness. *Journal of Personality Disorders, 9,* 143–159.

Millon, T. (1983). *Millon clinical multiaxial inventory.* Minneapolis, MN: Interpretive Scoring Systems.

Millon, T. (1987). *Millon Clinical Multiaxial Inventory–II (MCMI–II): manual.* Minneapolis, MN: Interpretive Scoring Systems.

Millon, T., Davis, R. D., & Associates. (1996). *Disorders of personality: DSM–IV and beyond.* New York: Wiley.

Molinari, V., & Marmion, J. (1995). Relationship between affective disorders and Axis II diagnoses in geropsychiatric patients. *Journal of Geriatric Psychiatry and Neurology, 8,* 61–64.

Patience, D. A., McGuire, R. J., Scott, A. I., & Freeman, C. P. (1995). The Edinburgh primary care depression study: Personality disorder and outcome. *British Journal of Psychiatry, 167,* 324–330.

Pfohl, B., Stangl, D., & Zimmerman, M. (1984). The implications of DSM–III personality disorders for patients with major depression. *Journal of Affective Disorders, 7,* 309–318.

Pilkonis, P., & Frank, E. (1988). Personality pathology in recurrent depression: Nature, prevalence, and relationship to treatment response. *American Journal of Psychiatry, 145,* 435–441.

Rathus, J. H., Sanderson, W. C., Millers, A. L., & Wetzler, S. (1995). Impact of personality functioning on cognitive behavioral treatment of panic disorder: A preliminary report. *Journal of Personality Disorders, 9*(2), 160–168.

Reichborn-Kjennerud, T., & Lingjaerde, O. (1996). Response to light therapy in seasonal affective disorder: Personality disorders and temperament as predictors of outcome. *Journal of Affective Disorders, 41,* 101–110.

Rose, J., Schwartz, M., Steffen, A., & Gallagher-Thompson, D. (1991, November). *Personality disorder and outcome in the treatment of depressed elders: Two year follow-up.* Paper presented at the Gerontological Society of America Annual Convention, San Francisco.

Rosowsky, E., & Gurian, B. (1991). Borderline personality disorder in late life. *International Psychogeriatrics, 3*(1), 39–52.

Sato, T., Sakado, K., Sato, S., & Morikawa, T. (1994). Cluster A personality disorder: A marker of worse treatment outcome of major depression? *Psychiatry Research, 53,* 153–159.

Segal, D. L., Hersen, M., Van Hasselt, V. B., Silberman, C. S., & Roth, L. (1996). Diagnosis and assessment of personality disorders in older adults: A critical review. *Journal of Personality Disorders, 10*(4), 384–399.

Shea, M. T. (1993). Psychosocial treatment of personality disorders. *Journal of Personality Disorders, 7*(Suppl.), 167–180.

Shea, M. T., Pilkonis, P. A., Beckham, E., Collins, J. F., Elkin, I., Sotsky, S. M., & Docherty, J. P. (1990). Personality disorders and treatment outcome in the NIMH treatment of depression collaborative research program. *American Journal of Psychiatry, 147,* 711–718.

Shea, M. T., Widiger, T. A., & Klein, M. H. (1992). Comorbidity of personality disorders and depression: Implications for treatment. *Journal of Consulting and Clinical Psychology, 60*(6), 857–868.

Spitzer, R., & Endicott, J. (1977). *The SADS–Change interview.* New York: New York State Psychiatric Institute.

Spitzer, R., Endicott, J., & Robins, E. (1978). Research diagnostic criteria: Rationale and reliability. *Archives of General Psychiatry, 35,* 773–782.

Spitzer, R. I., Williams J. B., Gibbon, M., & First, M. B. (1990). *Structured clinical interview for DSM–III–R personality disorders (SCID-II).* New York: New York State Psychiatric Institute, Biometrics Research.

Stangl, D., Pfohl, B., Zimmerman, M., Bowers, W., & Corenthal, C. (1985). A structured interview for the *DSM–III* personality disorders. *Archives of General Psychiatry, 42,* 591–596.

Thompson, L. W., Gallagher, D., & Breckenridge, J. S. (1987). Comparative effectiveness of psychotherapies for depressed elders. *Journal of Consulting and Clinical Psychology, 55*(3), 385–390.

Thompson, L. W., Gallagher, D., & Czirr, R. (1988). Personality disorder and outcome in the treatment of late-life depression. *Journal of Geriatric Psychiatry, 21*(2), 133–146.

Thompson, L. W., Gallagher-Thompson, D., Hanser, S., & Gantz, F. (1991, August) *Treatment of late-life depression with cognitive-behavioral therapy or Desipramine.* Poster presentation at the 99th American Psychological Association Convention.

Turkat, I. D., & Maisto, S. A. (1985). Personality disorders: Application of the experimental method to the formulation and modification of personality disorders. In D. H. Barlow (Ed.), *Clinical handbook of psychological disorders* (pp. 502–570). New York: Guilford.

Vine, R. G., & Steingart, A. B. (1994). Personality disorder in the elderly depressed. *Canadian Journal of Psychiatry, 39,* 392–397.

Winston, A., Pollack, J., McCullough, L., Flegenheimer, W., Kestenbaum, R., & Trujillo, M. (1991). Brief psychotherapy of personality disorders. *Journal of Nervous and Mental Disease, 179*(4), 188–193.

Zimmerman, M., Pfohl, B., Coryell, W., & Corenthal, C. (1988). Diagnosing personality disorder in depressed patients: A comparison of patient and informant interviews. *Archives of General Psychiatry, 45,* 733–737.

Zweig, R. A., & Hinrichsen, G. A. (1992, November). *Impact of personality disorder on affective illness in older adults.* Gerontological Society of America Annual Convention, Washington, DC.

CHAPTER 6

Dimensional Measures and the Five-Factor Model: Clinical Implications and Research Directions

PAUL R. DUBERSTEIN, PhD
LARRY SEIDLITZ, PhD
JEFFREY M. LYNESS, MD
YEATES CONWELL, MD
University of Rochester Medical Center

Why do some elders get sick while others stay well? Why are some more functionally limited by their disease than others? Why do some request a physician-assisted death, whereas others are more content to let nature take its course? Reductionistic explanations must be resisted. Of course, "personality" cannot account for most or even half of the observed interindividual variability in mental, physical, and social function across the second half of life. People and their lives are more complex than that. Yet, the contribution of personality to late life outcomes cannot be ignored. This survey of the literature illustrates the extent to which dimensional measures of personality have been, and could be, implicated in later life functioning. It concludes with a broad recommendation: Psychologists, psychiatrists, social workers, nurses, internists, family physicians, and other clinicians who work with older people need a working knowledge of the ways in which their patients' personality characteristics can engender or exacerbate the diseases, chronic strains, or life crises they are asked to alleviate or cure. Following a definitional and conceptual overview, there is a discussion of the intersection of personality with several late life issues and themes. The discussion is intended to be illustrative, not exhaustive; it is our hope that it will stimulate research in domains that are currently underinvestigated.

DEFINITIONAL AND CONCEPTUAL OVERVIEW

Definition of Personality

Colloquially, personality has been defined as "the totality of an individual's behavioral and emotional tendencies" (Woolf et al., 1977). A scientific approach to personality, in contrast, requires a working definition that suggests falsifiable hypotheses. Research on personality and health across the life course has conceived of personality as an organizing structure made up of constituent attitudes, patterns of behavior, cognitions, emotions, and other basic psychological processes, all of which have implications for how people affect and are affected by the social and physical environments.

In Search of a Common Personality Language: The Five-Factor Model (FFM)

This chapter focuses solely on self-reported or informant-reported traits. It does not discuss other important foci and methods of personality assessment, such as: self-reported motives and goals (Cross & Markus, 1991; Hooker & Kaus, 1994); implicit (or unconscious) motives, themes, and preoccupations (Masling, 1997; McClelland, Koestner, & Weinberger, 1989; Shedler, Mayman, & Manis, 1993); life narratives (Cohler, 1991; McAdams, 1992, 1994); behavioral observations in structured, laboratory situations (Kagan, 1994); and physiological responses to stressors (Kagan, 1994). Trait assessment typically uses natural language descriptions (John, 1990). Based on decades of factor analytic research on personality in the natural lexicon and questionnaires, there is considerable (Digman, 1990; John, 1990; McCrae & Costa, 1997), but not universal (Cloninger, Svrakic, & Przybeck, 1993; Livesley, Jang, & Vernon, 1998; Tellegen, 1985), agreement that the extensive number of personality attributes found in the dictionary can be grouped along five major dimensions: *Neuroticism, Extraversion, Openness, Agreeableness,* and *Conscientiousness.*

Although a number of researchers endorse this five-factor model (FFM) of personality, there is controversy concerning whether these labels are appropriate. Digman (1990), for example, preferred the label "Intellect" to Openness. Other disagreements concern the number (e.g., Cloninger et al., 1993; Livesley et al., 1998) and nature of basic personality dimensions. For example, Openness may not be a singular construct, but rather separate constructs represented by the tendency to enter unusual states of attentional awareness, heightened curiosity, and the propensity to endorse politically liberal values (Glisky, Tataryn, Tobias, Kihlstrom, & McConkey, 1991). Yet, proponents of the FFM argue that it provides a fixed reference point from which to assess a variety of different scales (Costa & McCrae, 1992a, 1992b, 1995; Marshall, Wortman, Vickers, Kusulas, &

Hervig, 1994). It therefore overcomes a perennial problem in personality psychology: Scales with different labels measure the same trait, whereas those with the same label measure different traits. Because the FFM promises a relatively comprehensive coverage of personality traits, it can be used to explore and generate hypotheses about a phenomenon that has been relatively underinvestigated, or about which there is relatively little theorizing.

Some readers may wish to consult Kagan (1994), McAdams (1992, 1994), and Block (1995) for dissenting, less optimistic opinions of the FFM. Kagan critiqued its basic premises, including the scientific utility of a natural language approach to personality, self-report measures, and factor analysis itself. He ultimately conceded that, even though the five factors "omit too much information" and are "insufficiently differentiated . . . [they] do tell us something of interest" (pp. 45–46). McAdams (1992) also took issue with the basic premises, and criticized trait assessments in general on the grounds that they fail to provide causal explanations for human behavior, disregard the conditional and contextual nature of human experience, and do not provide enough detailed information to predict specific behaviors in certain circumstances. Block (1995) generally accepted the basic premises, though he was somewhat critical of the "arbitrariness" (p. 189) of factor analysis and the overreliance on self- and peer-report, as opposed to behavioral, psychophysiological, and interview data. He also raised a number of technical concerns, such as the high intercorrelations among the ostensibly orthogonal (uncorrelated) five factors.

Most practitioners, especially those who wish to learn more about their patients' personalities, should have at least some familiarity with these important criticisms, as well as three tensions in the personality literature that have been exacerbated by the advent of the FFM. The first, and most significant, concerns the idiographic-nomothetic controversy (Runyan, 1983), an old debate that is alive and vibrant despite Holt's (1962) contention that these terms be dropped "from our vocabularies and let them die quietly" (p. 402). In some respects, the terms have fallen out of favor, but the tensions remain. Allport (1961) introduced the term *idiographic* to psychology to refer specifically to the study of individuals, the lawful regularities within single lives. Personality psychology has traditionally been "nomothetic," concerned with lawful regularities within a population. Block's (1961, 1971) distinction between person-centered and variable-centered assessment methods captures the spirit of the debate, while avoiding the linguistic clumsiness that afflicted Allport's terms. Interindividual and intraindividual are two additional terms that capture the same distinction, and are perhaps more widely used currently. Magnusson (1990; Magnusson & Törestad, 1993), among others (e.g., Runyan, 1983), forcefully argued in favor of the intraindividual approach. He emphasized individual agency and uniqueness, and maintained that the complexity of psychological phenomena cannot be captured by a score or set of scores on the sort of personality inventories that have gained credibility with increased acceptance of the FFM. For example, it cannot be assumed that a Neuroticism *T*-score of 60 means the same thing for two different people, or for the same person on two different occasions. The antecedents, correlates, and consequences of a high Neuroticism (or Extraversion, Openness, Agreeableness, and Conscientiousness) score are manifold. Although the FFM is the product of an interindividual approach to personality psychology, many of its proponents argue that interindividual and intraindividual approaches are neither competing nor mutually exclusive: A "combination of these two approaches . . . will shape the next generation of personality theories" (Costa & McCrae, 1995, p. 218).

A second issue concerns the debate about the relative merits of objective and projective approaches to personality assessment (Masling, 1997; Shedler et al., 1993). Given its grounding in natural language, the FFM encourages an objective (vs. projective) approach to personality assessment that relies on what people have to say about themselves. Block (1995), Masling (1997), and Shedler and colleagues (1993) decried the overreliance on self-report in personality assessments on the grounds that it can be easily faked and subject to numerous biases, such as the tendency to report socially desirable responses. Moreover, exclusive reliance on self-report is inconsistent with the possibility that some of the most important aspects of an individual's personality are outside conscious awareness. This is significant, given that projective assessments predict long-term behavioral patterns better than self-reports (McClelland, Koestner, & Weinberger, 1989, but see Garb, Florio, & Grove, 1998). Masling (1997) recommended supplementing self-report assessments with projective assessments, and is concerned about the elimination, as if by scientific fiat, of the latter from the clinical and research armamentaria. Of course, projective assessments are labor and time intensive, and are perhaps realistically better suited to the study of lawful regularities within single lives, rather than the lawful regularities within a population.

A third area of controversy concerns the extent to which personality is stable. The methodological and measurement issues are complex, in part because stability is relative, not absolute. Conceptually, instability (or "change," to use a colloquial term) can denote either systematic developmental maturation or simply the absence of stability (Caspi & Bem, 1990). More concretely, stability estimates in longitudinal studies of personality are, in part, a function of the manner in which questionnaire items are worded. Subtle changes in language can significantly influence the stability coefficient (McAdams, 1994), or any other psychometric statistic (Kagan, 1994). Perhaps more significantly, the assessment and interpretation of stability coefficients occurs against the backdrop of the idiographic-nomothetic controversy. Whereas most researchers are concerned (and content) with examining the consistency across time of an individual's score relative to other individuals within a group (differential stability), clinicians may actually be more interested in person-centered stability (Block, 1971), the stability of the configuration of personality variables within a particular individual across time.

To date, most research on the stability of personality traits that constitute the FFM has examined differential stability. In cross-sectional studies of mixed-age samples, the absolute values of correlations between age and each of the five factors falls between .1 and .2 (Costa & McCrae, 1992a). Therefore, age accounts for less than 4% of the variance in scale scores. Longitudinal studies show that test–retest correlation coefficients obtained over intervals greater than two decades exceed .90, after correcting for test unreliability (Costa & McCrae, 1992b, 1994). Among others, Costa and McCrae (1992a, 1992b, 1994, 1995) presented and reviewed convincing evidence that the traits constituting the FFM are, indeed, stable after age 30, at least as viewed through differential stability coefficients. Although Costa and McCrae cogently argued for the notion of personality stability, they recognized the limitation of this generalization. Personality "changes" could occur as a result of psychiatric disorder, psychotherapy, catastrophic stress, and dementing illness (Costa & McCrae, 1992b). Trying to explain why stability coefficients get smaller over time, Costa and McCrae admitted to some uncertainty, acknowledging that it may be due to "major changes in a few individuals . . . or to minor changes in many individuals" (Costa & McCrae, 1994, p. 33). It is hard to escape the idiographic-nomothetic debate.

Obviously, the FFM is not the only alternative to Axis II assessment, and exclusive reliance on either self- or informant-reported traits is probably unnecessarily limited. As far as natural language approaches to personality are concerned, however, the FFM has achieved apparently unparalleled consensus in the often vitriolic world of personality psychology, and has withstood criticism from those who do or do not share its basic assumptions. Those achievements alone may be sufficient justification for its continued application to questions of public health significance, especially issues that have been underinvestigated or about which there is little theorizing.

Few of the studies reviewed in this chapter were conducted by researchers who have adopted the FFM as a comprehensive measurement framework. More often, researchers focus on particular traits they deem most relevant to their topic. Some of the labels for these constructs (e.g., "Type A," "dependency," or "self-efficacy") are not used in the FFM literature. The label chosen usually reflects a particular theoretical or conceptual orientation. Yet, like personality disorders (Costa & Widiger, 1993; Soldz, Budman, Demby, & Merry, 1993; Trull, 1992; but see Coolidge, Becker, DiRito, Durham, Kinlaw, & Philbrick, 1994), they can be understood within the framework of the FFM. So as not to discard the baby with the bathwater, this chapter discusses studies of constructs, like dependency, that were labeled from a variety of theoretical perspectives.

Conceptual Model

The following are among the fundamental questions with which personality researchers have struggled: What is the relation between personality and environment? What is the relation between personality and health? Can personality "change"? The first two questions can be answered by invoking "interactionism," which in turn has implications for the third question. In its broadest sense, interactionism means both that people select and affect social environments, and that environments select and affect people. This idea is historically rooted in the writings of Allport (1961) and Murray (1981) and is manifest in contemporary personality (Caspi & Bem, 1990; Magnusson, 1990) and ecological psychology (Bronfenbrenner, 1979; Moen, Elder, & Luscher, 1995). With respect to the relation between personality and health, interactionism suggests that personality processes affect mental and physical health and vice versa, an old idea that has been fruitfully applied in contemporary health psychology (Contrada, Leventhal, & O'Leary, 1990). Given the bidirectional relations between personality on the one hand, and environments and health on the other, it seems reasonable to allow for the possibility of personality "change," reflecting inexorable instability in environments and health over time.

LITERATURE REVIEW

Derived from this conceptual model, Table 6.1 depicts a framework for articulating the ways in which personality in late life can be studied, and reflects how

TABLE 6.1
A Framework for Studying and Conceptualizing Personality in Late Life

	Question		
	Does Personality Measured at Time1 . . .		
Domain of Interaction	. . . Predict . . .	. . . Moderate the effect of a stressor on . . .	. . . Change significantly following . . .
Mental Health	. . . Major Depression at Time 2? . . . Generalized Anxiety Disorder at Time 2?	. . . Alcohol Dependence at Time 2? . . . Grief symptoms at Time 2?	. . . The onset of Alzheimer's Disease? . . . A major depressive episode?
Physical Morbidity and Mortality	. . . Death at Time 2? . . . Functional decline at Time 2?	. . . The risk of developing cancer at Time 2? . . . The risk of developing heart disease at Time 2?	. . . The diagnosis of lung cancer? . . . A cerebrovascular accident?
Social Environment	. . . Social isolation at Time 2? . . . Marital satisfaction at Time 2?	. . . Integenerational relations at Time 2? . . . Sibling relations at Time 2?	. . . The death of a spouse? . . . A change in residence?

the following literature review was organized. Most applied personality research is designed to answer one of the following three questions: *the Prediction Question*—Is Personality (or Independent) Variable A statistically associated with the onset of Outcome (or Dependent) Variable B?; *the Moderator Question* —Does Personality Variable A moderate the effects of a stressor on Outcome Variable B?; or *the Question of Change*—Are there "changes" in specific personality dimensions following a stressor?

These questions are interrelated and do not cover mutually exclusive terrain. A fourth question, that of mediation, is concerned with the basic psychological and behavioral processes that are interposed between personality and outcome. As Baron and Kenney (1986) put it, "Whereas moderator variables specify when certain effects will hold, mediators speak to how or why such effects occur" (p. 1176). Ths chapter does not cover mediation in part because very little mediational research has been conducted on older samples. Moreover, the wish is to emphasize the importance of personality dimensions, as opposed to basic behavioral and psychological processes.

The Prediction Question: Is Personality (or Independent) Variable A Statistically Associated With the Onset of Outcome (or Dependent) Variable B?

Data from cohort or longitudinal studies can be used to determine whether a personality trait truly predates a particular health-relevant outcome. Cross-sectional studies have also been used to draw such inferences, but the "state-trait" confound precludes unambiguous interpretation. Studies examining the prediction question are important because they identify risk factors and suggest potential treatments and primary prevention strategies.

Personality and Depression. Hirschfeld and Shea (1992) concluded that dependency is the trait most associated with predisposition to depression. Although there have been negative findings, numerous empirical studies have demonstrated that dependent persons are more likely to become depressed following loss and interpersonal rejection, conflict, and disapproval; those less prone to dependency are more likely to become depressed following events that threaten their need for independence, achievement, mastery, and power (Blatt & Zuroff, 1992; Bornstein, 1993; Nietzel & Harris, 1990; but see Coyne & Whiffen, 1995). Few, if any, of these studies have included participants who are over age 50.

There have been relatively few studies of personality traits and disorders in older depressives. Studies on that population in acute hospital settings have noted a high prevalence of comorbid *DSM–III–R* personality disorders with diagnoses from Cluster C predominating (Kunik et al., 1993; Kunik, Mulsant, Rifai, Sweet, Pasternak, & Zubenko, 1994). Personality disorders were associated with a younger age of onset of depression and poorer outcome (Abrams,

Rosendahl, Card, & Alexopoulous, 1994). These findings are robust, as they are consistent with those obtained using a different design. Schneider, Zemansky, Bender, and Sloane (1992) reported greater personality dysfunction among re-covered depressed elderly patients compared with nondepressed elderly. Just one study covers the contribution of personality factors to the prognosis of late life depression. Neither Neuroticism nor Extraversion predicted outcome in this elderly group (Burvill, Hall, Stampfer, & Emmerson, 1991).

At least one study has linked specific personality processes to response to pharmacological treatment (Peselow, Robins, Sanfilipo, Block, & Fieve, 1992). Autonomous personality traits were related to favorable antidepressant respon-siveness and unfavorable placebo responsiveness, whereas dependent personal-ity traits were associated with higher depression levels following the medication phase (Peselow et al., 1992). Such research on older samples is unavailable.

Personality and Mortality. Tucker and Friedman (1996) reviewed the litera-ture on associations of hostility, optimism, and Neuroticism with physical health and mortality. The strongest evidence of relations comes from research on hostility. They cited numerous prospective studies indicating that hostility and/or anger expression are risk factors for death in general and from coronary heart disease, cancer, and violence specifically. Optimism, although associated with a tendency to report fewer symptoms, quicker and better recovery after surgery, and more adaptive coping strategies, may be associated with increased mortality risk (Friedman et al., 1993), but findings are preliminary and inconsis-tent (cf. Rotton, 1992). Whereas Neuroticism is related more strongly to symp-tom reporting than to disease development (Costa & McCrae, 1987), there is growing evidence that it also is weakly but reliably related to a number of dis-eases, particularly coronary artery disease, and a general increase in mortality risk across the life span (Friedman et al., 1993; Friedman & Booth-Kewley, 1987).

Tucker and Friedman (1996) also discussed the results of their examination of the Terman Life Cycle Study data. In this study, 1,528 participants with IQs of at least 135 were assessed at 5- to 10-year intervals between 1922 and 1991 (approx-imately ages 11–80). Several measures of personality traits based on ratings made in 1922 were examined as predictors of mortality, including Extraversion (e.g., fondness for big groups), Conscientiousness (e.g., prudence, truthfulness), Neuroticism (e.g., self-esteem/high motivation), vulnerability to mood fluctu-ation, cheerful optimism, and physical energy/activity. Children who were rated as less Conscientious and those who were rated as more cheerful had an increased mortality risk in adulthood compared to their Conscientious and less cheerful counterparts. Those who tended to experience fluctuating moods were more likely to die than their counterparts. There were no effects of Neuroti-cism, Extraversion, or physical energy/activity level on mortality .

Secondary analyses of the Terman longitudinal database are significant in part because they demonstrate that some aspects of *childhood* personality and behavior are associated with mortality, longevity, and other health outcomes in late life. Put more dramatically, personality is literally a matter of life and death. Do personality data collected on middle-age and older adults have implications for mortality? It depends. Swan and Carmelli (1996) reported that scores on a self-report measure of curiosity (likely a dimension of Openness; see Marhall et al., 1994) administered to community dwellers with a mean age of 70 predicted mortality 5 years later. Highly curious respondents were less likely to have died during the follow-up interval. Associations between personality variables and mortality may, however, be determined in part by the age and diagnostic composition of the sample. Schulz, Bookwala, Knapp, Scheier, and Williamson (1996) showed that pessimism was associated with mortality in younger (age 30–59), but not older, cancer patients.

Personality and Social Isolation. The relation between social support and decreased morbidity and mortality (Berkman, 1995; House, Landis, & Umberson, 1988) may be explained in part by direct effects of social support on physiological outcomes (Uchino, Cacioppo, & Kiecolt-Glaser, 1996), meaning that physiological variables mediate the relation between social support and morbidity. These and similar findings have been used to justify implementing interventions to increase social support among the isolated. But this area of research and its implications are more ambiguous than these action-oriented calls for intervention may imply.

Understanding the determinants of social support is essential for the development of effective intervention programs (Thoits, 1995), especially given that targeted recipients may reject the social largesse (M. Clarke, S. J. Clarke, & Jagger, 1992). Yet, with the notable exceptions of studies on college students and other young adults, "almost no attention has been paid to social support as dependent variables" (House et al., 1988, p. 544). That changed dramatically in the late 1980s, in part due to the pioneering efforts of I. G. Sarason, B. R. Sarason, and their colleagues to integrate social support research with clinical developmental theory and personality research (e.g., I. G. Sarason, B. R. Sarason, & Shearing, 1986). A book devoted exclusively to the interface of personality and social support was published in 1997 (Pierce, Lakey, Sarason, & Sarason, 1997). Several recent studies conducted on older samples have demonstrated significant associations between personality and social support (Hooker, Monahan, Bowman, Frazier, & Shiffren, 1998; Krause, Liang, & Keith, 1990; Lang, Staudinger, & Carstensen, 1998; Oxman, Freeman, & Manheimer, 1995). For example, Oxman and colleagues (1995) showed that low Extraversion and high Neuroticism were positively associated with lack of group participation in a sample of 232 heart surgery patients. Hooker and colleagues (1998) reported a negative relation between Neuroticism and perceived social support among 175 spouse caregivers of elderly patients with neurodegenerative diseases. Structural modeling of the data led the authors to conclude that the lack of perceived social support "acts as a conduit for part of the effect of personality on stress and mental health" (p. P81). In a study of 516 community-dwelling German residents age 70 to 104 years, Lang and colleagues (1998) reported that Extraversion and Openness to Experience were positively associated with network size, and Neuroticism was negatively related to network size.

Two prospective studies reinforce these cross-sectional findings. Data analyses from the University of North Carolina Alumni Heart Study led Von Dras and Siegler (1997) to conclude that personality "during adolescence and young adulthood is an *antecedent* of the structural characteristics and functional dynamics of social support at midlife" (p. 240, emphasis added). Newman, Caspi, Moffitt, and Silva (1997) documented significant associations between temperament at age 3 and social support at age 21. Specifically, participants who were rated as inhibited (or introverted) at age 3 reported lower levels of material/practical support, companionship, and mentorship/guidance at age 21 than those who were not rated as inhibited.

The Moderator Question: Does Personality Variable A Moderate the Effects of a Stressor on Outcome Variable B?

Under what circumstances will a stressor lead to, or be associated with, a poor health outcome? By answering this question, researchers can generate information that allows for the development of treatments and interventions that are tailored to particular subgroups.

Personality Moderates Bereavement Response.   Many prebereavement characteristics, such as histories of separation and loss, level of functioning, health status, and religiousness have been hypothetically associated with bereavement outcome. These issues were extensively reviewed in two books published in the mid-1980s (Raphael, 1983; W. Stroebe & M. S. Stroebe, 1987). Although it might be expected that personality also has implications for bereavement outcome, Raphael (1983) noted that its role "remains unclear" (p. 63) and W. Stroebe and M. S. Stroebe (1987) indicated that the data are inconclusive, not because there have been negative findings, but because "very few personality traits have as yet been examined in the context of bereavement" (p. 198).

Empirical research on late life bereavement has typically been conducted without the benefit of personality data (Bass & Bowman, 1990; Dimond, Lund, & Caserta, 1987; Goldberg, Comstock, & Harlow, 1988; Hays, Kasl, & Jacobs, 1994; Murrell & Himmelfarb, 1989; Mullen, 1992; Murrell, Meeks, & Walker, 1991; Prigerson et al., 1997; Thompson, Gallagher-Thompson, Futterman, Gilewski, & Peterson, 1991). However, these carefully designed studies have confirmed that prebereavement characteristics, such as depression and strain, contribute to postbereavement psychological adjustment. Perhaps prebereavement dysphoria and strain reflect personality characteristics, which is another way of saying that postbereavement psychiatric symptoms develop in people with particular personality vulnerabilities (cf. Prigerson et al., 1997). Recognizing that postloss adjustment cannot be attributed solely to prebereavement characteristics, research on the contribution of personality to bereavement outcome is warranted.

Personality Moderates the Effect of Caregiving on Mental Health Outcomes. Caregiving is another common late-life issue that has been insufficiently informed by personality research. Dozens of articles have reported data on predictors and correlates of mental health outcomes in caregivers, but few research groups have systematically collected personality data. Hooker, Monahan, Shifren, and Hutchinson (1992) examined how the Neuroticism and optimism scores of spouse caregivers of dementia patients were related to their perceived stress and their self-rated mental and physical health. In a path analysis, they found that both Neuroticism and optimism were strongly related to perceived stress, Neuroticism was associated both directly and indirectly (via perceived stress) with self-report measures of mental health, Neuroticism was associated directly but not indirectly with self-reported physical symptoms, optimism was associated directly but not indirectly with self-reported depressive symptoms, and optimism was not associated with self-reported physical health. A subsequent study (Hooker, Frazier, & Monahan, 1994) on the same sample examined the relations of the FFM with the strategies used to cope with stress of caregiving. Controlling for gender, socioeconomic status, length of caregiving, and the other personality factors, Neuroticism was associated with less problem-focused and more emotion-focused coping strategies, and Extraversion was associated with less emotion-focused and more social support coping strategies.

The relation between care-recipient health and caregiver health remains one of the central themes in the caregiver burden literature. However, it is difficult to interpret many of these studies, because they are based on data provided by caregivers, but without data on caregiver personality. Similar problems arise in interpreting data on other constructs such as caregiver-perceived social support, stress, loneliness, depressive symptoms, and burden. Evidence that caregivers who obtain high Neuroticism scores may have somewhat distorted perceptions of care-recipients' functional and physical limitations comes from a carefully analyzed study of 393 caregivers (Bookwala & Schulz, 1998). Regression analyses showed significant relations between caregivers' personality (Neuroticism and mastery) and their reports of the care-recipients' behavior and functional limitations. Bookwala and Schulz concluded that data on the relation between care-recipient health and caregiver health can be reliable only if caregiver personality is taken into account.

Personality Moderates Recovery from Heart Disease.   Comorbid medical conditions contribute to the pathogenesis of later life depression (Caine, Lyness, & King, 1993; Katz, 1996). As scientific knowledge in this area grows, it is increasingly apparent that personality may moderate the relation between medical illness and depression. For example, coronary artery disease is a risk factor for depression. Personality processes might plausibly moderate this relation, such that patients high in Neuroticism may, as a result of their greater emotional vulnerability and tendency to exaggerate symptoms (Costa & McCrae, 1987), experience an increase in depressive symptoms or the onset of a depressive syndrome in the face of cardiac disease. Further, Neuroticism, but not Extraversion, is a risk factor for poststroke depression (Morris & Robinson, 1995), and Type A behavior pattern, among other personality constructs, is associated with negative emotions and poorer outcomes in patients with coronary artery disease (see Lesperance & Frasure-Smith, 1996, for a review). We are aware of no studies that have examined the hypothesis that the relation between coronary artery disease and depression in older persons is moderated by Neuroticism, or any other personality variable.

The Question of Personality Change: Are There Changes in Specific Personality Dimensions Following the Occurrence of Health-related Variable B?

Some readers may wonder why studies of personality change constitute one of the three most significant questions in applied personality research. After all, high test–retest stabilities, relative preservation of mean level, and the invariant factor structure across age and cohort all imply that personality is stable over time (Costa & McCrae, 1994). At the same time, there are hypotheses about lack of stability in specific personality dimensions that remain underinvestigated (e.g., Guttmann, 1980). This may be ascribed to the methodological and statistical complexities involved in the assessment of stability, the fact that stability is a relative, not an absolute concept, and the absence of a consensual, operational definition of stability. Despite these difficulties, Helson (1993) suggested that researchers have demonstrated stability in personality, and it is now time to "go on to questions about the nature and amount of change in personality at different periods of the life course and in different life contexts" (p. 95). Only by attempting to conduct this sort of research will the crucial definitional, methodological, and conceptual issues be identified and resolved.

Change in Specific Personality Dimensions Following Life Transitions.   Each society has its norms concerning the age-appropriateness of behaviors, goals, and major life transitions (e.g., marriage, employment). Neugarten (1968) referred to these norms as the "social clock," which presumably structure roles and tasks and thereby affect personality. In a longitudinal study based on the concept of the social clock, Helson and colleagues documented changes associated with life transitions among 140 members of the Mills college classes of 1958 and 1960 (Helson, Mitchell, & Moane, 1984; Helson & Moane, 1984; Wink & Helson, 1993). In one study, Helson et al. (1984) compared women who became mothers by age 27 with their childless age-peers. Compared to the scores obtained during their college years, the mothers obtained significantly higher scores on an inventory measuring responsibility, self-control, and femininity, and lower scores on sociability and acceptance. No pattern of change across the two measurement periods was detected for the childless women. Wink and Helson (1993) compared women and their partners on a measure of Conscientiousness at two timepoints, after college (mean age = 27 years) and 25 years later. In the interim, women obtained higher scores on the measure of Conscientiousness, but their partners' scores remained about the same.

For many older adults, spousal bereavement precipitates a major life transition. It, too, may be associated with empirically verifiable shifts in personality dimensions. Farberow, Gallagher-Thompson, Gilewski, and Thompson (1992) recruited subjects postloss and followed them over a 30-month period. Univariate analyses revealed significantly increasing brightness, emotional stability, enthusiasm, humility, practicality, and ability to relax. Multivariate measures for quadratic effects also revealed changes, but of a different sort. For example, enthusiasm increased between 2 and 6 months, then leveled off, then rose again between 12 and 30 months. Farberow et al. concluded that the observed changes in personality "probably reflect the acute effects of bereavement rather than any significant changes in enduring personality traits" (p. 365), but cautioned that their data are not definitive in that regard. More interpretable research in this area will require data collected prior to bereavement and longer follow-up.

Change in Specific Personality Dimensions Accompanying the Onset of Alzheimer's Disease. The decreased insight, impaired judgment, and cognitive deficits associated with this disease preclude the sole use of self-report measures. Informant reports are, therefore, essential to determine whether Alzheimer's disease is accompanied by an accentuation of premorbid characteristics or systematic changes in personality traits in particular subgroups of patients. The initial studies required informants to use bipolar adjective scales to rate target subjects both premorbidly and currently. Findings suggested personality changes associated with the onset of Alzheimer's disease, notably increased passivity, coarseness, and decreased spontaneity (Petry, Cummings, Hill, & Shapira, 1989). The FFM has enhanced the methodological rigor of more recent studies (Chatterjee, Strauss, Smyth, & Whitehouse, 1992; Siegler, Dawson, & Welsh, 1994; Strauss, Pasupathi, & Chatterjee, 1993). Informants have been asked to complete the NEO–PI twice, once to describe the patient prior to the onset of the illness, and again to describe the patient at the current time. In all three studies, informants have reported that the onset of AD is associated with increases in neuroticism and perceived decreases in Extraversion, Openness, and Conscientiousness. More definitive research in this area will require data collected prospectively from the subjects themselves, perhaps using existing biomedical databases.

DISCUSSION

From Science to Practice: Clinical Implications

The categorical approach to personality assessment and diagnosis predominates in clinical settings. The operationalized criteria sets and syndromes of the *Diagnostic and Statistical Manual of Mental Disorders* (*DSM–IV*) are used worldwide, facilitating communication and comparison of clinical and research findings. As with the literature reviewed in the preceding section, the multiaxial approach used in the *DSM* can also be understood in terms of the framework shown in Table 6.1. The prediction question asks whether a personality disorder predisposes to the development of a major Axis I condition; the personality disorder would be listed as a separate diagnosis on Axis II. Personality disorders moderate the course of major depressive disorder, such that patients with comorbid personality disorders have worse outcomes than those without a personality disorder. Finally, the group of diagnoses known as Mental Disorders Due to a General Medical Condition would be used to classify pathological states in which personality changes resulted from a specific medical illness, such as passivity following frontal lobe injury.

The FFM and other dimensional approaches to personality assessment complement categorical diagnosis in a number of respects that have important implications for clinical care. These implications apply both to the individual and to the population, and at each level of the framework proposed here. Dimensional approaches enable precise measurement of clinical features. For the individual, this advantage may lead to a sharper focus on particular areas of strength and vulnerability to illness, even when there is no demonstrable preexisting psychopathology.

Analyses designed to identify personality predictors of health outcomes may help define risk. With that knowledge, treatments can be more effectively designed and tested for their effectiveness as preventive measures. Efforts to decrease recurrent coronary artery disease and mortality in men following myocardial infarction through counseling to modify Type A behavior is one such example. It is a common clinical observation that personality traits change as a result of brain disorders. Further research is necessary to establish that other social and psychological factors may have the same result. The distinction of state from trait effects make such determinations elusive, but their clinical implications are profound. If clinicians were able to predict more reliably the personality changes that would likely occur as a result of particular circumstances, then they could help individuals and families prepare and adapt. Perhaps an understanding at the mechanistic level of the influence of environment on personality traits would suggest means for altering traits in treatment paradigms as well. Analyses designed to identify moderating variables have more extensive implications for illness treatment and prevention. The FFM and other dimensional approaches enable the study of relations between specific traits, and the relations between traits and both moderator and mediator variables, in determining vulnerability to morbidity and mortality. Examination of those relations may lead to a greater understanding of pathogenesis, and thus to more specific treatments and prevention. For example, Duberstein, Conwell, and Caine (1994) reported that the relation between Openness and completed suicide is moderated by age. Victims of completed suicide after age 50 had lower scores on the Openness factor of the NEO Personality Inventory than either younger suicide victims or age- and gender-matched community-dwelling elders. People who are low in Openness tend to be cognitively, affectively, and behaviorally constricted (see McCrae, 1993–1994, and McCrae, 1996, for reviews) and are hypothesized to be at increased risk for completed suicide because their rigidly defined self-concept complicates any effort they may make to experiment with new roles and identities following role loss (Duberstein, 1995; cf. Whitbourne, 1987). Unable to accommodate their superannuated self-concepts to the realities of their changing circumstances, yet needing to ward off undesirable negative affect, they descend into a state of "deconstructed awareness" (Baumeister, 1990), characterized by a sense of meaninglessness, concrete thinking, a distorted sense of time, and a focus on proximal goals. Deconstructed states are dangerous because they are accompanied by disinhibition, an increased willingness to violate social norms and standards (Baumeister, 1990).

A relatively brief duration of the events leading up to the suicide, functional decline, absence of prominent mood symptoms or communication of suicidal intent or ideation is frequently observed in older suicides who are not particularly open and receptive to novelty. The following case example, culled from a retrospective psychological autopsy study (Conwell, Duberstein, Cox, Herrmann, Forbes, & Caine, 1996), illustrates this scenario. As part of routine psychological autopsy procedure, the victim's wife of 42 years completed an informant-report version of the NEO–PI (Costa & McCrae, 1985), a questionnaire grounded in the FFM of personality, which yields five factor scores—Neuroticism (N), Extraversion (E), Openness (O), Agreeableness (A), and Conscientiousness (C)—as well as six constituent facets scores for each of the first three (N, E, and O).

Mr. A was a 66-year-old White, married, retired carpenter and father of six grown children. He died of a self-inflicted gunshot wound to the head 1 day after his discharge from the hospital following surgery. Psychological autopsy revealed a remote history of alcohol dependence but no active Axis I diagnosis. He stopped drinking nearly two decades prior to his death, shortly after he was diagnosed with insulin-dependent diabetes. Sufficiently frightened after awaking with chest pain one night, he remained sober thereafter.

The NEO–PI profile was remarkable for very low scores on Openness and Extraversion and a Neuroticism score that was just mildly elevated. Mr. A obtained very low scores on the aesthetics, ideas, and feelings facets of Openness. Low scorers on these facets do not enjoy playing with or discussing philosophical or abstract ideas, are not easily emotionally moved by poetry, music, or art, and rarely experience a wide range of emotions more generally.

Mrs. A noted that the events leading up to her husband's death unfolded over just 3 weeks. A day after a routine physical examination revealed nothing unusual, Mr. A. was admitted to the hospital for chest pain. A myocardial infarction was ruled out, but catheterization showed severe coronary artery disease. Notes from the hospitalization commented on his "tense look . . . and apprehension," as well as his complaint of "a pressure in my head." Two days after being discharged home for a trial of medication therapy, he was readmitted with unstable angina. He was again observed to be apprehensive and anxious, but he complained only of insomnia, had a good appetite, and reported "very positive feelings" about having elective coronary artery bypass surgery.

The surgery was as uneventful as the 8-day postoperative hospital course. Family noted no significant change after his arrival home, other than his request that first night that a light be left on. He was mildly tense and fatigued, but without any indication of hopelessness, helplessness, or suicidal ideation. The following morning, after she gave her husband breakfast and assisted in his bath, Mrs. A left the home to pick up a prescription. She found him dead when she returned. No suicide note was found.

One can only speculate about how Mr. A's surgery and functional limitations challenged his self-concept, as otherwise vital, independent, and productive. A man who earned a living by working with his hands and who had been able to live with diabetes for two decades without significant distress was suddenly dependent on his wife for some of his basic activities of daily living (ADLs). One can only wonder about what heart disease symbolically represented to Mr. A, who two decades earlier was sufficiently frightened by chest pain to stop drinking. Nor can one know for certain why Mr. A wanted a light to be kept on the night before his death, or the extent to which that request made him feel dependent or regressed. But the inscrutability of it all is precisely the point. Perhaps more so than other suicides, those elders who are low in Openness leave in their wake unanswered questions. The reasons for this uncertainty are unknown, but it has been suggested that elders with this trait tend not to share their feelings, perhaps reflecting a more general problem accessing, and attaching words to, emotions (Duberstein, 1995).

Openness may moderate the relation between medical illness and suicide, and this relation in turn may be mediated by affective dampening, cognitive constriction, and behavioral rigidity. If this is true, preventive measures could be designed specifically to augment the low-openness elder's coping in times of crisis. Individual or family counseling in anticipation of medical procedures or other specific stressful life events (e.g., retirement or bereavement) may be useful.

CONCLUSIONS

Even in late life, personality characteristics can engender or exacerbate the diseases, chronic strains, or life crises health care professionals are asked to alleviate or cure. This broad survey of the literature illustrates the extent to which dimensional measures of personality have been, and could be, implicated in mental and physical health in later life. It is intended to be neither comprehensive nor methodologically critical. Rather, it is hoped that it will stimulate research and clinical scholarship in domains that have been insufficiently informed by the advances (and tensions) in personality psychology. By focusing on the FFM, this does not mean to imply that it is superior to other approaches to personality assessment, or that it can stand alone. Indeed, more multimethod research is needed, incorporating assessments of implicit (McClelland et al., 1989) and explicit (Hooker & Kaus, 1994) motives and goals, life narratives (Cohler, 1991; McAdams, 1994), and physiological responses to stressors (Kagan, 1994). As for content, a number of topics have been reviewed, and others are listed in Table 6.1. No doubt, many readers will identify other topics that could be informed by personality research.

It is unknown whether the quantity of rigorous research on personality in late life (or any topic) reflects the extent to which researchers and practitioners acknowledge its significance. It would appear from this review that the contribution of personality to interindividual variability in health and function has been underacknowledged. A significant effort would be required to import personality into the lexicon of health care professionals who work with the elderly every day. Identifying the barriers impeding empirical pursuit of questions bearing on personality in late life may help move the field toward overcoming them. Some of the methodological barriers have been well-articulated, and include, perhaps most substantially, the possibility that the Axis II criteria sets are inappropriate for the elderly (Rosowsky & Gurian, 1991; Sadavoy & Fogel, 1992). The nonmethodological barriers may pose even greater difficulties. These include, but are not limited to, culturally biased beliefs that personality processes are less relevant to the development and understanding of late life disorders (Casey & Shrodt, 1989). Suicide provides one example. Suicide may be likely to be deemed more "pathological" in early adulthood than in later life. It may even be considered a reasonable response to medical illness and chronic pain in a lonely person who, even under better circumstances, had relatively little time to live.

Situational reductionism and biological reductionism also represent significant conceptual obstacles to the study of personality in later life. Guttmann (1997) described the "camel's back model of pathogenesis" in which "the laden beast endures until a critical mass of burden is reached, at which point any additional straw will cause a decisive rupture of its back" (p. 2). From this situationalist perspective, late life psychopathology is a product of terminal illness, caregiver burden, or the death of a spouse. Omitted from these formulations is any consideration of personality, perhaps out of a fear that doing so would be tantamount to "blaming the victim," despite the inextricable relation between personality and both the events people are exposed to and the events they are disturbed by (Caspi & Bem, 1990; but see Coyne & Whiffen, 1995). A similar criticism can be leveled against biological research that fails to consider the person from whom biological data are gathered.

This is the first book devoted to the clinical implications of personality disorders and dimensions in later life. It sounds a timely warning against reductionism, and thereby demonstrates the need for more rigorous research and clinical scholarship on the contributions of personality to interindividual variability in mental and physical health and function in later life.

ACKNOWLEDGMENTS

This project was financially supported in part by Public Health Service grants K07-MH01135, K07-MH01113, R03-MH55149, and R01-MH51201.

Jill Eichele provided helpful comments and bibliographic assistance, Nancy Talbot and the editors made a number of useful suggestions on a previous draft of this chapter, and Josephine Lauri assisted in manuscript preparation.

REFERENCES

Abrams, R. C., Rosendahl, E., Card, C., & Alexopoulos, G. S. (1994). Personality disorder correlates of late and early onset depression. *Journal of the American Geriatrics Society, 42,* 727–731.

Allport, G. (1961). *Pattern and growth in personality.* New York: Holt, Rhinehart & Winston.

Baron, R. M., & Kenney, D. A. (1986). The moderator-mediator variable distinction in social psychological research: Conceptual, strategic, and statistical considerations. *Journal of Personality and Social Psychology, 51,* 1173–1182.

Bass, D. M., & Bowman, K. (1990). The influence of caregiving and bereavement support on adjusting to an older relative's death. *Gerontologist, 31,* 32–42.

Baumeister, R. F. (1990). Suicide as escape from self. *Psychological Review, 97,* 90–113.

Berkman, L. F. (1995). The role of social relations in health promotion. *Psychosomatic Medicine, 57,* 245–254.

Blatt, S. J., & Zuroff, D. (1992). Interpersonal relatedness and self-definition: Two prototypes for depression. *Clinical Psychology Review, 12,* 527–562.

Block, J. (1961). *The Q-sort method in personality assessment and psychiatric research.* Springfield, IL: Thomas.

Block, J. (1971). *Lives through time.* Berkeley, CA: Bancroft Books.

Block, J. (1995). A contrarian view of the five-factor approach to personality description. *Psychological Bulletin, 117,* 187–215.

Bookwala, J., & Schulz, R. (1998). The role of neuroticism and mastery in spouse caregivers' assessment of and response to a contextual stressor. *Journal of Gerontology: Psychological Sciences, 53B,* P155–164.

Bornstein, R. F. (1993). *The dependent personality.* New York: Guilford.

Bronfenbrenner, U. (1979). *The ecology of human development.* Cambridge, MA: Harvard University Press.

Burvill, P. W., Hall, W. D., Stampfer, H. G., & Emmerson, P. (1991). The prognosis of depression in old age. *British Journal of Psychiatry, 158,* 64–71.

Caine, E. D., Lyness, J. M., & King, D. A. (1993). Reconsidering depression in the elderly. *American Journal of Geriatric Psychiatry, 1,* 4–20.

Casey, D. A., & Schrodt, C. J. (1989). Axis II diagnoses in geriatric inpatients. *Journal of Geriatric Psychiatry and Neurology, 2,* 87–88.

Caspi, A., & Bem, D. J. (1990). Personality continuity and change across the life course. In L. A. Pervin (Ed.), *Handbook of personality: Theory and research* (pp. 549–575). New York: Guilford.

Chatterjee, A., Strauss, M. E., Smyth, K. A., & Whitehouse, P. J. (1992). Personality changes in Alzheimer's disease. *Archives of Neurology, 49,* 486–491.

Clarke, M., Clarke, S. J., & Jagger, C. (1992). Social intervention and the elderly: A randomized control trial. *American Journal of Epidemiology, 136,* 1517–1523.

Cloninger, C. R., Svrakic, D. M., & Przybeck, T. R. (1993). A psychobiological model of temperament and character. *Archives of General Psychiatry, 50,* 975–990.

Cohler, B. J. (1991). The life story and the study of resilience and response to adversity. *Journal of Narrative and Life History, 1,* 169–200.

Contrada, R. J., Leventhal, H., & O'Leary, A. (1990). Personality and health. In L. A. Pervin (Ed.), *Handbook of personality: Theory and research* (pp. 638–669). New York: Guilford.

Conwell, Y., Duberstein, P. R., Cox, C., Herrmann, J., Forbes, N. T., & Caine, E. D. (1996). Relationships of age and Axis I diagnoses in victims of completed suicide: A psychological autopsy study. *American Journal of Psychiatry, 153,* 1001–1008.

Coolidge, F. L., Becker, L. A., DiRito, D. C., Durham, R. L., Kinlaw, M. M., & Philbrick, P. B. (1994). On the relationship of the five-factor personality model to personality disorders: Four reservations. *Psychological Reports, 75,* 11–21.

Costa, P. T., Jr., & McCrae, R. R.(1985). *The NEO Personality Inventory: Manual.* Odessa, FL: Psychological Assessment Resources.

Costa, P. T., Jr., & McCrae, R. R. (1987). Neuroticism, somatic complaints, and disease: Is the bark worse than the bite? *Journal of Personality, 55,* 299–316.

Costa, P. T., Jr., & McCrae, R. R. (1992a). *Revised NEO Personality Inventory and NEO Five Factor Inventory: Professional Manual.* Odessa, FL: Psychological Assessment Resources.

Costa, P. T., Jr., & McCrae, R. R. (1992b). Trait psychology comes of age. In T. B. Sonderegger (Ed.), *Nebraska symposium on motivation: Psychology and aging* (pp. 169–204). Lincoln, NE: University of Nebraska Press.

Costa, P. T., Jr., & McCrae, R. R. (1994). Set like plaster? Evidence for the stability of adult personal-
    ity. In T. F. Heatherton & J. L. Weinberger (Eds.), *Can personality change?* (pp. 21–40). Washington,
    DC: American Psychological Association.
Costa, P. T., Jr., & McCrae, R. R. (1995). Solid ground in the wetlands of personality: A reply to
    Block. *Psychological Bulletin, 117,* 216–220.
Costa, P. T., Jr., & Widiger, T. A. (Eds.). (1993). *Personality disorders and the five factor model of personal-
    ity.* Washington, DC: American Psychological Association.
Coyne, J. C., & Whiffen, V. (1995). Issues in personality as diathesis for depression: The case of socio-
    tropy-dependency and autonomy-self-criticism. *Psychological Bulletin, 118,* 358–378.
Cross, S., & Markus, H. (1991). Possible selves across the lifespan. *Human Development, 34,* 230–255.
Depue, R. A., & Monroe, S. M. (1986). Conceptualization and measurement of human disorder in
    life stress research: The problem of chronic disturbance. *Psychological Bulletin, 99,* 36–51.
Digman, J. M. (1990). Personality structure: Emergence of the five-factor model. *Annual Review of
    Psychology, 41,* 417–440.
Dimond, M., Lund, D. A., & Caserta, M. S. (1987). The role of social support in the first 2 years of
    bereavement in an elderly sample. *Gerontologist, 27,* 599–604.
Duberstein, P. R. (1995). Openness to experience and completed suicide across the second half of
    life. *International Psychogeriatrics, 7,* 183–198.
Duberstein, P. R., Conwell, Y., & Caine, E. D. (1994). Age differences in the personality characteris-
    tics of suicide completers: Preliminary findings from a psychological autopsy study. *Psychiatry,
    57,* 213–224.
Farberow, N. L., Gallagher-Thompson, D., Gilewski, M., & Thompson, L. (1992). Changes in grief
    and mental health of bereaved spouses of older adults. *Journals of Gerontology, 47,* P357–P366.
Friedman, H. S., & Booth-Kewley, S. (1987). The "disease-prone personality": A meta-analytic view
    of the construct. *American Psychologist, 42,* 539–555.
Friedman, H. S., Tucker, J. S., Tomlinson-Keasey, C., Schwartz, J., Wingard, D., & Criqui, M. (1993).
    Does childhood personality predict longevity? *Journal of Personality and Social Psychology, 65,* 176–
    185.
Garb, H. N., Florio, C. M., & Grove, W. M. (1998). The validity of the Rorschach and the Minnesota
    Multiphasic Personality Inventory. *Psychological Science, 9,* 402–404.
Glisky, M. L., Tataryn, D. J., Tobias, B. A., Kihlstrom, J. F., & McConkey, K. M. (1991). Absorption,
    openness to experience, and hypnotizability. *Journal of Personality and Social Psychology, 60,* 263–272.
Goldberg, E. L., Comstock, G. W., & Harlow, S. D. (1988). Emotional problems and widowhood.
    Journals of Gerontology, 43, S206–S208.
Guttmann, D. (1980). Psychoanalysis and aging: A developmental view. In S. I. Greenspan & G. H.
    Pollock (Eds.), *The course of life: Psychoanalytic contributions toward understanding personality devel-
    opment, Vol. 3: Adulthood and the aging process.* Washington, DC: National Institute of Mental
    Health.
Guttmann, D. (1997). *The human elder in nature, culture, and society.* Boulder, CO: Westview.
Hays, J. C., Kasl, S. V., & Jacobs, S. C. (1994). The course of psychological distress following threat-
    ened and actual conjugal bereavement. *Psychological Medicine, 24,* 917–927.
Helson, R. (1993). Comparing longitudinal studies of adult development: Toward a paradigm of
    tension between stability and change. In D. C. Funder, R. D. Parke, C. Tomlinson-Keasey, &
    K. Widaman (Eds.), *Studying lives through time: Personality and development* (pp. 93–119). Washing-
    ton, DC: American Psychological Association.
Helson, R., Mitchell, V., & Moane, G. (1984). Personality and patterns of adherence and nonadher-
    ence to the social clock. *Journal of Personality and Social Psychology, 46,* 1079–1096.
Helson, R., & Moane, G. (1984). Personality change in women from college to midlife. *Journal of Per-
    sonality and Social Psychology, 53,* 176–186.
Hirschfeld, R.M.A., & Shea, M. T. (1992). Personality. In E. S. Paykel (Ed.), *Handbook of affective dis-
    orders.* New York: Guilford.

Holt, R. R. (1962). Individuality and generalization in the psychology of personality. *Journal of Personality, 30,* 377–404

Hooker, K., Frazier, L. D., & Monahan, D. J. (1994). Personality and coping among caregivers of spouses with dementia. *Gerontologist, 34,* 386–392.

Hooker, K., & Kaus, C. R. (1994). Health-related possible selves in young and middle adulthood. *Psychology and Aging, 9,* 126–133.

Hooker, K., Monahan, D. J., Bowman, S. R., Frazier, L. D., & Shifren, K. (1998). Personality counts for a lot: Predictors of mental and physical health of spouse caregivers in two disease groups. *Journal of Gerontology: Psychological Sciences, 53B,* P73–P85.

Hooker, K., Monahan, D., Shifren, K., & Hutchinson, C. (1992). Mental and physical health of spouse caregivers: The role of personality. *Psychology and Aging, 7,* 367–375.

House, J. S., Landis, K. R., & Umberson, D. (1988). Social relationships and health. *Science, 241,* 540–545.

John, O. P. (1990). The "Big Five" factor taxonomy: Dimensions of personality in the natural language and questionnaires. In L. A. Pervin (Ed.), *Handbook of personality: Theory and research* (pp. 66–100). New York: Guilford.

Kagan, J. (with Snidman, N., Arcus, D., & Reznick, J. S.). (1994). *Galen's prophecy: Temperament in human nature.* New York: Basic Books.

Katz, I. R. (1996). On the inseparability of mental and physical health in aged persons. Lessons from depression and medical comorbidity. *American Journal of Geriatric Psychiatry, 4,* 1–16.

Krause, N., Liang, J., & Keith, V. (1990). Personality, social support, and psychological distress in later life. *Psychology and Aging, 5,* 315–326.

Kunik, M. E., Mulsant, B. H., Rifai, A. H., Sweet, R., Pasternak, R., & Zubenko, G. S. (1994). Diagnostic rate of comorbid personality disorder in elderly psychiatric inpatients. *American Journal of Psychiatry, 151,* 603–605.

Kunik, M. E., Mulsant, B. H., Rifai, A. H., Sweet, R., Pasternak, R., Rosen, J., & Zubenko, G. S. (1993). Personality disorders in elderly inpatients with major depression. *American Journal of Geriatric Psychiatry, 1,* 38–45.

Lang, F. R., Staudinger, U. M., & Carstensen, L. L. (1998). Perspectives on socioemotional selectivity in late life: How personality and social context do (and do not) make a difference. *Journal of Gerontology: Psychological Sciences, 53B,* P21–P30.

Lesperance, F., & Frasure-Smith, N. (1996). Negative emotions and coronary heart disease: Getting to the heart of the matter. *Lancet, 347,* 414–415.

Livesley, W. J., Jang, K. L., & Vernon, P. A. (1998). Phenotypic and genetic structure of traits delineating personality disorder. *Archives of General Psychiatry, 55,* 941–948.

Magnusson, D. (1990). Personality development from an interactional perspective. In L. A. Pervin (Ed.), *Handbook of personality: Theory and research* (pp. 193–222). New York: Guilford.

Magnusson, D., & Törestad, B. (1993). A holistic view of personality: A model revisited. *Annual Review of Psychology, 44,* 427–452.

Marshall, G. N., Wortman, C. B., Vickers, R. R., Jr., Kusulas, J. W., & Hervig, L. K. (1994). The five-factor model of personality as a framework for personality-health research. *Journal of Personality and Social Psychology, 67,* 278–286.

Masling, J. (1977). Klopfer award lecture: On the nature and utility of projective tests and objective tests. *Journal of Personality Assessment, 69,* 257–270.

McAdams, D. P. (1992). The five-factor model in personality: A critical appraisal. *Journal of Personality, 60,* 329–361.

McAdams, D. P. (1994). Can personality change? Levels of stability and growth in personality across the life span. In T. F. Heatherton & J. L. Weinberger (Eds.), *Can personality change?* (pp. 299–314). Washington, DC: American Psychological Association.

McClelland, D., Koestner, R., & Weinberger, J. (1989). How do self-attributed and implicit motives differ? *Psychological Review, 96,* 690–702.

McCrae, R. R. (1993–1994). Openness to experience as a basic dimension of personality. *Imagination, Cognition, and Personality, 13,* 39–55.

McCrae, R. R. (1996). Social consequences of experiential openness. *Psychological Bulletin, 120,* 323–337.

McCrae, R. R., & Costa, P. T., Jr. (1997). Personality trait structure as a human universal. *American Psychologist, 52,* 509–516.

Moen, P., Elder, G. H., Jr., & Luscher, K. (Eds.). (1995). *Examining lives in context: Perspectives on the ecology of human development.* Washington, DC: American Psychological Association.

Morris, P.L.P., & Robinson, R. G. (1995). Personality neuroticism and depression after stroke. *International Journal of Psychiatry Medicine, 25,* 93–102.

Mullen, J. T. (1992). The bereaved caregiver: A prospective study of changes in well-being. *The Gerontologist, 32,* 673–683.

Murray, H. A. (1981). *Endeavors in psychology: Selections from the personology of Henry A. Murray.* New York: Harper & Row.

Murrell, S. A., & Himmelfarb, S. (1989). Effects of attachment bereavement and pre-event conditions on subsequent depressive symptoms in older adults. *Psychology and Aging, 4,* 166–172.

Murrell, S. A., Meeks, S., & Walker, J. (1991). Protective functions of health and self-esteem against depression in older adults facing illness or bereavement. *Psychology and Aging, 6,* 352–360.

Neugarten, B. L. (1968). Adult personality: Toward a psychology of the life-cycle. In B. L. Neugarten (Ed.), *Middle age and aging* (pp. 137–147). Chicago: University of Chicago Press.

Newman, D. L., Caspi, A., Moffitt, T. E., & Silva, P. (1997). Antecedents of adult interpersonal functioning: Effects of individual differences in age 3 temperament. *Developmental Psychology, 33,* 206–217.

Nietzel, M. T., & Harris, M. J. (1990). Relationship of dependency and achievement/autonomy to depression. *Clinical Psychology Review, 10,* 279–297.

Oxman, T. E., Freeman, D. H., & Manheimer, E. D. (1995). Lack of social participation or religious strength and comfort as risk factors for death after cardiac surgery in the elderly. *Psychosomatic Medicine, 57,* 5–15.

Peselow, E. D., Robins, C. J., Sanfilipo, M. P., Block, P., & Fieve, R. R. (1992). Sociotropy and autonomy: Relationship to antidepressant drug treatment response and the endogenous-nonendogenous dichotomy. *Journal of Abnormal Psychology, 101,* 479–486.

Petry, S., Cummings, J. L., Hill, M. A., & Shapira, J. (1989). Personality alterations in dementia of the Alzheimer type. *Archives of Neurology, 45,* 1187–1190.

Pierce, G. R., Lakey, B., Sarason, I. G., & Sarason, B. R. (Eds.). (1997). *Sourcebook of social support and personality.* New York and London: Plenum Press.

Prigerson, H. G., Bierhals, A. J., Kasl, S. V., Reynolds III, C. F., Shear, M. K., Day, N., Beery, L., Newsom, J. T., & Jacobs, S. (1997). Traumatic grief as a risk factor for mental and physical morbidity. *American Journal of Psychiatry, 154,* 616–623.

Raphael, B. (1983). *The anatomy of bereavement.* New York: Basic Books.

Rosowsky, E., & Gurian, B. (1991). Borderline personality disorder in late life. *International Psychogeriatrics, 3,* 39–52.

Rotton, J. (1992). Trait humor and longevity: Do comics have the last laugh? *Health Psychology, 11,* 262–266.

Runyan, W. M. (1983). Idiographic goals and methods in the study of lives. *Journal of Personality, 51,* 413–437.

Sadavoy, J., & Fogel, B. (1992). Personality disorders in old age. In J. E. Birren, R. B. Sloane, & G. D. Cohen (Eds.), *Handbook of mental health and aging* (pp. 433–463). San Diego: Academic Press.

Sarason, I. G., Sarason, B. R., & Shearin, E. N. (1986). Social support as an individual difference variable: Its stability, origins, and relational aspects. *Journal of Personality and Social Psychology, 50,* 845–855.

Schneider, L. S., Zemansky, M. F., Bender, M., & Sloane, R. B. (1992). Personality in recovered depressed elderly. *International Psychogeriatrics, 4,* 177–185.

Schulz, R., Bookwala, J., Knapp, J. E., Scheier, M., & Williamson, G. M. (1996). Pessimism, age, and cancer mortality. *Psychology and Aging, 11,* 304–309.

Shedler, J., Mayman, M., & Manis, M. (1993). The *illusion* of mental health. *American Psychologist, 48,* 1117–1131.

Siegler, I. C., Dawson, D. V., & Welsh, K. A. (1994). Caregiver ratings of personality change in Alzheimer's Disease patients: A replication. *Psychology and Aging, 9,* 464–466.

Soldz, S., Budman, S., Demby, A., & Merry, J. (1993). Representation of personality disorders in circumplex and five-factor space: Explorations with a clinical sample. *Psychological Assessment, 5,* 41–52.

Strauss, M. E., Pasupathi, M., & Chatterjee, A. (1993). Concordance between observers in descriptions of personality change in Alzheimer's disease. *Psychology and Aging, 8,* 475–480.

Stroebe, W., & Stroebe, M. S. (1987). *Bereavement and health: The psychological and physical consequences of partner loss.* New York: Cambridge University Press.

Swan, G. E., & Carmelli, D. (1996). Curiosity and mortality in aging adults: A 5-year follow-up of the Western Collaborative Group Study. *Psychology and Aging, 11,* 449–453.

Tellegen, A. (1985). Structures of mood and personality and their relevance to assessing anxiety, with an emphasis on self-report. In A. H. Tuma & J. D. Maser (Eds.), *Anxiety and the anxiety disorders* (pp. 681–706). Hillsdale, NJ: Lawrence Erlbaum Associates.

Thoits, P. A. (1995). Stress, coping, and social support processes: Where are we? What next? *Journal of Health and Social Behavior, Extra Issue,* 53–79.

Thompson, L. W., Gallagher-Thompson, D., Futterman, A., Gilewski, M. J., & Peterson, J. (1991). The effects of late-life spousal bereavement over a 30-month interval. *Psychology and Aging, 6,* 434–441.

Trull, T. J. (1992). *DSM–III–R* personality disorders and the five-factor model of personality: An empirical comparison. *Journal of Abnormal Psychology, 101,* 553–560.

Tucker, J. S., & Friedman, H. S. (1996). Emotion, personality, and health. In C. Magai & S. H. McFadden (Eds.), *Handbook of emotion, adult development, and aging* (pp. 307–326). San Diego: Academic Press.

Uchino, B. N., Cacioppo, J. T., & Kiecolt-Glaser, J. K. (1996). The relationship between social support and physiological processes: A review with emphasis on underlying mechanisms and implications for health. *Psychological Bulletin, 119,* 488–531.

Von Dras, D. D., & Siegler, I. C. (1997). Stability in extraversion and aspects of social support at midlife. *Journal of Personality and Social Psychology, 72,* 233–241.

Whitbourne, S. K. (1987). Openness to experience, identity flexibility, and life change in adults. *Journal of Personality and Social Psychology, 50,* 163–168.

Widiger, T. A. (1998). Four out of five ain't bad. *Archives of General Psychiatry, 55,* 865–866.

Wink, P., & Helson, R. (1993). Personality change in women and their partners. *Journal of Personality and Social Psychology, 69,* 597–605.

Woolf, H. B., Artin, E., Crawford, F. S., Gilman, E. W., Ray, M. W., & Pease, Jr., R. W. (Eds.). (1977). *Webster's New Collegiate Dictionary.* Springfield, MA: Merriam.

CHAPTER 7

Determining Personality Disorders in Older Adults Through Self-Identification and Clinician Assessment

LINDA M. DOUGHERTY, PhD
Piedmont Geriatric Hospital

Identification and assessment of personality disorders is important for several reasons. Personality disorders exert significant clinical impact, but frequently go undiagnosed and disregarded in treatment planning and case management. The presence and severity of personality disorders predict subsequent development and severity of Axis I psychopathology (Johnson & Bornstein, 1992). Additionally, the presence of personality disorder has implications for treatment planning (Rosowsky, Dougherty, Johnson, & Gurian, 1997), as well as for predicting response to both psychological and pharmacological treatments (Andreoli, Gressot, Aapro, Tricot, & Gognalons, 1989). However, diagnosing personality disorders in older adults is problematic because standard diagnostic criteria (i.e., the *DSM* system) do not fit older adults as well as they do younger adults (Rosowsky & Gurian, 1991).

Age-related and life stage-related changes in symptom presentation of personality pathology can result in inappropriate or missed personality disorder diagnosis. Failure to diagnose personality disorder in the elderly may be due to several factors: the inherent difficulty in defining what "personality disorder" would be for this population and whether there are age-related differences in the definition of personality disorder, culturally based (and/or cohort-based) expectations that personality disorder does not exist in the elderly (Kroessler, 1990), or lack of consensus about diagnostic criteria (Perry, 1992).

Moreover, methodological problems contribute to the difficulty in identifying and assessing personality disorders (see chap. 3 in this volume). The chief conceptual problem is how to define personality disorder in late life. Related questions concern how to identify those criteria that serve as key markers for the diagnosis and what are relevant sources of diagnostic information. Finally, who is obliged to identify personality pathology or personality disorders—the patient, the clinician, or both? Although it is beyond the scope of this chapter to present a comprehensive discussion of theoretical and conceptual issues related to personality disorders in older adults (for an excellent review, see Clarkin and colleagues, chap. 1 in this volume), the way in which existing research measures and assessment instruments contribute to knowledge of personality disorders in late life is examined.

There are two general approaches to the identification and assessment of personality disorders: patient based and clinician based. Both approaches share similar methodology by collecting information about personality functioning through self-report and/or interview formats. This chapter reviews these approaches from the perspective of their psychometric properties (reliability, validity) and their utility (situational use, cost, efficiency). Whereas few assessment instruments have been developed specifically for use with older adults, applications for use with this population are highlighted here.

METHODOLOGICAL ISSUES

Personality disorders in late life have recently garnered attention from personality theorists and researchers alike. Conventional clinical wisdom maintains that personality disorders mellow or fade with age. Support for this came from studies (Kroessler, 1990; Sadavoy, 1987) reporting lower prevalence rates for "high energy" personality disorders (e.g., histrionic, antisocial). Recently, this position has been challenged by empirical evidence revealing a lack of congruence between the older patient's symptom portrayal and standardized diagnostic categories (Dougherty & Rosowsky, in press-a; Rosowsky & Gurian, 1991; Sadavoy & Fogel, 1992). Clinicians were more likely to overlook or disregard objective diagnostic criteria and instead relied on their countertransference responses to the older patient when diagnosing personality disorders.

Models of Personality

Personality functioning (and personality disorder) is commonly described by either categorical or dimensional models. Personality disorders differ from personality styles in that the traits are inflexible, pervasive, and impair social and occupational functioning and/or cause subjective distress. Dimensional models of personality propose that personality traits are possessed in some quantitative degree by all individuals and are not inherently adaptive or maladaptive. Within this dimensional framework, personality disorders are thought to reflect extreme variants of normal personality traits. These models provide flexible, specific, and comprehensive information that easily can be translated into a categorical system, if necessary. Empirical investigations of dimensional models have employed factor analytic techniques to identify key dimensions of personality. Five robust, recurrent personality domains are typically identified: Neuroticism, Extraversion, Openness, Agreeableness, and Conscientiousness. This Five-Factor Model of personality (FFM; Costa & McCrae, 1992; Digman & Takemoto-Chock, 1981; Tupes & Christal, 1961) has been generally accepted as the prevailing dimensional model of personality functioning.

Categorical models of personality functioning (e.g., the *DSM* system) conceptualize personality disorders as specific and unique constellations of personality traits. Advantages of categorical systems are consistency of personality disorder nomenclature, greater familiarity to clinicians, and greater ease in communication. Categorical models of personality have difficulty in classifying patients who manifest personality pathology that lies on the boundaries between categories. Further, the simplicity of categorical systems may be unsuited to a complex domain such as personality pathology (Frances & Widiger, 1986).

Both dimensional and categorical models of personality function struggle with the questions of relevant diagnostic criteria, differential importance of diagnostic criteria to the identification of personality disorder, and heterogeneity of diagnostic criteria to personality disorder membership. Despite extensive empirical research using the FFM, consensus has yet to be achieved as to which personality dimensions define the domain of personality disorders. Recently, several investigators (Dougherty & Rosowsky, in press-b; Widiger, Trull, Clarkin, Sanderson, & Costa, 1995) have identified Neuroticism as explaining most of the variance in measures of personality pathology. Whereas the importance of Neuroticism to identification of personality pathology seems to be robust with respect to method (e.g., self-report, family rating, clinician report) and age of patient (Dougherty & Rosowsky, in press-a, in press-b), Neuroticism has also been identified as the key personality domain in Axis I pathology (McCrae, 1991), adjustment to medical conditions (Wade, Dougherty, Hart, & Cook, 1992), and satisfaction with occupation (Tucker & Dougherty, 1997).

Reliability and Validity of Diagnostic Criteria

Reliability and validity of diagnostic criteria refers to the extent to which clinicians agree on diagnoses applied to a series of cases, and the extent to which observable behavior is a true representation of the underlying diagnostic construct. In other words, reliability is the extent to which patients with a particular diagnosis can be discriminated from patients with a different diagnosis. Validity is the convergence of observable behavior with the theoretical or abstract conceptualization of the diagnostic entity. A diagnostic classification may be reliable but have little validity. The converse is not true, however—validity is restricted by the extent of reliability (Spitzer & Williams, 1985).

Historically, personality disorder criteria have demonstrated poor levels of diagnostic reliability. Livesley (1985) suggested that one avenue to increase the reliability of personality disorder criteria would be to base diagnostic criteria on observable behavior rather than subjective impression. Behavioral criteria can be operationalized into concrete descriptors of personality disorder criteria. For example, terms such as aloof, emotionally cold, or social withdrawal could be replaced by behavioral descriptors such as "chooses to be alone in social situations," "did not respond to physical affection," or "facial expression blank or neutral". This reduces the amount of inference required to interpret diagnostic criteria. Although the most recent revisions of the DSM system (DSM–III–R, DSM–IV) have moved in this direction, clear behavioral descriptions of personality disorder criteria are still lacking for most personality disorders.

An additional problem related to the reliability and validity of diagnostic criteria is the juxtaposition of age changes on personality disorder manifestation. The aging process exerts considerable influence on the manner in which personality disorder criteria are exhibited. It is less common for older personality disordered patients to exhibit "high energy" diagnostic criteria (e.g., law breaking, identity disturbance, promiscuity), although these criteria may still be a part of the clinical picture. For example, Mr. R was a 72-year-old, widowed, White male admitted to an inpatient geriatric psychiatry unit for cognitive evaluation after he crashed his automobile into the drive-through window of his bank. Mr. R's history revealed a lifelong pattern of illegal and criminal behavior, as well as multiple concurrent sexual relationships. As he aged, his overt antisocial behavior became more passive. At the time of his admission, he had several prostitutes living in his home, he knew that crack cocaine was being sold at his home, and he admitted to advising his houseguests on how to engage in other illegal activities. Although he no longer met all of the DSM–IV criteria for antisocial personality disorder because he did not actually engage in the specific behaviors required for the diagnosis, his motivations, cognitions, and general pattern of behavior were clearly consistent with the diagnosis.

Representativeness of Clinical Subjects

The prevalence rate for personality disorders in the general population tends to be low, although it is much higher in selected subpopulations such as medical and psychiatric samples. Because prevalence rates are affected not only by who is assessed but also by how the assessment is conducted, estimates for prevalence of personality disorders in older adults vary widely from 10% in the general population to over 60% in geriatric medical/psychiatric patients. The question of who is being assessed is important because it will affect the external validity of the epidemiological research. It is not appropriate to generalize study findings from one sample to another, or from one age group to another. Consequently, a clear description of who is included in epidemiological studies is necessary in order to interpret the meaningfulness of prevalence rates.

Additional considerations are comorbidity of Axis II diagnoses with Axis I and Axis III diagnoses, and definitions of clinical signs and symptoms. Extensive research (see chap. 3 in this volume) has documented that Axis II prevalence rates increase dramatically when there is a concomitant Axis I condition (e.g., affective disorder) or Axis III condition (e.g., heart disease). Because personality disorder diagnostic criteria rely heavily on clinician judgment or self-report, consistent definitions of diagnostic criteria are critical. As Wetzler (1989) discussed, deciding if a patient has close friends (diagnostic criteria for avoidant, schizotypal, and schizoid personality disorders) is first complicated by the definition of "friend" and "close," and further confounded by whose definition is used—the patient's or clinician's.

Clinical research conducted by Dougherty and Rosowsky (in press-a, in press-b; Rosowsky & Dougherty, 1998) highlights the difficulty of getting a representative sample. Despite using deliberately broad inclusionary criteria (e.g., any patient over age 50 with an Axis II diagnosis), one entire statewide system of mental health outpatient clinics failed to provide any subjects. Clinic directors for this system reported they had very few patients in the targeted age range, and they very rarely diagnosed any patient, regardless of age, on Axis II. Interestingly, clinic directors could identify a multitude of "problem," or "difficult," patients but reported they had never considered whether these patients might also have a personality disorder.

PSYCHOMETRIC ISSUES

Three psychometric issues are discussed: reliability and validity of measures, norms and standards of measures, and instrumentation.

Reliability and Validity of Measures

Reliability measures the ability of an assessment instrument to produce consistent results from the same individual across multiple times of measurement and potential intraindividual change. It is a necessary but not sufficient cause for justifying the use of a measure. Demonstrating the reliability of a measure is important because it provides assurance that the measurement is consistent, stable, and accurate, and that the same procedure or method of measurement will yield the same results when used by different assessors at different times. Internal consistency, interrater reliability, and test–retest reliability measure reliability of assessment instruments.

Internal consistency assumes that items on a test measure only one underlying construct. The greatest threats to establishing internal consistency of a measure are age and cohort differences. For example, different age groups may engage in different patterns of social desirability responding. Additionally, generational changes in language usage and semantic interpretation may affect how test items are perceived and understood (Edelstein, Staats, Kalish, & Northrop, 1996).

Interrater reliability measures the consistency of scoring, rating, or direct observation by multiple assessors (Graziano & Raulin, 1989). This type of reliability is used when measurement includes a subjective, judgmental component. Interrater reliability can be influenced by assessor bias. For this reason, assessors or raters must be trained in a consistent, standardized manner so that assessment criteria are clearly defined and potential biases that may affect objective measurement are identified and restricted.

Test–retest reliability measures the extent to which scores can be generalized over different occasions. It is a measure of the temporal stability of the assessment instrument. Test–retest reliability is most meaningful when the construct being measured is assumed to be stable over time. Because it requires multiple administrations of the same instrument at different times by different raters, this type of reliability can be difficult and costly to demonstrate.

Validity refers to what an instrument measures and how well it does so. It is perhaps the most important factor to consider when selecting an assessment instrument because it pertains to the "appropriateness, meaningfulness, and usefulness of the specific inferences made from test scores" (American Psychological Association, 1985). Measurement validity is concerned with the relation between performance on a test or measure and other independently observable facts about the behavior characteristics under study. It is measured by content, criterion, construct, and external validity.

Content validity is a measure of the equivalence of the instrument items with the underlying construct being measured. This type of validity examines the appropriateness and thoroughness of test items to answer the question being asked by the assessment instrument (American Psychological Association, 1985). Assessment items need to be both age appropriate and symptom specific. Because personality disorder symptoms manifest themselves differently as a function of the aging process, the content validity of personality disorder measurement instruments may be compromised if a wide age range of individuals (e.g., adults over age 25) was used when normative information for the instrument was collected. For this reason, personality disorder instruments should report validity estimates separately for age groups (e.g., young, middle-age, young-old, old-old adults).

Criterion validity measures the effectiveness of a test in predicting an individual's performance in specified activities. Performance on the test is compared to a criterion that is a direct, independent measure of what the test was designed to measure. As it relates to personality disorder, a frequently used criterion is psychiatric diagnosis. When psychiatric diagnosis is based on extensive knowledge of the patient, it may be an appropriate criterion; however, when psychiatric diagnosis is determined using less detailed methods, its value as a validity criterion is greatly diminished.

Construct validity refers to the extent to which an instrument measures a theoretical construct. The question that construct validity estimates attempt to answer is whether observed behavior actually reflects the underlying construct. For example, do self-reports of brief, intense but volatile relationships, low frustration tolerance, low tolerance of boredom, and quickly shifting personal goals correspond with the construct of borderline personality disorder? As with content validity, the aging process affects construct validity. Constructs that are consistent for younger age groups may not hold true for older age groups. Rosowsky and Gurian (1991) provided evidence that the construct of borderline personality disorder is characterized by a different symptom profile for older adults than for younger adults.

External validity measures how well the results of a test can be generalized to other individuals, conditions, and places. Generalizability is a particular problem when using samples of older adults because both theoretical constructs and measurement instrument item content often differ for young as compared to older adults. Within the older adult population, external validity is difficult to establish because of the vast heterogeneity of this age group. The label "older adult" can encompass 30 years or more of the life span and includes a wide array of functional ability levels, ranging from elite senior athlete, elder statesperson, wise elder, and so on, to retired worker, homemaker, and so on, to nursing home patient, frail elder, and so on. An additional challenge to establishing external validity of a measure is the type of sample (i.e., clinical vs. research) on which the instrument was developed and normed. Clinical measures of personality disordered adults may not be adequately sensitive to personality disorder features when used with a community-based sample of older adults, whereas research-based measures of personality disorder may not be adequately specific when used with a clinical sample of personality disordered patients.

Norms and Standardized Information

Norms pertain to available test result data from individuals in a specified group or population (American Psychological Association, 1985). Demographic considerations such as age, gender, ethnicity, education, health, and functional status are extremely important normative considerations. Normative information specific to older adults is critically important when selecting a measurement instrument but is all too often not reported in the description of psychometric properties of an instrument. Reports of normative information typically include a description of the age of participants (mean, standard deviation, range);

however, most reports fail to fully delineate sample characteristics. For example, if the normative sample ranged in age from 25 to 78, then what percentage of the sample was over age 65?

This is a particular problem for measuring personality disorders in older adults. Although several instruments have included older adults in the normative sample, no personality disorder assessment instruments have been developed specifically with the older patient in mind. Normative information about personality disorders is scarce because of the low prevalence rate for personality disorders, changing diagnostic criteria, and varied diagnostic methods. When combined with the challenges of age changes and differences in psychiatric diagnosis, it is apparent why normative information on personality disorders in older adults is largely absent.

Attempts to standardize personality disorder measures have mainly focused on agreement of the measure with the current *DSM* system Axis II diagnostic criteria. Inventories and questionnaires are relatively easy to standardize because statistical procedures, such as factor analysis and Q-sort technology, can be employed to verify their measurement accuracy. Observational techniques of personality disorder using semistructured clinical interviews (e.g., SIDP and SCID–II) provide standardized administration techniques but have been limited in their ability to provide normative information on patients' performance. Most clinicians, in daily practice, do not have the time or research experience to use these standardized interviews, and so rely instead on a clinical interview they have developed from their clinical orientation, expertise, and experience. As Rosowsky and Dougherty (1998) indicated, in the absence of standardized measures, most clinicians rely on their clinical orientation and countertransference reactions to the patient when identifying personality disorder diagnostic criteria.

Instrumentation

Instrumentation refers to how information about personality disorders is compiled. Whereas there is much debate over the best way to measure personality disorder, all methods are flawed because of the underlying methodological problems associated with reliability and validity of diagnostic criteria and personality disorder labels. Despite this limitation, personality disorder measurement instruments can be classified according to the source of information (patient or informant) and the type of information collected (ratings or observations). As illustrated in Table 7.1, a 2 × 2 matrix can be used to classify personality disorder instruments. Using Zweig and Hillman's (chap. 3 in this volume) overview of assessment instrument content as an example, their four categories of measures (multiscale self-report inventories, structured clinical interviews, single trait measures, functional impairment measures) would serve as individual cell entries depending on who provides the information and how it is gathered.

TABLE 7.1
Classification of Personality Disorder Measurement Instruments

	Type of Information	
Source of Information	Ratings	Observations
Patient	Inventories, questionnaires	Behavioral logs, diaries
Informed Other (e.g., clinician)	Inventories, questionnaires	Clinical interviews

PATIENT IDENTIFICATION OF PERSONALITY DISORDERS

Patient identification of personality disorders uses self-reports from the patient to identify personality pathology. This information is useful clinically because it provides the clinician with a rare glimpse of the patient's intrapsychic experience from the patient's perspective. However, patient reports of personality pathology cannot be used solely as a basis for diagnosis and should be regarded as adjunctive information in the diagnostic process. Because the *DSM* system defines personality disorders as being ego-syntonic to the individual, it could reasonably be expected that patients will not—and cannot—be objective and fully appreciate the impact of their personality structure on others.

Patient Ratings

When patients are used as the source of information about their personality disorder(s), the most common approach is to use self-report questionnaires or inventories. They are asked to endorse frequency and intensity of behaviors, beliefs, and interactions that are representative of personality disorder criteria. One challenge to using these techniques with older adults is the length of time over which patients must evaluate themselves. For example, diagnostic criteria for antisocial personality disorder require the presence of certain behaviors (e.g., conduct disorder) before age 15. Requiring a 65-year-old patient to recall events from 50 years ago requires that this person interpret personal history from the perspective of current historical parameters and places a different cognitive demand on the patient as compared to a 25-year-old patient.

There are a variety of self-report questionnaires that differ dramatically in the breadth and depth of personality disorder data collected, and whether they are used for clinical or research purposes. Most have not been developed with the older adult in mind, although several have included adults over age 60 in the normative sample. The three most commonly used instruments are the Minnesota Multiphasic Personality Inventory (MMPI), Millon Clinical Multiaxial Inventory (MCMI), and Personality Disorder Questionnaire (PDQ).

MMPI.   The MMPI (Hathaway & McKinley, 1983) is a 550-item self-report true–false inventory designed to provide an efficient way for clinicians to arrive at psychodiagnostic labels based on patient reports of their symptomatology. Although it was not designed specifically to identify personality disorders, it is perhaps the most commonly used measure for identifying personality styles and clinical syndromes. The original MMPI did not include older adults in the normative sample although the restandardization process used to construct the MMPI–II (Hathaway & McKinley, 1989) included individuals up to age 85. Norms for older adults are absent from resource books on the MMPI–II (Graham, 1993). Segal, Hersen, Van Hasselt, Silberman, and Roth (1996) were unable to locate any research applying the MMPI or MMPI–II to older psychiatric patients or patients with specific personality disorders.

MCMI. The original MCMI (Million, 1983) and its subsequent revisions, the MCMI–II (Millon, 1987) and MCMI–III (Millon, 1994), are self-report inventories that assess and diagnose personality disorders. These instruments are widely used in clinical and research contexts and demonstrate good psychometric properties. They tend to be more reliable measures of personality disorder diagnosis than clinical syndrome discrimination. The MCMI has not been used extensively with older adults and norms for nonpsychiatric older adults are not available.

PDQ. The PDQ and its subsequent revisions (PDQ–R, PDQ–IV; Hyler, Rieder, Williams, Spitzer, Hendler, & Lyons, 1988) use a yes–no format to assess personality disorder according to current *DSM* criteria. Besides providing self-reported (or self-identified) personality disorder labels or diagnoses, the PDQ also provides an overall index of personality disturbance and an Impairment/Distress index that can be used as an indicator of personality pathology consistent with the diagnosis of personality disorder. A personality disorder diagnosis is assigned only when subjects reach the criterion on the impairment/distress scale, in addition to satisfying criteria for a personality disorder. Extensive research has examined the utility of the PDQ and supports its use as a global screening instrument for the assessment of clinically significant personality disorder pathology. This assessment tool appears capable of providing a "snapshot" of the impact of personality pathology from the perspective of the affected individual. Use with older adults has been limited, although normative and reliability data for psychiatric and normal older adults on the PDQ–IV is being collected (Segal et al., 1996).

Although the PDQ–R demonstrates commendable sensitivity, it appears to diagnose personality disorder more frequently than either structured interviews (i.e., Personality Disorder Examination [PDE], SCID–II) or other self-report measures (i.e., MMPI–PD). The PDQ–R may be useful in identifying clinically significant PD in nonclinical situations; however, it may overidentify certain personality disorders (e.g., borderline, paranoid, histrionic; Johnson & Bornstein, 1992). Because of this, the PDQ–R composite score may be a more useful index of Axis II symptomatology in nonclinical subjects than are the individual PDQ–R subscales. The PDQ may be most effective as a measure of the impact of personality pathology on the individual and as a tool to rule out personality disorder diagnosis.

Patient Observations

Patient observations of personality disorder criteria rely on patients' judgments regarding their maladaptive personality traits. Patients will vary considerably in their attribution of diagnostic criteria to themselves. Because many personality disorder criteria have socially undesirable features, patients may underreport or deny their occurrence. Additionally, because traits and behaviors associated with personality disorders are ego-syntonic, patients may fail to understand the negative impact these traits and behaviors have on others. For example, individuals with narcissistic personality disorder would be highly unlikely to be able to objectively observe when they are being interpersonally exploitative or lacking empathy (Wetzler, 1989).

Use of this technique for the initial identification and assessment of personality disorder has not been employed clinically. It holds promise, however, as an ongoing assessment technique to monitor change resulting from psychotherapy. Cognitive behavioral therapy frequently utilizes patients' personal diaries or behavioral logs as a measure of treatment progress. Patient observations could also be used a psychoeducational mechanism to illustrate a patient's stimulus value in interpersonal situations. When employed in this manner, the assessment information immediately becomes treatment data.

CLINICIAN ASSESSMENT OF PERSONALITY DISORDERS

Clinician assessment of personality disorders tends to be based on behavioral observations and clinical interviews conducted with the patient. Questionnaires tend to be used as ancillary or clinical research tools.

Most personality disorder diagnoses are based on clinical interviews that include a thorough history taking. Patient interviews have the advantage of providing the assessor with opportunities to more thoroughly evaluate the responses of the patient (Trull & Larson, 1994). As Loranger (1992) pointed out, most of the information elicited from interviews is based on what the patient is willing or able to report. Even when supplemented by behavioral observations, these techniques may not be able to get at long-standing behavior in a variety of real-life situations. Another major limitation is the assumption that respondents are capable of providing valid descriptions of disturbances to their personality. Because personality pathology is assumed to be ego-syntonic, patients may not be able to fully understand the impact of their personality on others.

Structured diagnostic interviews are expensive in staff and patient time while unpredictably increasing the reliability of the assessment process (Hunt & Andrews, 1992). Loranger (1992) discussed the abundant research that indicates how the age, gender, and personal style of the interviewer influenced the subjects' behavior and responses. An additional problem relates to the validity of structured interviews because there is no apparent "gold" standard for personality disorder diagnosis.

Structured Clinical Interview for *DSM–III–R* Personality Disorders (SCID–II)

The Structured Clinical Interview for *DSM–III–R* Personality Disorders (SCID–II; Spitzer, Williams, Gibbon, & First, 1990) is a semistructured clinical interview that provides an assessment of Axis II personality disorders. It was designed to provide rapid clinical assessment of personality disorder while maintaining adequate reliability and validity. There are two options for administration: full administration of the entire SCID–II or administration of sections of the SCID–II that are of particular interest. A unique feature of the SCID–II is the availability of a self-report questionnaire that can be used as a screening tool to shorten the administration time. Based on the respondent's self-report, the clinician can tailor the SCID–II interview to cover only those areas endorsed as problematic by the respondent.

The SCID–II has typically been used in three types of clinical research (First, Spitzer, Gibbon, & Williams, 1995). First, it has been used to profile personality disorders for a sample in either a particular setting or with particular characteristics (e.g., panic disorder). Second, it has been used to select individuals from a general setting who have a particular diagnosis (e.g., borderline personality disorder). Third, the SCID–II can be used for comparison with other personality disorder assessment measures.

Personality Disorder Examination (PDE)

The Personality Disorder Examination (PDE; Loranger, 1988; Loranger, Susman, Oldham, & Russakoff, 1987) is a semi-structured clinical interview developed to minimize confounding by Axis I symptoms. Each section begins with open-ended questions that are followed up with specific trait-based questions. It provides both dimensional scores and diagnoses for each *DSM–III–R* personality disorder and is designed to be administered by experienced and trained clinicians.

CONCLUSIONS

The identification and assessment of personality disorders remains problematic. Changing nomenclature and diagnostic criteria sets hamper reliability and validity of diagnostic criteria. Age changes in the manifestation of personality disorders further complicate assessment. Furthermore, there tends to be poor agreement between patients' and clinicians' identification and assessment of personality disorders. This is due to differing definitions of what is a personality disorder but it is also due to the intrapsychic impact of personality disorders. The ego-syntonic nature of personality disorders and the countertransference responses they create both contribute to difficulty in identification (see Rosowsky, chap. 9 in this volume).

Another critical issue in the identification and measurement of personality disorder is the lack of a gold standard for diagnosis. Spitzer (1983) recommended using a LEAD standard instead. Personality disorder diagnosis results from using the patient's longitudinal history (L), the clinician's expert opinion (E), and all available data (AD), including self-reports, structured interviews, and questionnaires and inventories. Although this multidimensional approach can potentially increase diagnostic reliability and validity, it still places ultimate responsibility for the identification of personality disorder on the clinician. It is unarguable that clinicians are ultimately responsible for assigning the diagnosis of personality disorder to a patient; however, assessment and identification of personality disorders is best done as a collaborative effort between patient and clinician. Patients may be equally accurate in interpreting the LEAD standard, and this may be even more the case for the older patient with personality pathology. L (longitudinal history) is frequently corrupted by unreliable reporting and/or inaccurate attention to historical detail; E (expert opinion) has been shown to be affected by countertransference responses to the patient; AD (all available data) may not be accesible to the clinician when working with an older patient with multiple social, medical, environmental, and psychological issues.

Clinical research indicates that self-report measures have high sensitivity but relatively low specificity in identifying personality disorders. For this reason, many experts have concluded that self-report measures should be used as a screening device and may be most useful in their ability to rule out diagnostic alternatives. Research findings indicate, however, that patients report more personality disorders and more psychological distress as a function of their personality pathology than do clinicians. Although *DSM* standards define personality disorders as being ego-syntonic, this body of research suggests that ego-syntonic is not analogous to lack of awareness. Individuals, regardless of age, who evidence ongoing, persistent personality pathology, are aware of their deficits and acutely experience the impact these deficits have on their day-to-day lives.

Finally, attention to the identification and assessment of personality disorders in older adults is gaining much needed attention. Increasingly, clinicians and researchers are focusing on methods and techniques to accurately, reliably, and validly measure personality disorders in this group. Strides are being made, but there is more work to be done and much knowledge to be gained.

REFERENCES

American Psychological Association. (1985). *Standards for educational and psychological testing.* Washington, DC: Author.

Andreoli, A., Gressot, G., Aapro, N., Tricot, L., & Gognalons, M. Y. (1989). Personality disorders as a predictor of outcome. *Journal of Personality Disorders, 3,* 307–320.

Costa, P. T., Jr., & McCrae, R. R. (1992). Normal personality assessments in clinical practice: The NEO Personality Inventory. *Psychological Assessment, 4,* 5–13.

Digman, J. M., & Takemoto-Chock, N. K. (1981). Factors in the natural language of personality: Reanalysis, comparison, and interpretation of six major studies. *Multivariate Behavioral Research, 16,* 149–170.

Dougherty, L. M., & Rosowsky, E. (in press-a). Who is responsible for diagnosing personality disorders in older adults? *Journal of Clinical Geropsychology.*

Dougherty, L. M., & Rosowsky, E. (in press-b). The NEO–PIR and personality disorder in older adults: Guiding the diagnosis. *Aging and Mental Health.*

Edelstein, B., Staats, N., Kalish, K. D., & Northrop, L. E. (1996). Assessment of older adults. In M. Hersen & V. B. Van Hasselt (Eds.), *Psychological treatment of older adults: An introductory text* (pp. 35–68). New York: Plenum.

First, M. B., Spitzer, R. L., Gibbon, M., & Williams, J.B.W. (1995). The Structured Clinical Interview for DSM–III–R personality disorders (SCID–II): Part I. Description. *Journal of Personality Disorders, 9,* 83–91.

Frances, A., & Widiger, T. (1986). Methodological issues in personality disorder diagnosis. In T. Millon & M. T. Klerman (Eds.), *Contemporary issues in psychopathology* (pp. 381–400). New York: Guilford.

Graham, J. R. (1993). *MMPI–2: Assessing personality and psychopathology* (2nd. Ed). New York: Oxford University Press.

Graziano, A. M., & Raulin, M. L. (1989). Hypothesis testing, validity, and threats to validity. In J. Rothman (Ed.), *Research methods: A process of inquiry* (pp. 153–177). New York: Harper & Row.

Hathaway, S. R., & McKinley, J. C. (1983). *The Minnesota Multiphasic Personality Inventory Manual.* New York: The Psychological Corporation.

Hathaway, S. R., & McKinley, J. C. (1989). *MMPI–2: Minnesota Multiphasic Personality Inventory–2: Manual for administration and scoring.* Minneapolis, MN: University of Minnesota Press.

Hunt, C., & Andrews, G. (1992). Measuring personality disorder: The use of self-report questionnaires. *Journal of Personality Disorders, 6,* 125–133.

Hyler, S. E., Rieder, R. O., Williams, J.B.W., Spitzer, R. L., Hendler, J., & Lyons, M. (1988). The Personality Diagnostic Questionnaire: Development and preliminary results. *Journal of Personality Disorders, 2,* 229–237.

Johnson, J. G., & Bornstein, R. F. (1992). Utility of the Personality Diagnostic Questionnaire—Revised in a nonclinical population. *Journal of Personality Disorders, 6*(4), 450–457.

Kroessler, D. (1990). Personality disorder in the elderly. *Hospital and Community Psychiatry, 41,* 1325–1329.

Livesley, W. J. (1985). The classification of personality disorder: II. The problem of diagnostic criteria. *Canadian Journal of Psychiatry, 30,* 359–362.

Loranger, A. W. (1988). *The Personality Disorder Examination (PDE) Manual.* Yonkers, NY: DV Communications.

Loranger, A. W. (1992). Are current self-report and interview measures adequate for epidemiological studies of personality disorders? *Journal of Personality Disorders, 6,* 313–325.

Loranger, A. W., Susman, V. L., Oldham, J. M., & Russakoff, L. M. (1987). The Personality Disorder Examination: A preliminary report. *Journal of Personality Disorders, 1,* 1–13.

McCrae, R. R. (1991). The five-factor model and its assessment in clinical settings. *Journal of Personality Assessment, 57,* 399–414.

Millon, T. (1983). *Millon Clinical Multiaxial Inventory.* Minneapolis, MN: Interpretive Scoring Systems.

Millon, T. (1987). *Millon Clinical Multiaxial Inventory II (MCMI II) manual.* Minneapolis, MN: National Computer Systems.

Millon, T. (1994). *Millon Clinical Multiaxial Inventory III (MCMI III) manual.* Minneapolis, MN: National Computer Systems

Perry, J. C. (1992). Problems and considerations in the valid assessment of personality disorder. *American Journal of Psychiatry, 149,* 1645–1653.

Rosowsky, E., & Dougherty, L. M. (1998). Personality disorders and clinician responses. *Clinical Gerontologist, 18*(4), 31–42.

Rosowsky, E., Dougherty, L. M., Johnson, C., & Gurian, B. (1997). Personality as an indicator of goodness of fit between the elderly individual and the health service system. *Clinical Gerontologist, 17*(3), 41–53.

Rosowsky, R., & Gurian, B. (1991). Borderline personality disorder in late-life. *International Psychogeriatrics, 3,* 221–234.

Sadavoy, J. (1987). Character disorders in the elderly: An overview. In J. Sadavoy & M. Leszcz (Eds.), *Treating the elderly with psychotherapy* (pp. 175–229). Madison, CT: International Universities Press.

Sadavoy, J., & Fogel, B. (1992). Personality disorders in old age. In J. E. Birren, R. B. Sloane, & G. D. Cohen (Eds.), *Handbook of mental health and aging* (pp. 433–462). San Diego, CA: Academic Press.

Segal, D. L., Hersen, M., Van Hasselt, V. B., Silberman, C. S., & Roth, L. (1996). Diagnosis and assessment of personality disorders in older adults: A critical review. *Journal of Personality Disorders, 10*(4), 384–399.

Spitzer, R. L. (1983). Psychiatric diagnosis: Are clinicians still necessary? *Comprehensive Psychiatry, 24,* 399–411.

Spitzer, R. L., & Williams, J.B.W. (1985). Classification in psychiatry. In H. I. Kaplan & B. J. Sadock (Eds.), *Comprehensive textbook of psychiatry* (4th ed., pp. 591–613). Baltimore: Williams & Wilkins.

Spitzer, R. L. Williams, J.B.W., Gibbon, M., & First, M. (1990). *Users' guide for the structured clinical interview for DSM–III–R.* Washington, DC: American Psychiatric Association.

Tucker, R. C., & Dougherty, L. M. (1997). *Concordance of perceived self and ideal personality traits of psychogeriatric nurses: Relation to job satisfaction.* Unpublished manuscript.

Trull, T. J., & Larson, S. L. (1994). External validity of two personality disorder inventories. *Journal of Personality Disorders, 8,* 96–103.

Tupes, E. C., & Christal, R. E. (1961). Recurrent personality factors based on trait ratings. *USAF ASD Technical Report,* No. 61–97.

Wade, J. B., Dougherty, L. M., Hart, R. P., & Cook, D. B. (1992). Patterns of normal personality structure among chronic pain patients. *Pain, 48,* 38–43.

Wetzler, C. (1989). *Measuring mental illness: Psychometric assessment for clinicians.* Washington, DC: American Psychiatric Press.

Widiger, T. A., Trull, T. J., Clarkin, J. F., Sanderson, C., & Costa, P. T., Jr. (1995). A description of the *DSM–III–R* and *DSM–IV* personality disorders with the five-factor model of personality. In P. T. Costa, Jr. & T. A. Widiger (Eds.), *Personality disorders and the five-factor model of personality* (pp. 41–56). Washington, DC: American Psychological Association.

CHAPTER 8

Conceptual and Methodological Issues in the Assessment of Personality Disorders in Older Adults

DANIEL K. MROCZEK, PhD
Fordham University

STEPHEN W. HURT, PhD
Joan and Sanford I. Weill Medical College of Cornell University

WILLIAM H. BERMAN, PhD
Fordham University

There are few guidelines for assessing personality disorders in older adults. Older adulthood represents a unique segment of the life span with novel contexts and singular difficulties that may render ordinary assessments questionable. Personality disorders, by definition, are characteriological problems that usually arise early in life, no later than young adulthood. When an older adult presents symptoms for a personality disorder, it is unlikely to be a first onset. For some, the disorder may have been present since youth but was never officially diagnosed. Some people, especially those with less severe disorders, may have gone decades without a formal assessment of their problem. Among others, a diagnosis may have been made, but the symptoms presented in older adulthood differ from those characterizing an individual's disorder earlier in life. Cases such as these highlight the need for assessments to be sensitive to age-graded differences in either the disorder or the person. Whether individuals are being diagnosed for the first time, or have been assessed many times in their past, the assessment needs to address symptoms present among older adults.

One key issue affecting the assessment of personality disorders in late life is whether they change with age. Very little is known about how personality disorders appear in later life, let alone how or if they change across the life span (Gatz, Kasl-Godley, & Karel, 1996). Rosowsky and Gurian (1991) and Sadavoy and Fogel (1992) indicated that some personality disorders may become mitigated with age, while others may become aggravated. Evidence suggests that borderline personality disorder may be in the former category (Rosowsky & Gurian, 1991), and compulsive, paranoid, and schizotypal personality disorder may fall in the latter (Sadavoy & Fogel, 1992). If this is true change, then why not continue to apply the same criteria that are applied to younger persons? Rosowsky and Gurian (1991) provided evidence that suggests age-specific criteria may be necessary. They found that a group of older adults judged as borderlines by their clinicians failed to meet *DSM–III–R* criteria for borderline personality disorder. Does this finding reflect problems with clinician judgment or with the *DSM* criteria? Rosowsky and Gurian (1991) believed the issue lies within the *DSM*, which may be age insensitive with regard to personality disorders.

This chapter discusses the important problems raised by Rosowsky and Gurian (1991) and Sadavoy and Fogel (1992). It also addresses the issues involved in constructing assessments for older adults by considering a number of factors that may affect the appraisal of personality disorders in older populations. The discussion is grounded in some pertinent theoretical ideas borrowed from developmental psychology, as well as what gerontologists have learned about assessing older populations in general. The bulk of the chapter concerns the first of these, and so the discussion begins with them.

MEASUREMENT ISSUES: CONTINUITY AND CHANGE IN PERSONALITY DISORDERS

It would make little sense to produce a book on personality disorders in later life if these constructs looked exactly the same in older age as they do in the rest of the life course. If the processes and characteristic behaviors are the same across the life span, then the same criteria and presumably the same measures can be used for persons of any age. This is not the assumption undergirding this volume. There is a uniqueness about personality disorders in late life that warrants special measurement. Many of these differences can be organized around a concept that has proven useful in life-span developmental psychology: heterotypic continuity.

Heterotypic Continuity

An issue of both theoretical and methodological importance is the extent to which a psychological entity undergoes a "face change" over time. Caspi and Bem (1990) and Kagan (1969) called this idea *heterotypic continuity* (see also Brim & Kagan, 1980; Kagan, 1980). This notion is distinct from outright change in a construct across time. For example, a person with antisocial personality disorder at age 20 may no longer possess the disorder at age 60. If it is truly gone, then this is outright change. Conversely, heterotypic continuity means that people still possess the underlying disorder or quality, but the behaviors that flow from it are distinct at different times across their life. Coherence is maintained in the long-term disorder or personality characteristic, but the behavioral manifestations are dissimilar. Latent continuity is ironically associated with manifest discontinuity.

Kagan (1969) and Caspi and Bem (1990) contended that heterotypic continuities are more readily observable in children than adults. Psychological constructs develop at a much quicker pace in childhood, giving rise to distinct surface behaviors as the underlying latent constructs move across different developmental epochs. Mussen, Conger, Kagan, and Huston (1990) illustrated this with the example of aggression. At age 4, a child may express the latent construct of aggression via blatant physical acts (e.g., hitting other children). However, by age 14, this same latent construct may manifest itself through verbal behaviors (e.g., insulting other adolescents) and other forms of more subtle antagonism (Mussen et al., 1990).

Despite a higher likelihood of heterotypic continuities in childhood, these types of stabilities can be observed in adulthood as well and even into late adulthood. Attachment provides a good example. The construct of attachment manifests itself in infant behavior via stranger anxiety and separation anxiety, and through various bonding behaviors. By age 7, attachment is no longer expressed through fear of strangers but rather is marked by more subtle cues such as time spent with caregivers. In adulthood, attachment is manifested differently yet again, through behaviors displayed in intimate relationships, friendships, and work associations. In older age, attachment may transform once more, perhaps manifesting itself in new interpersonal links to grandchildren or a second spouse. The underlying construct remains, even in adulthood, but the behaviors that represent it undergo marked "face changes" as time progresses and as contexts vary.

Mussen et al. (1990) used the term *functional equivalence* in reference to unique behaviors that emerge from the same latent construct at different ages. Functional equivalence is the primary feature of heterotypic continuity. A person who was cruel to animals as a child, set fires as an adolescent, and robbed gas stations as an adult has displayed functional equivalence. Through different age periods and changing contexts, this hypothetical person has clearly engaged in antisocial behavior. Whereas the specific behaviors exhibited at the different ages are quite diverse, they are presumed to spring from a relatively stable underlying construct that arises from genetic predispositions, reinforcement histories, parental influences, and other sources of antisocial personality disorder.

Heterotypic continuity and its subordinate concept, functional equivalence, have important implications for assessment. To measure reading ability over the course of a child's development, the same test would not be administered at different ages. It would be foolish to give an 8-year-old a reading test designed for a 16-year-old. Reading ability changes dramatically in its surface manifestations from age 8 to 16. It is still the same fundamental construct being assessed at the multiple time points, but the assessor must use different, age-appropriate meas-urement devices at the distinct developmental stages.

Personality disorders may function in much the same way, and the assess-ment of Axis II disorders in older adults should reflect the possibility of hetero-typic continuities. This is certainly true in personality disorder assessment earlier in the life span, where the requirements for children and adolescents to qualify for a diagnosis of conduct disorder are age specific and thus different from those for antisocial personality disorder (ASPD). The contrast between conduct disor-der and ASPD is an excellent example of heterotypic continuity. Although some scholars maintain these two should be considered separate disorders, many more recognize ASPD as the adult form of conduct disorder (Lytton, 1990), and vice versa, evincing a recognition of heterotypic continuities among clinicians, at least with respect to this particular disorder.

Changing Relevance of Symptoms

When assessing or constructing devices to assess personality disorders, clini-cians and researchers must not only keep in mind the possibility of functionally equivalent behaviors, but also potential increases and decreases in relevance of particular criteria. For instance, impulsivity and affective instability are two symptoms included among the diagnostic criteria for borderline personality dis-order in the *DSM–IV*. However, there is evidence that both of these qualities wane over the life span, at least in normal, community-dwelling samples (Costa & McCrae, 1994). If persons with borderline personality disorder follow this pattern and become less impulsive and more emotionally stable with age, then those diagnostic criteria may become much less relevant as people age. Simulta-neously, other criteria may become more relevant. For example, the criterion concerning the avoidance of real or imagined abandonment might intensify among late-adulthood borderlines. The social networks of many older adults often become reduced, especially after retirement or the death of a spouse. Such an event may increase the likelihood of borderline symptomatology involving the abandonment criterion in *DSM–IV*, relative to other criteria. This is a simple example of heterotypic continuity, but it does show how the weighting of par-ticular criteria may shift as a function of age, or the changing contexts that ac-company age.

Appearance or Disappearance of Symptoms

Independent of changes in the relative importance of different criteria, com-pletely new age-graded symptoms may emerge as well. For example, reclusive-ness may appear as an entirely new characteristic of paranoia as a person ages.

In youth, paranoia may include a host of suspicious behaviors and thoughts, but this mistrustfulness may not manifest itself in self-imposed isolation. For various reasons (e.g., believing one has enough physical strength to protect oneself), youthful paranoids may not be as reclusive as elderly paranoids. As such persons age, however, they may become increasingly solitary. Recent news reports describing the life of the convicted "Unabomber," Theodore Kaczynski, have revealed this very pattern. Although always shy and mistrustful of others, he did not become an isolated hermit until his early thirties. With age, a new manifestation of his paranoia, extreme reclusiveness, emerged.

Identifying age-graded symptoms that vary in relevance with time or appear only in a certain portion of the life span adds much complexity to the job of assessing personality disorders in late life. It takes an astute observer of disorders across wide swaths of people's lives to determine which behaviors, actions, thoughts, and emotions represent new manifestations.

Heterotypic Continuities as a Function of Contexts

To avoid making the mistake of attributing all heterotypic continuities to internal dispositions, it is essential to point out that changes in people's environments may underlie surface behavioral changes (Kagan, 1980; Patterson, 1993). New symptoms or behavioral manifestations of a disorder may be a function of age, but they can also emerge in reaction to new contexts. Patterson (1993) attributed heterotypic continuities in antisocial behavior to the changing contexts and environments encountered as they develop. He maintained that the real cause of functionally equivalent behaviors is variation in contextual variables—changing classes at school, moving to a new school, new friends, new family environments, and so forth—not age per se. Additionally, physical changes such as puberty create new contexts. In turn, these new environments give rise to new manifestations of antisocial and delinquent behavior. The underlying construct is still present, driving the boy to commit delinquent acts, but as his surrounding context changes, the specific social deviances transform.

Heterotypic continuities can also occur in small-scale contexts. It need not take the onset of puberty or retirement—a more large-scale context change— to bring about an alteration in the way an underlying construct is expressed. For instance, particular symptoms of a personality disorder may be expressed only around certain people. Individuals may express symptoms with greater frequency or intensity when around their spouse. Others may show symptoms only when around their children or parents. Still others may only show evidence of the disorder when in specific places, like school or work, or during specific seasons. Clinicians who work with children have reported the waning of attention deficit hyperactivity disorder (ADHD) symptoms in the summertime. While the child is out of the school context in the summer months, ADHD symptoms become more muted. When school begins in the autumn, the child is again required to concentrate, study, and sit still in class. Once again, the ADHD symptoms become amplified.

Bryk and Raudenbush (1992) observed a similar phenomenon with respect to math ability. Using hierarchical linear modeling (HLM) to estimate individual growth curves, they found that schoolchildren exhibit steady, linear progress in learning math skills during the academic year. However, in the summertime, the growth curves fall flat. No increase in math ability occurs between June and September, for it is the rare child who practices math in the summer months. The growth curves then resume their rise in the autumn. This is an excellent example of a phenomenon that shows relatively stable individual differences between children, but that also ebbs and flows in a systematic fashion depending on contexts. The ebb and flow is not random. It is measurable and orderly fluctuation, following a predictable pattern. Further, the incorporation of context-based influences need not subtract from the traditional notion of traits, syndromes, and abilities as stable. They may be stable in many ways, but are not completely static. Stability and change are best thought of as a spectrum. Rarely are psychological or psychiatric concepts entirely stable or changing. Rather, the amount that they change or fluctuate lie on a continuum. Conceiving these constructs in this manner makes it easy to think of them as both invariant over time in some ways, but also dynamic and changing in other ways. Such dynamisms may be explained with contextual factors, just as Bryk and Raudenbush (1992) explained the dynamic qualities of reading abilities with contextual (seasonal) factors. Reading ability is both stable and changing among youth.

Similarly, personality disorders in late life may reflect both stable and changing elements. The disorder itself may reside within a person beneath the surface, unchanging and continuous, but the changing contexts surrounding the individual act as a prism and change the way in which the disorder manifests itself in behavior. These contexts may be major life events, such as retirement, widowhood, or the launching of children. Sadavoy and Fogel (1992) suggested that such major life stressors may indeed aggravate personality disorders and make them more severe. They also suggested that long-term personality dimensions that may have been only slightly problematic in the past may transform into full-blown personality disorders when such late life stressors appear. There may also be smaller contextual changes of the type already described with regard to the growth of children's reading ability. The changing of the seasons, the visitation of a relative, or an appointment with a doctor may be potential triggers for heterotypic continuities of a smaller scale. Such manifestations, large and small, need to be considered when assessing personality disorders in older adults.

Dynamic Versus Static Variables

Nesselroade and Boker (1994) and Nesselroade and Featherman (1990) suggested that many of the variables in which psychologists and psychiatrists are interested are not static. Imagine that personality disorders, and perhaps other psychopathologies, are processes that oscillate over time rather than static diagnoses that are either present or not present. Picture the course of a disorder as akin to the rise and fall of the stock market during a typical week. The oscillations may correspond to regular cyclical patterns: The markets are often busy at the start of the trading day, become more quiet at midday, but then get busy again by the end of the day. The markets also react to contextual variables, as when new pieces of information are revealed about an individual company or the economy in general. Personality disorders may well be processes that ebb and flow in a similar manner. They may be stable and enduring in general, but do not sit still at all times. They may be dynamic rather than static entities, fluctuating over time in response to people's internal clocks, and in reaction to contextual factors.

If the overt symptomatology for personality disorders rises and falls with changing contexts and internal mechanisms, then what does this mean for measurement? Are these disorders impossible to pin down? How does one assess a moving target? It could be argued that two sources of data are required to adequately observe and measure the dynamic elements of personality disorders. First, longitudinal studies must be carried out using people with personality disorders to determine exactly how different Axis II disorders ebb and flow with time. Second, multiple assessments at different times and in different contexts are needed. It was suggested earlier that among older adults, personality disorders may become amplified or dampened when certain people are around, such as the client's children or spouse. Assessments can be performed across different contexts that are suspected to either amplify or suppress aspects of the disorder. If personality disorders are dynamic entities, then it should be possible to observe and assess the ups and downs that characterize them. This can help the clinician to treat the client more effectively, and would aid researchers by demonstrating how and when a dynamic disorder becomes magnified and when it subsides.

Using IRT to Identify Dynamic Symptoms

Thus far, the possibility has been raised that the symptoms marking a given personality disorder may manifest themselves differently in later life, either as a product of aging or of changed environments. The possibility was also introduced that symptoms may become more or less important with age or change of context. "Important" here means that different symptoms or *DSM–IV* criteria may have different weights among older adults. A symptom that is central to a disorder among younger individuals may not retain its centrality in older age.

What methods are available for identifying which symptom change in importance, either through the mechanism of changing contexts or via the aging process itself? The simplest way is to determine if the relation (via a part–whole correlation or factor loading) between a symptom and overall disorder decreases in magnitude with time. If the symptom of violent impulsiveness becomes less likely to occur as persons with ASPD age, then it would be expected that the correlation between that symptom and a measure of the overall disorder would shrink with time.

Another promising technique for detecting symptoms whose relation to an overall measure changes over time or across groups is item response theory (IRT). IRT refers to a family of psychometric models that allows the researcher to determine where a test item or symptom is yielding information along the underlying continuum defining the construct of interest (Lord, 1980). IRT models help an investigator to locate exactly where along a continuum a particular item, behavior, or symptom is measuring the construct best. It assumes that the construct being evaluated follows an underlying continuum, and the symptoms or behaviors that define the construct (in this case, *DSM–IV* criteria for personality disorders) are reasonably intercorrelated (Hambleton, Swaminathan, & Rogers, 1991; Lord, 1980). Personality disorders are usually characterized as dichotomies or syndromes, thus presenting a problem for those who wish to employ IRT, which requires an underlying dimension. However, like most other *DSM–IV* disorders, dichotomous diagnoses are easily translatable into continua. Symptom counts are often useful in transforming diagnoses into dimensions. Thus it would not be difficult to adapt dichotomies into dimensions in order to apply IRT.

As an example of how IRT might be used, consider impulsivity, a personality trait with important implications for many personality disorders. Suppose you have a multi-item measure of impulsivity. Further assume that impulsivity forms a continuum, and some items measure the low end of the trait, others the middle range, and still others the high end. An IRT model will first estimate your underlying continuum using the complete set of items, utilizing maximum likelihood estimation to gain the best approximation possible of the full impulsivity range. It will then calculate *location parameters* for each item, which mark exactly where on the underlying latent continuum of impulsivity each item is yielding the most information. Hypothetically, the item "I often take faraway trips on a whim" would indicate a relatively high level of impulsivity, and the IRT location parameter would tell you exactly how much underlying impulsivity it takes for a person to endorse that item. Thus, it tells the investigator where on the continuum each item falls, and where it maximizes information.

IRT can be used to determine if these location parameters differ across particular groups, like men versus women, or older versus younger. Ideally, a fair test is one where items function the same way across different groups. A man who is two standard deviations above the mean on impulsivity should endorse roughly the same set of items as a woman who is two standard deviations above the mean. If men and women who are at similar levels of impulsivity endorse a given item at different rates, then that item is said to display *differential item func-*

tioning (DIF; Holland & Wainer, 1993). DIF detection methods, most of which are based on IRT, have been used to identify items on the Scholastic Aptitude Test (SAT), the Law School Admissions Test, the Graduate Record Examination, and other standardized tests that do not have the same location parameter across two mutually exclusive groups, like Blacks versus Whites. If DIF is present in one or more items, then a researcher cannot tell whether a mean-level difference on the test is due to the biased items, or to a true mean difference between the two groups. Women may score higher than men on the verbal section of the SAT, but if there are differentially functioning items, then it is not possible to tell whether that difference was simply an artifact of the biased items, or a true mean-level difference in the population. The two are confounded until the items displaying DIF are deleted from the body of test questions.

An example from the depression literature illustrates the concept of DIF in a more familiar clinical context. Schaeffer (1988) analyzed a set of depression items from a survey of Chicago-area residents. She estimated IRT parameters for the whole sample, separately for women and men, taking appropriate actions to ensure that the separate estimates for the two genders were comparable. Schaeffer found the two sets of location parameters were quite similar for men and women, indicating that the items were functioning the same way across the genders, with one very notable exception. One item on the depression measure asked respondents if they had cried as part of their depressive experience. The location parameter for women on this item was in the middle of the depression range, indicating that medium levels of depression were what it took for an average woman to acknowledge that one of her symptoms was "crying." Men showed a quite different pattern on the crying item. The location parameter showed that it marked very high levels of depression. It took a high level of underlying depression as assessed by the IRT maximum likelihood estimate (almost two standard deviations above the mean) for the average man to concede that he had cried. The only other symptom among men with a location parameter near that of the crying symptom was the suicide item—an item asking whether one had considered suicide. Thus, admitting that one cried was tantamount to admitting that one considered suicide for men, but not for women, illustrating DIF.

Symptoms marking personality disorders may display DIF as well. Linking this concept with previous arguments, it may be that different age groups show biases across some test or interview items. A symptom that clearly marks compulsive personality disorder in younger adults may no longer be a representative symptom in older adulthood. The location parameter (the position on the underlying continuum of the construct where this item's maximum discrimination ability lies) may have shifted in a different direction. Further, the weighting of the symptom may also have either increased or decreased. For example, one of the *DSM–IV* criterion for compulsive personality disorder is excessive devotion to work at the cost of other activities. This criteria will clearly be irrelevant for retired persons with compulsive personality disorder. Their disorder may be as strong as it ever was, but is no longer manifested in work-related symptoms. Other, more age-relevant (or age-specific; Rosowsky & Gurian, 1991) symptoms may characterize their disorder in the postretirement years. Such an age-graded shift in the meaning of a *DSM* symptom will cause the weight or location of any measure of that symptom to shift. IRT can detect such shifts.

As long as the assumptions of the IRT models are met, investigators interested in improving measurement of personality disorders in older adults can use these new psychometric techniques to determine which *DSM–IV* criteria change in importance. IRT can help identify symptoms or criteria that display DIF either across age groups or across changing contexts. The results from applying these psychometric models may permit researchers to tailor tests for personality disorders to age groups that are known to present different symptom patterns. They may also help in building context-based personality disorder measures of the type described earlier.

Real Change or Heterotypic Continuity?

The aforementioned concepts may provide a useful framework for understanding how different aspects of personality disorders remain continuous over time and contexts despite changes in manifest behaviors. However, there is a fine line between heterotypic continuity and genuine change in the underlying construct. Whereas personality disorders have been shown to be quite stable over time (Vuchinich, Bank, & Patterson, 1992), it is possible that in some people the disorder may indeed disappear, or at least become less potent. Kagan (1980) warned against placing too much emphasis on finding continuities. It may blind people to authentic change. If personality disorders for certain people truthfully go away or subside, then an overemphasis on finding functionally equivalent symptoms may mask an individual's true recovery. Assessment methods that failed to detect real recovery would do a grave disservice to clients who have changed for the good. As a caveat, this section concludes with a caution invoked by Kagan (1980):

> The general popularity of [heterotypic continuity] is due, in part, to the fact that the intellectual community believes in stability and continuity in development. The community wants empirical proof of that supposition, and few are overly critical of the quality of the evidence or the logic of the argument. Recently this state of mind has emerged for studies of the inheritance of aspects of psychopathology and personality. When members of a society hold a presupposition with conviction, they tend to be permissive regarding the validity of the supporting facts, and eager for evidence that maintains the belief. It is time, therefore, to ask why so many Western scholars have favored the notions of stability of structure, continuity of process, and derivative change—a trio I shall call faith in connectedness. (p. 44)

Researchers and therapists should look for heterotypic continuity and functional equivalence, because they can help in designing more age-appropriate assessments; but at the same time, in heeding Kagan's caveat, they must practice vigilance about what is judged as continuity, and make sure they do not mislabel honest transformations.

GENERAL MEASUREMENT ISSUES
IN ASSESSING OLDER ADULTS

Now consider some general principles of assessment of older adults that may be useful in designing measures of personality disorders in those populations. When asking older adults to do any kind of self-report task, whether it be an intelligence test, an attitude survey, or an assessment of psychopathology, there are two factors that will affect their responses more than those of younger people. These are age equivalence in understanding and motivation (Dixon & Baltes, 1986; Schaie & Willis, 1996).

Age Equivalence in Understanding

Age equivalence in understanding means that the questions on the testing instruments or structured interview are understood the same way by people of different ages. Unless disorders are being assessed through behavioral observation or informer-report, accuracy of self-report will be crucial. If the interviews or test questions are not being understood the same way across different age cohorts, then age equivalence does not hold. As Stevens-Long and Commons (1992) pointed out, it is important that test or interview questions mean the same thing to 20-year-olds, 40-year-olds, and 60-year-olds. Schaie and Hertzog (1985) further argued that the different cohorts alive at a given moment can often differ dramatically from one another in terms of educational experience and language behavior.

As an example, the first version of the MMPI (an instrument often used to detect personality disorders) contained many outdated items that were baffling to younger test-takers, such as "I like to play Drop the Handkerchief," an item that would have made sense to someone who grew up in the 1940s, but not to a person who came of age in the 1960s or 1970s. The reverse can also be true. Psychological tests or structured diagnostic interviews that have been constructed in recent years by relatively young researchers may contain phrases that are unintelligible to older persons. Many tests contain very complicated questions that may not be immediately understandable to older people who received their educations 40 or 50 years ago, and perhaps even then only finished at eighth grade or early high school. Widely used instruments for assessing psychopathology, such as the DIS or SCID, often contain very long items that contain multiple ideas. Such questions are frequently confusing to intelligent, highly educated young people, let alone older persons who as a cohort possess less education. Additionally, declines in memory functioning may contribute to problematic answers to test or interview items among older adults.

Even more noteworthy, nearly every diagnostic test based on *DSM* criteria has been normed on young or middle-age populations (Gatz et al., 1996). As Schaie and Hertzog (1985) noted, educational and language usage differences between age groups can contaminate responses, leading to potentially false diagnoses. In the literature on intellectual functioning, this has often led to assignment of lower scores on intelligence tests (Schaie & Willis, 1996). In testing for personality disorders, it may lead to false positives and false negatives.

However, some instruments have been normed for older adults and thus may be better than others for assessing personality disorders. For example, the NEO–PI (Costa & McCrae, 1989) has the ability to assess personality disorders (Costa & McCrae, 1990; Widiger & Trull, 1992; Wiggins & Pincus, 1989) and provides norms for older adults, among other age categories, making it a useful tool that can circumvent some of the problems discussed earlier.

Age Equivalence in Motivation

A test can be no better than the cooperativeness of the test-taker. The importance of motivation in procuring valid responses from older interviewees or test-takers was first identified by gerontologists studying intellectual functioning (Dixon & Baltes, 1986; Schaie & Willis, 1996). Older persons will often question the relevancy of abstract test items. Intelligence tests often contain seemingly senseless items such as those from the block design or digit span sections of the Wechsler Adult Intelligence Scale–Revised (WAIS–R). Failing to see anything germane about reciting numbers backward and forward, older adults may lose enthusiasm and motivation for executing the task. Younger respondents, for whom test-taking is a part of their recent life experience, often are more likely to take tests seriously.

Moreover, cohort effects may exist with regard to this issue. Persons coming of age in the past 30 years or so have been bombarded with all manner of tests and assessments, especially involving school or work. Testing and evaluation of various types of performance are highly regular occurrences in the life of anyone younger than age 50. Persons who today are in the oldest cohorts have been tested more lightly than middle-age and younger cohorts. Thus, testing and assessment may seem more foreign and irregular to the older individual being testing for personality disorders. Not only may the questions seem impertinent and irrelevant, but the whole test-taking situation may be perceived differently, sapping motivation and perhaps yielding inaccurate or erroneous answers. Additionally, there may also be differences among cohorts of actual persons with personality disorders. Older persons with personality disorders are much less likely to have been tested for their problems than younger persons, who have come of age at a time when many instruments and methods are available for the detection of PDs. More widespread screening strategies are now also in use for personality disorders, another factor that may give rise to cohort differences in test-taking or interviewing motivation.

There is also some empirical evidence to suggest that older cohorts take personality tests less seriously than college undergraduates. Mroczek, Ozer, Spiro, and Kaiser (1998) compared older and younger samples on how consistently they had rated themselves on a personality trait test. Although most of the older respondents did the task and rated themselves in a consistent fashion, many did not, creating problematic total scores on the test. In comparison, almost none of the college students rated themselves inconsistently. It is not clear, however, whether these results are due to motivational differences between the younger and older samples, or to a lack of age equivalence in understanding the items or the task. In any case, there was a difference, showing that the issues discussed here are relevant outside of the realm of research on intellectual functioning. It is likely that the pitfalls mentioned here can plague tests for personality disorders as well.

Solutions

Diagnostic interview and test designers can combat a lack of understanding by piloting potential questions with older adults to make sure they are understandable. Groups of pretest subjects made up of older adults can be asked what was not understandable about particular questions. Focus groups can be also used to gain criticisms of potential test items. Sudman and Bradburn (1982) advocated these practices to any researcher designing a survey, interview, or questionnaire. Kessler and Mroczek (1994, 1996) similarly endorsed these techniques specifically when measuring quality of life or psychopathology. It is likely that adoption of these methods would improve tests for personality disorders specialized for older adults.

The issue of motivation is a trickier problem. It is often difficult to motivate people to do something that they think is useless. If an older adult cannot grasp the relevance of the array of *DSM–IV* diagnostic criteria that need to be asked, or the pertinence of MMPI items, there is often little the assessor can do to remedy the situation. However, there is one practice that is widely used in survey research that may help motivate older respondents. Cannell, Fowler, and Marquis (1968; Oksenberg, Cannell, & Kalton, 1991) advocated that interviewers should routinely ask the respondent to aid them by being honest, cooperating, and informing them about the importance of the interview. Cannell et al. found that motivating respondents through such simple actions can lead to more accurate reports and the resulting higher quality of data. Assessors of personality disorders in older adults may use such practices to fight a potential deficit of motivation.

CONCLUSIONS

Two major classes of factors that can influence the assessment of personality disorders in older adults have been considered. The first dealt with the possibility that the behaviors accepted as hallmarks of personality disorders may change and transform over time. These transformations may cause the disorder to look very different in older age than in younger adulthood or midlife. It may be no less a personality disorder, but it may be characterized by novel symptoms that arise only in later life, whether due to aging per se or to the changed contexts that accompany older age. A myriad of ways were discussed in which this concept, called heterotypic continuity, can affect the assessment of personality disorders in later life. It was argued that heterotypic continuity renders many behaviors functionally equivalent. This concept, functional equivalence, refers to seemingly different surface behaviors or symptoms that are made equivalent because they are caused by the same underlying construct. Also mentioned were some statistical models that may be useful in identifying heterotypic continuity, such as growth curve modeling and IRT.

The second major class of factors encompassed some general issues in assessing older adults. The discussion drew heavily from what has been learned from gerontological investigations of intellectual functioning, where age equivalence in understanding and motivation are crucial issues. It was suggested that test constructors and diagnostic interview designers adopt the practices endorsed by Sudman and Bradburn (1982) to solve problems stemming from difficulty in understanding, and those advocated by Cannell et al. (1968) to remedy motivational issues.

The solutions proposed herein, especially if applied in concert with one another, can lead to measurement tools that are sensitive to the problems that potentially plague the assessment of personality disorders in older adults. The issues discussed earlier are surely not the only ones that vex these measurements. However, they are among the most important assessment dilemmas in this area. They deserve at least some attention from those who hope to accurately and successfully detect personality disorders in late life.

ACKNOWLEDGMENTS

The authors wish to thank Avron Spiro III, David W. Evans, and Douglas Katz for helpful comments and criticisms of an earlier version of this chapter.

REFERENCES

Brim, O. G., Jr., & Kagan, J. (1980). Constancy and change: A view of the issues. In O. G. Brim, Jr. & J. Kagan (Eds.), *Constancy and change in human development* (pp. 1–25). Cambridge, MA: Harvard University Press.

Bryk, A. S., & Raudenbush, S. W. (1992). *Hierarchical linear models: Applications and data analysis methods.* Newbury Park, CA: Sage.

Cannell, C. F., Fowler, F. J., & Marquis, D. H. (1968). The influence of interviewer and respondent psychological and behavioral variables on the reporting of household variables. *Vital and Health Statistics, 26*, 1–65.

Caspi, A., & Bem, D. J. (1990). Personality continuity and change across the life course. In L. A. Pervin (Ed.), *Handbook of personality: Theory and research* (pp. 549–569). New York: Guilford.

Costa, P. T., Jr., & McCrae, R. R. (1989). *The NEO–PI/NEO–FFI manual supplement.* Odessa, FL: Psychological Assessment Resources.

Costa, P. T., Jr., & McCrae, R. R. (1990). Personality disorders and the five-factor model of personality. *Journal of Personality Disorders, 4*, 362–371.

Costa, P. T., Jr., & McCrae, R. R. (1994). Set like plaster? Evidence for the stability of adult personality. In T. F. Heatherton & J. L. Weinberger (Eds.), *Can personality change?* (pp. 21–40). Washington, DC: American Psychological Association.

Dixon, R. A., & Baltes, P. B. (1986). Toward life-span research on the functions and pragmatics of intelligence. In R. J. Sternberg & R. K. Wagner (Eds.), *Practical intelligence: Origins of competence in the everyday world* (pp. 203–235). Cambridge, England: Cambridge University Press.

Gatz, M., Kasl-Goldley, J. E., & Karel, M. J. (1996). Aging and mental disorders. In J. E. Birren & K. W. Schaie (Eds.), *Handbook of the psychology of aging* (4th ed., pp. 365–382). San Diego, CA: Academic Press.

Hambleton, R. K., Swaminathan, H., & Rogers, H. J. (1991). *Fundamentals of item response theory.* Newbury Park, CA: Sage.

Holland, P. W., & Wainer, H. (1993). *Differential item functioning.* Hillsdale, NJ: Lawrence Erlbaum Associates.

Kagan, J. (1969). The three faces of continuity in human development. In D. A. Goslin (Ed.), *Handbook of socialization theory and research* (pp. 53–65). Chicago: Rand McNally.

Kagan, J. (1980). Perspectives on continuity. In O. G. Brim, Jr. & J. Kagan (Eds.), *Constancy and change in human development* (pp. 26–74). Cambridge, MA: Harvard University Press.

Kessler, R. C., & Mroczek, D. K. (1994). Measuring the effects of medical interventions. *Medical Care, 33*, AS109–AS119.

Kessler, R. C., & Mroczek, D. K. (1996). Some methodological issues in the development of quality of life measures for the evaluation of medical interventions. *Journal of Evaluation in Clinical Practice, 2*, 181–191.

Lord, F. M. (1980). *Applications of item response theory to practical testing problems.* Hillsdale, NJ: Lawrence Erlbaum Associates.

Lytton, H. (1990). Child and parent effects in boys' conduct disorder: A reinterpretation. *Developmental Psychology, 26*, 683–697.

Mroczek, D. K., Ozer, D. J., Spiro, A., III, & Kaiser, R. (1998). Evaluating a measure of the five factor model of personality. *Assessment, 5*, 285–299.

Mussen, P. H., Conger, J. J., Kagan, J., & Huston, A. C. (1990). *Child development and personality* (7th ed.). New York: Harper & Row.

Nesselroade, J. R., & Boker, S. M. (1994). Assessing constancy and change. In T. F. Heatherton & J. L. Weinberger (Eds.), *Can personality change?* (pp. 149–174). Washington, DC: American Psychological Association.

Nesselroade, J. R., & Featherman, D. L. (1990). Intraindividual variability in older adults' depression scores: Some implications for developmental theory and longitudinal research. In D. Magnusson, L. R. Bergman, G. Rudinger, & B. Torestad (Eds.), *Problems and methods in longitudinal research: Stability and change* (pp. 47–66). Cambridge, England: Cambridge University Press.

Oksenberg, L., Cannell, C. F., & Kalton, G. (1991). New strategies for pretesting survey questions. *Journal of Official Statistics, 7,* 349–365.

Patterson, G. R. (1993). Orderly change in a stable world: The antisocial trait as a chimera. *Journal of Consulting and Clinical Psychology, 61,* 911–919.

Rosowsky, E., & Gurian, B. (1991). Borderline personality disorder in late life. *International Psychogeriatrics, 3,* 39–52.

Sadavoy, J., & Fogel, F. (1992). Personality disorders in old age. In J. E. Birren, R. B. Sloane, & G. D. Cohen (Eds.), *Handbook of mental health and aging* (2nd ed., pp. 433–462). San Diego, CA: Academic Press.

Schaeffer, N. C. (1988). An application of item response theory to the measurement of depression. In C. Clogg (Ed.), *Sociological methodology* (pp. 271–307). San Francisco: Jossey-Bass.

Schaie, K. W., & Hertzog, C. (1985). Measurement in the psychology of adulthood and aging. In J. E. Birren & K. W. Schaie (Eds.), *Handbook of the psychology of aging* (2nd ed., pp. 61–94). New York: Van Nostrand Reinhold.

Schaie, K. W., & Willis, S. L. (1996). *Adult development and aging* (4th Ed.). New York: HarperCollins.

Sudman, S., & Bradburn, N. M. (1982). *Asking questions.* San Francisco: Jossey-Bass.

Stevens-Long, J., & Commons, M. L. (1992). *Adult life* (4th ed.). Mountain View, CA: Mayfield.

Vuchinich, S., Bank, L., & Patterson, G. R. (1992). Parenting, peers, and the stability of antisocial behavior in preadolescent boys. *Developmental Psychology, 28,* 510–521.

Widiger, T. A., & Trull, T. J. (1992). Personality and psychopathology: An application of the five-factor model. *Journal of Personality, 60,* 363–393.

Wiggins, J., & Pincus, A. (1989). Conceptions of personality disorders and dimensions of personality. *Psychological Assessment, 1,* 305–316.

PART III

Clinical Issues:
Diagnosis and Treatment

The Patient–Therapist Relationship and the Psychotherapy of the Older Adult With Personality Disorder

ERLENE ROSOWSKY, PsyD
Harvard Medical School

Patients with personality disorders are typically those who are among the most challenging to treat, regardless of venue, clinician, or the patient's age. Indeed, "challenging" is a much softer term than others used to describe these patients: "difficult" (Powers, 1985; Starker, Baker, Drummond, & Pankratz, 1991), "crock" (Lipsitt, 1970), "over-demanding . . . long-suffering" (Kahana & Bibring, 1964), " malignant" (Sadavoy, 1996), and even "hateful" (Groves, 1978). It appears that the struggle to identify these patients and move toward a diagnostic consensus has been at least as challenging as the patients we purport to describe. The existence of books such as this exemplifies the need to recognize these disorders even in the absence of precise diagnostic criteria. There is a struggle to describe in a clinically meaningful way the qualities or aspects that prompt the widely held view that these patients are "difficult" or "hateful." The demographic shift to the older end of the life span results in an enlarging percentage, as well as greater absolute numbers, of people to be treated and cared for with increasingly limited resources. The psychosocial challenges of old and aging adults are mirrored in the challenges they present to mental health clinicians and other service providers. This is especially true for older adults with personality disorder (PD), who not only absorb resources but sap the energies of providers and programs. These clients and patients introduce chaos into systems and do more poorly in any treatment or program than do their "nondifficult" counterparts (Livesley, 1995; Thompson, Gallagher, & Czirr, 1988).

This chapter suggests that an essential key to the sought-after diagnostic refinement can be found within the relationship between the mental health clinician and the older adult patient with PD. The difficulties with the intimate relationships in which these individuals are engaged are neither arbitrary nor a collection of discrete happenings; rather, they are pathognomonic of—indeed are central to—the pathology itself. As efforts are continued to develop standardized measures to identify, and perhaps ultimately to quantify, PDs (see chap. 3 in this volume), it is suggested that diagnostic criteria should include adequate representation of the relational problems that describe the very core of the pathology.

Reasons to hesitate in advancing this suggestion are considerable and understandable. Diagnostic criteria generally mark cognitions, behaviors, and affects, all at least ostensibly measurable (observable and quantifiable) and allowing acceptable replicability. Some criteria identify symptoms, and others traits. It is daunting to attempt to describe and operationalize criteria describing the "effect on others in intimate relationships." But not doing so is to miss the most robust, age-resistant criteria of all. Stone (1993) defined personality as "a set of traits that intimates and acquaintances often perceive with greater clarity than the person who possesses these traits" (p. 14). Even moving from a categorical model of diagnosis toward a dimensional model predicts that reliability will suffer. It is clear that holding personality disorder diagnosis to a strict categorical model is less appropriate (not a good fit) than for Axis I conditions (Frances, 1982), even though it is consistent with the medical model, where a disorder is either present or absent. Greater diagnostic refinement or, perhaps with even greater clinical relevance, quantification of pathology (PDism) fits better with a dimensional model. It could be suggested that specific PD diagnoses, even respecting a categorical model, may be too narrow and therefore miss the diagnosis. In older adults, it appears that the *DSM* Axis II *clusters* may be closer to capturing a PD diagnosis (Dougherty & Rosowsky, in press; Molinari, Kunik, Mulsant, & Rifail, in press). This may be so because the clusters more closely reflect the way these individuals are perceived by others, whether as "odd," "dramatic," or "fearful."

Diagnosis becomes even more difficult when the "effect on others" is not adequately represented among clinical criteria. Although a "maladaptive interpersonal style" is represented among the diagnostic criteria (Kroessler, 1990), the response of the person in relation to the patient (the "inter" in interpersonal) is not.

For a number of reasons, clinicians hesitate to make the diagnosis of PD in their older adult patients. PD is often used as a pejorative label. It is not a diagnostic category that has a good treatment record or that is generally reimbursable by third parties. Reflecting ageist assumptions from which the clinician is not immune, older adults are perceived as rigid, and personality disordered older adults as exceptionally so. There is, in addition, the notion that PD is magically outgrown with increasing age, and, more relevant to the present discussion, a recognition that the current diagnostic gold standard does not "capture" these people (Rosowsky & Gurian, 1991). So although clinicians may not be formally making the diagnosis, they are experiencing and informally diagnosing these patients using idiosyncratic criteria that may not be quite so idiosyncratic on closer examination.

CLINICAL EMERGENCE OF PERSONALITY DISORDER IN THE OLDER ADULT: GENERAL COMMENTS

When older people come to the attention of a mental health professional, it is often because their usual way of being in the world has somehow failed. The diagnostic requirement for a PD is that the individual experiences impairment in social or occupational functioning and/or experiences subjective distress. Older adults with PD often "emerge" as a result of a comorbid condition or in response to an imperative for change with which they cannot cope. With regard to comorbidity, it is known that PD patients treated for an Axis I condition do more poorly in treatment and at follow-up then those without a PD diagnosis (Howard, Bandyopadhyay, & Cook, 1992). The inclusion of cultural considerations among *DSM–IV* Axis II criteria acknowledges the role of group identity in contributing to diagnostic labeling. It is also recognized that PD may be differentially diagnosed according to gender (Bornstein, 1997). Such considerations and assumptions, although they are not without merit, may contribute to the PD being underdiagnosed, untreated, and not considered in treatment planning (George, 1990).

The need to change often becomes a catalyst for the reemergence of PD after a quiescent phase during midlife, often following the loss of a significant relationship. This relationship is one that had previously served as a buffer between the patient and the world, to bind the expression of PD symptoms, or to bolster the more adaptive behaviors of the individual while reciprocally inhibiting maladaptive ones. Additionally, the loss of a role that had once served to contain the expression of pathology, or to support the individual by providing a "domain of success" (to be discussed later), may also be a catalyst. PD can also appear selectively in different contexts. For example, an individual whose life revolves around her home might be able to function adequately. This same person, needing to make independent decisions in a fast-paced work setting may become increasingly symptomatic and interpersonally disordered (see chap. 16 in this volume). It is not unusual for an older adult to become identified as "difficult" following the death of a spouse, a move to a new housing setting, or identified as a "resistant" patient while being treated for an Axis I or Axis III (medical) disorder. In addition, with regard to the presentation of serious character pathology in old age, certain criteria for clinical diagnosis appear to be altered with age. Conversely, some presumed expressions may be state dependent and may be confused with an "enduring" disposition. Some of the more florid cases of PD (greater PDism) may exhibit selective mortality, thus leaving the lesser ones to define the disorder in old age. This may be especially true for the Cluster B PDs, as a group highly impulsive and risk taking (Cohen et al., 1994). Other ways to understand the presumed reduced prevalence of PD in old age (Fogel & Westlake, 1990) may include physiological changes, specifically changes in brain neurochemistry (see chap. 1 in this volume) or the manifestation of geriatric variants of symptom expression, all resulting in underdiagnosis (Rosowsky & Gurian, 1992).

What we think we know about PD Clusters in old age can be summarized as follows: For *Cluster A* (odd and eccentric), there may possibly be some increase in paranoid tendencies; the individual may appear more eccentric, more withdrawn. However, the psychosocial environment is typically more indulgent of deviance in old age, and therefore the odd and eccentric character may actually fit in better, or at least less poorly, than at a younger age. For *Cluster B* (dramatic and erratic), less flagrant expression of impulsivity or overt aggressive, manipulative, and self-harming behaviors are anticipated. The narcissistic character might be expected to handle aging especially poorly. In general, their stock behaviors may become unavailable or limited. The pathology may be in response to their coping mechanisms being cut off at the pass. For *Cluster C* (anxious and fearful), it is anticipated that an individual may become more obsessive, more cautious, and more anxious in response to real or anticipated losses, especially losses of control and predictability.

THE FORM AND FUNCTION OF PERSONALITY DISORDER THROUGH THE LIFE COURSE

Personality traits serve the individual in the quest for self-righting in response to accommodations and adaptations to changes. They serve to support self-continuity, enabling the person to maintain a coherent identity through the life course (McCrae & Costa, 1984; Rosowsky & Gurian, 1992). This appears to be true even if certain personality features, more congruent with a younger age and lifestyle, are not present. Among the more robust features of the PD are the defensive structure and the effect individuals have on others with whom they are in a close relationship.

PDs have been discussed in the literature in terms of several major conceptual models, all essentially describing the same infrastructure through effects on others, self-report, and observations. Tyrer and Seivewright (1988) divided the PDs into "mature" and "immature" categories: borderline, antisocial, narcissistic, passive-aggressive, belonging to the latter; and obsessive-compulsive, schizotypal, schizoid, and paranoid belonging to the former. They suggested that the mature PDs appear somewhat later and are more likely to persist into old age. Kernberg (1975) elegantly described the genesis and manifestation of the character in Borderline Personality Organization. Sadavoy (1987) described the patient with "severe character disorder," rather than diagnosis of a specific PD. He posited five "core vulnerabilities," including intolerance of aloneness and fear of abandonment; inability to sustain appropriate interpersonal boundaries; inability to tolerate strong affect; inability to modulate anger; and a vulnerability to the loss of self-cohesion resulting in transient breaks with reality. These are likely identifying the same clinical syndrome as others have and the terms "residual," "core," and "essential" can be used interchangeably to identify those features that transcend place and age marking the pathological character.

The dominant defense mechanisms at work in these patients include splitting, denial, projection, projective identification, primitive idealization, reaction formation, and acting out (Schamess, 1981). The more primitive and aggressive the character to whom individuals relate, the greater is the regressive pull toward their own primitive core. This pull, together with their beliefs and attitudes about aging, create the essence of a special countertransference with this population to be considered shortly. The defenses are also the responses (e.g., dependency, somatization, withdrawal, etc.) allowing the elderly patient to avoid (further) disintegration, generally adaptive, and likewise avoid (necessary) reintegration, generally maladaptive.

The core features of severe character pathology include affective dysregulation and pathological object relations (Westen, 1990). Impulsively and flagrant acting out behaviors appear to lessen with age, perhaps due in part to constricted energy, limited opportunity, or social learning. An earlier work (Rosowsky & Gurian, 1991) suggested that behavioral variants observed in older adults may express stable lifelong psychodynamics, effectively serving as equivalents or behavioral proxies. In a study of the relation between defense mechanisms and the big five personality factors, where subjects were of mixed ages, Soldz, Budman, Demby, and Merry (1995) reported a significant relation between immature (more primitive) defenses and PDs in general, whereas withdrawal defenses were most consistent with Cluster A and Cluster C diagnoses.

HOW THE THERAPY RELATIONSHIP WORKS

The intellectual origins of the therapeutic encounter as an essential assessment and treatment tool is reflected in all aspects of the therapeutic relationship, including the working alliance, transference, and countertransference. For purposes of psychotherapy, it is essential that the clinician be able to structure, present, and preserve the therapeutic fame, and that the patient be able to tolerate and participate in the process of the therapy. This requires an ability to communicate, as well as an adequate memory, observing ego, and fantasy (Greenson, 1965).

Patients with severe PD, at any age, experience intense, rapid, broad swings in their interpersonal relationships. They vacillate between extremes of loving and hating, idealizing and devaluing, needing to be close and needing to be distant, seeking dependence and autonomy. They act out the conflict between the fear of abandonment (threatening annihilation) and the fear of domination (threatening fusion) (Melges & Swartz, 1989). Either way, there is a threatened loss of self. What is critical is that feedback from the interpersonal relationship (in this case, the therapeutic relationship) becomes the catalyst for movement toward the opposite pole. To this end, the effect on others is not only an expression of the psychopathology, but is inherent to maintaining it.

ISSUES RELATED TO THE ALLIANCE, CONTENT, AND PROCESS OF THE THERAPY

Clinicians in their practice use theoretical frameworks to better understand the experience of their patients and for guidance as to how best to help. They are only conceptual tools. Whereas there have been relatively few reports about treating the aged in the psychoanalytic literature, it is from this school that an understanding of defensive structure as well as the concepts of therapeutic alliance, transference, and countertransference emanate. In a thoughtful article on psychoanalysis and the aged, Reiss (1992) discussed a 70-year-old potential analysand, warning her that a possible negative effect of analysis might be depression when she considers all the things she may have missed in her life. "The patient responded with a chuckle, saying, "You do not have to be in analysis for that to happen" (Reiss, 1992, p. 20). For the older adult with PD the challenge is to guard against that happening; the breaking through of knowing can be life threatening (i.e., inducing regression, self-fragmentation, even transient psychosis).

THERAPEUTIC ALLIANCE

This refers to the ability of the therapist and patient to create an authentic relationship committed to the therapy, and to be able to do the work involved (Greenson, 1965). This assumes patients are able to cooperate, "follow the instructions and insights of his analyst" (p. 157), and ultimately observe themselves in order to confront resistance and direct the therapy. It requires of the therapist a capacity for empathy, an ability to tolerate, to like, perhaps even to love the patient, as well as a belief in the patient's capacity for change. Both patient and therapist need share a vision of the therapy as a context and catalyst for that change.

Transcending the bounds of the definition initially limited to psychoanalysis, therapeutic alliance requires that the patient acknowledge distress and believe that the therapist is someone who can help. From the perspective of the therapist, the therapeutic alliance builds on an accurate assessment of patients, including their strengths and weaknesses and their phenomenology and ability to create meaning of their universe. This requires that the therapist be able to abide the patient.

The working alliance defines the real patient–clinician relationship as opposed to the transference, to be discussed later in this chapter. Even with sincere acknowledgment of distress, and recognition of the therapist's contribution to the distress, the defenses will be mobilized, and resistance, reflecting the density of these defenses, will be activated. As Stone (1993) described it, "The therapist who works with personality disorders is more cabinetmaker than carpenter. We do not build and reshape as much as polish and sand down. . . . The shape stays as it was" (p. 161).

Stone (1993) suggested that the process of therapy can be viewed in three layers, or phases: the *support* phase, including establishing the alliance; *working through the neurotic transference;* and the *cognitive-behavioral,* or *skill-building* phase. This posits a sequence, but, as with any sequential schema, there is much deviation from a linear progression, especially as the therapy process mirrors the PD patient's oscillations of attachment. The individual with severe character pathology is exquisitely sensitive to interpersonal feedback, the necessary self-confirming nutrient that can only be supplied within a relationship. It is not an arbitrary occurrence (using a frequent example) that following an especially intimate therapy session the patient misses the next one, or that an expression of contriteness (even offers of flowers and candy) follows a particularly explosive, rage-filled session. Sometimes the therapeutic frame can endure the assault of the oscillations, and at other times it cannot. At those times, the treatment may not be able to get off the ground, as an alliance cannot be established, or else is ruptured and treatment prematurely abandoned.

DIFFERENTIAL IDENTIFICATION

A case can be made that, because of the ego-syntonic nature of PD, individuals would be less likely to perceive the disorder than individuals with whom they are in relationship. However, some studies do not support this position (Dowson, 1992). A lack of clinician–patient agreement regarding specific PD diagnosis has been reported (Hyler et al., 1989; Mellsop, Varghese, Joshua, & Hicks, 1982). Hyler reported greater discrepancy for Cluster A PDs and most agreement for Borderline PD (Hyler, Reider, Williams, Spitzer, Lyons, & Hendler, 1989). In another report of a mixed aged sample (Hyler, Rieder, Young, Williams, & Spitzer, 1990), a factor analysis of patient self-report data using the PDQ showed a weak relation between the self-report factors and the 11 *DSM–III* personality disorders, but a good relation between these factors and the three PD Clusters. Questions arise: Does the self-report questionnaire format use criteria that are not adequately specific? Can the patient with PD be an accurate reporter on any instrument (Segal, 1997)? Or, do the *DSM* criteria fit the diagnostic entities they purport to identify? It could be useful to replicate this design to see if there was a movement toward the mean with advancing age, which is suggested by the notion of "core," or "residual," PD. If confirmed, this would help explain the apparently repeated finding that there appears to be a reduction in Axis II specificity but increased agreement with regard to cluster and—even more—the presence (vs. absence) of the PD diagnosis.

As has been suggested in previous chapters, there may be movement toward a new nosology of PD, one specifically for geriatric diagnoses. Moreover, extended historical, informant, or other collateral data need to be gathered to make the diagnosis (Segal, 1997). These data need include self-report, informant data, historical review, as well as recognition of task, role, and context where the individual's pathology is most manifested. In other words, what, where, and how is this individual asked to be in order to be or not to be identified as having a personality disorder? A critical determinant is the enduring, consistent effect on others in an intimate relationship.

A series of patient–clinician dyads involving older adult mental health outpatients were analyzed (Dougherty & Rosowsky, in press). This study found that the patients identified themselves as meeting more PD criteria than did their clinicians, and the patients ascribed to themselves greater distress from their PD symptoms—referred to as *PDism*. There was good intradyad agreement that PD is present, as well as agreement that it was mixed PD (vs. a specific PD). This was consistent with reports that, among older adults, PD diagnoses are less specific and tend toward a diagnosis of PD, NOS. How might it be understood that the patients tended to report more subjective distress than was recognized by the clinicians? Are the diagnostic criteria only catching the behavioral expression of the PD and missing the experience of internal distress? Is there a clinical bias operating that in effect attenuates the degree of PDism identified? Is this bias a function of the patient's age? Is it a function of the countertransference? And, how is this self-greater-than-observer distress reconciled with the clinical premise that PD is ego-syntonic?

Another way to understand the patient–clinician disparity is by considering the core psychodynamic characteristics of PD: specifically, lack of personality integration, inability to sustain appropriate self–other distance in intimate relationships, inability to contain primitive aggression (resulting in anger dysregulation and acting out), and existential loneliness (emptiness, loss of self in the absence of others). The effects that these characteristics have on others (including professional "others") are great. Consider the following. The lack of integration presents a "moving target" to the clinician for the diagnosis and treatment. It is enormously difficult to provide care to the rapidly shifting person who feels, as he presents, disintegrated and inconsistent. The loneliness, emptiness, and regressive pull may appear initially like appropriate treatment foci, but, often quickly, the experience of the patient changes and starts to feel more like a threat than a challenge, and the clinician feels the urge to retaliate. The experience of the depth and degree of the patient's rage compounds the experience. The experience of the unbridled affect within the patient resonates within the clinician. It is powerful and creates the central criterion on which to base a diagnosis of PD in old age (Rosowsky & Dougherty, 1998).

WHEN WHAT WORKED NO LONGER DOES: DEFENSES, RELATIONSHIPS, CONTEXTS, AND TASKS

There are a number of ways to conceptualize what happens in old age that causes individuals to be unable to function in the way that they historically have. An explanatory model considers (a) physiological changes that are age specific, and organic changes that alter affect, behavior, cognition and memory, sensory acuity, and bring about a general slowing and the subjective experience of reduced energy; (b) responses to frequently occurring stresses of old age (Sadavoy, 1987; Solomon, Fallete, & Stevens, 1982); (c) loss of self-continuity. With PD, a sine qua non is the availability of fewer and more maladaptive coping mechanisms, further compromised in senescence secondary to loss of self-confirming roles and relationships. What may also become lost are the existential notions of purpose and meaning, as well as the image of self as an agent of change. These losses result in more limited and more rigid coping mechanisms and the tendency, under stress, to regress to more primitive ones. Although some have reported that "the frequency of personality disorders does not significantly change with aging" (H. Wylie & M. Wylie, 1987, p. 44), PD has also been reported to be less prevalent among older than younger adults in community samples (6.6% vs. 10.5%; Cohen et al., 1994). Moreover, older adults report fewer maladaptive personality traits. However, there is evidence that these traits emerge when they come under stress. It is known that older adults, in general, experience more losses and more stresses than younger adults.

THE DEVELOPMENTAL WORK AT OLD AGE AND THE PD PATIENT

Whereas traditional psychoanalysis embraced the belief that the old person was not amenable to analysis, developmental theorists have long championed the capacity for change throughout life and across stages of psychosocial development. This is the core premise, for example, of Erikson's epigenetic theory of life-span development (Erikson, 1969). Change is posited as emerging through resolutions of conflicts that are, in effect, developmental nodal points marking the parameters of discrete psychosocial stages. The nature of the conflicts, however, are not different than at younger ages. The processes of reminiscence, restitution, and reconciliation are implicitly woven into Erikson's final conflict between integrity and despair, with wisdom as the outcome of successful stage negotiation. This transition requires that the individual be able to do the work of the review process and come to acknowledge reasonable responsibility for and integration of his life (Solomon et al., 1982). Older adults with PD may not be up to this task. By definition, they have difficulty with self-integration and typically are unable to tolerate the anxiety generated by the processes of review and reflection. Patients may have developed a leitmotif that had supported an illusion of self-integration and a presentation of wholeness. Many adults with PD are wonderfully successful in a specific domain and only get into difficulty when this domain is no longer available to support them. This "domain of success" is the context for the personality style; without it, the personality disorder becomes revealed.

A reason why the dimensional versus the categorical model of personality disorder diagnosis appears more valid is that there are critical variables outside the individual that not only inform but actually create the diagnosis (Rosowsky & Gurian, 1992); these contribute to development of domains of success (enabling the expression of the personality *style*) and domains of stress (enabling the expression of the personality *disorder*). Although personality as a construct is regarded as generally stable, whether or not it is pathological reflects appraisal of the individual incorporating extra-individual concerns; these include roles, relationships, and tasks. Thus, personality traits (inherently neither adaptive nor maladaptive) can be understood to lie along continua where they can be identified as styles or disorders and, theoretically, according to how closely they approximate style or disorder. This speaks to the issue of quantification, or "PDism."

Consider an example.

Mrs. H was an 80-year-old woman who came to clinical attention with symptoms of anxiety and depression following the death of her middle-age son. His death occurred 1 year after that of her second husband. She had one earlier depressive episode and psychotherapy experience shortly after the death of her first husband. She stated that she was somewhat helped at that time by counseling, but still reported considerable distress. She was able to secure admission to a sanitarium, where she remained in a very protective environment for several months. She recovered fully when she was introduced to and later married her second husband. Both her marriages were long, over 25 years, and were, in her words, "So good. I was very, very lucky." Soon after the death of her second husband, Mrs. H again became symptomatic. At this time she was living in the same city as her son, who had just recently become divorced and was able to take over for his mother where her husband had left off. Again, Mrs. H became "whole and well" and resumed her life, which was committed to friends and involvement in charity work. She moved to a retirement community and made a good adjustment, but continued to rely on her son "for every-thing." After his sudden death, she decompensated dramatically. She was referred for "bereavement counseling" and was treated with selective sero-tonin reuptake inhibitors (SSRIs) for depression. She responded only min-imally to these interventions. After 8 months, she was able to plan and go on a long cruise (perhaps meeting similar needs as the sanitarium had ear-lier). There she met a widower and again fell in love. He was a retired CEO and quite happy to manage her life as well as his own. Her depression and anxiety remitted. Her obvious Dependent Personality Disorder was no longer a disorder, but rather a dependent personality "style" that fit well with her current life.

In addition to the negotiation of Erickson's final psychosocial stage, the older adult approaching the end of life needs also to attend to the more existential tasks of closure and legacy. The task of closure requires the ability to be able to tolerate existential anxiety in the service of discovering truth and creating a whole story of one's life. Older adults with PD are particularly defended against this and when the defensive structure is not able to adequately hold back the knowing, they become more symptomatic. This may have a special synergy with the awareness of the inexorable running out of time as a person nears the end of life. The task of legacy is the last step in ego transcendence. If the form of clo-sure is historical reconstruction and its function is to create a final story, the function of legacy is to be able to leave the created self (story) behind. The ther-apist who can be engaged is in the position of providing the context for closure, to facilitate / enable it by working through the resistance, and can also be there to receive the legacy. Therapy in late life provides an opportunity to make a new friend, and to have a new listener for the final story, at a time when such oppor-tunities are few.

ASPECTS OF THE THERAPEUTIC RELATIONSHIP CHALLENGED BY PERSONALITY DISORDERS

The Alliance

The contract to do psychotherapy requires hope and the possibility of loving the patient. The achievement of the therapeutic alliance implies the capacity of both partners of the dyad to do their part to commit to the work of the therapy and the possibility of positive change.

Transference

The therapeutic relationship promotes and reflects a combination of reactions to the real relationship as well as the transference. *Transference,* according to its original psychoanalytic definition, refers to the process of analysands reliving their early life in the therapy and displacing unconscious feelings stemming from relationships with early, primary objects (most notably parents), onto the analyst (Hinze, 1987). Transference embraces the whole of reactions that come from the past and are inappropriate to the current situation. In object relations theory, two broad areas organizing the transference include the Ideal (the missed and longed for selfobject) and the Real (the repeatedly experienced and anticipated selfobject).

Transference Issues and Personality Disorders.   With PD patients, the transference threatens to transcend the neurotic level, often becoming chaotic (sometimes psychotic) as they oscillate in attachment and fragment (dis-integrates) under stress, at times including the stress generated by the therapy. Many personality disordered individuals, especially those with primitive character structure, do not have the requisite ego resilience or strength to do the work of a depth therapy. Sometimes, unfortunately, this does not become apparent until a serious regression has been catalyzed by the therapy. For the clinician working with the PD patient, the special challenge of the transference is twofold: to tolerate the experience of the transference without reinforcing the pathology, and to be able to use it to come to know the phenomenology of the patient and guide the therapy (Stolorow, 1993).

In treatment, the transference enables a conservation of energy (familiarity vs. novelty) so that the elderly patient is able to become comfortably invested in replicating sameness. Novelty is not only energy draining, it is also stress generating. Self-development is also a dynamic and energy draining process, mutually shaping and being shaped by the individual and his world (Nemiroff & Colarusso, 1990), and the process of the shaping is likewise shaped by the course of therapy.

With personality disorders, the transference may be especially powerful because the individual does not have the necessary ability to maintain accurate, consistent reality testing of an intimate other. The maladaptive ways in which the PD patient uses the therapist are exhibited in the transference through a combination of flattery, cooperation and idealization, devaluing and threatening, often shifting with remarkable alacrity. These behaviors can be provocative and enraging, and can be destructive to both patient and the therapy. The result is the chaos and crises that define the disorder, that demand immediate attention, complex responses, and often put the therapy on the line.

The form of the transference provides valuable diagnostic information as well as "grist for the mill" for interpretation and confrontation. As individuals unconsciously strive to recreate the past in the present, they invest in the clinician and in the therapy what is needed to reinforce themselves. The odd and eccentric character is distrustful, uncomfortable with closeness, and hypervigilant, guarding against betrayal. The fearful and dependent character seeks unreasonable reassurance, never enough, in an effort to be taken over, held up, and cared for in order to feel like his or her self. The borderline character experiences and relates to the clinician in a devaluing or adoring manner, demanding care, railing against perceived insufficiencies and anticipating abandonment. The narcissistic character is loftier than the therapist, and shows disdain or conversely creates a collusion of entitlement: the therapist being pressed into service as an idealized selfobject.

Transference and the Older Adult. It may be especially hard for a young clinician to tolerate the feeling of being parent to an elderly child. "Both filial and parental images become part of the transference" (Reiss, 1992, p. 27). Special issues in transference work with older adults often reflect the many losses, the encroaching proximity of death, and increasing dependencies they experience (Martindale, 1988). Diminished resiliency, weakened resistance, and decreased independence all conspire to affect the transference; the therapist becomes experienced varyingly as child, parent, and ultimately as peer (Martindale, 1988; Stone, 1993).

CASE EXAMPLE

I treated Mrs. M, a nursing home resident, intermittently over the course of many years. Our relationship began when she was 82 and suffering a psychotic depression and continued until her death at age 95. Over time she had become progressively immobile and increasingly visually impaired. The transference was noteworthy, and although it was dramatic to experience, it was not unusual. In the early phase of the therapy relationship, I was the doctor, the parent, on whom she leaned and turned to for direction and support. Over time, and when her depression remitted, there was a movement away from a position of dependence as her own competence began to be restored. Then I was the young therapist and she the old patient. But transference is always dynamic. We were marking the occasion of her 95th birthday. I commented that my birthday had been a few days earlier. She asked how old I was. I demurred and asked how old she thought I was. She replied: "I know that you're not as old as I am. I would guess you're no more than 80." (At the time, I was in my early forties). In the transference she and I had finally achieved parity, or as close to it as she could reconcile with the reality.

Countertransference

Countertransference is a psychoanalytical term describing the responses of therapists to a patient that reflect the therapists' primary relationships, especially to their parents. According to Schroder (1985, p. 25), "Countertransference is the partly conscious but mostly unconscious responses that occur in response to our internal conflicts and cause a reactivation of primitive defenses." It is in essence "the analyst's reaction to his patient's transference" (Hinze, 1987, p. 467). The term *countertransference* has come to transcend the strict boundaries of psychoanalysis. It has been broadened to connote the full range of reactions engendered in the therapist by the patient. An important point is that countertransference embraces the unconsciously driven reactions of the therapist, as well as those that are more conscious responses to the patient's real expressions of self. Countertransference can be positive as well as negative. Examples of the former include protective feelings, rescue fantasies, heightened self-esteem, and an illusion of specialness. Examples of the latter include any negative affects, as well as fantasies of retaliation, sadism, and escape. The wise clinician values the countertransference and can use it well in formulating the diagnosis and interventions (Zinn, 1988).

Countertransference and Personality Disorders. The countertransference includes unconscious material from the clinician's past and the reaction of the clinician to the patient's transference. Just as the transference reflects both real and projected material, so does the countertransference as well. I have come to consider it as more helpful to be able to use and manage the "whole of responses," the "response Gestalt," elicited by PD patients. This can include the therapist's experience of feeling drained, angry, depleted, and frightened, as well as anger and frustration at patient's real behaviors and clinical demands; the response Gestalt includes real (nonneurotic) responses to provocative, intolerable behaviors.

Patients with severe personality disorders evoke strong negative feelings in their clinicians, feelings that are experienced at an unconscious level and are defended against. Clinical tools are used to manage the strong responses. These tools often involve departures from the clinicians' usual way of conducting their professional work, often involve boundary violations, and may result in the transfer of a patient or premature termination.

The intrapsychic states of these patients evoke in the clinician a reciprocal or complementary state, which may range from mirror to antithesis of the patient's own. This state, together with responses to the patient's real behaviors, comprise the *response Gestalt*, defined as the sum of all responses engendered by the patient. This Gestalt can and should be analyzed and used as essential data illuminating the patient's phenomenology. For example, therapists might respond to a patient's anxiety and irritability by feeling anxious and edgy themselves. They might feel the urge to be especially open and self-revealing, as a balance to a patient's hypervigilance and wariness. And, of course, they might feel frustration and anger in response to a patient's rage, and rejection and sabotage of any help they may propose. This fictitious patient's experience of being is watchful, wary, angry, irritable, and anxious. This is important information and provides a very different clinical picture than one, for example, of a patient who "feels" clingy, sad, and who experiences the clinician as an idealized rescuer.

Messner (1979) posited the term *autognosis* as incorporating all subjective responses to the patient including, among others, intuition, empathy, prejudices, "and other internal events." "The clinician's observations of him- or herself in relationship to the patient" (Lazare & Alonso, 1989, p. 207) is broader than the traditional definition of countertransference. As described by Messner, it includes conscious as well as unconscious responses, reflected through cognitions as well as affects.

That these patients are especially likely to draw atypical affective responses from professionals is pathognomonic of their psychopathology. The behavioral expressions on the part of the therapist may include neglect or abandonment, sadism, devaluing and scolding, withholding, or other aggressive acts (Maltsberger, 1982–1983). The key is that clinicians' behavior is a departure from their usual norm.

The therapist's formulation of the treatment and understanding of the patient may serve to rationalize abandonment or sadistic responses including, for example, cruel applications of limit setting, painful assignments, hostile interpretations, or anything reflecting unconscious hate for the patient. Alternatively, the therapist may turn aggression inward resulting, at the least, in burnout. Maltsberger (1982–1983, p. 127) associated the patient "who cries out to be rejected as hopeless" with the countertransference of heightened anxiety and lowered self-esteem. This parallels the patient's own experience. The clinical utility of the countertransference is too often underregarded. In truth, especially for the patient with PD, it often affords the receptive and self-aware clinician a clear reflection of the patient's phenomenology and allows for well-chosen interpretations and honest feedback, reflecting both the countertransferential and "real" reactions to the patient. Honest feedback works because it is authentic, reduces the patients' need to show their bad self, shows patients that they have a real effect on the relationship, that they matter, and that their badness does not mean destruction or abandonment.

The Dance of the Patient–Clinician Dyad. Groves (1978) in his seminal article on the "Hateful Patient" presented patient types that evoke especially powerful reactions in physicians caring for them: (a) "Dependent Clingers" constantly request reassurance, attention, and help, presenting themselves as extremely needy. The countertransference response is often aversion and weariness. Whereas Groves did not "diagnose" his patient types, the diagnosis suggested here is Dependent PD. (b) "Entitled Demanders" are devaluing, demanding, and present a posture of superiority. The response is to feel intimidated and ashamed. This suggests a diagnosis of Narcissistic PD. (c) "Manipulative Help-Rejectors" exhibit behaviors that evoke feelings of pessimism and hopelessness. This suggests a nonspecific Cluster C (anxious and fearful) PD diagnosis. (d) "Self-destructive Deniers" are extremely provocative and induce in the clinician rage and hateful malice. The suggested diagnosis clearly "feels" like Borderline PD.

Kahana and Bibring (1964) in their classic chapter described seven categories of personality types and how these informed the meaning and management of physical illness. The personality types suggest specific personality disorders. For example, the "dependent, over demanding" personality suggests Dependent PD; the "orderly, controlled" personality suggests Obsessive-Compulsive PD; the "dramatizing, emotionally involved" personality suggests Histrionic PD; the "long-suffering, self-sacrificing" personality suggests Paranoid PD; the "patient who feels uninvolved and aloof" suggests Schizoid or Schizotypal PD. These categories are presented as not describing personality disorders but rather as normal personalities who present as described under situations of great stress. Focus was on the need to cope with physical illness, a frequent stressor in older age, but other stressors as well can be catalysts for the heightening of core personality traits contributing to the appraisal of specific personality styles or even disorders.

The patient's aggression and demandingness can result in the clinician's urge to challenge, devalue, and correct the narcissistic inflation, reducing it to frustration, disappointment, shame, and rage. The clinician's reaction acted out in treatment with the hypersensitive PD, already fearful of rejection or abandonment, could have the effect of releasing primitive rage, devaluing the therapist or helpless clinging. This in turn leads to the unleashing of the clinician's frustration, disappointment, shame, and rage, and the dance goes on.

Westen (1991) reported specific countertransference responses to the Borderline PD patient (perhaps the most difficult to treat), including (p. 212) "wishes to save and wishes to kill," "suffocating pseudo-nurturance," "hostile interpretations or showdowns," and "aggressive use of multiple medication." Adler and Buie (1972) reported that countertransference may result in clinicians' misuse of confrontation stemming from rage or rescue needs. Confrontation matches demands with demands, but the patient may not be able to withstand the confrontation, resulting in further regression. In the service of the therapy, positive and hopeful feelings from therapists are optimal. The worst case may be clinicians bearing, without reacting to, the patient's impossible manipulations and provocations out of a sense of shame and guilt that they cannot be the idealized transference object. Patients may truly need to be able to induce the familiar, albeit negative feelings in their clinician. And, for their part, analysts may have some need to embrace them. One function of the therapy is to serve as a microcosm of the universe of the patient. It is essential then that the real relationship as well as the neurotic transference be addressed in the therapy.

Countertransference and the Older Adult.   There is an understandable reluctance to work with PD patients as they are at every age experienced as most difficult and worrisome. There is also a professional reluctance to work with older patents irrespective of their psychic state (Duffy, 1992). "People generally assume the 'road ahead' will be predictably similar to the road already traveled"

(Duffy, 1992, p. 433). This belief often preempts consideration of therapy in later life. "It is not uncommon that choosing to work with the elderly represents an unconscious, preconscious or conscious, attempt at reparation of difficulties and disappointments with one's own parents or grandparents" (Martindale, 1988, p. 70). Therapists have their way of seeing the elderly patient. Three assumptions have historically pervaded psychotherapy with the elderly. One is that change is not possible, thus clinical treatment is not suitable to old age (Freud, 1905; Sprung, 1989). Another is that there is a lack of a rich inner life in old age (Duffy, 1992), and thus the clinical work with this population is boring and dull, as well as futile. And, finally, common themes of therapy with older adults are considered not suitable foci for treatment, because they are "normal" in old age, reflecting confusion between what may be age related but not be inevitable and intractable.

Certain countertransference distortions have been identified as frequently occurring in work with older adults (Reiss, 1992). One results from the assumption that sexuality is expunged in old age, and thus little or no attention is directed to the role of defenses in managing libidinal urges. Another is a nihilistic position based on the assumption that distress and despair are a "normal part of aging" and thus not amenable to change. Yet another collusion between the patient and therapist supports a position of hopelessness and dependency (of the patient) and strength and omnipotence (of the therapist). "The countertransference issues with despair can lead therapist to condescension that leads to a synergy that enhances the despair" (Malamud, 1996, p. 36).

Specific issues reflecting the countertransference often present in clinical work with the elderly (Sobel, 1980). Among these are the therapists' fear of becoming drained or depleted as they are called on to treat ever more compromised patients as they grow older and decline further; feelings of aggression that develop as clinicians seek to meet the patient's increasing neediness; issues evolving from clinicians' relationships with their own parents (or grandparents); disillusionment as clinicians come to experience the futile struggle between maturation and time; guilt and shame about modifying the (sacred) therapy techniques to accommodate the aging patient; narcissistic wound to clinicians who feel there is less professional value to work with older adults than work with younger patients; the regressive pull resonating within clinicians as they experience the regression of the patient; and conflict between the wise elder (ideal) and the regressed child, both of which coexist in the patient. Collectively these provide a backdrop to the struggle to maintain hope in patients as they experience an increasingly hope-depleting reality.

It has been suggested that younger therapists have more problems working with older adults than older adults have being treated by younger therapists (Hinze, 1987). This suggests that the countertransference may be more a potential clinical land mine than the transference in work with older adults. Two overarching mandates for the provision of care to the elderly are worth noting. One is the clinician's function as an auxiliary ego for the aged patient during the extended crisis of failure and demise, and another is the need to cull and support the healthy narcissism that remains. That these appear to be in conflict underscores the challenge of the therapy.

   Countertransference: Older Adults with Personality Disorders.   Consistent with earlier reports (Rosowsky & Gurian, 1991), special countertransference with older adult PD patients is a robust and pathology-defining experience, as it is with these patients earlier in life. A recent study analyzed interviews with mental health clinicians exploring how they actually came to the Axis II diagnosis for their older adult PD patients. Three countertransference themes emerged as most informing the diagnosis. These were powerful experiences of the patient as disconnected/arelational, angry/rageful, or needy/helpless (Rosowsky & Dougherty, 1998).

CONCLUSIONS

Where does the diagnosis of PD lie and why bother considering it? What is the value of being able to identity and better understand the personality disordered older adult?

   Diagnostic assessment of PD must rely on historical review, collateral information, patient report, as well as the total experience of the clinician. Clinicians and health care providers need to better understand the catalysts for altering a personality style into a disorder and how, once expressed, this psychosocial pathology can be transmuted into the more adaptive and more tolerable style.

   Abraham (1919) advised that the age of the symptom was a better prognostic indicator than the age of the patient. In truth, the "old" then were not as old as the "old" are now. The suggestion is that PD lasts a lifetime, and that the diagnosis and clinical recognition of this pathology lies between individuals and the other person with whom they are in an intimate relationship. For purposes of this chapter, the mental health clinician is this "other person." The psychopathology of the personality disordered patient is reflected increasingly within casual relationships, relationships that matter, and especially within relationships that are counted on—those that are essential to the individual's functioning. As healthy old age relies on the capacity to allow and sustain mutual interdependence, the challenges and constraints of PD are particularly relevant. With PD, the prognosis is better if the symptom expression reemerges after a quiescent phase, suggesting that with treatment the individual can be restored to a better level of functioning. Reemergence of greater pathology may suggest increased probability of restoration of greater health.

   The goals of therapy are to restore, repair, and return the individual to his best level of functioning. Moreover, it should not be assumed that it is futile to expect to reshape the character of the patient. The older adult in treatment is there because there is distress; something is not working. There also is the ticking of the clock and the encroachment of the universal fears of pain and ending life alone. The individual approaches the end of life in consort with the intrapsychic mandate to somehow review, create, and integrate a life that was meaningful. There is also the need to express and bequeath that life story. Old people with personality disorders are not exempt from the press of time or its psychosocial imperatives, but they are less well equipped to do the work. It is unfortunate that Personality Disorders were assigned to Axis II rather than Axis I, implying a second rank importance. On the contrary, logic might suggest that personality/character is more central, more self-defining, than adventitious disorders or intermittent disorders that, regardless of severity, do not define the self in the essential way that personality does.

Little in life is linear except for aging. Intuitively it would seem reasonable to predict that the old PD patient would be more "calcified" in (maladaptive) structure, and that therapy would be more likely to fail than at a younger age. This is not borne out in experience and there are a number of ways to understand this. There is in old age a narrowing range of symptom expression and a diminution of intensity, consonant with the "economy" of old age observed along many dimensions. With fewer roles and relationships defining a person's life, there are fewer foci of expression, effectively reducing practice, reinforcement and generalization effects; this appears to be true, despite Freud's position that by age 50 (hardly old by today's standards) the "mental processes" were too rigid (and the anticipated future too short) to justify therapy. The current health service delivery climate tends increasingly to value expedience and pragmatism, and for the older adult this can unfortunately translate into preemptive exclusion from psychological treatment.

There is an inherent empathic inadequacy in work with the old that is exclusive to this population. People hold no memory of ever having been at this stage. They do not know what it means or feels like to be very old. Therapy-promoted change in older adults may derive more from the outside than the inside, but the change effected through therapy is change nonetheless and can contribute enormously to the patient's whole of life.

REFERENCES

Abraham, K. (1919). The applicability of psychoanalytic treatment to patients at an advanced age. In S. Steury & M. H. Blank (Eds.), *Readings in psychotherapy with older people* (pp. 78–409). Washington, DC: NIMH, DHEW (Adon), 1978.

Adler, G., & Buie, D. H. (1972). The misuses of confrontation with borderline patients. *International Journal of Psychoanalytic Psychotherapy, 1,* 109–119.

Bornstein, R. F. (1997). Dependent personality disorder in the *DSM–IV* and beyond. *Clinical Psychology Science and Practice, 4,* 175–187.

Cohen, B. J., Nestadt, G., Samuels, J. F., Romanoski, A. J., McHugh, P. R., & Rabins, P. V. (1994). Personality disorder in later life: A community study. *British Journal of Psychiatry, 165,* 493–499.

Dougherty, L., & Rosowsky, E. (in press). Who is responsible for diagnosing personality disorders in older adults? *Journal of Clinical Geropsychology.*

Dowson, J. H. (1992). Assessment of *DSM–III–R.* Personality disorders by self-report questionnaire: The role of informants and a screening test for comorbid personality disorders (STCPD). *British Journal of Psychiatry, 161,* 344–352.

Duffy, M. (1992). Challenges in geriatric psychotherapy. *Individual Psychology, 48,* 432–440.

Erickson, E. (1969). Identity and the life cycle. *Psychological Issues, 1,* 101–164.

Fogel, B. S., & Westlake, R. (1990). Personality disorder diagnosis and age in patients with major depression. *Journal of Clinical Psychiatry, 51,* 232–235.

Frances, A. (1982). Categorical and dimensional systems of personality diagnosis. A comparison. *Comprehensive Psychiatry, 23,* 516–527.

Freud, S. (1905). *On psychotherapy. Standard Edition* (Vol. 7, pp. 255–268). London: Hogarth Press.

George, L. (1990). Gender, age and psychiatric disorders. *Generations,* Summer, 22–27.

Greenson, R. (1965). The working alliance and the transference neurosis. *Psychoanalytic Quarterly, 34,* 155–181.

Groves, J. F. (1978). Taking care of the hateful patient. *New England Journal of Medicine, 298,* 883–887.

Hinze, E. (1987). Transference and countertransference in the psychoanalytic treatment of older patients. *International Review of Psycho-Analysis, 14,* 465–474.

Howard, R., Bandyopadhyay, D., & Cook, M., (1992). Dissocial personality disorder in the elderly: A case history. *International Journal of Geriatric Psychiatry, 7,* 527–532.

Hyler, S. E., Rieder, R. O., Williams, J. B., Spitzer, R. L., Lyons, M., & Hendler, A. (1989). A comparison of clinical and self report diagnoses of *DSM–III* personality disorders in 552 patients. *Comprehensive Psychiatry, 30,*170–178.

Hyler, S. E., Lyons, M., Rieder, R. O., Young, L., Williams, J. B., & Spitzer, R. L. (1990). The factor structure of self-report *DSM–III* Axis II symptoms and their relationship to clinicians' ratings. *American Journal of Psychiatry, 147,* 751–757.

Kahana, R., & Bibring, G. L. (1964). Personality types in medical management. In N. E. Zinberg (Ed.), *Psychiatry and medical practice in the general hospital* (pp. 108–123). New York: International Universities Press.

Kernberg, O. (1975). *Borderline conditions and pathological narcissism.* New York: Aronson.

Kroessler, D. (1990). Personality disorder in the elderly. *Hospital and Community Psychiatry, 41,* 1325–1329.

Lazare, A., & Alonso, A., (1989). The mental status examination III. Psychodynamic dimensions. In A. Lazare (Ed.): *Outpatient psychiatry: Diagnosis and treatment* (2nd ed., pp. 200–208). Baltimore: Williams & Wilkins.

Lipsitt, D. R. (1970). Medical and psychological characteristics of "crocks." *International Journal of Psychiatry & Medicine, 1,* 15–25.

Livesley, W. J. (Ed.). (1995). *The* DSM–IV *Personality Disorders.* New York: Guilford.

Malamud, W. I. (1996). Countertransference issues with elderly patients. *Journal of Geriatric Psychiatry, 29,* 33–42.

Maltsberger, J. T. (1982–1983). Countertransference in borderline conditions: Some further notes. *International Journal of Psychoanalytic Psychotherapy, 9,* 125–134.

Martindale, B. (1988). Becoming dependent again: The fears of some elderly persons and their younger therapists. *Psychoanalytic Psychotherapy, 1,* 67–75.

McCrae, R. R., & Costa, P. T., Jr. (1984). *Emerging lives, enduring dispositions: Personality in adulthood.* Boston: Little, Brown.

Melges, F. T., & Swartz, M. S. (1989). Oscillations of attachment in borderline personality disorder. *American Journal of Psychiatry, 146,* 1115–1120.

Mellsop, G., Varghese, F., Joshua, S., & Hicks, A. (1982). The reliability of Axis II of *DSM–III*. *American Journal of Psychiatry, 139,* 1360–1361.

Messner, E. (1979). Autognosis: Diagnosis by the use of self. In A. Lazare (Ed.), *Outpatient psychiatry* (pp. 231–237). Baltimore: Williams & Wilkens.

Molinari, V., Kunik, M., Mulsant, B., & Rifail, A. H. (1998). The relationship between patient, informant, social worker, and consensus diagnosis of personality disorder in elderly depressed inpatients. *American Journal of Geriatric Psychiatry, 6*(2), 136–144.

Nemiroff, R. A., & Colarusso, C. A. (1990). *New dimensions in adult development.* New York: Basic Books.

Powers, J. S. (1985). Patient–physician communication and intervention: A unifying approach to the difficult patient. *Southern Medical Journal, 78,* 145–147.

Reiss, B. F. (1992). Some thoughts and material on age-related psychoanalysis of the aged. *Psychoanalysis and Psychotherapy, 10,* 17–32.

Rosowsky, E., Dougherty, L., Johnson, C., & Gurian B. (1997). Personality as an indicator of "goodness of fit" between the elderly individual and the health service system. *Clinical Gerontologist, 17*(3), 41–53.

Rosowsky, E., & Dougherty, L. (1998). Personality disorders and clinician responses. *Clinical Gerontologist, 18*(4), 31–42.

Rosowsky, E., & Gurian, B. (1991). Borderline personality disorder in late life. *Intergenerational Psychogeriatrics, 3,* 221–234.

Rosowsky, E., & Gurian, B. (1992). Impact of borderline personality disorder in late life on systems of care. *Hospital and Community Psychiatry, 43,* 386–389.

Sadavoy, J. (1987). Character disorders in the elderly: An overview. In J. Sadavoy & M. Leszcz (Eds.), *Treating the elderly with psychotherapy* (pp. 175–229). Madison, CT: International Universities Press.

Sadavoy, J. (1996). Personality disorders in old age: Symptom expression. *Clinical Gerontologist, 16,* 19–36.

Schamess, G. (1981). Boundary issues in countertransference: A developmental perspective. *Clinical Social Work Journal, 9,* 244–257.

Schroder, P. I. (1985). Recognizing transference and countertransference. *Journal of Psychosocial Nursing, 23,* 21–26.

Segal, D. (1997). Structured Interviewing and DSM Classification. In S. M. Turner & M. Hersen (Eds.), *Adult psychopatholgy and diagnosis* (3rd ed., pp. 24–57). New York: Wiley.

Sobel, E. F. (1980). Countertransference issues with the later life patient. *Contemporary Psychoanalysis, 16,* 211–222.

Soldz, S., Budman, S., Demby, A., & Merry, J. (1995). The relation of defensive style to personality pathology and the big five personality factors. *Journal of Personality Disorders, 9,* 356–370.

Solomon, J. D., Fallete, M., & Stevens, S. (1982). The psychologist as geriatric clinician. In T. Miller, C. Green, & R. Meagher (Eds.), *Handbook of clinical health psychology* (pp. 229–230). New York: Plenum.

Sprung, G. M. (1989). Transferential issues in working with older adults. *Social Casework, December,* 597–602.

Starker, S., Baker, L., Drummond, D., & Pankratz, L. (1991). Treating the "difficult" medical patient: Organizational strategies. *VA Practitioner, 8,* 91–97.

Stolorow, R. D. (1993). An intersubjective view of the therapeutic process. *Bulletin of the Menninger Clinic, 57,* 450–457.

Stone, M. H. (1993). *Abnormalities of personality: Within and beyond the realm of treatment.* New York: Norton.

Thompson, L., Gallagher, D., & Czirr, R. (1988). Personality disorders and outcome in the treatment of late-life depression. *Journal of Geriatric Psychiatry, 21,* 133–146.

Tyrer, P., & Seivewright, H. (1988). Studies of outcome. In P. Tyrer (Ed.), *Personality disorders: Diagnosis, management, and course* (pp. 119–136). London: Wright.

Westen, D. (1990). Towards a revised theory of borderline object relations: Contributions of empirical research. *International Journal of Psycho-Analysis, 71,* 661–693.

Westen, D. (1991). Cognitive-behavioral interventions in the psychoanalytic psychotherapy of borderline personality disorder. *Clinical Psychology Review, 11,* 211–230.

Wylie, H., & Wylie, M. (1987). The older analysand: Countertransference issues in psychoanalysis.
International Journal of Psycho-Analysis, 68, 343–352.

Zinn, W. M. (1988). Doctors have feelings too. *JAMA, 259,* 3296–3298.

CHAPTER 10

The Influence of Personality on Reactions of Older Adults to Physical Illness

MILTON VIEDERMAN, MD
Joan and Sanford I. Weill Medical College of Cornell University

This chapter addresses the issue of the way in which personality in older patients influences their experience and behavior when physically ill. Other chapters deal with theories of personality disorder, its stability and instability over time, and its relations to behavior and aging, among other subjects. This chapter provides a framework to aid clinicians in their confrontation with older physically ill patients. As such, it does not address the formal diagnostic criteria for personality disorder and does not distinguish between personality traits and personality disorders.

The early psychoanalytic literature focused on the relation between conflicts, personality, and physical illness, particularly as it was referred to in those days as "psychosomatic disorders." The evolution of the ideas about what was called psychosomatic medicine may be seen as analogous to the main theme of this chapter, namely, a movement away from the specificity in early conceptualization to a recognition of the uniqueness of each individual's experience. Alexander (Alexander & Szasz, 1952), often considered the father of psychoanalytic psychosomatic medicine, originally considered certain physical diseases (i.e., peptic ulcer, ulcerative colitis, hypertension, migraine, hyperthyroidism, rheumatoid arthritis, neurodermatitis) to have been primarily caused by intrapsychic conflict. Central to his thesis was the idea that specific conflicts led to specific diseases and there was a predictable relation between the specific conflict and the disease. Gradually he came to recognize that other factors participated in the causation of disease. Then it became apparent that the specific conflict was not always a predictor of specific disease. Moreover, it was necessary to distinguish between etiology and the precipitation of disease. Genetic and environmental rather than psychological factors were causal in many diseases. Ultimately, Alexander's specificity shifted to Engel's (1977) biopsychosocial model in which there were varying contributions emanating from the biological, psychological, and social domains. Dunbar (1947) was more specific in her view that specific personality types were associated with specific diseases. However, the clarity of these relations tended to dissolve under the impact of empirical evidence or the lack of it.

Nonetheless, the idea that psychogenic causes of a particular sort caused physical illness reemerged with the work of the French psychosomaticians; in particular, Marty and De M'Uzan (1962) developed the concept of *penseé operatoire*. They postulated that early in development the body was a vehicle for the expression of needs and feelings, and as development proceeded and as psychological processes became more developed, expression occurred through fantasy or symptom formation. Arrested development led to continuing expression through physical channels and ultimately to physical disease. This idea is closely related to the concept of alexithymia developed by Sifneos (1972) in this country. *Alexithymia,* essentially a personality construct, is defined as the inability to put feelings into words. Alexithymics are concrete in their thinking, have a poverty of fantasy life, and are often unaware of their feelings. Hence, they are generally not easily accessible to psychological intervention. Alexithymic individuals are much more likely to present with somatoform disorders, such as conversion and somatization, than with physical disease (Viederman, 1985). There has been a gradual movement away from the idea that psychological conflict or personality relate to specific physical disorders, although psychosocial factors may precipitate disease.

With decreased concern about etiology, interest then turned to the understanding of how personality affects response to illness, as mediated by the characteristic ways in which different personalities view the world. With such understanding, specific recommendations could be made as to how physicians might respond to patients of different character types.

Kahana and Bibring's (1964) work, although written almost 40 years ago, remains useful in its rich description of the dynamic underpinnings of character types, their manifestations in behavior in the medical setting and recommended management approaches. Indeed, this work is a tribute to the usefulness of the older psychoanalytically derived personality constructs that are close to experience.

Kahana and Bibring described seven character types: the dependent overdemanding (oral) personality; the orderly, controlled (compulsive) personality; the dramatizing, emotionally involved, captivating (hysterical) personality; the long-suffering, self-sacrificing (masochistic) patient; the guarded, querulous (paranoid) person; the patient with the feeling of superiority (narcissistic); and the patient who seems uninvolved and aloof (schizoid). The descriptive titles immediately suggest the nature of the patient's presentation and predominant concerns. For example, the authors emphasized that the needy, dependent patient transforms the anxiety accompanying illness into the wish for "boundless interest and abundant care, associated with a deep fear of being abandoned, helpless, and starving" (page 110). Based on this understanding, physicians will attempt to satisfy these needs for special attention in some measure, but they may also be required to set limits. A willingness by the treating staff to convey its readiness to care for the patient as completely as possible is essential. In contrast, the compulsive personality fears a loss of control over impulses with a need to master aggression and to be good. His effort is to be "responsible and orderly, and to suppress uncontrolled emotions" (page 112). Hence, a person of this sort finds the scientific medical approach to be a congenial one. He admires the doctor's application, his attention to detail, and the patient must be informed step-by-step of the physician's understanding and attention to treatment.

Friedman (1993) pointed out that some of the most useful personality descriptions in work with the medically ill are not easily subsumed by the formal diagnostic classification. For example, Groves (1978) described the "hateful patient," which includes dependent clingers, entitled demanders, manipulative help rejecters, and self-destructive deniers. In a similar way, Lipsitt (1970) described the "crock" and Breslau (1980) the "exaggeratedly helpless."

All of these conceptualizations describe persons frequently seen on the medical services. The recognition of these personality types not only leads to recommendations about management, but also permits the formulation of limited and achievable goals, thereby decreasing staff frustration in the struggle for what cannot be attained. Moreover, by describing the patient's behavior and showing the logic of this behavior as a product of life history, the consultant can often mute the intensity of the staff's hostile reaction.

Strain and Grossman (1975) developed a concept of "pseudo-hypochondriasis of the aged" that describes the behavior of many elderly patients. As individuals age, their social world becomes more and more constricted through deaths and decreased functional capacity. In this context, attention is increasingly focused on bodily processes and physical symptomatology that become vehicles for social exchange, particularly with physicians. The pseudohypochondriasis of the aged differs from more deeply ingrained hypochondriasis, which has been present as a lifelong symptom. Often, reassurance in this situation by the physician and the commitment to continue caring for the patient through regular contact diminishes anxious concerns about bodily function.

Friedman outlined some useful general approaches to the management of the medically ill elderly patient. First, he emphasized the need to be alert to the impact of organic changes on personality. Second, he cited what Mehlman (1977) called a narcissistic alliance with the patient, namely, an alliance directed toward the maintenance of self-esteem. The family must not be ignored and communication about the state of the patient and their need for support is essential. Another issue is that the increasing dependence of older people on others evokes latent conflicts about dependency. The dependency object frequently becomes the target of rage and resentment (Sadavoy, 1987a, 1987b). Finally, and a point that is emphasized in what follows, is the importance of establishing a coherent narrative for the patient that places the meaning of his response in the context of his life story (Viederman 1983).

It is also important to emphasize the idea that persistent behavioral traits, as well as consistent motivations, values, and modes of perceiving the world, are imbedded in the concept of personality. Although observable behavioral patterns are easier to categorize than subjective modes of perceiving the world, the latter are often determinants of behavior in situations of crisis.

The richness of psychiatric work lies in part in the enormous variations of human experience and behavior that often defy categorizations. The individuality of each patient demands special nuances in response. Diagnosis of personality disorders in *DSM–IV* is based almost exclusively on the external description of behavior. In many respects, this limits the usefulness of personality constructs as predictors of behavior in general and of response to physical illness. For this reason the chapter focuses on the special and individual meanings in response to illness and later describes a specific psychotherapeutic intervention, the Psychodynamic Life Narrative (Viederman, 1983; Viederman & Perry, 1980).

The following is an example of the subtle influence of the mixture of personal meanings and the personality as it affects a patient's response to physical illness in old age.

CASE I

The patient was an 86-year-old man, a highly successful artist, who described his life as having been charmed. He came from a wealthy background and had great talent that was recognized early on. He was married to a nondemanding, giving, and supportive woman interested in family who was perfectly happy to ignore the fact that he was, as he called himself, a "sexual miscreant." This meant he had many sexual relationships with women, each lasting a significant period of time, none of which manifestly interfered with his marriage. These relationships ended amicably. He had a natural charm, a mischievous eye, and at 86 was cognitively intact with excellent memory. As he put it, he was constantly gratified in his vanity, as people asked him to speak and responded to him with admiration and pleasure.

When the patient was younger, he decided that age 80 was a good round number and that he would choose to die—perhaps kill himself. He did not want to experience a decline in his powers. He was surprised at the present time, now having passed this venerable age, to discover himself so vigorous, so alert, and so able to continue in his artistic endeavors. He was clear in his affirmation that if he were to experience decline, then he would kill himself. Although the patient had been referred to evaluate depression, he was not at all depressed. He was enjoying life.

Six years earlier he discovered that he had nonsymptomatic cancer. He handled this well, bolstered as he was by his continued professional success.

However, he did have a nagging problem. For the past 20 years he was involved in a love relationship with a woman collaborator 40 years his junior. She had a traumatic childhood background that left her vulnerable. Though talented, she had become dependent on him emotionally and materially. He was very concerned about what would happen to her when he died. This concern echoed a fundamental attitude he had maintained throughout life after his mother died when he was 10 years old: He took a supportive, caregiving role with people. He was extremely pained and troubled by the thought that she would be alone and helpless during his decline and after his demise. His identification with the helpless waif reflected his early experience.

This patient illustrates how a benign narcissistic attitude, his "vanity," which hurt neither himself nor others, was reflected in his highly valued artistic activity and the pleasure he received from the admiration he evoked in others. This was the experiential centerpiece for his view of illness and ultimately of death. Essential to his sense of himself, to his values, to his anticipation of continued existence, was the picture of himself as a productive creature. This was, in part, a defense, a need to flee the fear of gradual deterioration that had accompanied his mother's prolonged illness. In this situation an aspect of his personality, his vanity, made it imperative that even in illness, decisions about life and death should remain in his control. These would hinge on maintaining his intellectual and artistic powers. His area of vulnerability lay in his need to protect the woman who was important in his life. His failure to achieve his ego ideal, to care for others, made him narcissistically vulnerable.

THE SPECIAL ISSUE OF MEANINGS EMBEDDED
IN PERSONALITY STYLE

More important than personality style itself in response to illness are the special meanings attached to illness, functional loss, and treatment as they reflect vulnerabilities and strengths developed through early life experience (Viederman 1983, 1974a, 1974b; Viederman & Hymowitz, 1988). People are much more different than they are alike, whether they are obsessive, histrionic, or narcissistic. Indeed, it is the enormous variability in human behavior that makes the work of the psychodynamic psychiatrist so fascinating.

There is, however, a general dictum that has some pertinence to illness. In the context of the regressive forces of physical illness, a situation in which dependent care is required and trust must be placed in giving figures, it is often found that individuals who have had poor early nurturant experiences adapt more poorly, experience greater distress, and in particular have significantly more difficulty in a hospital setting (Viederman, 1974a). As with any generalization, this is contradicted by certain patients who reveal discontinuities in development, which means the development of highly adaptive coping patterns that might have seemed unlikely given their early traumatic life experiences. This is more the exception than the rule.

Some personality designations, such as narcissistic personality disorder, seem to have more pertinence than others to expectable patterns of response to physical illness. Borderline personality disorder seems to be less in evidence, perhaps as a reflection of an "aging-out" process. However, in some situations, the intense regressive demands of physical illness do evoke primitive defensive reactions in borderline patients that may create havoc on the ward.

Friedman and Lister (1987) also emphasized how the process of aging inevitably encompasses a succession of losses, each requiring some resolution through mourning. If these losses are experienced as profound narcissistic injuries, damaging self-esteem, difficulties, and "compensatory narcissistic reactions" (e.g., entitlement, jealousy, grandiosity, and illusion of self-sufficiency), then hoarding, depression, and hypochondriasis may ensue (Cath, 1965; Levin, 1977). Certainly self-esteem and the need to find value in themselves are important aspects of how well individuals will negotiate both age, physical illness, and decreasing functional capacity.[1] The following anecdote illustrates this theme.

CASE 2

The patient was a 74-year-old married lawyer, referred for evaluation of depression after a complicated medical course requiring a 6-month hospitalization. It had begun with ventricular fibrillation requiring the placement of an automatic defibrillator, followed by a bypass operation with replacement of a mitral valve, tracheotomy, and ultimately an infection in the sternum that led to a long period of respiratory treatment and rehabilitation. His residual symptomatology involved difficulties that awakened him at night with fear of death. The illness had affected a dramatic change in his life.

Before his illness he had prided himself on his continuing vigor and excellent physical form. His past history had included a dissecting aneurysm that was treated successfully with surgery. His wife, generally disinter-

---

[1]Hamburg (1974) and Visotsky, Hamburg, Gross, and Lebovits (1961) have usefully delineated general criteria for evaluating effectiveness of coping in physical illness. These include keeping distress within manageable limits, maintaining a sense of personal worth and self-esteem, restoring relationships with significant others, enhancing prospects for recovery of bodily functions, increasing possibility of working out a personally valued and socially acceptable situation after maximum physical recovery, and maintaining pleasure and security sources.

ested in sex before, now avoided it altogether; he still maintained sexual desire.

There had been considerable irritability on the patient's part in the context of negotiating the initial appointment. At the beginning of this first session I brought this up. He had incorrectly felt that I was impatient. I had seemed to be conveying that I was a busy practitioner with little time for him. This had not been my experience and I asked him whether this was a familiar experience. He responded by speaking of his relationship with his former partner, an extremely powerful man and the friend of major political figures. They had established a partnership to their mutual profit because the partner was gregarious, histrionic, and brought in many clients, whereas the patient was a careful, obsessional, and competent person. Yet the patient felt that he had paid a heavy price by being subservient and felt diminished in the relationship. He had retired 10 years earlier. The firm had been turned over to his son. It was then that he turned to physical activity.

At the end of the first session I offered the following narrative (Viederman, 1983): You have come from a family anxious and concerned about money and law was imposed on you by your domineering mother as a safe conduit to the future. Though you established yourself very successfully and have done well, for years you were subservient to this partner and felt resentment about his domination, just as you did with your mother. Ten years ago you were liberated and established a good sense of yourself, not only as a success in business but also as a vigorous man and an accomplished tennis player. This illness has come as a terrible blow to your physical being and your sense of masculinity and it has damaged your sense of worth. The patient responded by saying that this assessment was exactly on target.

In the second session, he revealed that he had been relieved of his depression but was preoccupied with something else. For many years he had a close relationship with his executive secretary, who maintained an interest in him. Though 25 years younger than he, she had a great deal of affection for him and gave signals that she was interested in a sexual relationship. He had never been unfaithful to his attentive but unaffectionate wife and he recognized that he had begun to have fantasies about a sexual relationship with this other person. I commented that these fantasies were quite understandable, which relieved him because in his obsessional and self-condemnatory way he felt the desire to be inappropriate.

In the third session, the patient revealed that he had spent a day with this woman, and although they had fondled one another, they had decided that they should go no further in a sexual relationship given the circumstances of their lives. This seemed to him to be a reasonable solution and he was gratified by the affection that they expressed toward one another and with the idea that they would have a continued platonic relationship.

The patient clearly fell into the category of an obsessional character style, though he does not meet the criteria of Obsessive Personality Disorder. Although the style was manifested in his behavior, the description of him as obsessional in no way encapsulated his struggle with physical illness.

The special meaning of the illness as it pertained to the impairment of the patient's sense of masculinity had been threatened by both his mother and his partner. This was the special meaning of the illness that had been distressing to him. And, when the significance was appropriately communicated, he felt relieved of his depression and tentatively acted or acted-out on a basis of the renewed strength that he felt, as if to confirm his masculinity, only then to recognize the potential difficulties with this behavior. Meaning was an intervening variable, and the appropriate communication of this meaning led to relief (Viederman, 1984). Respect was clearly consistent with his obsessional character, but the experience was not dominated by his personality style.

THE SPECIAL PROBLEM OF THE DEMENTED PATIENT

Limitation in the use of personality constructs as predictors of behavior are nowhere more evident than in patients with dementia, as is evident in the general hospital where there has been a gradual increase in the average age of the population. The following is a prototypic case.

CASE 3

A 94-year-old woman is found on the floor of her apartment confused and dehydrated. The apartment has not been cleaned recently and is in disarray. Neighbors indicate that the bills have not been paid. The patient has been lost on occasion and unable to find her way home. After admission to the hospital, rehydration, and the treatment of the expectable urinary tract infection, the patient appears to return to a homeostasis with significant cognitive impairment. Medical evaluation reveals no primary source, and Alzheimer's dementia is diagnosed. The patient can no longer care for herself, but she absolutely refuses nursing home placement and adamantly insists on returning home even though she does not have the resources to support the 24-hour care that she requires. In the past she had rapidly discharged home health aides.

An examination of the histories of these patients makes it clear that they encompass a wide range of personality styles and disorders. The ferocious demand for independence that dominates these women (many now widowed) may not have characterized them before. In this situation, context supersedes personality style or disorder in determining their behavior. There is a desperation and a pathos in the patient's request to return home as she seeks to find a wall of familiarity and a barrier to stimuli that she cannot integrate. Although cognitive impairment may accentuate previous personality traits, this is not found universally. The paranoia associated with dementia, for example, may occur in people who have no history of a suspicious or paranoid view of the world, and rather represents an aspect of the brain dysfunction itself.

SPECIFIC PERSONALITY DISORDERS

Although personality constructs are limited in organizing thinking about the reaction of elderly people to physical illness, three personality categories do present particular problems: the narcissistic character, the paranoid character, and the schizoid character.

The Narcissistic Personality Disorder

CASE 4

Consultation was requested on an 89-year-old man hospitalized for pneumonia and requiring a nasogastric tube for feeding. He was said to be an extremely demanding person, dissatisfied with all aspects of hospital care, and had evoked very negative feelings in the staff by his constant complaints. He was reluctant to have the tube removed for fear that he would not have adequate nutrition and even requested a percutaneous endoscopic gastrostomy (PEG).

Having inferred in discussion with the resident that the patient was a narcissistic character, I responded to his question of what my title was by indicating that I was a professor. Clearly status was a central issue. He proceeded to establish his credential by indicating that he had been a delegate to the United Nations for a South American country during a previous regime (a significant exaggeration). This was followed by a long and furious diatribe on how he had been treated with disrespect in the hospital, and dealt with "like a Puerto Rican." When I indicated that I could understand his need and desire for dignity and respect, the patient relaxed and proceeded with a litany of complaints about how he was required to sit up for 2 or 3 hours a day when only 1½ hours were possible for him, how people did not respond to his calls for help, and so on. He was enraged at the insistence that his tube be removed. I acknowledged this but emphasized the desirability of his taking food by mouth, which would be more effective. He agreed, but outlined in detail what he considered to be the nurses' responsibilities in monitoring his food intake.

In response to my inquiry about his occupation, he indicated that he had been the head of a real estate business. I emphasized that as an executive it was natural for him to control things. Being a patient in the hospital, helpless and out of control, with people who did not know him was very difficult—especially for such a man as he. The patient was appeased when I emphasized that his being accustomed to power and control in his world created more difficulty for him in such a situation than would be the case with individuals who were used to less control to over their experiences. Each intervention of this sort diminished the tension and anger, although it was clear that he was exaggerating his exalted status and was defending against a damaged self-image. A discussion with his wife revealed that his narcissistic character was well-entrenched.

The threat to this man's integrity and his confrontation with possible death and decline filled him with anxiety because it so threatened his ideal and vulnerable representation of himself. In order to engage him, it was important to solidify his self-esteem, to convey respect, and to acknowledge his need for dignity. This became a vehicle for facilitating collaboration with the staff.

There are times when a personality trait, such as narcissism, may be used in an aggressively defensive way. Take the following patient, for example.

CASE 5

The patient was a 96-year-old man, a former physician who contended that he had an impressive previous curriculum vitae. He variously called himself a neurologist, a neurosurgeon, and a neuropathologist. History from others strongly suggested that he had a narcissistic personality disorder but had functioned well. He was now demented, having been found filthy and incontinent in his apartment. In a previous examination by a resident, he revealed severe impairment in recent memory and orientation, although he rapidly refused participation and became aggressive as the exam continued. When I asked about his professional career, he arrogantly indicated that I should read his curriculum vitae. He stated that he had no knowledge of who I was. He had never heard of me. He persisted in emphasizing the contributions he had made in medicine and remained arrogant and contemptuous.

His vague awareness of his serious impairment was a narcissistic injury and intensified a narcissistic and aggressive refusal to deal with even the most benign inquiries about his current state.

The Schizoid Patient

Schizoid patients have special problems in their adaptation to life in a general hospital, although this is not specific to the geriatric age group. Their very need to protect themselves from others they see as threats makes either the constant intrusions or the need to share a room with other patients painful experiences.

These patients press to leave the hospital quickly because they find the experience intolerable.

CASE 6

A 72-year-old MIT graduate whose life had been dominated by extreme passivity and self-doubt had managed to maintain an isolated homeostasis until he was forced to leave his job at the post office some years before. Although he had diabetes with relatively minor complications, he orchestrated his physical symptomatology and embraced the sick role in such a way as to seek a dependency adaptation. He had taken little responsibility for his life and had always had the appearance and the psychological attributes of an old man. Yet even these wishes conflicted with his intolerance of the intrusive hospital experience and he pressed for discharge. His transfer to a single room helped to mute his pressing need for a protective bubble.

The Problem of Paranoia

One is often confronted in the general hospital with elderly paranoid patients. A history obtained from someone who has known the patient over time may help to determine whether the patient is chronically psychotic, or if the person has a paranoid character disorder. Occasionally, paranoia appears in old age for the first time. Under these circumstances, the clinician must determine whether or not it is part of a dementing process.

Two anecdotes illustrate this problem.

CASE 7

A 67-year-old man was admitted with mild Parkinson's disease and dementia with severe cognitive impairment associated with paranoid delusions. He believed that invisible marks had been placed on him and were evident to others. Further, he stated that there was another person using his name and spreading rumors about his inappropriate sexual behavior. He was uncertain in his conviction about these delusions.

On examination, the patient was friendly, cooperative, and aware of his cognitive impairment, emphasizing that it was improving, although in fact he remained severely impaired, disoriented, with very limited short-term memory, an inability to spell "world" backward or repeat three digits backward, or to draw a coherent clock. He remained friendly and cooperative, although earlier in the hospitalization he had torn out an intravenous line in a state of disorganization.

The paranoia was an extension of his cognitive defect, his difficulty in integrating and interpreting his experiences of the world. His cooperative, even trusting relationship with his physicians was striking.

CASE 8

An 81-year-old woman insisted that her relatives had stolen the fortune that she had brought with her from Europe. She had previously been a friendly and coherent woman, but now in the context of increasing poverty, both materially and socially, she interpreted her personal world as hostile and complained that her relatives were taking her money. She was cognitively intact. In other respects she related well to those around her. Her paranoid stance in old age reflected her defense against awareness of her confined social and material world and was a projection of her experience of continuing physical and material loss.

CONCLUSIONS

In my view, there are important limitations in the use of conventional descriptive personality constructs for predictions of the responses of elderly patients confronted with medical illness. There are those, particularly in the research community who understandably seek regularities in behavior and precise definitions of disorders that have clear boundaries in order to do systematic research. Clinicians trained in the psychoanalytic tradition are more likely to search for the individuality and uniqueness of each patient. Moreover, many personality disorders, as defined in the *DSM–IV*, are less useful indicators of treatment approaches than those of the Axis I disorders. The limitation of formal diagnostic categories of personality disorders are perhaps nowhere more evident than in work with the aged patient confronting medical illness. Here, as elsewhere, one is compelled to seek the inner experience of the patient, his past experience in the world, and the way it affects his construction of his current view of reality. This search for the special and unique experience of the patient, for the individualized meanings in response to illness, is not only a source of fascination but invites interventions designed to undo the isolation of the seriously ill patient and to alleviate his distress.

REFERENCES

Alexander, F., & Szasz, T. S. (1952). The psychosomatic approach in medicine. In F. Alexander & H. Ross (Eds.), *Dynamic psychiatry* (pp. 369–400). Chicago: University of Chicago Press.
Breslau, L. (1980). The faltering therapeutic perspective toward narcissistically wounded institutionalized aged. *Journal of Geriatric Psychiatry, 13,* 193–206.
Cath, F. H. (1965). Some dynamics of middle and later years: A study of depletion and restitution. In M. Berezin & F. H. Cath (Eds.), *Geriatric psychiatry: Grief, loss and emotional disorder in the aging process* (pp. 21–72). New York: International Universities Press.
Dunbar, F. (1947). *Mind and body.* New York: Random House.

Engel, G. L. (1977). The need for a new medical model: A challenge for biomedicine. *Science, 196,* 129–136.

Friedman, R. S. (1993). When the patient intrudes on the treatment: The aging of personality types in medical management. *Journal of Geriatric Psychiatry, 26*(2), 149–177.

Friedman, R. S., & Lister, P. (1987). The current status of psychodynamic formulation. *Psychiatry, 50,* 126–141.

Groves, J. (1978). Taking care of the hateful patient. *New England Journal of Medicine, 298,* 883–887.

Hamburg, D. (1974). Coping behavior in life-threatening circumstances. *Psychotherapy and Psychosomatics, 23,* 13–25.

Kahanna, R. J., & Bibring, G. L. (1964). Personality types in medical management. In N. E. Zinberg (Ed.), *Psychiatry and medical practice in the general hospital* (pp. 108–123). New York: Internatioal Universities Press.

Levin, S. (1977). Normal psychology of the aging process, revisited—II: Introduction. *Journal of Geriatric Psychiatry, 10,* 3–7.

Lipsitt, D. R. (1970). Medical and psychological characteristics of "crocks." *International Journal of Psychiatry in Medicine, 1,* 15–25.

Marty P., & De M'Uzan, M. (1962). La Pensée opiratoire. Intervention sur le rapport de M. Fain et Ch. David [Operational thoughts. Discussion of the report of M. Fain and Ch. David]. (1963) *Revue française de psychanalyse, 27*(6), 345–356.

Mehlman, R. D. (1977). Normal psychology of the aging process, revisited—II: Discussion. *Journal of Geriatric Psychiatry, 10,* 53–60.

Sadavoy, J. (1987a). Character disorders in the elderly: An overview. In J. Sadavoy & M. Leszcz (Eds.), *Treating the elderly with psychotherapy* (pp. 175–229). Madison, CT: International Universities Press.

Sadavoy, J. (1987b). Character pathology in the elderly. *Journal of Geriatric Psychiatry, 20,* 165–178.

Sifneos, P. E. (1972). *Short-term psychotherapy and emotional crisis.* Cambridge, MA: Harvard University Press.

Strain, J., & Grossman, S. (1975). Psychological reactions to medical illness and hospitalization. In J. Strain & S. Grossman (Eds.), *Psychological care of the medically ill* (pp. 138–148). New York: Appleton-Century-Crofts.

Viederman, M. (1974a). Adaptive and maladaptive regression in hemodialysis. *Psychiatry, 37,* 68–77.

Viederman, M. (1974b). The search for meaning in renal transplant. *Psychiatry, 37,* 283–290.

Viederman, M. (1983). The psychodynamic life narrative: A psychotherapeutic intervention useful in crisis situations. *Psychiatry, 46,* 236–246.

Viederman, M. (1984). The active dynamic interview and the supportive relationship. *Comprehensive Psychiatry, 25,* 147–157.

Viederman, M. (1985). Somatoform disorders. In R. Michels (Ed.), *Psychiatry* (Vol. 1, chap. 35). Philadelphia: Basic Books.

Viederman, M., & Hymowitz, P. (1988). A developmental-psychodynamic model for diabetic control. *General Hospital Psychiatry, 10,* 34–40.

Viederman, M., & Perry, S. (1980). Use of a psychodynamic life narrative in the treatment of depression in the physically ill. *General Hospital Psychiatry, 3,* 177–185.

Visotsky, H. M., Hamburg, D., Gross, M. E., & Lebovits, B. Z. (1961). Coping behaviors under extreme stress: Observations of patients with severe poliomyelitis. *Archives of General Psychiatry, 5,* 423–448.

CHAPTER 11

Neuropsychological Contributions to Differential Diagnosis of Personality Disorder in Old Age

JOHN H. MINER, PsyD
Harvard Medical School

This chapter concerns personality change in old age, as opposed to actual personality disorders. Although personality disorders do exist and can be modified by stress in old age, there are both subtle and obvious manifestations of personality change as the brain ages, secondary to neurologic permutations. Personality change often precedes physical symptoms of brain disease and can serve as a prodromal warning. It should be emphasized, however, that the research literature has generally shown personality to be stable over the life span into old age. The changes described are the exception rather than the rule.

The fourth edition of the *Diagnostic and Statistical Manual of Mental Disorders* (*DSM–IV;* American Psychiatric Association, 1994) differentiates between personality disorder and "personality change due to a general medical condition or due to dementia" (p. 171). It states that personality disorder is a long-standing psychiatric condition in which onset is in adolescence or early adulthood and is stable over time, leading to distress or impairment in social, occupational, or other important areas of functioning. It is manifested in at least two of the following areas: cognition, affectivity, interpersonal functioning, or impulse control. It is important to note that the *DSM* does recognize that individuals may not come to clinical attention until relatively late in life, with exacerbation following the loss of significant supporting persons or previously stabilizing social situations (e.g., a job). It nevertheless emphasizes the need to distinguish between the development of a change in personality in later life versus one due to the direct physiological effects of a medical illness (e.g., mood disorder due to brain tumor, with depressive features, or personality change secondary to delirium or dementia). When due to a medical condition, the personality disturbance represents a change from the individual's previous characteristic personality pattern. Common manifestations of such change include affective instability, poor impulse control, outbursts of aggression or rage grossly out of proportion to a precipitating psychosocial stressor, marked apathy, suspiciousness, or paranoid ideation. Various subtypes have been designated: labile, disinhibited, aggressive, apathetic, paranoid, as well as "other, combined, and unspecified." Although it shares the term *personality* with the Axis II Personality Disorders, this diagnosis is coded on Axis I and is distinguished by its specific etiology, different phenomenology, and more variable onset and course.

NEUROANATOMICAL SUBSTRATES OF PERSONALITY FUNCTIONING

In the development of personality, contributing emotional and cognitive factors are mediated by neural circuitry and transmitters in the brain. A person's ability to manage feelings or action is affected by the functioning of those brain areas that are the physical substrates of abilities to remember; to perceive the subtleties of social interaction; to develop, implement, and regulate a plan for action; and to modulate the experience and expression of affect (Hodel-Malinofsky, 1994). For the sake of clarity, the areas might be divided into cortical and subcortical, although in actuality no sharp division exists, as efferent and afferent projections link the two. Moreover, brain–behavior correlates are not so precise, and variability does occur.

Frontal Lobes

In the human cortex, the frontal lobes play the major role in controlling behavior and organizing responses to stimuli from the environment. The frontal lobes receive input from other cortical and subcortical structures and integrate the incoming information before regulating a response. These lobes are anatomically the largest in the human brain and are composed of several parts, the largest being the dorsolateral and the orbitomedial areas. The dorsolateral frontal cortex mediates surveillance of the environment for drive-relevant stimuli, attention, spatial orientation, and emotional arousal. The orbitomedial frontal region regulates the acquisition and storage of emotional associations to stimuli, including social restraints (Bear, 1983). Damage to either part leads to a different personality syndrome. A dorsolateral lesion creates a condition of apathy, dulled affect, and lack of spontaneity. Just the opposite, orbitomedial dysfunction is characterized by behavioral disinhibition, emotional lability, and indifference to social decorum (Lishman, 1987). Decreased concern can ensue from either condition, resulting in impairment of activities of daily living and personal hygiene. Cognitively, people suffering from frontal lobe dysfunction may have difficulty with any number of functions, including self-observation and monitoring, impulse control, abstract reasoning, development and execution of a complex plan of action, sustained attention, and ability to filter distractions. Interference with attention may be caused by either hyper- or hypoarousal, leading to agitation and distractibility on the one hand, and anergia and abulia on the other. The lobes are functionally asymmetrical, as suggested by lesions to the left side, which reduce verbal fluency, and those to the right, which release talking without regard to appropriateness or interest to others (Kolb & Wishaw, 1985).

A variety of clinical states can produce frontal lobe cognitive and emotional change. Some of the more common conditions affecting the elderly are cerebral atrophy of normal aging, stroke, Alzheimer's disease, and Pick's disease. In addition, other conditions affecting other parts of the brain or metabolism of neurotransmitters can produce frontal-like symptoms of apathy. In the elderly, two common causes are Parkinson's disease and thyroid dysfunction.

Temporal Lobes

The temporal lobes play a central role in the processing of information as they mediate memory functions. Together with their limbic connections to subcortical structures (particularly the hippocampus and the amygdala), the temporal lobes lend affective tone to sensory input, that is, associating them with motivational or emotional significance. This function is crucial for learning because stimuli become associated with their positive, negative, or neutral consequences, and behavior is modified accordingly (Kolb & Wishaw, 1985). The lobes are functionally asymmetric in the processing of information, with verbal memory lateralized to the left and visual memory to the right. Damage to the right temporal lobe produces impairment in the formation of new visual memories, whereas insult to the left can cause impaired verbal recall and word-finding difficulty. Older memory traces are more resistant to degradation, although these, also, gradually fade as deterioration of the lobes proceeds in dementing conditions. Difficulties with naming and memory can lead to such emotional reactions as irritability, depression, insecurity, and either dependence on others or avoidance. On occasion, paranoia may emerge when the afflicted believe that other people are deceiving them, as they cannot remember what has occurred. Personality disturbances identical to those accompanying frontal lesions may occur, but will more commonly be associated with intellectual and neurological defects. Chronic temporal lobe lesions have been associated with emotional instability and aggressive misconduct. They also contribute to an increased risk of psychotic disturbances similar to schizophrenia. Depersonalization and dissociation may occur, as well as a disturbance in sexual function. Epileptic phenomena are common with temporal lobe lesions.

Parietal Lobes

In comparison with other cortical areas, the parietal lobes have less clear boundaries. Their functions are accordingly quite complex. They regulate the processing of somatic sensations and perceptions, as well as the integration of sensory
input from the somatic, visual, and auditory regions. In their "cross-modal
matching" of input from various thalamic and cortico-cortical connections, the
parietal lobes mediate functions that relate to such cognitive activities as reading, word finding from a visual stimulus (confrontation naming), writing, math-
ematical reasoning, spatial orientation, recognizing an object from touch, as
well as control of limb movement that requires accurate internal representation
of moving body parts and changes in their spatial positions. Because a person's
behavior is influenced by the integration of sensory stimuli to produce a unified
perception of the world, lesions to the parietal lobes are associated with a per-
plexing array of complex cognitive and emotional disturbances. The nature of
the deficits depends on the lateralization of the lesion. Left hemisphere parietal
lobe lesions can produce deficits in language and number sense, motor apraxia,
alexia in association with agraphia, finger agnosia, and right–left orientation.
Right hemisphere lesions are associated with disturbances in visuospatial perception and drawing, topographical orientation, body image, and sometimes facial recognition. Luria (1973) described a group of patients with such lesions:

> They firmly believed that at one and the same time they were in Moscow and also
> in another town. They suggested that they had left Moscow and gone to the other
> town, but having done so, they were still in Moscow where an operation had been
> performed on their brain. Yet they found nothing contradictory about these con-
> clusions. Integrity of the verbal-logical processes in these patients, despite the pro-
> found disturbance of their direct self-perception and self-evaluation, led to a char-
> acteristic overdevelopment of speech, to verbosity, which bore the character of
> empty reasoning and masked their true defects (p. 168).

In some cases, the disability may be ignored or denied ("anosognosia"). Such
denial is most often accompanied by hemiattentional neglect of the contralat-
eral side of space or of the body. Neurologically based denial is extremely difficult to overcome, as it produces a personality change of blithe indifference. In
extreme cases, paranoia can ensue, whereby others are perceived as lying to
them about their deficits.

Hemispheric Lateralization

In addition to differentiation according to lobe, the lateralization of brain has
produced hemispheric asymmetries, resulting in specialization for cognitive
modalities as well as emotional states. The left hemisphere has been associated
with several characteristic functions affecting personality: Its processing is cognitive and neutral; its emotional-attentional bias is unconcerned and inattentive;

its cognitive preference is temporal, sequential, and analytic; its focus is on the central field of vision and intentional; and its response style is reflective. Lesion to the left hemisphere generally causes catastrophic reactions characterized by fearfulness and depression. In contrast, the right hemisphere has very different characteristics: Receptively, it is sensitive to emotional material, such as visual social cues (e.g., facial emotion) and nonverbal auditory cues of emotion (e.g., tone of voice); it is concerned and vigilant in its emotional-attentional bias, allowing for a more immediate or powerful affective reaction to stimuli, characterized, for example, by greater autonomic responses; it processes spatial information simultaneously and holistically; it is attentive to data in the peripheral fields and is incidental in its learning; its response style tends to be more spontaneous and impulsive. As a result of a lesion to the right hemisphere, a person is more likely to experience indifference. It should be understood that a simple left/right distinction of catastrophic experiencing versus indifference belies the true complexity underlying brain functioning, and one must take into account both hemispheric and lobar specialization. In addition, a third dimension of brain anatomy and functioning, the subcortex, must be considered.

Subcortical Structures

At the subcortical level, the limbic system, basal ganglia, and white matter have been implicated in the functioning of personality. The limbic structures were referred to earlier in relation to the temporal lobes, to which they are closely connected. The limbic system is the border between the cortex and the brainstem and includes the hippocampus, amygdala, septum, mammillary bodies, olfactory bulbs, cingulate gyrus, and fornix. This system is the physical substrate of the moods and drives forming the basis of temperament, including such primitive feelings and impulses as sexual drive, rage/fight, and terror/flight. The limbic system also plays a critical role in memory, which permits a person to learn from experience, to connect emotional associations to behavior, and to regulate survival behaviors. Lesions in the limbic system can produce dramatic changes in the arousal and expression of emotions and drives.

The basal ganglia comprise the putamen, globus pallidus, caudate, lenticular nucleus, and amygdala. In addition to their role in the extrapyramidal motor system, they serve an integrative role for the limbic system, facilitating coherent and goal-oriented action and emotional expression, and inhibiting unwanted responses (Modell, Mountz, & Beresford, 1990). The amygdala is associated with the primitive feelings of anger and fear. A compromise in functions of the basal ganglia can lead not only to disordered movement but also to impairments of personality and cognition, including reduced insight, decreased judgment, and impulsivity—changes similar to those seen with orbitofrontal lesions (Welch & Bear, 1990). Obsessive-compulsive disorder, as well as craving and loss of control in addictions, have been associated with neurophysiologic dysfunction in pathways connecting the basal ganglia, striatum, thalamus, and cortex. Subcortical white matter consists of neuronal axons covered with myelin sheathing, thereby lending a characteristic pallor. Destruction of myelin and resultant decrease in conduction velocity occur in such conditions as multiple sclerosis, AIDS, dementia, diffuse axonal injury in brain trauma, alcoholism, ischemia, and to some extent normal aging. Symptoms of damage here include both cognitive and emotional change: inattention, impaired memory retrieval, slowed thinking, word-finding difficulty, impaired problem solving, apathy, depression, and irritability.

The diencephalon (thalamus and hypothalamus) and brain stem control basic functions of arousal, sleep, appetite/thirst, breathing, and sensory reception. Focal lesions here may produce rapidly progressive change in cognition and emotion. Features similar to those seen in frontal lobe lesion may occur, including disinhibition, indifference, carelessness, and fatuous euphoria. Insight into the changes is said to be better preserved than in frontal lobe dysfunction. Emotional lability and sudden violent outbursts are typical. In bilateral lesions to diencephalon and upper brain stem, pseudobulbar palsy occurs, which is characterized by extreme emotional lability. A person laughs or cries excessively to trivial stimuli, but denies experiencing the degree of emotion displayed and may be distressed over this inability to control reactions.

NEUROPSYCHOLOGICAL COMPONENTS OF PERSONALITY

In order to understand better how organic change contributes to personality change in aging, it is important first to clarify the most important cognitive functions affecting individuals' perceptions of and interactions with the world and themselves. They are attention, visual representation, verbal mediation, memory, and executive control.

Attention

Attention is the most basic factor affecting the amount of incoming stimuli on which perceptions and thoughts are formed and emotional reactions are based. Without the ability to attend, a person cannot process information accurately and therefore can become confused, disoriented, and subject to false impressions. Attention can be subdivided into several types. At the most elementary level, it is auditory or visual, depending on the modality of the stimuli involved. It can be relatively brief (i.e., a few seconds) or sustained (i.e., several minutes). Sustained attention allows a person to maintain focus on a particular activity and goal. Divided attention permits a person to carry on several tasks at a time and to keep track of both simultaneously. Selective attention is the ability to focus on a particular task or target and filter out distracting stimuli. Concentration is that type of attention that also involves working memory, such as when a person is asked to hold information in short-term storage and simultaneously manipulate it (e.g., digits backward). Sequential attention involves accurate processing of information in a linear series of successive data (e.g., digits forward or chained commands). Problems of attention can derive from impairment in any one or any combination of types, with most older people having difficulty with the more demanding aspects (divided, concentration, selective). Disruptions to attention are a common characteristic in such Axis I psychiatric conditions as schizophrenia, depression, and anxiety, as well as schizotypal personality disorder (Siever, 1985; Siever & Davis, 1991.)

Visual Perception

Assuming adequate ability to attend to incoming stimuli, visual perception is one step more differentiated, involving how a person perceives and comes to understand the external world through visual information. Visual properties of an object must be apprehended, such as contour, size, and color, before it can be identified and dealt with in a meaningful way. In addition, visual relations among parts of an object or among various objects must be discerned and integrated accurately. For example, the top of a stove is a complicated pattern of a combination of shapes, each part with its particular purpose. When visual perception is disrupted, the array becomes meaningless and confusing. Similarly, social interactions comprise a series of many simultaneous events involving both verbal and visual stimuli. Without accurate perception of visual cues, a person's view of the interpersonal world may become idiosyncratic and distorted, thereby limiting effective social intercourse. Problems perceiving visual information accurately have been found in most of the major psychiatric disorders, including schizophrenia, paranoia, depression, and manic depression, and are also present in borderline personality disorder (O'Leary, Brouwers, Gardner, & Cowdry, 1991).

Verbal Mediation

Verbal mediation is frequently used in problem solving to talk one's way through a series of steps or strategies. It is a way of organizing and keeping track of an approach to a task, used most frequently in multistep, sequential activities. In addition to problem solving, verbal mediation is used as a mnemonic by which information is encoded, stored, and subsequently retrieved. Developing semantic associations to data, using acronyms, or tagging and clustering data by categories are three common examples of verbal mediation as a memory tool. Processing visual information through verbal channels is another facet very important for effective social communication. Without verbal mediation, a person's capacities to engage in more complex and intellectually demanding activities may become more limited, and they may become slower, less secure, and possibly more dependent on others to solve problems. In more catastrophic situations, such as stroke involving Broca's area, deficits in expressive language function are almost always accompanied by serious depression. In subtler ways, verbal mediation and use of words have significant implications for borderline personality disorder, where words may lack utility for encoding or communicating meaning; instead, they function more concretely, to manipulate other people in an effort to regulate an unstable sense of self (Robbins, 1989). Moreover, inadequate use of inner speech may partly account for the lack of memory consolidation and poor self-regulatory functions seen in more primitive personalities, including borderline, histrionic, and antisocial (Miller, 1987; Watt, 1990).

Memory

Memory itself is an extremely important cognitive function in personality functioning, for without it a person reacts to each event as if it were the first time, without any prior experience or associations. Memory allows a person to draw on past experience to solve problems and to regard events in the environment as continuous and hence logical, rather than mere random, isolated happenings. Consequences of events can be remembered, obviating the need for repeated trial and error. Memory thus provides the connection between past and present that permits a personality to evolve in an integrated way. Without memory, a person loses a sense of meaningful flow of daily events; responsibilities are neglected and tasks left unfinished or undone. Hence, personality change often accompanies memory impairment. Evidence of such personality change might include greater dependence on family members, avoidance of social situations outside the family, emotional reactivity to forgetting, and sometimes paranoia. Memory problems have been found to occur in borderline personality disorder (Judd & Ruff, 1993; O'Leary et al., 1991), where they may contribute to the difficulties the borderline patient experiences in maintaining a continuous sense of self and others and in using the past to anticipate future consequences.

Executive Functions

Executive functions include planning, impulse control, and regulation of attention to complex tasks involving shifting of set. They are expressed in such activities as problem solving wherein a person must induce from feedback whether a trial solution is right or wrong, monitoring of one's own responses, and delaying immediate action in order to weigh matters and bring judgment to bear in decision making. Without executive control a person operates willy-nilly, reacting to each stimulus as it comes along, often to the neglect of social decorum or appropriateness to the situation. Hence distractibility is a key feature in disruption to executive functioning. In addition, perseveration may occur due to the person's inability to shift set or keep track of prior responses. Personality change is most striking in executive dysfunction, exemplified by change in emotional expression (either hyper- or hypoaroused), inappropriate social behavior (possibly even antisocial), and narcissistic focus on the individual's own needs and wishes.

PERSONALITY CHANGE SECONDARY TO DISEASE

In discussing personality disorders in the elderly, personality change due to illness must be differentiated from exacerbation of preexisting personality traits under stressful conditions that are part of normal aging. This section focuses on those personality symptoms attributable to medical conditions. In such conditions, dramatic personality changes can occur. Frequently, the personality symptoms precede the emergence of clear pathological signs of disease and can be used by the sensitive clinician to identify and refer the older person for early diagnosis and treatment. In order to evaluate carefully for personality change, a detailed psychosocial history is crucial, drawn from both self-report and the observations of a reliable "objective" family member or friend. Lishman's (1987) description of prodromal symptoms of "chronic organic reactions" applies here:

> Intellectual deficits are absent in the early stages, or pass unnoticed in consequence of curtailment of activities and the use of props and evasions. Deterioration of manners may be the earliest sign, or diminished awareness of the needs and feelings of others. Some social blunder may disclose the illness, such as an episode of stealing or disinhibited sexual behavior out of character for the individual. Sometimes the earliest change is merely the aggravation of long-standing personality traits such as depression, suspiciousness, or selfishness. Neurotic traits may be elaborated with the production of obsessional, hysterical or hypochondriacal symptoms. More rarely still the illness may present with the picture of a functional psychotic illness of depressive, paranoid, or schizophrenic type in especially predisposed individuals. It is then only by careful examination that the intellectual deterioration is revealed. (p. 13)

Dementia and Related Disorders

The most common neurologic condition causing personality change in old age is dementia, of which there are several subtypes, each causing a somewhat different psychiatric presentation. The most common type of dementia, Senile Dementia of the Alzheimer's Type (SDAT), presents with several personality manifestations, typically affecting the control of emotions and impulses and aspects of motivation and social judgment. Behavioral change is often insidious in onset, with early signs of loss of interest and initiative, inability to perform up to previous standard, and transient episodes of bizarre inappropriate behavior. As intellectual impairment becomes more pronounced in its effect on behavior, a person loses the capacity for decisive action, fails to maintain attention, and develops impersistence, fatiguing quickly on tasks requiring mental effort. Responses to stimuli may be appropriate so long as the person understands; nevertheless, sustained attention and concentration are reduced, thereby limiting the extent of interests and activities, with rigid adherence to routines and stereotyped behavior (Goldstein, 1939). When taken out of this circumscribed sphere, a person may become evasive or sullen, or react abruptly with anger, anxiety, or tears. Social interaction is limited by lack of concern for others, self-focus, and withdrawal. Thinking becomes concrete, inflexible, and stimulus bound to irrelevant incidental detail. As a consequence, judgment becomes impaired, with poor insight or little awareness shown about the cognitive and social deficits. Misperceptions or misinterpretations of reality may give rise to paranoid ideation and delusions of being robbed, poisoned, threatened, or deprived. Verbal production becomes limited, in which words are used with disregard for the use of language as a code of communication: References to the self and to things in the immediate environment tend to limit the extent of word usage (thereby leading to reduction of verbal mediation, described earlier). Memory problems often involve confabulation and overendorsement of items on recognition cuing, which further contribute to false notions. The person may be unaware of memory difficulties or, conversely, may try to hide or explain them away with facile excuses. More adaptively, those cognizant of their memory difficulties may try to compensate for them by adhering to a rigid daily schedule or by using a notebook.

Emotional changes in dementia may be linked to cognitive change in that a person may react to perceived decline with uncharacteristic indifference, anxiety, or depression with agitation and hypochondriacal features. Suicidal ideation and attempts may occur in the early stage. General irritability may be punctuated by explosive outbursts of anger. Further deterioration during midstage leads to bland flat affect, apathy, or unfounded euphoria. Emotions become more childlike in their petulant and brief excessive responses to minor inconvenience. "Emotional control may show a characteristic threshold effect in which there is little response to mild stimulation but thereafter an excessive and prolonged disturbance. Emotional lability may be extreme, with episodes of pathological laughing and crying for little or no cause" (Lishman, 1987, p. 16). Premorbid personality features may become more pronounced, such as hysterical conversion symptoms deriving from increased suggestibility, or obsessive traits emerging as a way of coping with reduced faculties. Hallucinations may occur, frequently of a visual nature, such as seeing bugs or strangers in the home (Beats, 1989).

Frontal lobe dementia (e.g., Pick's disease) generally begins in a gradual and insidious manner. It presents with a constellation of symptoms characterized by problems with executive control, described earlier. Changes in personality are most noticeable in this type of dementia. A person may exhibit disinhibition in social behavior, such as overfamiliar tactless garrulity, overexcitement, or inappropriate joking. Mood may shift in a dyscontrolled way, with giddiness suddenly changing to irritability. Some patients evidence obsessive-compulsive behavior, developing stereotyped routines or obsessions with specific activities (e.g., urge to eat specific foods, often accompanied by large weight gain early in the disease). Impulsivity is more common than apathy. Perseveration and tangentiality mark their verbal production. Spontaneous language output diminishes gradually (Moss, Albert, & Kemper, 1992).

Vascular dementia secondary to many small strokes (formerly called multi-infarct dementia), or to diffuse arteriosclerotic damage of subcortical white matter (Binswanger's disease), can produce personality changes of varying nature. Lishman (1987) pointed out that vascular dementia may lead to loss of ability to adjust to any unusual circumstances; consequently, small matters can create anxiety, irritability, or depression. A person tends to avoid new experiences, narrowing the field of activities to an unvarying routine. Confrontations with new responsibilities or social demands may trigger extreme reactions of rage, fear, or weeping. Irritability and resistance are typical responses to any demands made that require effort; on the other hand, when left unbothered, the person may be affable and obliging. Hypochondriacal complaints may occur to minor physical disturbances (primarily around sleep or bowels) to a degree that they appear neurotic. Premorbid personality features may be exaggerated: For example, loneliness may evolve into suspiciousness, or mild dysphoria may turn into more serious depression. At later stages of illness, the emotions are unmistakably abnormal, with dull, flat affect, irritability, or inflexible, stereotyped reactions. For example, vascular patients may show no pleasure or concern where the interests of others are concerned, but extreme and prolonged catastrophic reaction to disturbance of their own security. Often these personality changes precede decisive evidence of failing memory and reduced cognitive functioning. Magnetic resonance imaging studies have been done with elderly complaining of depression; they show an unexpectedly higher incidence of periventricular white-matter lesions in the frontal lobes and basal ganglia. Although these lesions are the result of infarction, they do not result in motor or sensory symptoms and hence are termed "silent." The biggest risk factor appears to be carotid atherosclerosis, and secondarily a history of myocardial infarction (Brown & Lempa, 1997).

More recent studies have not supported the preceding description. Several studies have differentiated the personality changes typical of vascular dementia from those related to Alzheimer's type dementia. Personality was affected in both groups, but vascular subjects exhibited less severe alterations in mature coping mechanisms than did Alzheimer's patients, who showed significant changes in behavioral control, engagement, self-reliance, and practical judgment. In contrast, those with vascular dementia showed greater constancy in interpersonal relatedness and were more affectionate and easy-going but did show some change in self-reliance and apathy (Cummings, Petry, Dian, & Shapira, 1990). Premorbidly, Alzheimer's patients tend to have been passive, submissive, and conflict-avoiding, whereas those with vascular dementia tend to have been dominant and assertive (Bauer, Stadtmuller, Qualmann, & Bauer, 1995). It may be hypothesized that the loss of self-reliance in vascular patients leads to change in the way they now deal with others—less domineeringly and more relatedly than before. Hypertensive patients who showed personality change tended to have reduced drive and energy and flatter affect than before; they did not show frank dementia or depression but only mild intellectual impairment suggestive of frontal lobe dysfunction. On magnetic resonance imaging, multiple small infarcts were revealed involving deep subcortical structures (Habib et al., 1991).

Stroke

In cases of stroke, localized physical signs present themselves first, and personality change subsequently becomes manifest and progresses even though the focal effects of the stroke may improve. Depression is the most common effect of left hemisphere strokes, and within the left hemisphere the more anterior the lesion, the worse the depression. Left frontal brain lesions produce more depression than lesions in any other location (Robinson & Szetela, 1981). The depression may derive from the special aspects of cognitive dysfunction in such patients, for example, the frequent loss of speech and use of the dominant hand (Lishman, 1987). Anterior strokes in either hemisphere appear to be more susceptible of producing depression than posterior strokes due to disruption of catecholamine-containing pathways in the brain passing from subcortical centers through the frontal cortex (Robinson & Bloom, 1977). Strokes in the right hemisphere typically produce disturbances in self-awareness, recognition of the effects of illness (anosognosia), neglect of the left side of space, and sometimes psychotic hallucinations and persecutory delusions (Levine & Finklestein, 1982). Premorbid personality factors play a role in adjustment to handicap: Achievement-oriented, independent patients react more adversely than those with strong dependency needs. Those with a history of anxiety and depression in reaction to previous stress will be at even greater risk (Lishman, 1987).

Alcohol and Medications

As the brain ages, it becomes more sensitive to neurotoxic effects of exogenous substances, such as alcohol and medications. Substantial alcohol use can produce personality change in older people, characterized by frontal lobe type symptoms, including circumstantiality, plausibility, and weakness of volition (Lishman, 1987), and, in the case of Korsakoff's syndrome, flattening of drives, unconcern about incapacities, and apathy (Victor, Adams, & Colling, 1971).

Medications, in particular their side effects or cumulative effects of interactions with other medications, can have a profound effect on both cognitive and personality functioning, clouding mentation and triggering such wide-ranging reactions as anxiety, depression, mania, paranoia, and hallucinations.

Medical Conditions

Pathological medical conditions also can produce personality change. Space-occupying cerebral lesions are commonly attended by depression and anxiety, sometimes irritability or emotional lability, but rarely elation. Henry (1932) outlined the typical sequence of mood changes during the growth of cerebral tumors: first irritability, giving way to increasing anxiety and depression, and culminating in indifference and apathy or euphoria or emotional lability. Impulsive suicide attempts may follow tumor-induced paroxysms of headache. Hallucinations and any form of psychotic illness may accompany cerebral tumor at any stage of its evolution. The nature of the hallucinations depends on the location of the tumor. Delusions when they occur may have an organic flavor, being poorly elaborated, shallow, or fleeting (Lishman, 1987). The most common form of space-occupying lesion among the elderly, subdural hematomas, can produce transient obfuscation and such personality changes as depression, dullness, and lethargy.

Systemic illness is frequently accompanied or preceded by changes in mood and disposition. For example, affective disorder has been found as a prodromal feature in patients who develop cancer, particularly among men (Kerr, Shapira, & Roth, 1969). Neuropsychological impairment secondary to metastasis to the brain may precede overt signs of cancer and create a dementing condition that impairs job performance and activities of daily living and consequently leads to depression, anxiety, and sometimes paranoia. Chronic airflow obstruction (seen in such diseases as chronic bronchitis and emphysema) typically produces manifest personality symptoms of irascibility and impatience. These symptoms appear to be a depressive equivalent, as depression, tension, and anxiety have been found on psychological testing using the Minnesota Multiphasic Personality Inventory (Prigatano, Wright, & Levin, 1984). They may be underpinned by neuropsychological problems involving perceptual-motor learning and problem solving, as well as motor speed and strength that limit performance of activities of daily living (Prigatano & Levin, 1988). Parkinson's disease is attended by general slowing of cognitive processes and difficulty with executive functioning; depression may result from these neuropsychological problems as well as from neurotransmitter change. Cardiac conditions treated surgically have resulted postoperatively in anxiety and depression and sometimes brief psychotic features. There was a tendency for cardiac patients with neuropsychological problems, which were reportedly to be general rather than specific, to have greater functional symptoms (Tienari, Outakoski, Hirvenoja, Joulasmaa, Takkunen, &

Kampman, 1982). Endocrine disorders, most notably hyper- and hypothyroidism, can produce problems with concentration and memory and have characteristic emotional effects: anxietylike symptoms in hyperthyroidism, and depression in hypothyroid state. Cushing's disease may disturb cognitive functions of concentration, comprehension, memory, and orientation, as well as trigger irritability, decreased libido, and depressed mood without depressing thought content (Starkman & Schteingart, 1981).

EPILOGUE: THE EFFECT OF NEURODEVELOPMENTAL CHANGE ON PRE-EXISTING PERSONALITY DISORDERS

Not all change is bad. In old age various normal neurologic events occur that can temper some personality problems and may explain in part the declining prevalence of personality disorder in later life (Cohen, Nestadt, Samuels, Romanoski, McHugh, & Rabins, 1994). For example, frontal, parietal, and temporal association cortices are not fully myelinated until the third or fourth decade (Elliott, 1992). As myelination of the frontal lobes enhances executive planning and impulse control, the behavioral improvement noted in longitudinal studies of personality disorders in those decades may be attributed to this neurologic change. As people age, serotonin activity remains stable or actually increases in relation to decrease in dopamine (McEntee & Crook, 1990, 1991; Morgan, May, & Pinch, 1987). Studies in both animals and humans suggest that lower serotonin activity correlates with irritable, impulsive aggression, which can be directed at either the self or others (Coccaro, 1989). Thus, serotonin increase may explain the diminution of impulsive, aggressive acting out among aging patients with personality disorders. In addition, progressive decline in the testosterone level of men with age may account for a lower frequency of impulsive aggression (Gray, Jackson, & McKinlay, 1991).

The mitigating effects of neurologic change with age, which stand in contrast to most of the effects described in this chapter, bring to mind the words of Samuel Butler in his novel, *The Way of All Flesh* (1903/1925): "Youth is like spring, an over-praised season more remarkable for biting winds than gentle breezes. Autumn is the mellower season, and what we lose in flowers we more than gain in fruits."

REFERENCES

American Psychiatric Association. (1994). *Diagnostic and statistical manual of mental disorders* (4th ed.). Washington, DC: American Psychiatric Association.

Bauer, J., Stadtmuller, G., Qualmann, J., & Bauer, H. (1995). Premorbid psychological processes in patients with Alzheimer's disease and in patients with vascular dementia. *Gerontologie Psychiatrische, 38*, 179–89.

Bear, D. (1983). Hemispheric specialization and the neurology of emotion. *Archives of Neurology, 40,* 195–202.

Beats, B. (1989). Visual hallucinations as the presenting symptom of dementia—a variant of the Charles Bonnet syndrome? *International Journal of Geriatric Psychiatry, 4,* 197–201.

Brown, A., & Lempa, M. (1997). Late-life depression. *National Alliance for Research on Schizophrenia and Depression Research Newsletter* (Winter Suppl.), 10–15.

Butler, S. (1903/1925). *The way of all flesh.* New York: Macmillan.

Coccaro, E. F. (1989). Central serotonin and impulsive aggression. *British Journal of Psychiatry, 155,* 52–62.

Cohen, B. J., Nestadt, G., Samuels, J. F., Romanoski, A. J., McHugh, P. R., & Rabins, P. V. (1994). Personality disorder in later life: A community study. *British Journal of Psychiatry, 165,* 493–499.

Cummings, J. L., Petry, S., Dian, L., Shapira, J. (1990). Organic personality disorder in dementia syndromes: An inventory approach. *Journal of Neuropsychiatry and Clinical Neurosciences, 2,* 261–267.

Elliot, F. A. (1992). Violence, the neurologic contribution: An overview. *Archives of Neurology, 49,* 595–603.

Goldstein, K. (1939). *The organism: A holistic approach to biology derived from pathological data in man.* New York: American Book Company.

Gray, A., Jackson, A. N., & McKinlay, J. B. (1991). The relation between dominance, anger, and hormones in normally aging men: Results from the Massachusetts Male Aging Study. *Psychosomatic Medicine, 53,* 375–385.

Habib, M., Rovere, M. L., Habib, G., Bonnefoi, B., Milandre, L., Poncet, M., Luccioni, R., & Khalil, R. (1991). Changes in personality and hypertension. *Archives de Mal Coeur et Vaisseaux, 84,* 1225–1230.

Henry, G. W. (1932). Mental phenomena observed in cases of brain tumor. *American Journal of Psychiatry, 89,* 415–473.

Hodel-Malinofsky, T. (1994). Neuropsychological perspective on personality disorders. In J. M. Ellison, C. S. Weinstein, & T. Hodel-Malinofsky (Eds.), *The psychotherapist's guide to neuropsychiatry: Diagnostic and treatment issues* (pp. 329–368). Washington, DC: American Psychiatric Press.

Judd, P. H., & Ruff, R. M. (1993). Neuropsychological dysfunction in borderline personality disorder. *Journal of Personality Disorders, 7,* 275–284.

Kerr, T. A., Schapira, K., & Roth, M. (1969). The relationship between premature death and affective disorders. *British Journal of Psychiatry, 115,* 1277–1282.

Kolb, B., & Wishaw, I. Q. (1985). *Human neuropsychology* (2nd ed.). New York: Freeman.

Levine, D. N., & Finklestein, S. (1982). Delayed psychosis after right temporoparietal stroke or trauma: Relation to epilepsy. *Neurology, 32,* 267–273.

Lishman, W. A. (1987). *Organic psychiatry* (2nd ed.). Oxford, England: Blackwell.

Luria, A. R. (1973). *The working brain.* New York: Penguin.

McEntee, W. J., & Crook, T. H. (1990). Age-associated memory impairment: A role for catecholamines. *Neurology, 40,* 526–530.

McEntee, W. J., & Crook, T. H. (1991). Serotonin, memory, and the aging brain. *Psychopharmacology. 103,* 143–149.

Miller, L. (1987). Neuropsychology of the aggressive psychopath: An integrative review. *Aggressive Behavior, 13,* 119–140.

Modell, J. G., Mountz, J. M., Curtis, G. C., & Greden, J. F. (1989). Neurophysiologic dysfunction in basal ganglia/limbic striatal and thalamocortical circuits as a pathogenetic mechanism of obsessive-compulsive disorder. *Journal of Neuropsychiatry and Clinical Neuroscience, 1,* 27–36.

Modell, J. G., Mountz, J. M., & Beresford, T. P. (1990). Basal ganglia/limbic striatal and thalamocortical involvement in craving and loss of control in alcoholism. *Journal of Neuropsychiatry and Clinical Neuroscience, 2,* 123–144.

Morgan, D. G., May, P. C., & Pinch, C. F. (1987). Dopamine and serotonin systems in human and rodent brain: Effects of age and neurodegenerative disease. *Journal of the American Geriatric Society, 35,* 334–345.

Moss, M. B., Albert, M. S., & Kemper, T. L. (1992). Neuropsychology of frontal lobe dementia. In R. F. White (Ed.), *Clinical syndromes in adult neuropsychology: The practitioner's handbook* (pp. 287–303). Amsterdam: Elsevier.

O'Leary, K. M., Brouwers, P., Gardner, D. L., & Cowdry, R. W. (1991). Neuropsychological testing of patients with borderline personality disorder. *American Journal of Psychiatry, 148,* 106–111.

Prigatano, G. P., Wright, E., & Levin, D. (1984). Quality of life and its predictors in mildly hypoxemic COPD patients. *Archives of Internal Medicine, 144,* 1613–1619.

Prigatano, G. P., & Levin, D. C. (1988). Pulmonary system. In R. E. Tarter, D. H. Van Thiel, & K. L. Edwards (Eds.), *Medical neuropsychology: The impact of disease on behavior* (pp. 11–26). New York: Plenum.

Robbins, M. (1989). Primitive personality organization as an interpersonally adaptive modification of cognition and affect. *International Journal of Psychoanalysis, 70,* 443–459.

Robinson, R. G., & Bloom, F. E. (1977). Pharmacological treatment following experimental cerebral infarction: Implications for understanding psychological symptoms of human stroke. *Biological Psychiatry, 12,* 669–680.

Robinson, R. G., & Szetela, B. (1981). Mood change following left hemisphere brain injury. *Annals of Neurology, 9,* 447–453.

Siever, L. J. (1985). Biological markers in schizotypal personality disorder. *Schizophrenia Bulletin, 11,* 564–574.

Siever, L. J., & Davis, K. (1991). A psychobiological perspective on the personality disorders. *American Journal of Psychiatry, 148,* 1647–1658.

Starkman, M. N., & Schteingart, D. E. (1981). Neuropsychiatric manifestations of patients with Cushing's syndrome. *Archives of Internal Medicine, 141,* 215–219.

Tienari, P., Outakoski, J., Hirvenoja, R., Juolasmaa, A., Takkunen, I., & Kampman, R. (1982). Psychiatric complications following open-heart surgery: a prospective study. In R. Becker, J. Katz, M-J. Polonius, & H. Speidel (Eds.), *Psychopathological and neurological dysfunctions following open-heart surgery* (pp. 48–53). Berlin: Springer.

Victor, M., Adams, R.D., & Colling, G.H. (1971). *The Wernicke–Korsakoff syndrome.* Philadelphia: Davis.

Watt, D. F. (1990). Higher cortical functions and the ego: Explorations of the boundary between behavioral neurology, neuropsychology, and psychoanalysis. *Psychoanalytic Psychology, 7,* 487–527.

Welch, L., & Bear, D. (1990). Organic disorders of personality. In D. M. Adler (Ed.), *Treating personality disorders* (pp. 87–102). San Francisco: Jossey-Bass.

CHAPTER 12

Personality Disorders
in Older Adults: Some Issues
in Psychodynamic Treatment

WAYNE A. MYERS, MD
Joan and Sanford I. Weill Medical College of Cornell University

This chapter describes the psychodynamic therapy of two older patients, one with a narcissistic personality and the other with a borderline personality disorder. It focuses on those aspects of the treatments that illustrate the impact of aging on the typical features of these disorders. The patient with the borderline personality, in particular, offered a unique opportunity, inasmuch as she had been a patient some 25 years earlier and the differences in her behavior then and now could directly be observed.

The literature on the effects of aging on the treatment of personality disorders is extremely limited. Probably the only references that directly apply to this area are those by Sandler (1978), Kernberg (1980), and Myers (1987). These authors pointed out that some narcissistic patients may become more amenable to dynamic psychotherapy as they get older. This is especially true when these individuals become depressed and humbled as a result of life circumstances, which lead them to realize that their fantasies of their grandiose selves are no longer as viable as they once thought.

CLINICAL MATERIAL

CASE I

Mr. A is a patient briefly described elsewhere (Myers, 1987). I saw him in four-times-a-week psychoanalytic treatment on the couch for a period of 7 years, beginning when he was in his late fifties and ending in his mid-sixties. When I first saw him, he told me that he was homosexual and had been happy with his lifestyle for over 35 years. What he was alluding to was his pattern of having brief encounters with "beautiful boys" in the bars and bathhouses of the major cities and elegant watering holes of several continents. He informed me that he never would have come for therapy had it not been for his intense fear of contracting AIDS. He had known a number of friends who had already died of the disease and he did not wish to join their ranks. Hence he had a desire to form a long-lasting relationship with a single person. Because he had not been able to accomplish this feat on his own, he opted for treatment.

The patient was the only child of middle-class parents. His father was a passive academician with little interest in his son and his mother was an overbearing woman who was obsessed with keeping her home clean. She refused to allow other children into the house, thus turning her son's life into an isolated existence. As Mr. A thought about his mother's continual intrusions into his life, his room, and his person in her endless pursuit of dirt and grime, his eyes would well up with tears of self-pity and rage. He saw his homosexuality in part as a flight from the clutches of his mother and of other women, a threat that men did not seem to pose for him. When I asked him why, if that was the case, that he had never managed to form a close relationship with a man, he saw the question as a problem that "we" would have to figure out in the treatment.

I was encouraged by his response, inasmuch as it seemed to indicate a willingness to include me into his thinking. In my consideration, this indicated a capacity for object relatedness and for a reasonably healthy transference potential that he might not have had earlier in his life. In addition, he had largely given up his impulse driven style of life, except for occasional afternoons of anonymous "safe" sex in the porno bookstores and movie theaters catering to the gay community. This capacity for delay of gratification also boded well for a more psychodynamically oriented form of therapy. In addition, the patient exhibited an intense sense of pain and a desire to change his life. "I've never wanted to be attached to just one person in the past. It's always seemed too limiting. I don't know that I really want it now, but it's the only way that's safe. I don't know how to begin to look for someone. That's why I'm here. I can't accomplish this by myself. I've never acknowledged that about anything before in my life. You've got to help me, doctor." The coupling of these several features led me to suggest starting a psychoanalysis to the patient, which he readily agreed to.

The early phase of the analysis centered on the patient's rage at his mother and his intense sense of how unfairly treated he had been by life and fate. Both his parents died when he was in his early twenties, and he was finally freed up to pursue his quest for pleasure. And pursue it he did

—for decades. Now AIDS had come along and changed everything. Again, life was proving to be unfair.

In the first months of the treatment, the patient also managed to deny his earlier acknowledgment of needing the analyst's help. Many attempts at transference interpretations on my part were met with irritation, as if I were intruding on his person in the manner that his mother had done earlier in his life. When I tried, for example, to link a spate of visits to porno theaters to his anxiety over an impending vacation separation, he became angry at me for my comments. He insisted that the chance of contracting AIDS was the reason for his anxiety, not my going away.

After my return, however, Mr. A mentioned having had a dream of being at the baths and of being scorned by younger men for being too old. In this context, he revealed the idea that it was not only the fear of AIDS that kept him away from his prior homosexual activities, but the fact of his being too old to be invited to join in the "fun." The recognition of the affront posed by his getting older to his former grandiose image of himself gave him considerable pause. It was almost more than he could bear to think of. And he responded to this narcissistic humbling by immediately thereafter engaging in a mutual masturbatory episode with a younger man in a gay movie theater, which temporarily buoyed up his spirits by taking his mind off the idea of his having gotten older.

Several months later, shortly before my first summer vacation of the treatment, the patient formed a monogamous relationship with an attractive younger man. He preempted any possible transference implications by denying out of hand any connection between the romantic liaison and my going away. When I returned in the fall, I was greeted with the news that the relationship had been aborted. Mr. A seemed saddened by the turn of events and I commented to him that he appeared to have invested more energy in the relationship, both sexually and emotionally, than in any other one he had described before.

He said that my comment had surprised him, inasmuch as he had expected me to connect the demise of the encounter with his not needing it anymore because of my return . He noted that what I had said was true, but then went on to observe that what he had thought I might say was also true. This first tentative acknowledgment of the transference was immediately followed by a considerable period of anger toward me and other heterosexuals for our lack of empathy to the plight of homosexuals dealing with the AIDS crisis. After he dreamt of the analyst as a teacher indifferent to the problems of his students, he was able to connect his anger to the analyst and other heterosexuals to his long buried feelings toward his indifferent father.

Following this, he observed that he had tried to blank out any feelings for me in the analysis, in much the same manner that he felt his father had dealt with him during his growing up. I agreed with this idea and noted how hard it was for him to acknowledge any feelings of dependence on me. Thus his acting like his father served to protect him from getting hurt by anyone who might serve as a surrogate for the father. I further noted that this must have interfered with his capacity to establish close relationships with me in the past, and he agreed.

In the second year of the treatment, Mr. A noted how much more difficult it was for a homosexual man to get older, inasmuch as age and looks and penis size were the only currencies that counted in the world of the bars and baths. The idea that he would no longer be able to get all the men he desired was an appalling one. So was the thought that he had nearly reached the age at which his father had died. He wanted to get more out of life than his parents had realized, especially in terms of achieving closeness with another human being. It was as if the treatment was affording him his "last chance" to change his patterns of a lifetime and he had to make the most of this opportunity.

As the months and years unfolded, the patient began to express more and more feelings toward the analyst, including both his anger and his dependency at times of separation. Despite this apparent evidence of progress, his capacity to view the analyst as a complete object was never quite up to the levels seen with neurotic patients. He clearly continued to regard the analyst as a "part object," who performed a calming and normalizing function for him during periods of separation or loss.

Mr. A sequentially became involved with a number of men, beginning with younger ones and gradually allowing his lovers to come closer to his own age as the treatment progressed. Although the desire to slip off for interludes of anonymous sex was never totally lost, after a period of years it was no longer acted on, even during periods in which the analyst was away.

In the seventh and final year of the analysis, Mr. A and his lover moved into a new apartment together. In his dreams of the time, he saw both his lover and the analyst as latter-day replicas of the intrusive mother, penetrating his emotional guardedness with phallic intensity. Long submerged feelings of love and dependency on the mother began to surface, however, especially in the context of our setting a termination date.

When the time for the termination of the treatment drew near, Mr. A expressed much fear about his need for me to continue my soothing "function" for him, lest he be unable to sustain the relationship with the lover. He even suffered brief episodes of erectile impotency at this time, which were especially humiliating for him. In this setting, he expressed the idea that the analytic sessions were serving as daily injects of manliness for him and he had a difficult time envisioning functioning without me. He also mentioned that he would truly miss the feelings of warmth and humor that I communicated to him, which was the closest representation of me as a total object that he had ever made. We did manage to terminate nonetheless, and in follow-up cards and letters to the analyst, Mr. A wrote that although he missed me, he and his lover were even closer than they had been before.

CASE 2

Mrs. B was a woman I had seen for a period of months a quarter of a century earlier, when she was nearing her 40th birthday. At that time, the man she was involved with decided to terminate his chaotic love relationship with her. Because this had happened to her several times before, she was intensely anxious and depressed. She spoke of feeling empty and began gorging herself on food and alcohol and then attempted suicide with an overdose of tranquilizers. Following a brief hospitalization, during which time she was placed on antidepressant medication, she was referred to me by her internist because of his feeling that he could no longer manage her case without psychiatric assistance.

In our brief period of twice-weekly psychoanalytically oriented psychotherapy, she scratched her wrists on several occasions. When I questioned her about these occurrences, she expressed the idea that the pain and the blood from the scratches eased her anxiety. We came to understand that the physical sensations at such times helped to enable her to demarcate her bodily boundaries during periods in which her self-image felt especially unstable. Just prior to these mutilatory moments, she reported a number of mirror dreams in which her face seemed ugly and distorted, with the sense of deformation carrying over into her waking state. Her feelings about her former lover, at such times, showed high amplitude, rapid oscillations between a totally unrealistic overidealization and a massive devaluation and denunciation.

During my summer vacation, I had her see the covering physician. Despite this, she became hypomanic and spent money in a dramatically reckless and flagrant manner. She also managed to sleep with a half a dozen men she barely knew in a short period of time. When she again attempted suicide with an overdose of antidepressant medications, she was hospitalized by the covering doctor. On my return, she spoke of feeling angry at me for having abandoned her and stormed out of the treatment.

To my surprise, Mrs. B called me one day, nearly 25 years later. Even on the phone, she sounded different. Her tone seemed muted, though not especially depressed. When she came into my office, she seemed a different person. Although she spoke about having been left by her most recent lover, this event had occurred nearly a year earlier. Even though she had not become markedly depressed, the psychopharmacologist she consulted at that time had placed her on fluoxetine. This only led to a minimal mood elevation and when she stopped the drug after 9 months, she decided she wanted to once and for all change her repetitive pattern of failed love affairs. As for why she chose to see me, she said that she felt I had understood her better than any of her other therapists and she had long ago come to realize that I had not willfully abandoned her by going off on vacation.

During the early months of our second treatment, Mrs. B reviewed for me what had transpired during the intervening years. When she spoke of the lovers who had left her, there were still oscillations in her reports between idealization and devaluation, but the amplitude of the waves and the rapidity of the transitions seemed markedly diminished. Even when she was angry at me for short periods of separation, her rage seemed considerably more constrained than it had been 25 years earlier. The eating and drinking binges had largely ceased, as had much of the wrist scratching and other self-mutilatory and suicidal behaviors. She still frequently spoke of feeling empty, but there were no longer any mirror dreams or waking periods in which her self-image appeared ugly and deformed. It was as if age had taken its toll on her personality.

In the next year and a half of the treatment, we worked on her distortions and misperceptions of the interactions with the important people in her life, including her aged mother and her older siblings. The rage at these individuals was still there (as when she spoke of her mother's early "abandonment" of her or her mother's preference for her two older brothers), but the office walls did not shake as they had in the past when she verbalized it. Indeed, she was able to recognize that the periods of so-called abandonment by the mother during her childhood were very brief ones at best and were more likely only connected with reasonable vacation trips that the parents took without their three children. Although she never came to feel any significant upsurge of warmth toward her mother, she was able to considerably modify her long-standing negative image of the woman.

She had a similar experience with the two older brothers, with whom she had barely spoken for years. When she came to recognize that they, too, had more than their share of painful experiences throughout their lives, her image of them as selfish and ungiving became less vitriolic. She reinstituted her relationship with them and their families and was pleased at their responsiveness to her. The feeling of finally having the family she had always wished for was a very good one indeed. She spoke of feeling "grounded" in a way that she had never felt before and noted that even her sense of the stability of her self and of her bodily boundaries felt more secure than at any time before.

The idealization of the patient's long-dead father also began to modify in the second treatment. The mere mention of his name no longer elicited tears of longing and of sorrow, as it had done for so long. She was even able to recall instances in which the father had not always been so loving and attentive to her needs as she had previously remembered him to be. Though she never came to devalue, as she had done with her earlier lost lovers, she definitely came to recognize that her long-standing idol did indeed have clay feet.

These realizations about the significant figures in her life caused her many anxious moments in the treatment. The new modifications also did not occur in any simple linear fashion. They only came after considerable work on both our parts. What is of interest, however, is the fact that she was able to carry this therapeutic work out without any major interruptions in the treatment and without any self-destructive attempts directed against her own person.

As for her feelings toward me in the transference, they were still strong, but not as intense as they once had been. She would occasionally get up out of her chair and pace about the room when she was angry with me, but she never left the office or the treatment as she has previously done, though she would still periodically miss a session or two after an especially intense realization in the therapy. Even at her most paranoid moments of thinking that I was malevolently working against her best interests, the distortions were only fleeting and her healthy reality testing would soon return. The therapeutic alliance seemed stronger than I would have ever imagined her being capable of forging in the past and it carried us past many a tense moment.

During the third year of the new therapy, she met a man a few years her senior while on a bicycle trip in Provence. Contrary to her usual modus operandi, she did not immediately enter into an intense sexual relationship with him. She let it develop over a period of some weeks, and verbalized the hope that this time the encounter might be more lasting and even culminate in marriage. Even when the man appeared to be backing off from her for a brief period of time, she did not let her rage out with the overpowering intensity she had expressed previously. This salutary change led to a deepening of their relationship and they eventually did marry.

Shortly after their wedding, she decided to decrease the frequency of her visits to me because she did not want her feelings toward me to interfere with her feelings toward her husband. "I can't handle two strong positive feelings at the same time," she said, "and I don't want to turn one or the other of you into a negative." She told me that she did not quite ever envision terminating our treatment because it provided a necessary safety valve for her. "I always want to have a forum for my feelings," she said, "so I don't have to inflict them on my husband. Besides, you've become so much a part of my day-to-day existence, I can't imagine not ever seeing you again. You're my good family. I don't want to let go of you."

She also saw our relationship as having allowed her to rise, like the Phoenix, from the ashes of her muted state, but not to soar too high or too intensely so as to be seared by the sun, in the manner of Icarus. She initially cut down from twice a week to once a week and from there to once every other week, before finally arriving at a once-a-month schedule. This seems to serve her needs quite well, functioning as the safety valve that she envisioned it to be.

DISCUSSION

Turning now to the clinical material presented here, the discussion focuses on the manner in which the two patients described here differed from younger narcissistic personalities and borderline patients. First consider the first patient, Mr. A. Here is an individual who would not have come for treatment at the time that he did, if ever, had it not been for a confluence of factors. One was the spread of AIDS in gay men. In order to appease his sexual appetites in a way that would not be life threatening, he was forced to deal with the idea of attempting to relate to a single "object" in a manner that he had never managed to do in the past. To achieve this goal, he needed therapeutic help. Getting this help, however, necessitated his becoming dependent on another human being, the therapist, in a manner that would have been an anathema to him at an earlier period in his life.

A second factor of importance was the patient's recognition that he was aging and that he envied the youth of others, as well as his own lost youth. He also had to acknowledge that he could no longer regularly enhance his narcissistically depleted grandiose self-image with regular injections of the masculinity of the beautiful boys as he had done before, because they no longer desired him. All of these factors operating in concert made him feel anxious and depressed and provided him with the motivation—which had never been present before —to seek out therapy. Needless to say, this confluence of factors is simply not present in younger narcissistic personality patients.

During the course of the treatment, Mr. A became increasingly aware that his advancing age made it essential that he resolve his issues at the present time, and not in some indefinite future. His time span was no longer infinite and this might be the only opportunity he had to work things through; this is what King (1980) referred to as the "last chance" syndrome. When he neared the age at which his father had died, his motivation for change was further enhanced by the realization that he wanted to get more out of whatever time remained in his life than his father had gotten out of his.

A number of features about Mr. A's treatment are notable to point out here. From the very beginning of the analysis, the patient was able to acknowledge the presence of the analyst as something more than a simple "part object," in a way that few narcissistic personality patients are able to do. This was apparent in the manner in which he spoke of the need for the analyst's help to work his problems through. Though he frequently utilized the analyst largely as a part object-soothing function, he also would often acknowledge the singularity of the therapist and of his own dependency on him.

He repeatedly stated that time had taken its toll on him and that he had been "humbled" in a way that he had never imagined. His earlier illusion that he would remain young and desirable and be an object of envy for all the men at the baths and bars had been "shot down" by the ravages of time and the repeated rejections he had suffered. All of this had depressed him and made him need other people, most notably the analyst, in a fashion that he had not been capable of experiencing in the past.

The mutability of life experience on the personality, and the consequently heightened availability of narcissistic patients for psychodynamically oriented treatments, are the most important effects of again which I have observed in a number of older narcissistic personalities whom I have treated in psychotherapy or psychoanalysis. Not all narcissistic patients exhibit these salutary effects. Some seem untouched by the effects of aging and remain as difficult to treat as they would have been when they were younger And others remain difficult because of the extreme envy they feel for the youth of others or of the therapist, if the therapist happens to be much younger than they are. But a good number are better treatment cases in their older age than in their youth.

Now turn to Mrs. B, the borderline personality. In the abortive earlier treatment, she exhibited many of the typical features that have come to be associated with this disorder. The rapid and extreme oscillations of her feelings toward herself and the significant individuals in her life, the empty unstable sense of self, the suicide attempts, and the multiple examples of impulsive behavior are almost a textbook description of the disorder. Her mirror dreams, however, were an interesting and inconsistent feature that I have seen in other such patients (Myers, 1976) in the past.

In her second treatment incarnation with me, Mrs. B was practically another person. Everything about her seemed muted, from the rapid oscillation of her feelings to the very intensity of the feelings themselves. Her capacity for forming a therapeutic alliance and for actually examining her relationships with the important people in her life was vastly enhanced. She seemed considerably more capable of delay of discharge and gratification than she had been 25 years earlier.

It is not easy to account for these changes in any other manner than to suggest that the diminution in the intensity of the drives that people experience as they age, is responsible for the "burnt out" feeling reported by Mrs. B. I have seen this decreased ardor in other older borderline patients and have heard the phrase "burnt out borderlines" being bandied about in geriatric clinical conferences. I believe that the phenomenon is not an infrequent one and hope that by calling attention to it here, more reports about its frequency will follow.

These case reports emphasize that certain difficult-to-treat personality disorder patients are more amenable to dynamic psychotherapeutic treatments in their old age than they were in their younger years. It behooves us to maintain an open mind with such people, and not to limit treatment suggestions solely to the psychopharmacologic sphere.

CONCLUSIONS

Case reports of an older narcissistic male and a borderline female treated with psychodynamically oriented psychotherapeutic treatments are presented here. Both patients showed themselves to be more amenable to such treatments in their elder years then they would have been, or actually were, in their youth. The impact of life experience and the effects of the decrease in drive intensity on the typical features of these personality disorder is discussed.

REFERENCES

Kernberg, O. F. (1980), *Internal world and external reality: Object relations theory applied.* New York: Aronson.

King, P. (1980). The life cycles as indicated by the nature of the transference in the psychoanalysis of the middle-aged and the elderly. *International Journal of Psycho-Analysis, 61,* 153–160.

Myers, W. A. (1976). Imaginary companions, fantasy twins, mirror dreams and depersonalization. *Psychoanalytic Quarterly, 45,* 503–524.

Myers, W. A. (1987). Age, rage and the fear of AIDS. *Journal of Geriatric Psychiatry, 20,* 125–140.

Sandler, A. M. (1978). Psychoanalysis in later life. Problems in the psychoanalysis of an aging narcissistic patient. *Journal of Geriatric Psychiatry, 11,* 5–36.

CHAPTER 13

Cognitive-Behavioral Therapy, Personality Disorders, and the Elderly: Clinical and Theoretical Considerations

Robert M. Goisman, MD
Harvard Medical School

The growth of cognitive-behavioral therapy (CBT) for psychiatric disorders in the past 20 years is well documented. In particular, there has been a recent increase in the use of cognitive-behavioral approaches in the treatment of personality disorders, as reviewed by Marshall and Serin (1997) and especially as exemplified in Linehan's (1993a) work with borderline personality disorder. Simultaneously, after a period of underreporting and underutilization (Wisocki, 1991a), the use of CBT in the treatment of geriatric mental health problems has grown, so that CBT is now the most frequently researched form of psychotherapy for the elderly (Teri & McCurry, 1994).

Despite this, there have been no attempts to systematically examine the CBT literature as it applies to the treatment of geriatric patients with personality disorders. To derive specific behavioral treatment approaches in this area has generally required extrapolating from adult CBT rather than turning to literature specific for this age group (P. A. Wisocki, personal communication, June 1997). In fact, a computer-assisted literature search did not yield one article on the subject of the cognitive-behavioral treatment of elderly persons with such disorders.

This chapter hopes to remedy this deficiency. In doing so, it discusses general issues in behavior therapy with this population, examines aspects of the presentation of geriatric personality disorders of particular relevance from a CBT standpoint, and then presents examples of cognitive-behavioral techniques likely to be useful in this population. The chapter remains mindful of the assertion from

Lazarus and Sadavoy (1996) that "age per se defines neither indications nor contraindications for specific therapies" (p. 819).

CHARACTERISTICS OF COGNITIVE-BEHAVIORAL TREATMENT

The definition of CBT employed here should be stated at the outset. As identified by Lazarus and Fay (1984), some characteristics of behavior therapy include an emphasis on treating presenting problems in their own right, rather than as "symptoms" of a hypothesized underlying disorder; a focus on factors immediately maintaining a behavior rather than those that may have remotely caused it; and the use of structured therapy sessions, with an active therapist and homework assignments between sessions to promote skill acquisition and generalization. These characteristics are largely shared by cognitive therapy methods as well, although the focus here may be on self-reported intrapsychic experiences (especially thoughts), as well as on specific externally observable behaviors (Beck, 1976).

This chapter refers to treatment methods generated by either of these approaches as "CBT," regardless of whether the focus of the intervention is intrapsychic or external. Some authors have cautioned against involving severely character-disordered patients in psychoeducational or CBT-oriented group psychotherapy programs (Thompson & Gallagher-Thompson, 1996). Others have warned that some of the literature supporting the use of these interventions is only a series of uncontrolled case reports, rather than controlled trials or formally designed single case studies (Wisocki, 1991a). Nonetheless, the usefulness here of a structured, time-efficient approach relying on specific goal attainment and teaching skill acquisition and independent functioning is readily apparent (Zeiss & Steffen, 1996).

COGNITIVE-BEHAVIORAL TREATMENT AND PERSONALITY DIAGNOSIS

The field of cognitive-behavioral therapy has been slow to enter the arena of the treatment of personality disorders. A major reason was the vague, theory-bound, nonoperationalized nature of personality diagnosis embodied in the second edition of the *Diagnostic and Statistical Manual of Mental Disorders* (*DSM–II*; American Psychiatric Association, 1968), which did not include borderline personality disorder but did contain categories such as "asthenic personality" and "inadequate personality." Further, some behaviorists have opposed devising behavioral treatments for personality disorders, viewing the concept of personality itself as a nonempirical reification of hypothesized global traits and hence incompatible with a more typically behavioral state-oriented analysis of individual behaviors (Koerner, Kohlenberg, & Parker, 1996; Linehan, 1993a; Sperry, 1995).

However, the *DSM–III* (APA, 1980) and its successors have included a far more empirical and much less theory-bound approach to personality diagnosis, as well as specific operationalized criteria for the diagnosis of borderline personality disorder. Further, accompanying *DSM–III* was an introductory chapter specifically inviting behavioral approaches to formulation and treatment planning for all diagnoses in the manual (Spitzer, 1980). Highly operationalized revisions of diagnostic criteria for geriatric personality disorders have already been proposed (Sadavoy, 1996).

PERSONALITY DISORDERS, TREATMENT EFFICACY, AND TARGET SYMPTOMS

Some caveats about cognitive-behavioral treatment of personality disorders are in order. Although Linehan (1993a, 1993b) certainly demonstrated good results with her borderline patients using a combination of group and individual approaches, some have cautioned that the presence of a personality disorder may worsen the prognosis for comorbid psychopathology (Lazarus & Sadavoy, 1996; Thompson, 1987). Various personality disorders may have differing effects on prognosis, with dependent or avoidant personalities doing better and compulsive or passive-aggressive personalities more poorly (Thompson, Gallagher, & Czirr, 1988).

In addition, personality disorder symptoms can be fluid. The severity of such symptoms may increase during a major depressive episode (Thompson et al., 1988), but the frequency of symptoms meeting full criteria for a personality disorder diagnosis may diminish with age (Agronin, 1994), as may the overall prevalence of these disorders (Marshall & Serin, 1997). Further, some degree of personality change, including male–female role reversal or a tendency of both genders toward androgyny, may be normative in this population, so that a change in behavior (e.g., aggressiveness) may to some extent represent a normal age-related adaptation and therefore not always be an appropriate treatment target (Carstensen, 1988). See Fogel and Sadavoy (1996) for a more complete discussion of phenomenological issues in the presentation of geriatric personality disorders.

However, from a CBT perspective, it could be argued that target symptoms, rather than the personality disorder itself, should be attacked. Thase (1996) cautioned against drawing overly simplistic conclusions about the relation between personality disorder and treatment response, and Dreessen, Arntz, Luttels, and Sallaerts (1994) found that the presence of comorbid personality disorders did not diminish response to cognitive-behavioral therapy of panic disorder. Similarly, AuBuchon and Malatesta (1994) found that patients with obsessive-compulsive disorder (OCD) and comorbid personality disorder did not respond to behavior therapy as well as those without personality disorder. But, when treatment was aimed more broadly at psychosocial functioning, those with both syndromes did improve more than they did when the treatment was more narrowly focussed. If these findings apply to a geriatric population, then concern about the negative effects of personality disorders on prognosis may be misdirected.

The identification of target symptoms may not be straightforward. Rosowsky and Gurian (1991) found decreases in both symptomatology and in characteristic psychological test findings—including impulsivity, parasuicidality, acting-out, and substance abuse—in elderly borderline patients; any of these could, in theory, be appropriate target symptoms. Young (1994) overtly advocated educating all his personality-disordered CBT patients as to the schemas ("extremely stable and enduring themes that develop during childhood and are elaborated upon throughout an individual's lifetime," p. 9) that characterize their personality dysfunction and form the targets for his approach; these may include beliefs in individuals' incompetence, sense of defectiveness, feeling of isolation, sense of vulnerability, and others particularly characteristic of this population. Two recent textbooks with extensive coverage of behavioral approaches to geriatric psychiatry (Carstensen, Edelstein, & Dornbrand, 1996; Wisocki, 1991b) include chapters on such topics as mood and anxiety symptoms, social skills deficits, substance abuse, and aggression, all potential symptoms of personality disorder, without any chapter on the treatment of personality disorders as such!

One further caveat pertains to identification of the recipient of the interventions. Many CBT approaches useful in this population are treatments in which the patient's caretakers, in addition to or instead of patients themselves, participate directly (e.g., Gallagher-Thompson & Steffen, 1994; Thompson & Gallagher-Thompson, 1996; J. M. Zarit & S. H. Zarit, 1991; Zeiss & Steffen, 1996). This may both directly benefit the caretakers and also prevent a "vicious circle" (e.g., of depression leading to decreased interaction, followed by diminished positive reinforcement for patient and caretaker, then exacerbated by further withdrawal and negativism, etc.; Leszcz, 1996). Thus, selection of symptoms to be ameliorated must include discussion of whose symptoms should be ameliorated.

SPECIFIC TREATMENT CONSIDERATIONS

Treatment can proceed in terms of specific symptoms or by addressing the personality disorder as a discrete entity. Regardless of which approach is adopted, certain modifications of technique may make CBT more useful in this population. Zeiss and Steffen (1996) divided these modifications into those taking into account whatever cognitive deficits may be present and those utilizing specific strengths likely to appear. The former include slowing the pace of material presented, utilizing multiple sensory and educational modalities and memory aids, and devising strategies for staying focused within sessions and promoting generalization outside of them. The latter include demonstrating respect for the elder's role and status, an activity that may be particularly powerful with patients with schemas of inadequacy or incompetence (Sperry, 1995; Young, 1994); inviting the patient to demonstrate areas of strength relevant to the topic at hand; and discussing parallel or related problems already handled in the patient's life or in other ways allowing the patient to demonstrate wisdom.

In general, the general characteristics of all CBT interventions—short duration, problem and goal orientation, deemphasis on interpretation, corresponding emphasis on directiveness and teaching, and use of written materials—make this a modality well-suited to the needs of this population (Wolfe, Morrow, & Frederickson, 1996; Zeiss & Steffen, 1996). But, particularly regarding the cognitive end of the CBT spectrum, Sadavoy (1994) cautioned that not all adverse or negative cognitions are automatically cognitive distortions, especially in individuals who have already suffered many severe reality losses. Similarly, he recommended not treating cognitive distortions directly if the patient's reality situation unalterably reinforces the distortion. For example, working directly on schemata of lack of autonomy may be very difficult with a patient whose medical condition has dictated entrance into a nursing home.

Conversely, the presence of a personality disorder should not blind the clinician to the possible existence of a treatable Axis I illness. Major depression in particular is common among the elderly and may exacerbate personality symptoms but otherwise remain occult (Agronin, 1994; Thompson et al., 1988; Wolfe et al., 1996). This necessitates careful assessment and consideration of antidepressant medication along with more purely psychosocial approaches.

Given these considerations, how should the CBT clinician proceed when treating an elderly individual with a personality disorder, apart from ruling out or treating any Axis I psychopathology? Thompson, Davies, Gallagher, and Krantz (1986) focused on the initial establishment of a warm, concerned relationship in which the patient and therapist work to define complaints as solvable problems and in which the patient is educated as to the nature of the treatment approach, including what will be required of both parties in order for treatment to succeed. Attempting to isolate at least a few symptoms on which patient and therapist can agree to work is essential.

Establishing this contract may not be a straightforward matter, because by the nature of the schemas intrinsic to personality disorders the patient is likely to hold negative beliefs about the likelihood (or even desirability) of change (Beck, Freeman, & Associates, 1990; Thompson et al., 1986; Young, 1994). It may be possible to elicit the patient's collaboration in viewing these beliefs as themselves symptoms to be worked on (e.g., hopelessness or passivity); but, even if that is not possible, the collaborative, active, homework-oriented, optimistic, and structured nature of the treatment needs to be made explicit and agreed to in order for the therapy to proceed (Thompson et al., 1986; Zeiss & Steffen, 1996).

Beyond the establishment of the treatment alliance, therapy will be determined in part by the specific symptoms being addressed. When personality disorder manifestations are closely tied to painful symptoms such as panic attacks or depressed mood, treatment can be a combination of symptomatic relief, (e.g., cognitive restructuring or relaxation training), and more global work on the patient's assumptions or schemas. Examples of the former include Handen's (1991) work on stress and anxiety management, Engels' (1991) ingenious role-playing techniques to remedy social skills deficits, and Patterson's (1992) more operant approach to activities of daily living and social skills training.

However, the contribution of the comorbid personality disorder in these situations must still be addressed. Patients may need help to see the role that beliefs or expectations about self and others play in influencing their current state, and that those cognitions can be altered for their benefit. A psychoeducational approach to the role these cognitions might be playing may help (e.g., "How can thoughts and beliefs affect feelings?"), as outlined by Thompson et al. (1986) and Young (1994). But this still assumes some degree of treatment alliance between patient and therapist around reducing certain personality disorder symptoms (e.g., "being too emotional" or "not relying on myself enough"). In psychodynamic terms, it assumes an egodystonic quality to some manifestations of the personality disorder. Obviously, this is not always the case.

For example, Sadavoy (1996) briefly described a case of "malignant personality disorder" (probably narcissistic) ending in suicide. Also, Thompson et al. (1986) presented the case of a depressed elderly woman with mixed dependent and compulsive personality disorder who failed to respond to conventional CBT. In both of these cases there was no agreement between patient and therapist as to what truly was wrong; the former situation involved a woman who was rigid, demanding, and frequently rejected by her family, whereas the latter involved a woman who insisted on blaming herself for the circumstances around her father's death. Both patients felt their worldviews to be correct and did not believe their schemas to be inaccurate or even dysfunctional, and both did not improve.

Some suggestions made by Teri (1991) regarding assessment and treatment of depression in the elderly can be adapted here in an attempt to demonstrate the potential usefulness and likelihood of change. For example, even patients with severe narcissistic or borderline personality disorders may feel that there are insufficient pleasant events in their life; thus, attempts to engage such individuals around how to increase the frequency of such reinforcers may be likely to proceed with a minimum of struggle. Similarly, patients with avoidant or dependent personality disorders may feel easily overwhelmed in social situations and prefer to remain withdrawn rather than feel such overpowering anxiety; for such patients, breaking down the approach to independent socialization into small increments may significantly allay anxiety. Abundant reinforcement for small change from the therapist, plus the spirit of "collaborative empiricism" (Beck et al., 1990), which views therapy activities as "experiments" from which people can learn whether or not they are overtly successful, can also help make an attempt to change their behavior more acceptable.

Another set of approaches involves working with family members or significant others of the personality-disordered elderly patient. As outlined by J. M. Zarit and S. H. Zarit (1991), family meetings should focus on a six-step process: assessment, generation of alternative solutions, selection of one specific alternative, behavioral rehearsal of this selection, implementation, and outcome evaluation (p. 448). For the family of an individual with a personality disorder, assessment might involve determining the triggers of angry outbursts, as well as any family behaviors that might be maintaining the outbursts, such as ignoring patients when they are not angry. Alternative solutions might include paying more attention to the patient when not upset; asking for alternative behaviors at the first sign of an outburst; devising a consistent, nonreinforcing response for all family members to follow in the event of an episode; and so on. Using this method, the therapist would then help family members rehearse their choice and assist them in implementation strategies and assessment of their efficacy.

The purpose here is both to teach new skills and also to alter reinforcement contingencies that may have inadvertently been maintaining problematic behavior. Thompson and Gallagher-Thompson (1996) also outlined a series of interventions to help support caregivers who have become angry, overwhelmed, or depressed at the longevity or intensity of making such efforts. Designed in a classroom-style format, their "Coping with the Blues" and "Coping with Frustration: Anger Management" programs include psychoeducational and CBT interventions to meet the emotional needs of caregivers in dealing with the problematic behaviors of those in their care. Such programs can make caregivers more effective behavior modifiers while also preserving their own mental health under stressful circumstances.

A CASE EXAMPLE

The utility of some of these approaches may be illustrated in a brief case presentation. This hypothetical case includes some aspects of cases in which this author was involved directly or consultatively, and it is intended to depict a manner in which these techniques might be applied.

Ms. A is a 70-year-old widow referred for outpatient follow-up after a hospitalization for major depression with suicidal ideation without actual attempt or plan. She was described by her daughter, Ms. B, a 45-year-old married attorney living in a neighboring community, as having been "depressed and clingy" for much of her life. Her daughter noted that after Ms. A's husband had died 2 years previously she had become much worse, frequently calling her daughter or old friends and crying on the phone that "no one loves me anymore." Ms. B had found these calls increasingly demanding and, without discussing her feelings with her mother for fear of "hurting her feelings," had recently begun hanging up on her. Feeling guilty, she had called her mother back after one of these occurrences and had gotten no answer. She became frightened, went to Ms. A's apartment, found her mother sitting silently except for whispers of "I want to die," and noticed that there were days' worth of unopened mail in the house and almost no food in her refrigerator. She called her mother's internist, who admitted her to a local general hospital psychiatry service; she received the diagnoses of major depression and mixed narcissistic and dependent personality disorder and was started on paroxetine 10 mg daily.

Ms. A was angry about having been referred for outpatient psychiatric care, but did agree that she had been feeling more depressed than usual recently, angrily adding "Wouldn't you be depressed too if everyone ignored you?" When the therapist listened empathically and did not challenge the concept of being ignored by everyone, she seemed to relax a bit. She agreed that she felt better on medication than she had before she began taking it, but wondered why she would need to talk to a professional regularly when the problem was clearly the manner in which she was treated by others.

The therapist stated that it was a shame that their behavior was affecting her so strongly and wondered if she would want to learn ways in which she could learn not to let injuries from others bother her so much. While not agreeing that her daughter or her friends were any the less unfaithful, she did agree to work on these new ways of thinking "for my own protection."

Over the course of the next 6 months, Ms. A received a fairly standard course of cognitive-behavioral therapy, working particularly on mood monitoring, scheduling of pleasant events, and analysis of her schemata regarding dependence and isolation. For example, mood monitoring disclosed that she would typically awaken at 6 AM and then stay in bed until 10 AM, ruminating about how unfair life had been and about how abandoned she felt. She was grateful for the recommendation to get out of bed earlier, although the task felt overwhelmingly difficult. When the therapist advised her to first put her feet on the floor, then stand up, then walk to the bathroom, then brush her teeth, and so on, she found this much easier to accomplish and noted a rapid improvement in her mood. She also identified a task—buying a new chest of drawers for her bedroom—which she had wanted to accomplish but had felt too depressed to take on. Using a similar graded task assignment approach, she went to three secondhand stores, identified one she liked, made arrangements for it to be delivered, and cleaned up her room and put her clothes in the new chest. She felt tremendous satisfaction in accomplishing this over about 8 weeks of treatment and reported a lifting of her mood.

Beyond the more purely behavioral exercises already described, she tolerated some minimal written disputation of some of her distortions (e.g., "If you don't want to talk to me right now it means you don't care about me at all, therefore I'm worthless"). She and her daughter accepted some "coaching" from the therapist about how to make and decline specific requests, and they agreed that they would speak every other day on the phone. Ms. B was also grateful for information from the therapist about depression in the elderly, and found that when she reminded her mother gently that they would surely speak with each other again in 2 days, Ms. A would become less upset and accusatory. At the end of 6 months, Ms. A was still on paroxetine, was speaking with her daughter every other day as agreed, and was more active in redoing other portions of her apartment. There had been no more than three disagreements between mother and daughter, and she had not been rehospitalized.

A number of points discussed earlier can be found in this vignette. First, the patient clearly had an Axis I major depression, and treatment definitely needed to include medication as well as psychotherapy. Second, the therapist used Ms. A's overt distress as leverage to approach her more characterologic issues, but in doing so did not ignore the patient's own understanding of why she was depressed. Third, concrete, incrementally arranged behavioral exercises were attempted before much cognitive work was done in order to help instill a sense of success in the patient. Finally, her daughter was brought into the treatment and given support, psychoeducation, and specific technical assistance.

CONCLUSIONS

A full review of outcome data regarding cognitive-behavioral therapy is beyond the scope of this chapter. Among sources already discussed herein, there certainly is evidence for the efficacy of CBT among depressed elders (Thompson, 1987; Wolfe et al., 1996). Cognitive-behavioral treatment and psychodynamic psychotherapy for depressed caregivers have each been found effective, the former more for those in caregiving roles for more than 44 months and the latter for those in such roles for less than that time (Thompson & Gallagher-Thompson, 1996). Koder, Brodaty, and Anstey (1996), Lazarus and Sadavoy (1996), and Zeiss and Steffen (1996) discussed other outcome studies with CBT among the elderly.

These data are of course only suggestive, as they pertain only to the CBT of Axis I disorders in an elderly population. There are in fact no outcome studies on the efficacy of any form of psychotherapy for older patients with personality disorders (Lazarus & Sadavoy, 1996). Why, then, recommend the use of this method in this population?

The answer lies in the theory, methodology, and structure of CBT. It is difficult to argue with Zeiss and Steffen (1996) when they pointed out that cognitive-behavioral "therapies are based on theoretical approaches that emphasize life-long learning and the optimistic belief that people can make important changes in their thoughts, feelings, and actions at any point in their lives" (p. 372); this is a CBT application of Lazarus and Sadavoy's (1996) caution against excluding any treatment modality due to patient age. Similarly, the reluctance of cognitive-behavioral therapists to regard personality traits as fixed and ingrained permits the legitimate expression of hope and the expectation of a good outcome. Finally, the incremental approach, clear specification of short-term goals, and use of written work to facilitate skill acquisition and generalization that characterize CBT all seem compatible with the needs of this population.

Furthermore, there are some data supporting the usefulness of CBT in the treatment of personality disorders in general adult populations that include (but are not limited to) elderly persons. Linehan (1993a; Linehan, Armstrong, Suarez, Allmon, & Heard, 1991) is the best source of efficacy data regarding CBT of borderline personality disorder, although her study group includes adults of all ages. Beck et al. (1990) provided an excellent summary of the state of outcome research among 11 DSM–III–R personality disorders. In their book it is notable that all 11 disorders have uncontrolled clinical reports regarding the use of CBT in their treatment, but only 7 disorders have had single-case design studies reported, 6 have been studied regarding their effect on treatment outcome, and only 3 (antisocial, avoidant, and borderline) have been investigated with controlled outcome studies (p. 12).

Thus, the outcome literature is not even uniform across all personality diagnoses. Knowledge in this area could be advanced by collecting a large enough sample of elderly patients meeting criteria for each of the disorders and then carefully operationalizing the interventions to be utilized, perhaps in the form of a treatment manual (e.g., Linehan, 1993b; Young, 1994). It is to be expected that some disorders would be easier to study than others, due to differential prevalences and to varying degrees of clinical salience, so that antisocial and borderline diagnoses might again predominate. Further, it would be easier to simply describe the course of the patients thus treated than to compare their course with a matched control group treated, say, with psychodynamic psychotherapy, although there has been some work with borderline adults that attempts such a comparison (Linehan et al., 1991).

This report has emphasized individual psychotherapy approaches. But Beck et al. (1990) described a number of situations in which group CBT would be appropriate for personality-disordered adults, and Linehan's work (1993a, 1993b) is explicitly designed as a combination of group and individual treatment.

Furthermore, a number of the social skills training interventions described earlier are best carried out in a group format (e.g., Patterson, 1992; Thompson & Gallagher-Thompson, 1996). As already discussed, the literature contains citations regarding group CBT of personality-disordered adults and of the elderly in general, but nothing specifically on group CBT of the personality-disordered elderly; so again it is necessary to extrapolate its usefulness based on limited data.

In the absence of more specific guidance than is currently obtainable, the clinician looking for a CBT approach to a personality-disordered elderly patient will probably most benefit from examining the work of Beck et al. (1990). Their work is recommended because it is based on extensive clinical experience, individualizes approaches to the various personality disorders, validates the typical thinking of the patient by virtue of its focus on schemata, and includes behavioral as well as cognitive interventions (p. 90). The comments of Zeiss and Steffen (1996) regarding adaptation of standard CBT approaches to an elderly population should guide the clinician around such issues as pacing of the treatment, abstraction versus concreteness of interventions, keeping the list of target symptoms small, and so on.

Thus, in closing, the track record of cognitive-behavioral therapy with Axis I disorders among the elderly and with Axis II disorders in the general population can be viewed as optimistic preliminary findings regarding the utility of CBT with personality-disordered older adults. The field of psychotherapy outcome research is very much in its infancy, and it may be unreasonable to expect it to be able to further confirm or disconfirm these impressions at this point in its development. It will more likely fall to future psychotherapists and investigators to determine whether or not these early indications that cognitive-behavioral therapy can be useful in the treatment of elderly individuals with personality disorders prove accurate in the long run.

REFERENCES

Agronin, M. (1994). Personality disorders in the elderly: An overview. *Journal of Geriatric Psychiatry, 27*, 151–191.

American Psychiatric Association (1968). *Diagnostic and statistical manual of mental disorders* (2nd ed.). Washington, DC: Author.

American Psychiatric Association (1980). *Diagnostic and statistical manual of mental disorders* (3rd ed.). Washington, DC: Author.

AuBuchon, P. G., & Malatesta, V. J. (1994). Obsessive compulsive patients with comorbid personality disorder: Associated problems and response to a comprehensive behavior therapy. *Journal of Clinical Psychiatry, 55*, 448–453.

Beck, A. T. (1976). *Cognitive therapy and the emotional disorders.* New York: International Universities Press.

Beck, A. T., Freeman, A., & Associates (1990). *Cognitive therapy of personality disorders.* New York: Guilford.

Carstensen, L. L. (1988). The emerging field of behavioral gerontology. *Behavior Therapy, 12*, 259–281.

Carstensen, L. L., Edelstein, B. A., & Dornbrand, L. (Eds.). (1996). *The practical handbook of clinical gerontology.* Thousand Oaks, CA: Sage.

Dreessen, L., Arntz, A., Luttels, C., & Sallaerts S. (1994). Personality disorders do not influence the results of cognitive behavior therapies for panic disorder. *Comprehensive Psychiatry, 35,* 265–274.

Engels, M.-L. (1991). The promotion of positive social interaction through social skills training. In P.A. Wisocki (Ed.), *Handbook of clinical behavior therapy with the elderly client* (pp. 185–202). New York: Plenum.

Fogel, B. S., & Sadavoy, J. (1996). Somatoform and personality disorders. In J. Sadavoy, L. W. Lazarus, L. F. Jarvik, & G. T. Grossberg (Eds.), *Comprehensive review of geriatric psychiatry* (2nd ed., pp. 637–658). Washington, DC: American Psychiatric Press.

Gallagher-Thompson, D., & Steffen, A. (1994). Comparative effectiveness of cognitive/behavioral and brief psychodynamic psychotherapies for the treatment of depression in family caregivers. *Journal of Consulting and Clinical Psychology, 62,* 543–549.

Handen, B. L. (1991). Stress and stress management with the elderly. In P. A. Wisocki (Ed.), *Handbook of clinical behavior therapy with the elderly client* (pp. 169–183). New York: Plenum.

Koder, D.-A., Brodaty, H., & Anstey, K. J. (1996). Cognitive therapy for depression in the elderly. *International Journal of Geriatric Psychiatry, 11,* 97–107.

Koerner, K., Kohlenberg, R. J., & Parker, C.R. (1996). Diagnosis of personality disorder: A radical behavioral alternative. *Journal of Consulting and Clinical Psychology, 64,* 1169–1176.

Lazarus, A. A., & Fay, A. (1984). Behavior therapy. In T. B. Karasu (Ed.), *The psychosocial therapies* (pp. 485–538). Washington, DC: American Psychiatric Association.

Lazarus, L. W., & Sadavoy, J. (1996) Individual psychotherapy. In J. Sadavoy, L. W. Lazarus, L. F. Jarvik, & G. T. Grossberg (Eds.), *Comprehensive review of geriatric psychiatry* (2nd ed., pp. 819–850). Washington, DC: American Psychiatric Press.

Leszcz, M. (1996). Group therapy. In J. Sadavoy, L. W. Lazarus, L. F. Jarvik, & G. T. Grossberg (Eds.), *Comprehensive review of geriatric psychiatry* (2nd ed., pp. 851–879). Washington, DC: American Psychiatric Press.

Linehan, M. M. (1993a). *Cognitive-behavioral treatment of borderline personality disorder.* New York: Guilford.

Linehan, M. M. (1993b). *Skills training manual for treating borderline personality disorder.* New York: Guilford.

Linehan, M. M., Armstrong, H. E., Suarez, A., Allmon, D., & Heard, H. L. (1991). Cognitive-behavioral treatment of chronically parasuicidal borderline patients. *Archives of General Psychiatry, 48,* 1060–1064.

Marshall, W. L., & Serin, R. (1997). Personality disorders. In S. M. Turner & M. Hersen (Eds.), *Adult psychopathology and diagnosis* (3rd ed., pp. 508–543). New York: Wiley.

Patterson, R. L. (1992). Psychogeriatric rehabilitation. In R. P. Liberman (Ed.), *Handbook of psychiatric rehabilitation* (pp. 276–289). New York: Macmillan.

Rosowsky, E., & Gurian, B. (1991). Borderline personality disorder in late life. *International Psychogeriatrics, 3,* 39–52.

Sadavoy, J. (1994). Integrated psychotherapy for the elderly. *Canadian Journal of Psychiatry, 39 (Suppl. 1),* S19–S26.

Sadavoy, J. (1996). Personality disorder in old age: Symptom expression. *Clinical Gerontologist, 16,* 19–36.

Sperry, L. (1995). *Handbook of diagnosis and treatment of the DSM–IV personality disorders.* New York: Brunner/Mazel.

Spitzer, R. L. (1980). Introduction. In American Psychiatric Association, *Diagnostic and statistical manual of mental disorders* (3rd ed., pp. 1–12). Washington, DC: APA.

Teri, L. (1991). Behavioral assessment and treatment of depression in older adults. In P.A. Wisocki (Ed.), *Handbook of clinical behavior therapy with the elderly client* (pp. 225–243). New York: Plenum.

Teri, L., & McCurry, S. M. (1994). Psychosocial therapies. In C. E. Coffey, J. L. Cummings, M. R. Lovell, & G. D. Pearlson (Eds.), *The American Psychiatric Press textbook of geriatric neuropsychiatry* (pp. 662–682). Washington, DC: American Psychiatric Press.

Thase, M. E. (1996). The role of Axis II comorbidity in the management of patients with treatment-resistant depression. *Psychiatric Clinics of North America, 19,* 287–309.

Thompson, L. W. (1987). Comparative effectiveness of psychotherapies for depressed elders. *Journal of Consulting and Clinical Psychology, 55,* 385–390.

Thompson, L. W., Davies, R., Gallagher, D., & Krantz, S. E. (1986). Cognitive therapy with older adults. *Clinical Gerontologist, 5,* 245–279.

Thompson, L. W., Gallagher, D., & Czirr, R. (1988). Personality disorder and outcome in the treatment of late-life depression. *Journal of Geriatric Psychiatry, 21,* 133–153.

Thompson, L. W., & Gallagher-Thompson, D. (1996). Practical issues related to maintenance of mental health and positive well-being in family caregivers. In L. L. Carstensen, B. A. Edelstein, & L. Dornbrand (Eds.), *The practical handbook of clinical gerontology* (pp. 129–150). Thousand Oaks, CA: Sage.

Wisocki, P. A. (1991a). Behavioral gerontology. In P. A. Wisocki (Ed.), *Handbook of clinical behavior therapy with the elderly client* (pp. 3–51). New York: Plenum.

Wisocki, P. A. (Ed.) (1991b). *Handbook of clinical behavior therapy with the elderly client.* New York: Plenum.

Wolfe, R., Morrow, J., & Fredrickson, B. L. (1996). Mood disorders in older adults. In L. L. Carstensen, B. A. Edelstein, & L. Dornbrand (Eds.), *The practical handbook of clinical gerontology* (pp. 274–303). Thousand Oaks, CA: Sage.

Young, J. E. (1994). *Cognitive therapy for personality disorders: A schema-focused approach.* Sarasota, FL: Professional Resource Press.

Zarit, J. M., & Zarit, S. H. (1991). Behavioral programs for families of dependent elderly. In P.A. Wisocki (Ed.), *Handbook of clinical behavior therapy with the elderly client* (pp. 439–458). New York: Plenum.

Zeiss, A. M., & Steffen, A. (1996). Treatment issues with elderly clients. *Cognitive and Behavioral Practice, 3,* 371–389.

CHAPTER 14

Pharmacologic Treatment of Personality Disorders in Late Life

Marc Agronin, MD
Miami Jewish Home & Hospital for the Aged
University of Miami School of Medicine

Despite intense interest among both clinicians and researchers in the pharmacologic treatment of personality dysfunction and personality disorders, there is virtually nothing in the literature that focuses on their use in elderly individuals. Mental health clinicians who treat elderly individuals with personality disorders are thus faced with the dilemma of using psychotropic medications without clear guidelines, or based on extrapolations from their use in adults with personality disorders or from the treatment of other psychiatric disorders. There are, however, important treatment considerations that apply across the life span, and several that are specific to late life. These considerations stem, in part, from informative studies that have been conducted with younger individuals with several types of personality disorders. This chapter explores these guidelines with the specific goal of applying them to late life.

Most mental health clinicians have worked with elderly individuals with personality disorders, and many of their patients end up on one or more psychotropic medications. Given the challenging and often unremitting nature of personality dysfunction, clinicians can easily get locked in a battle to find any and all medications that will prove effective. More often than not, therapeutic progress remains elusive.

CASE EXAMPLES

CASE I: THE PASSIVE-AGGRESSIVE PROFESSOR

Professor P had been seen in an outpatient mental health clinic for over 30 years, and was well known to half-a-dozen clinicians who had treated him over the years. He had chronic complaints of anxiety and intermittent panic attacks, and a long-standing diagnosis of a personality disorder with passive-aggressive and narcissistic traits. In the last 4 years, the clinic's geriatric psychiatrist had treated him unsuccessfully with four antianxiety medications (alprazolam, clonazepam, lorazepam, and buspirone), six antidepressant medications (nortriptyline, fluoxetine, sertraline, bupropion, trazodone, and nefazodone), and two antipsychotic medications (perphenazine and risperidone). Professor P agreed to try each medication, but with each trial he would immediately discontinue after one or two doses, and describe at his next appointment how he had a "catastrophic reaction" consisting of tremendous and "incapacitating pain" in the back of his head. Professor P would accuse the physician of trying to kill him, and then complain bitterly of his unremitting anxiety and panic. He would beg for another medication, but then repeat the same pattern of resistance. The physician reported that each session was a recapitulation of the last, with this supposedly brilliant academician demonstrating little insight into his overdramatized reactions and refusal to give the medications adequate time to work.

Professor P's presentation illustrates the complexity of personality disorders in late life. He demonstrated both a heterogeneous cluster of maladaptive personality traits, as well as comorbid symptoms of anxiety and panic. Like Professor P, many elderly individuals with personality dysfunction are not easily fit into the categorical diagnostic model of *DSM–IV*. Instead, they often have maladaptive traits from multiple disorders, and sometimes traits that do not appear in the current nomenclature. In addition, most elderly patients with an Axis II diagnosis have one or more comorbid Axis I disorders. These comorbid disorders are often the pathologic result when a dysfunctional personality is placed under increased stress. In turn, their symptoms can exacerbate underlying personality dysfunction.

Given both the complexity and chronicity of personality disorders in late life, the goal of pharmacologic treatment is not to cure the personality disorder, but to diminish the intensity of expression of maladaptive personality traits and the dysfunctional behaviors they inspire. Davis, Janicak, and Ayd (1995) proposed three avenues to accomplish this: target the personality disorder itself, focus on treating discrete symptom clusters, and/or reduce the effects of comorbid Axis I disorders. Given their heterogeneous presentation, however, it is extremely difficult to develop consistent pharmacologic treatment strategies for the entire range of dysfunctional traits and behaviors subsumed under individual personality disorders. It is more practical to target specific maladaptive traits and behaviors that lend themselves to pharmacologic treatment. Treatment of comorbid Axis I disorders usually means reducing symptoms of depression, anxiety, or psychosis that are preventing therapeutic progress with core symptoms of the personality disorder.

Identification of target traits does not, however, guarantee the success of pharmacologic treatment. The act of prescribing medications has unique meaning to individuals with personality disorders, and their specific psychopathology can easily present the most formidable barrier to treatment. For this reason, the use of pharmacologic agents is sometimes contraindicated. Consider the following case vignettes:

CASE 2: PROFESSOR P REVISITED

Despite obvious noncompliance with medications and spurious side effects, Professor P became fed up with his psychiatrist's failed attempts to treat him. He requested transfer to a new physician, who also tried and failed to find a satisfactory medication. Professor P then complained to the hospital's patient representative that the psychiatry staff was incompetent.

CASE 3: MULTIPLE MEDS OF MR. M

Mr. M. had a history of alcohol abuse, major depression, and personality disorder with antisocial and narcissistic traits. Over the years he had managed to get himself on an antidepressant, two benzodiazepines (lorazepam for anxiety and temazepam for sleep), a narcotic analgesic for arthritic pain, and a muscle relaxant. Despite warnings from his psychiatrist, Mr. M continued to drink alcohol intermittently while on this medication regimen.

CASE 4: WHY PRESCRIBE TO MS. Y?

Ms. Y had a history of personality disorder with obsessive-compulsive and dependent traits. She had been on a benzodiazepine for many years, but for unclear reasons. Her current psychiatrist had not prescribed it initially, but was reluctant to discontinue it because Ms. Y had been on it for so long. Ms. Y spent most of the time during visits with her psychiatrist discussing ways to alter its dose and schedule to maximize several vaguely described benefits.

At the heart of each of these cases of personality disorder lies an impairment in interpersonal relationships, which is manifest in maladaptive and idiosyncratic responses to both the prescribing of a medication as well as to the ingestion of it. In the case of Professor P, multiple medications were prescribed to address symptoms of anxiety, panic, and dysthymia, but he never took any of them long enough to experience benefit. The very act of ingesting a pill given to him by a physician elicited strong unconscious resistance, experienced by him in the form of panic and headaches. Mr. M was clearly dependent on several psychotropics, and demonstrated an abusive and frankly hazardous pattern of medication use. Ms. Y did not have a clearly established clinical need for her medication, but she relied on it to maintain a sense of dependency and control within the therapeutic relationship. These maladaptive ways in which individuals with personality disorders manage relationships with physicians must be clearly understood before a decision is made to use a pharmacologic agent. Table 14.1 outlines some of the most common complications and forms of resistance to psychopharmacologic treatment for various personality disorders. The table divides these problems into three areas: noncompliance, poor treatment relationships, and abuse of medications.

TABLE 14.1
Common Complications and Forms of Resistance
in the Pharmacologic Treatment of Personality Disorders (PDs) in Late Life

Resistance and Complications	Associated Personality Disorders
NONCOMPLIANCE WITH MEDICATIONS	
Refusing to take medication	Odd[1] and dramatic[2] cluster
Frequent forgetting of doses	Passive-Aggressive
Experiences of repetitive, suspect, idiosyncratic, and/or inconsistent side effects that derail treatment	Passive-Aggressive PD Odd cluster
Excessive or unrealistic fear of side effects	Anxious cluster[3] Depressive
Angry, belligerent response to side effects	Paranoid Passive-Aggressive Borderline Narcissistic
POOR RELATIONSHIP WITH PRESCRIBING CLINICIAN	
Difficulty forming stable working relationship	Odd cluster Antisocial Borderline Passive-Aggressive
Distrust of psychopharmacologist	Paranoid Schizotypal
Repetitive questions, complaints, or demands that derail treatment	Dependent Passive-Aggressive Obsessive-Compulsive Narcissistic
ABUSE OF MEDICATIONS	
Polypharmacy/abusive patterns of use	Antisocial Borderline
Self-injurious or suicidal use of medications	Antisocial Borderline
Unsupervised and/or unwarranted use of medications	Obsessive-Compulsive Narcissistic

[1] Odd cluster = Paranoid, schizoid, and schizotypal
[2] Dramatic cluster = Antisocial, borderline, histrionic, and narcissistic
[3] Anxious cluster = Avoidant, dependent, and obsessive-compulsive

Several treatment guidelines may help minimize the occurrence and/or impact of these pharmacologic pitfalls, and are important in terms of risk management. First, a prescriber must establish a clinical need and target symptoms for a medication, and focus on the affected individual rather than on the concerns or complaints of health care staff or caregivers. Noncompliance is a likely response to treatment when patients feel forced into it by individuals who are fed up with their behaviors. The prescriber must then obtain and document informed consent from the patient, and devote ample clinical time to discussing the purpose of the medication in an honest and open manner. Such efforts might inevitably provoke the psychopathology under treatment, but will certainly help establish the best possible working relationship under the circumstances. Finally, the judicious use of the fewest possible agents with clear refill limitations is often preferred, especially when there is a history or likelihood of abusive use of medications or other substances, or of self-injurious or suicidal behaviors. The use of medications on a PRN or "as needed" basis should be discouraged, because such schedules often play into a patient's maladaptive needs for dependency, control, or angry retribution.

In approaching an elderly patient with a personality disorder, it is critical for the clinician to first conduct a thorough psychiatric examination that includes gathering information from the patient, available informants, past clinicians, and previous records. In the case of personality disorders, patient reports may be discordant with these other sources of information. Elderly patients may be reluctant to confide problematic or socially inappropriate behaviors, especially if they are participating in the psychiatric evaluation against their will. Paranoid, schizotypal, antisocial, narcissistic, and borderline patients may experience the psychiatric evaluation as noxious, and refuse to fully cooperate. Passive-aggressive patients may intentionally withhold critical and revealing history. Most individuals with personality disorders experience their behaviors as ego-syntonic, despite the ego-dystonic distress they cause, and may not consider them to be problematic enough to report. Without adequate and/or accurate psychiatric and psychosocial history, clinicians' resultant diagnoses are often impressionistic, and can be highly influenced by ageist stereotypes, countertransferential reactions, and salient but inconsistent clinical features.

A second critical step for clinicians during the diagnostic process is to allow enough time to observe the patient in multiple sessions and settings. The very definition of personality disorders notes their chronicity and pervasiveness, and a clinician should observe this firsthand. Adequate clinical time will enable the clinician to build a therapeutic relationship with some patients, and to gain an understanding of the underlying dynamics and typical resistance of their personality dysfunction. This step is especially important when comorbid Axis I disorders alter the clinical picture, because the stress of depression, anxiety, or psychosis may exacerbate and/or distort dysfunctional personality traits. Eventually, the clinician will arrive at both a reliable working diagnosis and a clinical formulation on which to frame treatment. At this point, psychotropic medications can be invaluable therapeutic tools.

Before pharmacologic treatment begins, however, a thorough diagnostic workup must also determine whether personality dysfunction actually represents a more recent personality change. The term "organic personality disorder" that appeared in *DSM–III–R* (1987) had been changed in *DSM–IV* (1994) to "personality change due to . . ." a specified medical condition. Common medical causes of personality change include head injury, dementing disorders, stroke, seizure disorders, cerebral neoplasm, and endocrine dysfunction. The 10th revision of the *International Classification of Diseases* (ICD–10; WHO, 1992) retains the diagnosis of organic personality disorder, but offers a broader classification of enduring personality change after a catastrophic experience or a psychiatric illness. This diagnosis would encompass personality change seen in posttraumatic stress disorder and substance abuse, or after episodes of depression, mania, psychosis, and other psychiatric disorders.

Manifestations of organic personalities vary with etiology, but are characterized by impaired control of affect and impulses. Frontal lobe injury is associated with two syndromes, one characterized by affective lability, lack of judgment and forethought, jocularity, irritability, and disinhibition, and a second one characterized by apathy, behavioral slowing, and lack of affective range and spontaneity. Temporal lobe epilepsy is associated with a "sticky," or "viscous," personality, characterized by affective deepening, verbosity, hypergraphia, hyposexuality, and preoccupation with religious, moral, and cosmic issues. This syndrome is sometimes referred to as an "interictal personality disorder," or Geschwind syndrome. Alzheimer's disease is associated with several early onset personality changes, including apathy (withdrawal, passivity, and decreased interest and initiative), egocentricity, and increases in irritability, aggression, and impulsivity (Rubin, Morris, & Berg, 1987; Petry, Cummings, Hill, & Shapira, 1988; Bózzola, Gorelick, & Freels, 1992).

The use of pharmacologic agents to treat personality disorders does have some theoretical basis. Two particular psychobiologic models have described a relation between certain biologic trait vulnerabilities and underlying neurotransmitter systems. Cloninger (1987) and Cloninger, Svrakic, and Przybeck (1993) described four dimensions of personality: novelty seeking, harm avoidance, reward dependence, and persistence. They believe that empirical evidence points to the first three traits being mediated by respective neurotransmitter pathways containing dopamine, serotonin, and norepinephrine. Siever and Davis (1991) presented a psychobiological model for personality disorders based on four behavioral dimensions they believe are also mediated by monoamine pathways: cognitive-perceptual organization (impairment leads to symptoms of paranoia, transient psychosis, and perceptual distortions), affective regulation (symptoms of depression and anger), impulse control (symptoms of self-injurious or reckless behaviors), and anxiety modulation. Each dimension is anchored in specific Axis I syndromes, with personality disorders representing less extreme forms of disturbance. At the other side of each dimension lie healthier points consisting of specific defensive mechanisms and adaptational strategies.

The researchers behind these psychobiologic models agree that there is empirical support for the link between neurotransmitter pathways and personality traits. In particular, there is strong evidence linking serotonergic dysfunction to compulsive behaviors, impulsive aggression, and suicidality (Coccaro et al., 1989; Stein et al., 1996). Pharmacologic strategies that modulate monoamine activity would be expected, then, to alter corresponding trait vulnerabilities. In fact, the models just described are based in part on observations of how certain pharmacologic agents affect behavior. Soloff (1990, 1997) argued, however, that pharmacologic treatment cannot be reduced to a one-to-one correspondence between a selective medication with its target neurotransmitter and a single behavior or personality trait. Rather, it is the complex interaction among multiple neurotransmitters that gives rise to certain behaviors and traits, and pharmacologic strategies that try to modulate these complex interactions are only modestly effective at best. Soloff further noted that the use of pharmacologic agents with personality disorders is usually targeted at acute symptoms rather than long-standing traits.

TREATMENT STRATEGIES
FOR INDIVIDUAL PERSONALITY DISORDERS

This section describes each personality disorder, with a focus on target traits or behaviors that are potentially amenable to pharmacologic treatment. A summary of these clinical targets is presented in Table 14.2.

It is important to note that none of the cited studies focused on elderly individuals, or even included them in overall samples. In general, there have been very few specific studies on pharmacologic treatment of personality disorders, and Soloff (1997) was only able to locate 83 abstracts in a search of Medline for a 10-year period of time between 1984 and 1995. Of these abstracts, 77% looked at treatment of borderline personality disorder and 12% looked at schizotypal personality disorder, leaving only 9 abstracts on other categories. Many of these studies do not look at pharmacologic treatment for maladaptive traits; rather, they focus on treatment strategies for comorbid symptoms of anxiety, depression, or psychosis.

The Odd Cluster (A):
Paranoid, Schizoid, and Schizotypal Personality Disorders

Paranoid Personality Disorder. Individuals with paranoid personality disorder are characterized by a tendency to view other people with suspiciousness

TABLE 14.2
Pharmacologic Treatment
of Individual Personality Disorders (PDs) in Late Life:
Target Traits, Behaviors, and Comorbid Symptoms

Personality Disorder	Clinical Targets
Paranoid	Paranoid stance
	Belligerence, rages
	Transient psychosis
Schizoid	Social anxiety
Schizotypal	Odd beliefs
	Paranoid ideation
	Transient psychosis
Antisocial	Impulsivity
	Aggression/belligerence
	Depression/Anxiety
	Substance abuse
Borderline	Affective instability
	Depression/Anxiety
	Impulsivity
	Agitation/belligerence/rages
	Rejection sensitivity
	Self-injurious behaviors
	Transient paranoia
	Substance abuse
Histrionic	Emotional lability
	Impulsivity
	Somatization/hypochondriasis
Narcissistic	Anger/belligerence/rages
	Depression/Anxiety
	Rejection sensitivity
Avoidant	Social phobia
	Isolative behaviors
	Anxiety
Dependent	Depression
	Anxiety, panic
	Somatization/hypochondriasis
Obsessive-Compulsive	Depression/Anxiety
	Somatization/hypochondriasis
	Anger/belligerence
Passive-Aggressive	Depression/Anxiety
	Somatization
Depressive	Depression/Anxiety
	Somatization/hypochondriasis

and distrust. As a result, benign behaviors by others may be interpreted as demeaning, threatening, or malevolent. In day-to-day interactions, these individuals may sometimes appear rather serious and rational. However, their pervasive distrust and sensitivity to perceived insults frequently leads to irritability, hostility, accusations, and grudges. Not surprisingly, such behaviors result in a history of occupational and marital problems in middle age, and can severely impair relationships with caregivers in late life. Projection is the characteristic defense mechanism, in which internalized anger or hostile impulses are perceived as coming from external sources. Differential diagnosis is important, because the paranoid stance of paranoid personality disorder must be distinguished from paranoid psychosis. The paranoia of a delusional disorder is more fixed, severe, and resistant to therapeutic intervention. Paranoid ideation in schizophrenia may be more bizarre or fragmented, and is often accompanied by delusions and hallucinations. The long-term course of paranoid personality disorder is not known, although it is believed to be chronic. In late life, individuals with paranoid personality disorder may respond with increased paranoia to changes in location or reliance on strangers for assistance (Solomon, 1981; Straker, 1982). As a result, their introduction to long-term settings may precipitate threats to leave, or litigiousness toward staff for holding them against their will.

The patient with suspected paranoid personality disorder should always be screened for an underlying paranoid psychosis, which may result from another psychiatric or medical disorder, or from transient decompensation of the personality disorder. Treatment of acute psychotic symptoms with an appropriate antipsychotic medication, along with treatment of an underlying medical illness, may diminish the intensity of paranoia, agitation, and belligerence. Antipsychotic medications may also be helpful in treating paranoid personality disorder itself, although without the same established efficacy as with paranoid psychosis. Antianxiety and antidepressant medications may play a role in reducing the intensity of rage and belligerence that may erupt secondary to perceived slights and insults. In general, standing doses may be more effective and better utilized than PRN doses.

Not surprisingly, medication compliance is a major difficulty with the paranoid personality. Medications may be viewed as a hostile extension of the physician or psychiatric system, and thus may be rejected. Paranoid individuals often dismiss the need for medication because they view their suspiciousness as perfectly justified. It is important for the prescribing physician to recognize the intense fear and anger experienced by the paranoid individual, and attempt to empathize with these feelings. It is possible to acknowledge the paranoid person without having to accept the paranoid accusation, perhaps by wondering aloud to the patient how difficult it must be for them to face such worries. The physician can then present the medication as a way for the patient to reduce stress and worry. Overt attempts should be made to respond to and reduce side effects that may aggravate distrust of the prescribing physician.

It is never wise to challenge paranoid ideas outright, unless they are leading to behaviors that pose imminent risk of danger to the patient or others. Overly solicitous or friendly approaches, on the other hand, may be interpreted as patronizing or threatening. A straightforward, honest, and businesslike description of medications will minimize such reactions. Commitments made to the patient (such as providing for follow-up phone calls to monitor medication effects) should be met promptly and as agreed on. An apology or honest admission made to patients when they feel slighted will minimize conflict. None of these approaches are meant to suggest that clinicians must tiptoe around such patients and avoid confrontation at any cost; in fact, limits are often needed to help contain a patient's belligerence. In the long run, however, a focus on consistent and well-structured routines and relationships will increase the chance of medication compliance by helping the patient cope with a profound sense of distrust and projected anger.

Schizoid and Schizotypal Personality Disorders. Schizoid individuals are often viewed by others as isolated, eccentric, or lonely. They appear uncomfortable or aloof in social situations, and demonstrate a constricted, flat, and detached affect. Their inner experience, however, is characterized less by loneliness and anxiety and more by a lack of desire for social relationships. As a result, they do not usually have close ties with friends, caregivers, or relatives outside of immediate family. To maintain their isolation, they may work odd hours in solitary jobs or pursuits, or spend time with their own fantasies or imaginary friends. It is important to distinguish such behaviors from the acute social withdrawal and constricted affect of schizophrenia, schizoaffective disorder, and mood disorders, and from the more profound deficits in social relatedness seen in pervasive developmental disorder. It is also important to distinguish them from individuals with avoidant personality disorder, who may appear equally isolative due to fears of embarrassment and social scrutiny that are not characteristic of schizoid individuals.

Schizotypal individuals are also described as odd or eccentric, and demonstrate a lack of close friends and social relationships. However, schizotypal behaviors are more bizarre and inappropriate, and may manifest in paranoid ideation, ideas of reference, superstitious or supernatural beliefs, and odd speech. These cognitive and perceptual distortions are less extreme forms of psychotic behaviors seen in schizophrenia, but may increase in intensity during periods of stress.

Solomon (1981) believed that schizoid and schizotypal individuals become more eccentric, withdrawn, and anxious in late life, and often develop secondary psychopathology. McGlashan (1986a) studied a sample of schizotypal individuals, and found that after a mean follow-up of 15 years, 50% were married, 30% had children, and their global outcome was slightly better than in a comparison group of schizophrenic individuals. Because they were studied in middle age, it is not known what follow-up in late life would reveal. Several aspects of schizoid and schizotypal personality disorders may actually prove adaptive in late life. These individuals may tolerate social losses better, and value the enhanced social isolation brought about by limited mobility and resources. On the other hand, chronic impairment in cognitive-perceptual functioning that underlies many schizotypal symptoms would seem particularly vulnerable to age-associated decreases in sensory acuity and cognitive processing speed. Odd or inappropriate behaviors can impair relationships with needed caregivers. Institutionalization can be particularly devastating, because schizoid and schizotypal individuals have no choice but to face multiple social interactions.

Elderly schizoid and schizotypal individuals will rarely seek psychiatric care, and will often resist pharmacologic therapy. However, their odd or minimal social interactions and reluctance to participate in activities or therapy groups in residential, inpatient, and long-term settings often bring them to the attention of mental health clinicians. Establishing a therapeutic relationship on which to start treatment can be extremely difficult, and must be based on clearly problematic behaviors that both clinician and patient can recognize. For example, psychotropic agents can help treat comorbid symptoms of psychosis, anxiety, or depression that the schizoid or schizotypal individual will agree are painful. Several studies have found low dose neuroleptics (specifically haloperidol and thiothixene) to be useful in treating individuals with schizotypal personality disorder, particularly psychotic symptom clusters (Goldberg et al., 1986; Hymowitz, Frances, Jacobsberg, Sickles, & Hoyt, 1986; Schulz, 1986). The antidepressants fluoxetine (Markowitz et al., 1991) and amoxapine (Jensen & Anderson, 1989) have also shown benefit for schizotypal patients. To date, there are no published studies on specific pharmacologic agents for schizoid personality disorder.

The Dramatic Cluster (B): Antisocial, Borderline, Histrionic, and Narcissistic Personality Disorders

Antisocial Personality Disorder. The antisocial individual has a long-standing inability to conform to social norms, illustrated by a history of aggressive, reckless, irresponsible, impulsive, deceitful, and criminal behavior. In fact, it is estimated that up to three fourths of the prison population suffers from antisocial personality disorder. Substance abuse is a common comorbid complication. Men are more frequently diagnosed with antisocial personality disorder than women. The terms *sociopathy* and *psychopathy* are sometimes used interchangeably with antisocial personality disorder, although historically there have been diagnostic distinctions between all three terms. The antisocial patient may initially come across in a deceptively charming manner. However, beneath this facade lies an angry and hostile personality, with little anxiety or remorse over the consequences of behaviors directed toward other people or their property. These individuals rarely seek psychiatric treatment for antisocial traits, and when they do it is often ineffective. However, they often present seeking treatment for substance abuse and symptoms of depression and anxiety.

Longitudinal research indicates eventual improvement in antisocial traits, with individuals displaying less impulsivity, aggression, and violent crime (Solomon, 1981). A study by Robins (1966) found full remission in one third of an antisocial sample by age 31, but with one fourth to one third of the sample developing alcoholism. The most aggressive and least socialized individuals had the poorest prognosis. Weiss (1973) found improvement in antisocial tendencies in both Minnesota Multiphasic Personality Inventory (MMPI) scores and hospital records for successively older cohorts in a sample of outpatients. A longitudinal study of 71 men with antisocial personality disorder by Black, Baumgard, and Bell (1995) found that symptoms in over half the sample either remitted or improved after an average of 30 years, but that many of them experienced chronic symptoms of substance abuse, anxiety, and major depression. Robins (1990) believed that the excess of symptoms in young adults tends to diminish in middle age, although with a high risk of death in early years. There is a decline in the amount of criminal behavior, number of arrests, and degree of aggressiveness, with a shift from property and person-related crimes to conduct offenses such as public drunkenness. Brandler (1992) also believed that there is a decline in the most flagrant symptoms such as criminal behavior, promiscuity, and acting out. Not surprisingly, epidemiologic studies have found a decreased prevalence of antisocial personality disorder with age (Blazer et al., 1985; Robins et al., 1984).

In earlier diagnostic systems, antisocial personality disorder was defined by personality dynamics that gave rise to a variety of antisocial behaviors. Since *DSM-III-R,* however, the diagnosis has been based primarily on the presence of those specific behaviors. Age-related changes in behavior may thus make it more difficult to diagnose antisocial personality disorder in late life. As an older individual retires, loses physical strength, has less contact with children, and has less mobility due to physical and financial constraints, *DSM-IV* diagnostic criteria (i.e., inconsistent work behavior, criminal behavior, physical fighting, reckless driving, using aliases, and irresponsible parenting) will not apply in the same context as with a much younger person. Within the confines of a long-term care or nursing home setting, however, a smaller but equally disruptive repertoire of behaviors can be seen. These behaviors may include belligerence or assaultiveness toward staff or patients, stealing property from other residents, disregarding dietary restrictions, surreptitious substance abuse, sexually inappropriate behaviors, and general noncompliance. These individuals often attempt to leave facilities without authorization, putting themselves in dangerous situations.

The first step in treatment is to rule out other causes of apparent antisocial behaviors, such as substance abuse, manic or psychotic states, impulse control disorders, and dementia. In particular, a history of stroke, head injury, or dementia with frontal or temporal lobe damage may lead to antisocial behaviors.

Numerous psychotropic medications can then be used to target aggressive, impulsive, or disinhibited behaviors that are common to antisocial individuals. These include antipsychotics, lithium carbonate, propranolol, benzodiazepines, valproic acid, carbamazepine, trazodone, and clonidine. Penick et al. (1996) found that antidepressants benefited alcoholic men with comorbid antisocial personality disorder. In another study, however, the presence of antisocial personality disorder limited the efficacy of desipramine in cocaine abusers (Arndt, McLellan, Dorozynsky, Woody, & O'Brien, 1994). Selection of an agent will depend on previous trials, medical and pharmacologic contraindications, and the presence of comorbid psychiatric disorders. It is imperative to take note of comorbid substance abuse (or a history of it) that might interfere with psychotropic medications, or increase the chances of medication-seeking behaviors, polypharmacy, and frank medication abuse.

Noncompliance is a common problem with antisocial individuals, and physicians frequently do not have a lot of leverage. In long-term care settings, however, staff should respond to antisocial behaviors that disrupt treatment with firm limit setting. This process may require a meeting between the patient and a figure of authority, such as a medical director or administrator. Patients should understand clearly what the rules are, that they are not arbitrary but apply to all patients, they are mandated by the facility's highest authority, and they are meant not as punishment but for the patient's protection. Rules may need to be written out for the patient, perhaps in the form of a signed contract. A behavioral contract may also be helpful, in which compliance with medication regimens and the absence of antisocial behaviors entitles the patient to desired privileges (e.g., cigarettes or passes).

Borderline Personality Disorder.   Individuals with borderline personality disorder (BPD) are characterized by their intense, unstable interpersonal relationships, poor affective control, impulsive behaviors, and tentative identity and self-image. They often employ a defense mechanism known as splitting, in which they view other people as either all good or all bad. The borderline patient frequently appears to be in a state of crisis, which may culminate in brief psychotic episodes.

CASE 5: BORDERLINE BELLIGERENCE

Mrs. S was a 70-year-old woman admitted to a nursing home after a stroke left her unable to walk. Prior to placement, she had lived in a spare bedroom of her daughter's house for 5 years after her husband's death. During that period of time, the relationship with her daughter was severely strained by Mrs S's frequent rages and obscenity-laced screaming. On several occasions, Mrs. S had threatened to kill herself after having a fight with her daughter. She would often say, "What's the use, you're going to abandon me anyway!" Sometimes she would refuse meals or medications.

Mrs. S was calm and charming when visited by a psychiatrist from a local mental health center, but then refused to take the recommended prescription for an antidepressant, or to attend a day program.

In the six months that she had lived at the nursing home, Mrs. S was described by staff as difficult, hateful, and vicious. She would scream at aides and tell them that they were "fired" when she was unhappy with their care. She had constant complaints about the food and cleanliness of the ward. She did not tolerate her first roommate, and accused her second roommate of stealing from her. Her behavior escalated when she was moved unexpectedly to another floor: She spent her days wheeling up and down the hallways and yelling at other residents about how "terrible" the staff was. She began to throw her linens into the hallway each day after her bed was made. After an angry confrontation with her physician, Mrs. S threatened to throw herself out of the window. She was transferred to an inpatient psychiatric ward, with the expressed hope that an alternate placement could be found.

Because Mrs. S was so belligerent to staff and exhibited paranoid ideation, she was started on a low dose of an atypical antipsychotic medication along with a benzodiazepine with a relatively long half-life. This calmed her immediately, and after several days she seemed less paranoid. However, her moods were quite labile, alternating between tearful cries of despair and angry complaints of being confined against her will. Despite her overall hostility, Mrs. S did take a liking to one nurse, and agreed to a trial of an antidepressant. Over the course of 3 weeks, her lability decreased significantly, and she was discharged back to the nursing facility.

The case of Mrs. S. illustrates many characteristics of elderly borderline patients. She was unable to maintain consistent relationships with her daughter, roommates, or nursing home staff. She was always worried about being abandoned or mistreated, and reacted with hostility, rages, transient paranoia, self-injurious behaviors (e.g., refusing food and medication), and frequent suicidal threats. Much of her symptom profile was echoed by Rosowsky and Gurian (1992), who found that qualities of younger borderline patients such as identity disturbance, impulsivity, self-mutilation, risk-taking, and substance abuse did not appear to define the disorder in elderly patients. They proposed instead that several of the core symptoms may manifest differently in late life; for instance, identity disturbance may be seen in an inability to formulate future plans or pursue goal-directed activities, whereas self-mutilative impulses may manifest in symptoms of anorexia, polypharmacy, and noncompliance with treatment.

Follow-up studies of BPD have not looked at individuals in late life. Short-term follow-up studies in younger patients have found persistence of symptoms (Gunderson, Carpenter, & Strauss, 1975; Masterson, 1980; Pope, Jonas, Hudson, Cohen, & Gunderson, 1983). A long-term follow-up study by McGlashan (1986b) found decreased expression of borderline and depressive symptoms, improved occupational functioning, but persistence of impaired social relationships and suicide risk. Paris, Brown, and Nowlis (1987) found that 75% of subjects with borderline personality disorder did not retain their diagnosis at 15-year follow-up. Although these studies have shown selective decreases in symptoms throughout middle age, several researchers have suggested that there is eventually a re-emergence of symptoms in late life (Agronin, 1994; Reich, Nduaguba, & Yates, 1988; Rosowsky & Gurian, 1991).

For the borderline individual, relevant age-associated losses such as retirement, death of a spouse or other social supports, and the onset of and awareness of physical deterioration or cognitive impairment can precipitate crises. Goldstein (1992a) warned that many of these individuals enter late life without enough social supports, emotional stability, or self-esteem to balance those losses. Conflictual feelings toward significant relationships may impair the process of mourning. Moreover, borderline individuals may lack the skills to replace such devastating losses. Placement in a long-term care setting can lead to feelings of abandonment, depression, and rage. It may be extremely difficult for borderline individuals to form stable relationships with staff and other residents. They may idealize certain staff members while vilifying others, leading to conflict between patients' "supporters" and "enemies." Frequent crises erupt from emotional outbursts, refusal to comply with treatment plans, hostility, and suicidal threats. As a result, staff members often dislike borderline patients, describing them as difficult and hateful.

Psychopharmacologic consultation should be an early step in treatment, and a necessary step during periods of crisis. Numerous studies have looked at the psychopharmacologic treatment of symptom clusters in borderline personality disorder, and have found a variety of medications to be useful in treating acute symptoms. However, there is no single medication of choice, and little research to support the long-term efficacy of any agent (Soloff, 1994). The selective serotonin reuptake inhibitors (SSRIs) fluoxetine and sertraline have been shown to be efficacious in treating impulsive, self-injurious, and depressive behaviors (Coccarro et al., 1990; Kavoussi, Liv, & Cocarro, 1994) and anger (Salzman et al., 1995), but no SSRI appears to be superior. Other antidepressants, including the monoamine oxidase inhibitors (MAOIs; Cowdry & Gardner, 1988; Links et al., 1990; Soloff et al., 1993), tricyclics, and venlafaxine (Markowitz & Wagner, 1995), have also been shown to benefit acute symptoms of borderline PD.

Antipsychotic medications may be helpful for transient paranoia, agitation, or rages (Goldberg et al., 1986; Leone, 1982), including the atypical antipsychotics risperidone (Khouzam &Donnelly, 1997) and clozapine (Frankenburg & Zanarini, 1993). Mood stabilizers such as valproate, carbamazepine, and lithium carbonate have reduced symptoms of anxiety and agitation (Gardner & Cowdry, 1986; Stein et al., 1995; Wilcox, 1995). Antidepressant and antianxiety medications are helpful in younger patients with dissociative symptoms, but it is not clear whether such symptoms are prominent in elderly borderline patients. Benzodiazepines with short half-lives should be used with caution: One study found increased behavioral dyscontrol in borderline patients treated with alprazolam (Gardner & Cowdry, 1985).

It is important to coordinate a consistent treatment approach among all clinicians working with the borderline patient. This will prevent the patient's defense mechanism of splitting from leading to conflict within a treatment team. Interactions with the patient should be consistent, respectful of boundaries, and supportive while not being inappropriately friendly. In response to outrageous behaviors in acute and long-term care settings, staff anger should be vented in staff meetings rather than at the patient. Otherwise, it may be highly reinforcing for the patient to see staff acting out their inner feelings of anger or rage. Suicidal or self-injurious threats should be acknowledged, taken seriously, and responded to with compassion and yet firm limit setting. A behavioral contract that spells out the consequence of such outbursts or threats (e.g. immediate hospitalization, lost inpatient privileges, restricted passes or visitation) may serve over time to extinguish them. A detailed written contract, signed by the patient and by all clinicians involved, will also minimize confusion among treatment teams as to the best way to deal with the patient's behaviors. Pharmacotherapy for the borderline patient should always be provided with adjunctive cognitive-behavioral, dialectical behavioral, or insight-oriented psychotherapy.

Histrionic Personality Disorder.   Individuals with histrionic personality disorder are extroverted, seductive, and provocative, and demonstrate excessive and dramatic expressions of emotion. These emotional displays are brief and lacking in depth, and are not accompanied by much insight or consistency. Histrionic patients distance themselves from their true emotions through defense mechanisms of *repression,* in which emotions are kept unconscious, and *dissociation,* in which individuals temporarily assume an altered sense of identity. The lability, impulsivity, and provocative nature of histrionic emotional displays may mimic those seen in borderline personality disorder. Histrionic and narcissistic individuals are similar in their desire for attention, approval, and reassurance, and in the superficial nature of their relationships. In contrast, histrionic individuals are more trusting, sometimes to the point of gullibility, and are more reactive to a lack of attention and gratification than to narcissistic injury. Excessive and dramatic affective expression can also reflect more acute states of mania, agitation, and intoxication. Given its historical relationship to hysterical personality, histrionic personality disorder may include symptoms of conversion and/or somatization disorder. Although there are no studies that have looked at histrionic personality disorder in the elderly, it is thought to show gradual improvement (Solomon, 1981; Vaillant & Perry, 1990).

Because of their seductive behavior, need for attention, and concern with physical attractiveness, histrionic patients are sensitive to many of the age-related stressors that also affect borderline and narcissistic patients, such as losses in physical strength, beauty, and sexual responsiveness. Clinicians and staff members may feel overwhelmed by their dramatic emotional expressiveness, and exhausted by their attentional needs. The histrionic individual can benefit from participation in group activities, which provide attention along with constructive feedback and appropriate limits. Psychotherapy may help them clarify their true feelings. There have been virtually no studies of pharmacologic treatment of histrionic personality disorder in adults, and absolutely no studies in late life. One study found that patients with histrionic personality disorder had an increased number of hypochondriacal complaints, and these complaints decreased after treatment with fluoxetine (Demopulos et al., 1996). It is not clear whether this decrease represented a true change in a personality trait (in this case a decreased tendency to focus on bodily symptoms) versus an improvement in more acute affective symptoms, which in turn resulted in fewer somatic complaints.

Narcissistic Personality Disorder. Healthy narcissism is critical to the aging personality; it underlies self-esteem and helps an individual adapt to losses. In narcissistic personality disorder, however, narcissism manifests in a grossly exaggerated sense of entitlement, grandiosity, and arrogance. Such individuals have a strong need for admiration, success, and power, and often demand special treatment. Like antisocial individuals, they often lack empathy for others, but more out of a sense of superiority than from manipulative intent. Like the paranoid individual, they may be acutely sensitive to slights or rejection, but this is due to a fragile sense of self that requires constant stroking, rather than from paranoid fears. Individuals with narcissistic personality disorder may be especially devastated by age-related losses in physical function and attractiveness, occupational opportunities, independence, self-esteem, and self-identity. Their maladaptive attempts to cope with such losses may include excessive entitlement, hostility, rage, paranoid ideation, controlling behaviors, and depression (Goldstein, 1992b).

Clinicians on the frontline of care often feel inadequate, devalued, and angry when dealing with the narcissistic individual's inappropriate entitlement and angry sensitivity to perceived slights. They may feel put off by narcissistic individuals' attempts to manage their own medications, or by their impatience and angry responses to medication side effects or therapeutic failure. It is important, however, for clinicians to identify the losses that are especially devastating to the patient, and to acquire an understanding of the fragile personality underlying the patient's attitudes. Supportive and friendly interactions with the patient will bolster their self-esteem and need for admiration. At the same time, prompt attention to fulfilling treatment-related commitments (e.g., appointments, prescription refills, requests for information) will prevent a patient from feeling unimportant. When complaints arise, extra attention such as phone calls may defuse anger by gratifying narcissistic needs. If available, the narcissistic patient can benefit from psychotherapy. As with histrionic individuals, there has not been research into pharmacologic treatments of narcissistic personality disorder in late life. Clinical experience has shown, however, that antianxiety, antidepressant, and antipsychotic medications may be needed to treat the individual in frequent crisis from narcissistic blows.

The Anxious Cluster (C): Avoidant, Dependent, and Obsessive-Compulsive Personality Disorders

Avoidant and Dependent Personality Disorders. Individuals with avoidant personality disorder have a sense of inadequacy, coupled with a pervasive fear of exposure and rejection. As a result, they appear timid and inhibited, and avoid social situations. Avoidant and schizoid individuals are similar in that both have few friends, and spend their time alone or with trusted family members. However, avoidant individuals genuinely desire companionship, but are too afraid. Individuals with dependent personality disorder are also afraid of rejection, but they cling to relationships instead of avoiding them. Their dependency makes it difficult for them to be alone, make decisions, or take initiatives without constant advice and nurturance from other people. In order to avoid such losses, they are often exceptionally cooperative and submissive. When dependency needs are frustrated, however, they can react with anger, clinging, and urgent demands, or become hopeless, depressed, apathetic, and withdrawn (Kahana & Bibring, 1964). The longitudinal course of avoidant and dependent personality disorders is not known, although both are felt to be chronic disorders (Vaillant & Perry, 1990). Prevalence studies of personality disorders in elderly inpatients have found high incidences of dependent and avoidant personality disorders and traits, in particular with comorbid major depression (Abrams, Alexopoulos, & Young, 1987; Mezzich, Fabrega, Coffman, & Glaven, 1987; Thompson, Gallagher, & Czirr, 1988). These findings suggest that major depression may be a common endpoint for both disorders.

Differential diagnosis can be complicated for avoidant and dependent personality disorders. Diagnostic criteria for dependent personality disorder (e.g., allowing other people to make decisions, difficulty initiating projects, feeling uncomfortable or helpless when alone, and fears of being abandoned) are common in light of age-associated decreases in physical and cognitive ability, and losses of social supports due to death and disability. Individuals who have experienced some of these losses might become exceptionally dependent on surviving family members who are willing to be invested in their care, and display many symptoms of a dependent disorder. Likewise, an individual restricted or embarrassed by physical constraints (e.g., amputation, arthritis, hemiparesis) or symptoms (e.g., incontinence, shortness of breath, visual loss) may display avoidant traits such as avoiding social or occupational activities with significant interpersonal contact, reticence in social situations, fears of being embarrassed, or seeming exaggeration of the risks or difficulties in ordinary tasks. These examples illustrate how an individual could develop behaviors consistent with a diagnosis of a personality disorder without a long-standing history of pervasive, maladaptive behaviors. The diagnosis of a personality change disorder might be appropriate in such circumstances.

Individuals with avoidant and dependent disorders may be particularly vulnerable to numerous age-specific stressors. For example, both disorders are extremely vulnerable to losses of family members or other caregivers who serve as primary social supports. Placement in long-term care settings can have variable effects; avoidant individuals may be unable to tolerate the scrutiny of communal living, whereas dependent individuals may resent having to share staff members with other residents. On the other hand, several aspects of both disorders may conceivably be adaptive in late life. Avoidant (and schizoid) individuals may value the enhanced social isolation brought about by limited mobility and resources. Dependent individuals may welcome newly available health and social services, and value having less social and occupational responsibilities that require decisions (Gurland, 1984).

A first step in treatment is to identify legitimate losses and fears that may result in avoidant and dependent behaviors. Many of these factors can be addressed by providing appropriate medical and rehabilitative support. For example, a patient who avoids social situations due to frequent incontinence can be treated with medications, exercises, and protective undergarments. Patients dependent on assistance for dressing changes can be taught to do it on their own. Avoidant individuals will need consistent reassurance and encouragement. Chastising them or calling attention to their isolative or timid behaviors may only reinforce their sense of inadequacy and fear of rejection. In addition, comorbid major depression or anxiety disorders must be treated. Research has indicated a high overlap between avoidant personality disorder and social phobia (Fahlén, 1995; Schneier et al., 1992), the latter of which can be treated with antidepressant and antianxiety medications (Reich, Noyes, & Yates, 1989). Both fluoxetine and MAOIs have been found to decrease avoidant behaviors (Deltito & Stam, 1989; Versiani et al., 1992).

The dependent individual, on the other hand, can easily irritate clinicians with excessive questions and neediness. As noted, failure to obtain enough nurturance can create a feeling of helplessness, and elicit more clinging behaviors, perhaps in the form of frequent somatic complaints. One way to preempt such behaviors while meeting dependency needs at the same time is to provide the patient with brief, supportive, regularly scheduled clinical contact. In response to excessive demands, clinicians should explain limits in their ability to provide care, while also conveying their willingness to help and offering reasonable concessions (Kahana & Bibring, 1964). There are no specific pharmacologic studies of dependent PD. Treatment will often focus on comorbid symptoms of anxiety and depression.

CASE 6: ANXIOUS AND ODD AVOIDANCE

Mr. W was a 68-year-old single man who was admitted to a VA hospital long-term care unit for treatment of a chronic leg ulcer. Prior to admission, Mr. W had lived by himself in a small, rural house. Ever since his mother died 10 years ago, he spent all of his time alone, and had infrequent contact with several neighbors. He had never had any close friends or romantic relationships, and had never married. Following a psychiatric hospitalization in the early 1950s for an unspecified "nervous condition," Mr. W had been unemployed and on disability. Hs mother took care of managing meals, household duties, and finances, and Mr. W helped out. However, he was able to assume most of these responsibilities when she died. In the last several years, he spent all of his holidays alone, but stated that he was not bothered by this.

A judge had mandated his hospitalization and had assigned a temporary guardian after county social workers reported that Mr. W was refusing to allow visiting nurses to enter his house. This was apparently due to his faithful adherence to instructions his mother had left before her death not to let anyone in the house. Mr. W was described as nervous and shaky on the ward. He kept to himself, often spending time in the bathroom. He was timid when approached by staff, and spoke in a soft, high-pitched voice. His affect was flat, and he demonstrated odd hand posturing and facial tics. He told a psychiatric consultant that he was "nervous around people," and worried that his whiskers "make me look awful." Mr. W was started on an SSRI antidepressant to treat his social anxiety and rejection sensitivity, and within several weeks he demonstrated significantly less anxiety in social interactions. He was able to establish relationships with several nurses as he became more familiar and comfortable with their presence. These nurses were sensitive to his fears, and maintained regular, friendly contacts with Mr. W without being intrusive or critical. After several weeks of successfully residing on the ward, he agreed to remain voluntarily.

Mr. W demonstrated a variety of long-standing, maladaptive traits. Avoidant traits included his timidness and inhibitions in social situations, and lack of social or occupational pursuits due to fears of embarrassment and rejection. He also demonstrated many schizoid traits, including a flat, detached affect, solitary pursuits, and at times a genuine disinterest in relationships. He had a pronounced dependency on his parents when they were living, but had managed to adapt to more independent living. Although the antidepressant medication did not fundamentally alter his personality or "cure" him of personality dysfunction, it diminished his maladaptive traits to the point where he could interact more comfortably in a treatment setting.

Obsessive-Compulsive Personality Disorder. Obsessive-compulsive behaviors are quite common, and often considered a necessity for successful professionals. The individual with obsessive-compulsive personality disorder (OCPD), however, has taken them to an extreme. Preoccupation with orderliness and perfectionism, coupled with a rigid and overly conscientious approach to activities, can be maddening for family members and other caregivers who must submit to such zealous control. Interpersonal relationships are hampered when the obsessive-compulsive person is unable to compromise or act spontaneously. Such behaviors serve as defense mechanisms to control anxious and aggressive impulses. This pattern of behavior must be distinguished from obsessive-compulsive disorder (OCD), in which an individual has specific irresistible, intrusive thoughts (obsessions) or behaviors (compulsions) that are performed to ward off intense anxiety.

Symptoms of OCPD may be exacerbated by changes in daily routine and environment that disrupt an individual's sense of control and self-continuity. As a result, these individuals may redouble their efforts at control, leading to marked inflexibility, hesitation, doubting, and indecisiveness (Kahana & Bibring, 1964). In late life, obsessive-compulsive individuals are especially vulnerable to a loss of self-worth and integrity provided by occupational activities (Bergmann, 1978). The loss of control over their environment and personal space in hospitals and nursing homes is an even more noxious stress. As a result, individuals with OCPD are thought to become more rigid and demanding in late life (Solomon, 1981), and more vulnerable to depression, secondary physical illness, and psychosomatic disorders (Vaillant & Perry, 1990). The presence of cognitive impairment can unleash many impulsive, disruptive behaviors if the patient is unable to remain in control of a daily routine.

Treatment strategies for obsessive-compulsive individuals must recognize this need for control. In clinical settings, it may manifest itself in repeated requests for detailed descriptions of disease states, medication actions, and side effects. Obsessive-compulsive individuals might insist on precise routines for scheduling, ingesting, and managing medication regimens. It is often difficult for clinicians to adapt their prescribing modus operandi, such as when and in what manner medications can be dispensed and refilled, to meet these needs. Instead, clinicians should attempt to focus the energies of obsessive-compulsive individuals on tasks in which they can invest time and have a sense of control. All medications, doses, and scheduling suggestions should be explained with sufficient detail, and with plenty of advance preparation (Kahana & Bibring, 1964). Instructions should be written out in simple language, without ambiguity, especially when prescribing PRN medications. Ample time for questions and provisions for follow-up phone calls should be provided. All of these efforts can prove fruitless when individuals with OCPD are overwhelmed by major medical or psychiatric illness, especially when mental status changes are involved. In those cases, antidepressant medications can treat depressive symptoms, and antipsychotic and antianxiety medications can ameliorate symptoms of belligerence and agitation. Pharmacologic agents used to treat OCD (e.g., fluoxetine, fluvoxamine, and clomipramine) have not been established as efficacious in treating OCPD.

PASSIVE-AGGRESSIVE AND DEPRESSIVE PERSONALITY DISORDERS

Passive-aggressive personality disorder was included as a formal diagnostic entity in *DSM–III–R,* but is now classified (with the added title of "negativistic personality disorder") in the appendix of *DSM–IV* as requiring further study. It is characterized by a pattern of resistance to demands placed on the individual, and manifested by complaining, half-hearted efforts, noncompliance, criticism and resentment of authority, and procrastination. When provided with treatment plans, these individuals will slow or derail progress, and frustrate and anger staff with their complaints and noncompliance. As in the case of Professor P, passive-aggressive patients may derail pharmacologic treatment by failing to adhere to recommended doses or schedules, or may present with repeated, vague side effects. Psychotherapy can provide an opportunity for these individuals to verbalize their true feelings, rather than by indirectly acting them out. Similarly, passive-aggressive behaviors can sometimes be diminished by a patient staff member who is willing to listen to the individual and acknowledge feelings of dissatisfaction or frustration. Pharmacologic treatment frequently focuses on comorbid anxiety and depression, or on chronic somatic complaints.

Depressive personality disorder is characterized by a gloomy, pessimistic, and critical outlook on life and others, guilt-proneness, and a sense of personal inadequacy or lack of self-esteem. Depressive personality disorder is also classified in the appendix of *DSM–IV* as a disorder requiring further study. Although there has not been much research on this current conceptualization, there have been many similar concepts throughout the psychiatric literature (Phillips & Gunderson, 1994). Not surprisingly, there is nothing in the literature on its presence in late life. The main diagnostic concern has been whether this personality disorder can be distinguished from major depression and dysthymic disorder, but data have supported its phenomenologic distinctiveness (Klein, 1990). Unpublished data from a research database of personality disorders in a geriatric psychiatry outpatient clinic at the Minneapolis VA Medical Center indicate that it is a relatively common personality disorder in late life, found in 11 of 48 individuals (23%) with personality disorders, representing roughly 2% of the clinic population (Agronin & Orr, 1998).

Target symptoms for depressive personality disorder might include the characteristic gloomy or dysphoric mood and the tendency to worry or brood. Antidepressants would be the obvious pharmacologic treatment for these traits, although anxiolytics might play a role with more pronounced worrying that inspires frank anxiety or even occasional panic. Adjunctive cognitive therapy would certainly play a key role for target symptoms such as pessimistic and critical attitudes, and low self-esteem. Engaging depressive individuals in pharmacologic treatment might be challenged by their pessimistic and critical attitudes toward the efficacy of medications. It is likely that patients will cooperate with pharmacotherapy, but that medications will bring only modest benefit at best. As a result, prescribing clinicians often end up switching to alternate agents or using augmentation strategies. It is more likely that the most beneficial use of antidepressants will be their use in treating more acute depressive symptoms that have developed on top of chronic depressive traits (Akiskal, 1983).

CONCLUSIONS

Pharmacotherapy is an important and viable treatment strategy for personality disorders across the life span. Despite the lack of research into the pharmacologic treatment of late-life personality disorders, and the limited spectrum of studies in younger individuals, there is a growing body of knowledge that can be applied to elderly cases. This knowledge is based in part on research findings that suggest a relation between the monoamine neurotransmitter systems in the brain and certain biologic personality trait vulnerabilities. The use of medications to treat personality disorders should only occur once a thorough medical and psychiatric evaluation have allowed the clinician to establish a likely diagnosis and case formulation, and to select target symptoms. Pharmacologic treatment must sometimes be avoided when the act of prescribing medications takes on symbolic importance to a particular personality disorder, resulting in disruptive behaviors. Treatment strategies vary with each personality disorder, but the goal of pharmacotherapy is not to cure the disorder but to ameliorate select maladaptive traits and to treat comorbid psychopathology.

REFERENCES

Abrams, R. C., Alexopoulos, G. S., & Young, R. C. (1987). Geriatric depression and *DSM–III–R* personality disorder criteria. *Journal of the American Geriatrics Society, 35*, 383–386.

Agronin, M. (1994). Personality disorders in the elderly: An overview. *Journal of Geriatric Psychiatry, 27*(2), 151–191.

Agronin, M., & Orr, W. (1998, March). *Personality disorders in a geriatric psychiatry outpatient clinic* [Abstract]. American Association for Geriatric Psychiatry Annual Meeting, San Diego, CA.

Akiskal, H. S. (1983). Dysthymic disorder: Psychopathology of proposed chronic depressive subtypes. *American Journal of Psychiatry, 140*, 11–20.

American Psychiatric Association (1987). *Diagnostic and statistical manual of mental disorders* (3rd ed. rev.). Washington, DC: Author.

American Psychiatric Association (1994). *Diagnostic and statistical manual of mental disorders* (4th ed.). Washington, DC: Author.

Arndt, I. O., McLellan, A. T., Dorozynsky, L., Woody, G. E., & O'Brien, C. P. (1994). Desipramine treatment for cocaine dependence: Role of antisocial personality disorder. *Journal of Nervous and Mental Disease, 182*(3), 151–156.

Bergmann, K. (1978). Neurosis and personality disorder in old age. In A. D. Isaacs & F. Post (Eds.), *Studies in geriatrics psychiatry* (pp. 41–76). New York: Wiley.

Black, D. W., Baumgard, C. H., & Bell, S. E. (1995). A 16- to 45-year follow-up of 71 men with antisocial personality disorder. *Comprehensive Psychiatry, 36*(2), 130–140.

Blazer, D. G., George, L. K., Landerman, R., Pennybacker, M., Melville, M. L., Woodbury, M., Manton, K. G., Jordan, K., & Locke, B. (1985). Psychiatric disorders, a rural/urban comparison. *Archives of General Psychiatry, 42,* 651–656.

Bózzola, F. G., Gorelick, P. B., & Freels, S. (1992). Personality changes in Alzheimer's disease. *Archives of Neurology, 49,* 29–300.

Brandler, S. (1992). Antisocial behavior in old age. In F. J. Turner (Ed.), *Mental health and the elderly* (pp. 304–327). New York: The Free Press.

Cloninger, C. R. (1987). A systematic method for clinical description and classification of personality variants. *Archives of General Psychiatry, 44,* 573–588.

Cloninger, C. R., Svrakic, D. M., & Przybeck, T. R. (1993). A psychobiologic model of temperament and character. *Archives of General Psychiatry, 50,* 975–990.

Coccaro, E. F., Astill, J. L, Herbert, J. A., & Schut, A. (1990). Fluoxetine treatment of impulsive aggression in *DSM–III–R* personality disorder patients. *Journal of Clinical Psychopharmacology, 10,* 373–375.

Coccaro, E. F., Siever, L. J., Klar, H. M., Maurer, G., Cochrane, K., Cooper, T. B., Mohs, R. C., & Davis, K. L. (1989). Serotonergic studies in patients with affective and personality disorders: Correlates with suicidal and impulsive aggressive behavior. *Archives of General Psychiatry, 46,* 587–599.

Cowdry, R. W., & Gardner, D. L. (1988). Pharmacotherapy of borderline personality disorder. Alprazolam, carbamazepine, trifluoperazine, and tranylcypromine. *Archives of General Psychiatry, 45,* 111–119.

Davis, J. M., Janicak, P. G., & Ayd, F. J. (1995). Pharmacotherapy of the personality-disordered patient. *Psychiatric Annals, 25*(10), 614–620.

Deltito, J. A., & Stam, M. (1989). Psychopharmacological treatment of avoidant personality disorder. *Comprehensive Psychiatry, 30,* 498–504.

Demopulos, C., Fava, M., McLean, N. E., Alpert, J. E., Nierenberg, A. A., & Rosenbaum, J. F. (1996). Hypochondriacal concerns in depressed outpatients. *Psychosomatic Medicine, 58*(4), 314–320.

Fahlén, T. (1995). Personality traits in social phobia. II: changes during drug treatment. *Journal of Clinical Psychiatry, 56*(12), 569–573.

Frankenburg, F. R., & Zanarini, M. C. (1993). Clozapine treatment of borderline patients: A preliminary study. *Comprehensive Psychiatry, 34*(6), 402–5.

Gardner, D. L., & Cowdry, R. W. (1985). Alprazolam induced dyscontrol in borderline personality disorder. *American Journal of Psychiatryiatry, 142,* 98–100.

Gardner, D. L., & Cowdry, R. W. (1986). Positive effects of carbamazepine on behavioral dyscontrol in borderline personality disorder. *American Journal of Psychiatryiatry, 143,* 519–522.

Goldberg, S. C., Schulz, S. C., Schulz, P. M., Resnick, R. J., Hamer, R. M., & Freidel, R. O. (1986). Borderline and schizotypal personality disorders treated with low-dose thiothixene vs. placebo. *Archives of General Psychiatryiatry, 43,* 680–686.

Goldstein, E. G. (1992a). Borderline personality disorders. In F. J. Turner (Ed.), *Mental health and the elderly* (pp. 220–248). New York: The Free Press.

Goldstein, E. G. (1992b). Narcissistic personality disorder. In F. J. Turner (Ed.), *Mental health and the elderly* (pp. 249–270). New York: The Free Press.

Gunderson, J. G., Carpenter, W. T., & Strauss, J. S. (1975). Borderline and schizophrenic patients: A comparative study. *American Journal of Psychiatry, 132,* 1257–1264.

Gurland, B. J. (1984). Personality disorders of old age. In D.W.K. Kay & G. D. Burrows (Eds.), *Handbook of studies on psychiatry and old age* (pp. 303–318). New York: Elsevier.

Hymowitz, P., Frances, A. Jacobsberg, L. B., Sickles, M., & Hoyt, R. (1986). Neuroleptic treatment of schizotypal personality disorder. *Comprehensive Psychiatry, 27,* 267–271.

Jensen, H. V., & Anderson, J. (1989). An open, comparative study of amoxapine in borderline disorders. *Acta Psychiatrica Scandinavica, 79,* 89–93.

Kahana, R. J., & Bibring, G. L. (1964). Personality types in medical management. In N. Zinberg (Ed.), *Psychiatry and medical practice in a general hospital* (pp. 108–123). New York: International Universities Press.

Kavoussi, R. J., Liv, J., & Cocarro, E. F. (1994). An open trial of sertraline in personality disorder patients with impulsive aggression. *Journal of Clinical Psychiatry, 55,* 137–141.

Khouzam, H. R., & Donnelly, N. J. (1997). Remission of self-mutilation in a patient with borderline personality during risperidone therapy. *Journal of Nervous and Mental Disease, 185*(5), 348–349.

Klein, D. N. (1990). Depressive personality: Reliability, validity, and relation to dysthymia. *Journal of Abnormal Psychology, 99,* 412–421.

Leone, N. (1982). Response of borderline patients to loxapine and chlorpromazine. *Joural of Clinical Psychiatry, 43,* 148–150.

Links, P. S., Steiner, M., Boiageo, B. A., & Irwin, D. (1990). Lithium therapy for borderline patients: Preliminary findings. *Journal of Personality Disorders, 4,* 173–181.

Markowitz, P. J., & Wagner, S. C. (1995). Venlafaxine in the treatment of borderline personality disorder. *Psychopharmacology Bulletin, 31*(4), 773–777.

Markowitz, P. J., Calabrese, J. R., Schulz, S. C., & Meltzer, H. Y. (1991). Fluoxetine treatment of borderline and schizotypal personality disorders. *American Journal of Psychiatry, 148,* 1064–1067.

Masterson, J. F. (1980). *From borderline adolescent to functioning adult: The test of time.* New York: Brunner/Mazel.

McGlashen, T. H. (1986a). Schizotypal personality disorder. The Chestnut Lodge follow-up study: IV. Long-term follow-up perspectives. *Archives of General Psychiatry, 43,* 329–334.

McGlashen, T. H. (1986b). The Chestnut Lodge follow-up study: III. Long-term outcome of borderline personalities. *Archives of General Psychiatry, 43,* 20–30.

Mezzich, T. E., Fabrega, H., Coffman, G. A., & Glaven, Y. (1987). Comprehensively diagnosing geriatric patients. *Comprehensive Psychiatry, 28,* 68–76.

Paris, J., Brown, R., & Nowlis, D. (1987). Long-term follow-up of borderline patients in a general hospital. *Comprehensive Psychchiatry, 2,* 530–535.

Penick, E. C., Powell, B. J., Campbell, J., Liskow, B. Í., Nickel, E. J., Dale, T. M., Thomas, H. M., Laster, L. J., & Noble, E. (1996). Pharmacological treatment for antisocial personality disorder in alcoholics: A preliminary study. *Alcoholism, Clinical & Experimental Research, 20*(3), 477–484.

Petry S., Cummings J. L., Hill, M. A., & Shapira, J. (1988). Personality alterations in dementia of the Alzheimers type. *Archives of Neurology, 45,* 118–190.

Phillips, K. A., & Gunderson, J. G. (1994). Personality disorders. In R. E. Hales, S. C. Yudolsky, & J. A. Talbott (Eds.), *Textbook of psychiatry* (2nd ed., pp. 701–728). Washington, DC: American Psychiatric Press.

Pope, H. G., Jonas, J. M., Hudson, J. I., Cohen, B. M., & Gunderson, J. G. (1983). The validity of *DSM–III* borderline personality disorder. *Archives of General Psychiatry, 40,* 23–30.

Reich, J., Nduaguba, M., & Yates, W. (1988). Age and sex distribution of *DSM–III* personality cluster traits in a community population. *Comprehensive Psychiatry, 29*(3), 298–303.

Reich, J., Noyes, R., Jr., & Yates, W. (1989). Alprazolam treatment of avoidant personality traits in social phobic patients. *Journal of Clinical Psychiatry, 50,* 91–95.

Robins, L. N. (1966). *Deviant children grow up: A sociological and psychiatric study of sociopathic personality.* Baltimore: Williams & Wilkins.

Robins, L. N. (1990). Epidemiology of antisocial personality. In R. Michels & J. O. Cavenar (Eds.), *Psychiatry* (Vol. 3, pp. 1–14). Philadelphia: Lippincott.

Robins, L. N., Helzer, J. E., Weissman, M. M., Orvaschel, H., Gruenberg, E., Burke, J. D., & Regier, D. A. (1984). Lifetime prevalence of specific psychiatric disorders in three sites. *Archives of General Psychiatryiatry, 41,* 949–958.

Rosowsky, E., & Gurian, B. (1991). Borderline personality disorder in late life. *International Psychogeriatrics, 3*(1), 39–52.

Rosowsky, E., & Gurian, B. (1992). Impact of borderline personality disorder in late life onsystems of care. *Hospital and Community Psychiatry, 43*(4), 386–389.

Rubin, E. H., Morris, J. C., & Berg, L. (1987). The progression of personality changes in senile dementia of the Alzheimers type. *Journal of the American Geriatrics Society, 35,* 21–25.

Salzman, C., Wolfson, A. N., Schatzberg, A., Looper, J., Henke, R. Albanese, M., Schwartz, J., & Miyawaki, E. (1995). Effect of fluoxetine on anger in symptomatic volunteers with borderline personality disorder. *Journal of Clinical Psychopharmacology, 15*(1), 23–29.

Schneier, F. R., Chin, S. J., Hollander, E., & Liebowitz, M. R. (1992). Fluoxetine in social phobia. *Journal of Clinical Psychopharmacology, 12,* 62–64.

Schulz, S. C. (1986). The use of low-dose neuroleptics in the treatment of "schizo-obsessive" patients. *American Journal of Psychiatryiatry, 143,* 1318–1319.

Siever, L. J., & Davis K. L. (1991). A psychobiological perspective on the personality disorders. *American Journal of Psychiatry, 148,* 1647–1658.

Soloff, P. H. (1990). What's new in personality disorders? An update on pharmacologic treatment. *Journal of Personality Disorders, 4*(3), 233–243.

Soloff, P. H. (1994). Is there any drug treatment of choice for the borderline patient? *Acta Psychiatrica Scandinavica* (Supp. 379), 50–55.

Soloff, P. H. (1997). Psychobiologic prespectives on treatment of personality disorders. *Journal of Personality Disorders, 11*(4), 336–344.

Soloff, P. H., Cornelius, J., George, A., Nathan, S., Perel, J. M., & Ulrich, R. F. (1993). Efficacy of phenelzine and haloperidol in borderline personality disorder. *Archives of General Psychiatry, 50,* 377–385.

Solomon, K. (1981). Personality disorders and the elderly. In J. R. Lion (Ed.), *Personality disorders, diagnosis and management* (pp. 310–338). Baltimore, MD: Williams & Wilkins.

Stein, D. J., Simeon, D., Frenkel, M., Islam, M. N., & Hollander, E. (1995). An open trial of valproate in borderline personality disorder. *Journal of Clinical Psychiatry, 56*(11), 506–510.

Stein, D. J., Trestman, R. L., Mitropoulou, V., Coccaro, E. F., Holander, E., & Siever, L. J. (1996). Impulsivity and serotonergic function in compulsive personality disorder. *Journal of Neuropsychiatry & Clinical Neurosciences, 8,* 393–398.

Straker, M. (1982). Adjustment disorders and personality disorders in the aged. *Psychiatric Clinics of North America, 5*(1), 121–129.

Thompson, L. W., Gallagher, D., & Czirr, R. (1988). Personality disorder and outcome in the treatment of late-life depression. *Journal of Geriatric Psychiatry, 21*(2), 133–153.

Vaillant, G. E., & Perry, J. C. (1990). Personality disorders. In H. I. Kaplan & B. J. Sadock (Eds.), *Comprehensive textbook of psychiatry* (5th ed., vol. 2, pp. 1352–1387). Baltimore, MD: Williams & Wilkins.

Versiani, M., Nardi, A. E., Mundim, F. D., & Alves, A. B. (1992). Pharmacotherapy of social phobia: A controlled study with meclobemide and phenelzine. *British Journal of Psychiatry, 161,* 353–360.

Weiss, J.A.M. (1973). The natural history of antisocial attitudes. What happens to psychopaths? *Journal of Geriatric Psychiatry, 6,* 236–242.

Wilcox, J. A. (1995). Divalproex sodium as a treatment for borderline personality disorder. *Annals of Clinical Psychiatry, 7*(1), 33–37.

World Health Organization. (1992). *The ICD–10 classification of mental and behavioural disorders: Clinical descriptions and diagnostic guidelines.* Geneva: Author.

PART IV

Systems and Social Issues

Personality Disorders and the Difficult Nursing Home Resident

ERLENE ROSOWSKY, PsyD
Harvard Medical School

MICHAEL A. SMYER, PhD
Boston College

Consider the following case:

> Mrs. F, a woman in her 80s, who entered the nursing home requiring significant medical care and assistance with most activities of daily living (ADL). Initially she was haughty and demanding, imperious in her dealing with staff. She aligned herself with the head nurse, bearing to her tales of every perceived failure of the aides. The nurse would confront the aides and smooth over the latest incident, but never before the next complaint was filed by the resident.
>
> The staff labeled her in negative terms and soon tried to avoid being assigned her care. When assigned, they limited their contact with Mrs. F to what was minimally necessary, if that. Being ignored had a dramatic effect on Mrs. F. She escalated and was rude to staff even before they began their work with her. She began to reveal suicidal ideation, saying that she'd like to be dead and hinting that she would find a way. The staff, enraged at her, ignored her distress and dismissed her threats. Over time she became withdrawn, stopped eating, and lost weight.
>
> A staff nurse, rotated from another floor, who did not have the negative history of managing Mrs. F's care, recognized a clinical depression and requested treatment. Mrs. F was started on a course of medication and psychotherapy. A diagnosis was made of Depression on Axis I and Narcissistic Personality Disorder on Axis II.

A therapeutic intervention at the level of the nursing home staff was made. This included introducing them to Mrs. F's history: who she was, what had provided purpose and meaning in her life, and how she had engaged and related to others. The staff identified which of Mrs. F's behavioral repertoire facilitated or impeded her care. In a creative brainstorming session, they anticipated how their approach to Mrs. F could advance or sabotage their professional agenda.

Through the intervention, the staff made relevant, self-selected behavioral changes, and felt more empowered and less hostile. Mrs. F, of course, mirrored these changes. She felt more appreciated and better cared for. When her irritating and difficult behaviors did appear—and they did— the staff was better protected by a reasonable working distance and understanding . They were able to avoid acting out or acting in as a reflection of Mrs. F's psychopathology. Over time, the staff valued Mrs. F's special talent and expertise as a fashion consultant, taking her advice in selecting their attire for upcoming social events.

As this case illustrates, many significant factors affect the quality of life of nursing home residents: the culture of the nursing home, the physical setting, the administrative and clinical staffs. However, the effect of the residents' personalities on their nursing home experience is often overlooked. This chapter provides a framework for assessment and treatment of personality disorders (PDs) in the nursing home setting.

It begins with a discussion of "the difficult patient," because this label is more frequently used than the diagnostic category of personality disorder. The second section considers the role that nursing homes play in the current mental and physical health care system. This section draws on epidemiological data from national studies on the rates of disordered behavior in nursing homes. The third section focuses on the subtle but important distinction between personality style and personality disorder. The fourth section describes assessment and treatment approaches, with emphasis on organizational consultation strategies. The chapter concludes with a discussion of the policy and practice incentives and disincentives for recognizing personality disorders more clearly within the nursing home setting.

NURSING HOMES:
PHYSICAL AND MENTAL HEALTH CARE SETTINGS

Nursing homes are both mental health and physical health treatment settings for society (Smyer, Cohn, & Brannon, 1988). They are also family care settings (Freedman, Berkman, Rapp, & Ostfeldt, 1994).

The majority of nursing home residents have a mental disorder in addition to their physical health problems. For example, Strahan and Burns (1991), using the 1985 National Nursing Home Survey, concluded that 65% of nursing home residents have at least one mental disorder. Lair and Lefkowitz (1990) reached the same conclusion drawing on the 1987 National Medical Expenditure Survey (NMES). The most common form of mental disorder among nursing home residents is Alzheimer's disease or another dementia (German, Rovner, Burton, Brant, & Clark, 1992). Although dementia and organic mental disorder are the most frequent diagnoses, Tariot, Podgorski, Blazina, and Leibovici (1993) reported that 18% had primary diagnoses on Axis I and Axis II, and it is recognized that Axis II diagnoses are typically underrecorded.

Most nursing home residents face the dual challenge of mental and physical illness. For example, in the 1985 National Nursing Home Survey, a majority of nursing home residents needed assistance with self-care activities, a common proxy for the effects of physical disability (Cohen, Van Nostrand, & Furner, 1993). A similar pattern emerged in the 1987 NMES data (Lair & Lefkowitz, 1990).

The patterns described thus far are drawn from data gathered in the mid-1980s, just prior to a major congressional intervention. Following an Institute of Medicine study (IOM, 1986), Congress passed the Nursing Home Reform Act of 1987 (NHRA; Smyer, 1989). The intent was clear: Congress wanted to improve nursing home care through regulatory reform. One means of achieving this goal was to focus attention on who sought admission to nursing homes. Under the NHRA, each potential resident was to be screened. Those who only needed mental health care (and not physical health care or nursing care) were to be excluded.

Unfortunately, regulatory reform has not altered the patterns of mental and physical disorders among nursing home residents. For example, the 1996 Medical Expenditure Panel Survey (MEPS) found that over 80% of nursing home residents needed help with three or more activities of daily living, a proxy for physical incapacity. Nearly half of the residents had some form of dementia (Krauss et al., 1997). In short, nursing homes continue to serve as a major receiving site for older adults who are both physically and mentally ill.

PATTERNS OF MENTAL DISORDERS:
PSYCHIATRIC EPIDEMIOLOGY

Thus far, the patterns of mental illness in nursing homes have been presented using national data (e.g., Burns et al., 1993; Lair & Lefkowitz, 1990). The national studies have used structured questionnaires or administrative record keeping and reporting to develop their portrayals of nursing home residents' functioning.

In contrast, several investigators have followed small cohorts of residents using a full psychiatric examination to assess the presence or absence of mental illness. For example, German and her colleagues (German et al., 1992) prospectively studied a cohort of 454 residents admitted to eight nursing homes in the Baltimore area. They found that 80% of the newly admitted residents had a mental illness, with 36% receiving a diagnosis of dementia; 32% receiving a diagnosis of dementia, complicated; and 13% being diagnosed with another psychiatric disorder. It is important to note that this study occurred soon after the implementation of the 1987 NHRA.

Tariot and his colleagues (Tariot et al., 1993) also undertook a psychiatric examination of a cohort of nursing home residents. In contrast to German's study, Tariot et al. (1993) concentrated on a single county-owned long-term care facility in Rochester, New York. The sample was representative of the county hospital's census. In particular, 10% of the sample were Black and 86% were White. A randomly selected cohort of 80 residents was examined by a geriatric psychiatrist. The results were striking, with 91% of the sample having at least one psychiatric diagnosis and at least one behavioral problem and 50% having four or more behavioral problems. At the same time, 61% of the sample received some form of psychiatric care after admission. This study was carried out in 1989, after the implementation of the NHRA preadmission screening criteria.

Class and his colleagues (Class, Unverzagt, Gao, Hall, Baiyewu, & Hendrie, 1996), by contrast, focused attention specifically on rates of mental disorders among African American nursing home residents in six nursing homes in Indianapolis, Indiana. They found that 90% of their subjects had at least one primary psychiatric diagnosis, most often dementia. Moreover, 71% exhibited at least one behavioral problem, and 26% had five or more behavioral problems. In contrast with the Tariot sample, only 23% had contact with a mental health professional within the previous 6 months. Again, it should be noted that this study was carried out in 1990, after implementation of the 1987 NHRA.

These small sample studies complement the large national studies in two ways. First, their reliance on psychiatric examination for diagnoses assures greater reliability and validity of the determination of a mental illness. Second, they provide snapshots of resident functioning before and after the NHRA. The conclusion from these studies is clear: Nursing homes remain an important mental health treatment setting. As noted earlier, mental health problems are often a major (or the major) factor for the individual's transfer from the home in the community into the nursing home.

Nursing homes often serve as a setting of last resort turned to by family members after they have exhausted emotional and economic resources (Zarit, 1996). This may be especially true for "difficult" elders who overwhelm the family's ability to provide effective structure and care. As Gurland (1980) pointed out, older adults who exhibit disruptive behavior, excessive dependence on others, and social maladjustment are likely to elicit some sort of organized help from formal and informal resources. Commonly, the last resort of informal caregivers of difficult older adults is the nursing home.

As noted elsewhere in this volume (see chap. 4), reports of a slight decline in the prevalence of personality disorders in old age (Blazer et al., 1985) may reflect several aspects of clinical practice and the disorder itself: poor recognition of personality disorders in late life, an inability to make a clinical diagnosis using criteria designed to capture the expression of the pathology at a younger age, and a potential selective mortality effect for those with the more severe personality disorders because of lives marked by risky behaviors and poor support networks (Rosowsky & Gurian, 1991; Sadavoy, 1996). However, there may be a positive selective bias overrepresenting older adults with personality disorders in nursing homes. Such elderly are likely to have been especially difficult to maintain at home and to have had a history of unstable, conflictual relationships with potential caregivers (Sadavoy, 1996).

The Difficult Nursing Home Resident

Gauging the rates of personality disorders among nursing home residents is problematic because of the nature of the setting and the nature of the disorder. The nursing home is both a medical setting and a residential setting. As such, it is a place where the world of the resident encounters the universe of the medical and mental health systems. Sometimes this coming together can be described as a gentle rendezvous. At other times, the impact of collision is detrimental to both the resident and the community of the nursing home. This is often the case with the "difficult" resident. As illustrated in Mrs. F's case, the label "difficult" has a dramatic effect on the care provided and the experience of the care received. The resident who clashes most with the culture of the nursing home often has a personality disorder; moreover, this disorder may become increasingly apparent in the context of the nursing home.

The difficult nursing home resident may not have a need for "heavy" physical care. However, this type of resident typically does not fit well with the system, often engendering negative feelings among the setting's caregivers (Trexler, 1996). Fit itself is a fluid concept that reflects universal and idiosyncratic realities, as well as attitudes and expectations (Rosowsky Dougherty, Johnson, & Gurian, 1997). Whatever the concept embraces, a good fit enables a positive outcome, and a poor fit enables a negative one.

Difficult patients have been recognized and discussed in the medical and psychiatric literature (Anstett, 1980; Chrzanowski, 1980; Drossman, 1978; Gerrard & Riddell, 1988; Groves, 1978; Kahana & Bibring, 1964). These patients can evoke strong feelings, cognitions, and behaviors, even in the encounter of the psychotherapy session (see chap. 9 in this volume). Their impact may be even greater in the more constrained environment of total care. In addition, this "hateful," "difficult" or "problem" patient can have an enormous rippling effect throughout the whole nursing home system.

In the community, these difficult patients use a disproportionate share of services and medical resources. They are also labor intensive and evoke enormous affect in their treatment providers (Lin et al., 1991). Overall, they have comparatively poorer outcomes for psychotherapeutic interventions than their nondifficult counterparts (see chap. 5 in this volume).

Within the nursing home, they also disproportionately consume "resources," either through direct care, consultation time, administrative time, or the affective energies of the staff. Indeed, in the nursing home there may be a number of labels for this resident that are, in effect, proxies for the term *personality disorder*. These residents may be described, for example, as making a poor adjustment, not fitting in, complaining, or being withdrawn, asocial, nasty, deviant, demanding, a nuisance, and so on. Further compounding the situation is the principle that the more formal the setting, the less tolerance the system has for deviance (Goffman, 1961). Thus, the staff may be more likely to experience and to label a resident moving from the community into an institutional setting as "difficult" (Trexler, 1996).

Even without a label, certain staff behaviors may identify these residents: departures from usual and expectable professional behaviors, a different amount of time spent on a given procedure, withholding eye contact or verbal exchange, or lack of smiling or touching. At the extreme, it is likely that residents with personality disorders—difficult to treat and abide—are those who are most likely to provoke sadistic behaviors in their care providers. Although abuse in the nursing home setting is not prevalent, it does exist and is likely to be underreported.

Personality traits at the core of the individual are lifelong (Sadavoy, 1996), and continue to define the individual regardless of context, relationship or task (see chap. 9 in this volume). Thus, if the resident's needs are not well met by the system, the resident may intensify the deviant behaviors in a heightened display of self that is inflexible, maladaptive, and distressing to others, the sine qua non of a personality disorder. This does not cause the PD, but it can exacerbate the negative behaviors. The ripple effect promotes conflict throughout the nursing home system and can have a cascading effect on other residents, directly and indirectly. For example, as the difficult resident consumes disproportionate staff attention, less time is available for care of the nondifficult residents. Staff negative attitude, lowered morale, and displaced frustration compromise the care of all residents. Inadequate training in how to care for the difficult resident and inadequate institutional support can produce staff burnout, high turnover, and absenteeism. Thus, personality disorders among nursing home residents can have important effects on the residents and the staff.

PERSONALITY STYLE VERSUS PERSONALITY DISORDER: A CRITICAL DISTINCTION

Personality traits are neither inherently adaptive nor maladaptive. To assess them as such, a referent needs to be considered. The referent, for example, can be a task individuals are asked to perform, a context of the behavior, or a problem or stressor to which they are responding. Traits, although neither inherently normal nor pathological, can be envisioned as distributed along a continuum representing the intensity of expression. Dimensional models of personality support the view that personality disorders are maladaptive expressions of normal personality traits, which are at least theoretically possessed to some degree by everyone. The five-factor model is an exemplar of a dimensional model. Although personality as a construct implies remarkable stability, whether or not it gets assessed as adaptive or maladaptive, normal or pathological, depends in part on variables outside the individual. The extent to which such variables have an impact on the assessment of personality style or disorder directly reflects the point along the continuum on which the trait lies. Thus, extreme outliers are most likely to be assessed as having a personality disorder, regardless of the referent, whereas those closer to the median, falling under the curve, are less likely to be assessed in this way.

Stage models of psychosocial development emphasize stage-related tasks consistent with specific life stages (Erikson, 1982). Successful mastery of these de facto define successful adaptation, and also contribute to the assessment of "normalcy" or pathology. Thus, an individual may be diagnosed with a personality disorder at one stage of psychosocial development, and at another stage may not be so diagnosed even while exhibiting the same profile of personality traits. The position along the personality style–personality disorder continuum is dynamic, whereas the specific trait expression may be static.

Another person, functioning as an auxiliary personality, can play a role in binding, bolstering, or buffering the expression of personality traits and thus influence the assessment of a personality style or disorder (Rosowsky et al., 1997). The context also can serve a similar function. In addition, the context can be understood in terms of the personality traits that the system positively endorses— those it is designed to serve and those who will exert the least pressure to modify the standard service delivery.

PREMISES UNDERLYING THE GOODNESS OF FIT MODEL

The complementarity of the templates describing the individual's personality profile, and the profile of personality traits the system values, define the "goodness of fit" model. Three premises are posited as underlying a goodness of fit model for personality disorder.

Personality traits lie along continua where they can be identified as styles or disorders.

Contexts of care or service delivery systems value certain personality traits and devalue certain others.

"Goodness of fit" between the context and the individual affects how the individual is diagnosed, the adaptation to the system, and the care received. The individual who is assessed as a "good fit" or a "poor fit" is differentially accepted and cared for by the system.

Personality and the Nursing Home: Traits Expressed by the "Difficult" Resident and Traits Valued by the "Typical" Nursing Home

The conventional nursing home is a model of a formal system, and as such is generally less able to tolerate deviance in its members than informal systems (Litwak, 1985). What is highly prized or most valued varies not only between systems, but within systems. For example, for the administrative staff, most valued aspects of a nursing home may be fiscal solvency and compliance with regulations. Residents and families that financially stress the home's per diem/per case allotment are not valued. In addition, the facility can only be successful if the word of mouth publicity is satisfactory. The unhappy family can be harmful to the bottom line. The difficult patient is more likely to have an unhappy family, and generally an impaired and impoverished social support system (Rose, Soares, & Joseph, 1993).

The direct care staff of the nursing home consists mainly of nurses: registered nurses (RNs), licensed practical nurses (LPNs), and aides. RNs make up about 14% of the full-time direct care staff, LPNs another 20%, and aides about 64% (Strahan, 1997). Most are caring professionals. Among them, most highly prized is their ability to provide care and maintain a smooth daily routine. Residents who disrupt the routine because of an acute medical crisis are generally well-managed by the system. Residents who chronically disrupt the system, especially with perceived volition, are not. These are residents who are aggressive, unpredictable, impulsive, disinhibited, display angry outbursts, and engage in intense, labile interpersonal relationships. These residents especially threaten and challenge the system, and provoke atypical, unprofessional responses (Trexler, 1996). Clearly, this description is of the residents with a personality disorder.

There is a noteworthy exception. Residents who have a dependent personality, who may indeed have been diagnosed with a dependent personality disorder earlier in life, now may be assessed as having a dependent style—no longer a disorder—within the context of the nursing home.

PREMISES UNDERLYING THE ABILITY OF THE NURSING HOME TO PROVIDE CARE

Five premises underly the interdependence of the resident's personality traits and the ability of the system to provide care:

Resident cognitions, affect, and behaviors influence the system of care delivery.

Any system strives to maintain homeostasis.

Deviance in the resident is regarded as pathology.

Pathology in the system is perceived as a threat to the homeostasis of the system and is experienced as a threat to its integrity.

The system will respond to correct the deviance, eliminate the threat, and restore the homeostasis.

Assessment and Treatment Approaches

A team approach is required for effective treatment of personality disorders in nursing homes. The task of the mental health professional reflects a complicated combination of goals. On one hand, the goal is to help the resident negotiate the demands of the setting that stem from both regulatory and resource constraints, and on the other hand, the goal is to help the staff respond effectively to the mental health needs of the residents (Spayd & Smyer, 1996).

The basic elements of geriatric assessment apply well to assessment for personality disorders in nursing homes. Key elements include a thorough chart review; clinical interview with the resident; interviews with key informants in the setting (including nursing assistants); interviews with family members to assess the duration, variability, and progression of the symptom complex; and use of standardized assessment approaches (Spayd & Smyer, 1996). To make a diagnosis of PD, however, other elements need to be added. Included is a detailed history, especially of intimate relationships, their quality and stability, adequacy of general social functioning, ability to tolerate frustration and manage anger. Informant data from the resident's family, as well as past medicosocial records, provide important data in support of the diagnosis.

Approaches for assessing and treating personality disorders within nursing homes must also take advantage of several aspects of the setting: already-existing assessment information and the culture of the nursing home, especially the staffing pattern. Earlier chapters have addressed a number of treatment approaches to the older adult with personality disorder (see chaps. 5, 12, 13, and 14 in this volume). The focus here is on approaches that are unique to the nursing home setting.

One outcome of the 1987 NHRA was a mandated set of specific assessment procedures: the Minimum Data Set (MDS) and the Resident Assessment Protocols (RAPs). As Morris and his colleagues (Morris et al., 1990) noted, an outcome of the 1987 NHRA was the development and evaluation of the two interrelated components:

> The first, the Minimum Data Set (MDS), contains the core items necessary for a comprehensive assessment of nursing facility residents. It also provides triggers (individual items or combinations of MDS elements) to identify residents for whom specific Resident Assessment Protocols (RAPS) . . . will be completed. Each RAP is a structured framework for organizing MDS elements that can be used to inform the care planning process. The intent in developing these modules is education rather than 'prescription.' They provide additional assessment items and background information to develop a context in which information about residents, their strengths, preferences, and needs is linked to care plan options. (Morris et al., 1990, p. 294)

The MDS was developed with special attention to the issues of the reliability and validity of the information gathered in the structured process. For example, Hawes and her colleagues reported that the MDS achieved a "standard for excellent reliability (i.e., intraclass correlation of .7 or higher)" in several important areas of resident functioning; physical functioning (ADLs; disease diagnoses; oral/nutritional status); and medication use (Hawes, Morris, Phillps, Mor, Fries, & Nonemaker, 1995). At the same time, though, Hawes and her colleagues acknowledged that the MDS is not a panacea. There are diagnostic areas that need additional work (e.g., delirium). In addition, the area of personality, whether style or disorder, is another candidate for further development, because personality disorder is not even among the psychiatric disorders on the diagnoses list.

The initial version of the MDS has been revised, and nursing homes are now using the MDS Plus (MDS+; Frederiksen, Tariot, & DeJonghe, 1996). Recent work suggests that the MDS+ scales in the areas of functional status, cognitive impairment, and communications were highly correlated with research scales in these areas. However, behavior and mood scores did not correlate as well with research scales.

In assessing personality disorders in nursing homes, then, it is important to take advantage of information already assembled that may support the diagnosis of a personality disorder. In particular, certain specific MDS items, rather than scale scores, may be of use in assessment and treatment of personality disorders. For example, the domains and associated items in Table 15.1 may be especially evident to the assessment and treatment process.

In summary, the clinician who works in the nursing home setting must use the already-existing data sources for the diagnosis of personality disorder. There remains a major need for future research to address the relation between PDs and MDS items. This could then inform future iterations of the MDS. Unfortunately, currently these sources are not designed to "red flag" the possible presence of personality pathology. Therefore, the MDS items become general grist for the diagnostic mill, without providing specific diagnostic indicators of personality disorders.

Once a diagnosis is made, the emphasis shifts to treatment. As with assessment, the basic principles of geriatric treatment and treatment approaches for personality disorders in later life apply to nursing home settings (Sadavoy, 1987). A major challenge in treating personality disorders in nursing homes, however, is achieving a standard observation, assessment, and treatment approach because of the differential effect these residents typically have on their care providers and the number of providers involved in their care.

As noted, nursing assistants form the majority of the direct care staff (Strahan, 1997). They are paid slightly above minimum wage for providing direct, personal assistance to residents. They are often the first to notice changes in the resident's behavior and functioning. Despite the stresses of the work, they view their jobs as having important personal significance. They recognize that their

TABLE 15.1
MDS Items

Domain	Sample Items
Customary Routine	Eating patterns ADL patterns Involvement patterns
*Mood & Behavior Patterns	Indicators of depression/anxiety Mood persistence Behavioral symptoms
*Psychosocial Well-being	Sense of initiative/involvement Unsettled relationships Past roles
Health Conditions	Pain symptoms
Activity Pursuit Patterns	Time awake Preferred settings/times
Special Treatments & Procedures	Psychological therapy
Intervention Programs for Mood, Behavior, Cognitive Loss	Special behavior evaluations

*Likely of greatest significance

care has a direct impact and this differentiates it from other minimum wage work (Brannon, Cohn, & Smyer, 1990; Brannon et al., 1988). Thus, they may be motivated to provide good quality care, even for difficult residents; or conversely, they may resent being paid near minimum wage.

At the same time, there are real constraints to engaging nursing assistants as effective mental health caregivers. For example, nursing assistants often lack basic information and understanding about the types of mental disorders and behavior problems that occur frequently in nursing homes (e.g., Spore, Smyer, & Cohn, 1991). In addition, cultural and class differences between residents and nursing assistants may especially elicit more primitive defenses in the resident with PD, and provoke retaliatory responses from the assistant. Thus, the mental health provider must find a way to use the primary caregivers in the setting— nursing assistants—in the assessment and treatment approaches for personality disorders.

One element of the NHRA was a mandate of increased attention to mental health treatment in nursing homes. However, Schnelle and his colleagues have warned that the NHRA may have mandated "policy without technology" in an effort to improve the quality of care in nursing homes (Schnelle, Ouslander, & Cruise, 1997). The result is that any treatment protocol must be developed and implemented with the input and cooperation of the nursing assistants and nursing administration. For example, registered nurses are responsible for the mandated resident assessment data in nursing homes. Similarly, they play key leadership roles in developing, implementing, and evaluating mental health interventions.

Developing assessment and treatment approaches for personality disordered residents in nursing homes must take into account the staffing patterns and caregiving resources of the setting. To be effective, traditional assessment and treatment approaches must accommodate the dominant role of nursing assistants. Unfortunately, there are no well-documented treatment protocols for treating personality disorders in nursing homes that capitalize on the patient contact and expertise of the nursing assistants.

NURSING HOME CONSULTATION

A CASE EXAMPLE

Mrs. M is a 78-year-old woman admitted to the nursing home 5 months ago. Prior to the admission, she had been living alone in her own home. She has two daughters living nearby, each married and with their own families, who were increasingly unable to support her living alone. Always a difficult woman, Mrs. M became more hostile and demanding following the death of her husband from a sudden myocardial infaction (MI) 2½ years ago. She was enraged at him for dying and leaving her to cope with everything by herself. After his death, she took comfort from the attention and support that typically follows. After this was withdrawn, she felt more and more abandoned and increasingly angry.

She had many fallings out with her sister. Finally her sister, a few years older and with her own health problems, confronted Mrs. M with her impossible behavior. The result was that the two have not spoken for over a year.

Mrs. M developed numerous physical symptoms due to self-neglect, and vague complaints for which no medical cause could be found. Her physician became frustrated and irritated with her, giving her pills to help her sleep and others to treat her irritability and anxiety.

Whereas Mrs. M and her husband had always enjoyed an evening cocktail, she now began drinking more heavily on a daily basis. She became erratic in her diet and medication compliance. Her management of her chronic medical conditions, diabetes and hypertension, went out of control. When confused and disinhibited from the effects of alcohol and psychotropic medications, she would call her daughters and vent her rage, accusing them of hating her, wishing she were dead, and plotting to take her money.

She fell, fractured her hip, and was sent to a rehabilitation facility for 5 weeks. While there, she was physically reconditioned, but she was verbally abusive toward the staff. They discharged her to home a week earlier than originally scheduled. She had orders at home for physical therapy three times per week. Mrs. M fired the first therapist because she was "rude," but very much liked her replacement. She enjoyed her visits and cooperated with the treatment.

When the treatment was completed, and services withdrawn, Mrs. M became more demanding of her daughters and started her alcohol abuse and self-neglecting behaviors. One evening, she called her older daughter and intimated suicide. Her daughter, concerned, rushed over and stayed the night. Mrs. M continued to make veiled threats, but would not see a mental health specialist. Finally, an exhausted daughter refused to leave her own home and family and run to her mother's house whenever she threatened to end her life. Mrs. M took "what was left in the bottle" of her sleep medication and called her younger daughter to tell her what she had done and "to say goodnight."

The daughters consulted with her physician and a social worker affiliated with the council on aging. They arranged for admission to a nursing home in the area. Mrs. M was furious with her daughters and her physician. She ultimately agreed to the placement and was very charming when she arrived. After the attention given to new residents subsided, she started to become more and more demanding of the staff. Soon she developed favorites, to whom she would proffer praise, compliments, appreciation, and cooperation. She would harass other staff, being negativistic and belligerent. She was especially hostile to the aides, insisting that she wanted "a real nurse" for her care. "After all, this is a nursing home, isn't it?" She was abusive, hurling racial slurs and other epithets at staff members that she hated. Her roommate was seriously troubled by all the "yelling and fighting" going on, and was also resentful of the extra attention Mrs. M received.

After numerous attempts at accommodation, the charge nurse finally "had it" with Mrs. M, when for one shift she was unable to find an aide or LPN who was on Mrs. M's "good list." A staff member was assigned, endured one more outburst, gave minimal care, and got out of Mrs. M's way as quickly as possible. A mental health consultation was ordered.

The Consultation

The overall goal of the consultation is to create the greatest amount of positive change, while meeting the least amount of resistance, between the resident and the system.

Procedure

An interview with the staff was conducted to determine the following: (a) What specific behaviors does Mrs. M exhibit that have a significant negative impact on her care? (b) What are the context of these behaviors? These include the antecedents, the behaviors themselves, and the consequences (Cohn, Smyer, & Horgas, 1994). (c) Regarding the consequences, which have been successful, which have had no effect, and which have exacerbated the undesirable behaviors?

Next, clarify with staff what minimal changes in behaviors, if achieved, would make Mrs. M acceptable to the system. The emphasis here is twofold: understanding that Mrs. M's basic personality style will not be altered but can become less disruptive. It is up to the system to accommodate this. Behaviors that cannot be tolerated by the system are most considered for modification.

Then prepare for modification. This requires staff commitment, patience, and consistency. Who will be a part of the process? Ascertain with staff what will be the short-term and long-term indicators of success. Explore the likelihood of staff continuity for treatment and identify sources of possible treatment sabotage.

There are, as well, resistance considerations. Identify who among the participating staff are Mrs. M's favorites. Discuss splitting and how this mechanism can be used in the service of minimizing resistance and affecting behavioral change. Also, determine who in each shift will be responsible for the behavior request and the consequence.

Finally, there is a need for reinforcement and shaping. Determine what in the context can be used to cultivate Mrs. M's positive behaviors and diminish the undesirable ones. Ask how Mrs. M can contribute to the nursing home community. What can the staff identify as likely providing meaning and purpose to her life that is reasonably available in the system?

Using the Countertransference

The consultation will include an educational component leading to the understanding that the effect the resident has on staff is the same effect she has had on others in other contexts as well; it is an integral part of her personality. When Mrs. M is distressed, the negative behaviors and affects will increase promoting a downward spiral. The theoretical and practical question is the same: How might her personality traits be used to support her personality style, lessen the probability of a personality disorder becoming manifested, and reduce the distress she engenders in the system.

CHALLENGES AND CONTINUING ISSUES: POLICY AND RESEARCH

Geriatric mental health providers face a number of emerging and continuing challenges in nursing homes. Because the difficulty of assessing and treating personality disorders in this setting has already been discussed, this section focuses on policy-related challenges that form an economic context for service development and implementation.

A major challenge in the coming years will be defining and paying for mandated mental health services in nursing homes. For example, Shea and his colleagues (Shea, Smyer, & Streit, 1993) estimated the costs of implementing the mental health services mandated by the 1987 NHRA. The costs for those mandated services are a function of two basic elements: definitions of the target group of mentally ill nursing home residents and costs of basic mental health service provision (e.g., medication supervision and psychotherapy). Shea et al. found that the costs of providing mandated mental health treatment ranged from $480 million to $1.34 billion per year. Of course, the NHRA mandated treatment without mandating additional payment mechanisms to cover the costs of the treatment. Thus, there may be policy incentives for underestimating the need for treatment in nursing homes—incentives that would work against greater diagnostic refinement and treatment regimens that include personality disorders, especially as these have a poor treatment efficacy record.

On the level of an individual institution, there are also disincentives for identifying rates of mental disorders (including personality disorders) more accurately. For example, if more than 50% of nursing home residents have a primary diagnosis of mental disorder, then the nursing home may be reclassified as an institution for mental disorders. The IMD rubric carries with it a lower federal reimbursement rate, presumably because of "lighter" staff requirements. In short, there are also important incentives at the institutional level for underdiagnosing, or, in the case of physical and mental health comorbidity, for specifying physical disorders as the primary diagnoses.

In the end, these policy challenges must be viewed within the larger context of the continuing crisis in funding for long-term care. For example, there are current pressures to allow older adults increased flexibility in choosing among several health care plans under Medicare, including health maintenance organizations. But as Shea (1998) pointed out, this cost-containment trend may adversely affect the mentally ill elderly, including those with personality disorders:

> If there is any lesson that can be drawn from the economics of insurance applied to mental health care, it is that providing comprehensive mental health benefits in a system with competing health plans is a very difficult proposition. . . . No clear model exists of cost-effective delivery of mental health care for older adults with serious mental illness. . . . In the meantime, Medicare appears to be heading down a road that holds great danger for persons with mental illness. (pp. 10–11)

CONCLUSION

There is an essential distinction between Axis I and Axis II disorders that has special significance to the care received by nursing home residents. The goal for the careproviding staff is not to cure the Axis II condition. Rather, it is to limit its negative impact, the collateral damages on the overall care, and quality of life in the nursing home. For research and clinical application, the challenge is how to use generally available information to help the nursing home achieve that goal. Prerequisites for this include, minimally, that there be systemic recognition that some residents are difficult, and that their being difficult is a clinical presentation. This implies the need for a common vocabulary, with predictive value. Such an approach will help prevent behavioral problems and allow staff to provide a context for their care. (For example, the MDS should include markers for the dominant manifestations of PD in older adults in the nursing home setting.)

To the extent that it is known that personality is remarkably robust over the life course, and stable across contexts, resident and informant data regarding personality should be routinely collected and integrated into the admission or new resident history-taking process. Research could confirm the cost-effectiveness of this information, and its clinical relevance in terms of staff satisfaction, absenteeism, and turnover. Additionally, cost savings may be found in reduced transfers of difficult residents to acute care settings and from reductions in consultation orders. Perhaps most significant of all would be evidence of increased comfort and decreased distress in staff and resident, contributing to an improved quality of life for the difficult nursing home resident.

REFERENCES

Anstett, R. (1980). The difficult patient and the physician-patient relationship. *Family Practitioner, 11,* 281–286.

Blazer, D., George L. K., Landeman, R., Pennybacker, M., Melville, M. L., Woodbury, M., Manton, K. G., Jordan, K., & Locke, B. (1985). Psychiatric disorders: A rural–urban comparison. *Archives of General Psychiatry, 42,* 651–6.

Brannon, D., Cohn, M. D., & Smyer, M. A. (1990). Care giving as work: How nurse's aides rate it. *Journal of Long Term Care Administration,* Spring, 10–14.

Brannon, D., Smyer, M. A., Cohn, M. D., Borchardt, L., Landry, J. A., Jay, G. M., Garfein, A. J., MaloneBeach, E., & Walls, C. (1988). A job diagnostic survey of nursing home caregivers: Implications for job redesign. *Gerontologist, 28,* 246–252.

Burns, B. J., Wagner, R., Taube, J. E., Magaziner, J., Permutt, T., & Landerman, L. R. (1993). Mental health service use by the elderly in nursing homes. *American Journal of Public Health, 83,* 331–337.

Chrzanowski, G. (1980). Problem patients or troublemakers? Dynamic and therapeutic considerations. *American Journal of Psychotherapy, 34,* 26–38.

Class, C. A., Unverzagt, F. W., Gao, S., Hall, K. S., Baiyewu, O., & Hendrie, H. C. (1996). Psychiatric disorders in African American nursing home residents. *American Journal of Psychiatry, 153,* 677–681.

Cohen, R. A., Van Nostrand, J. F., & Furner, S. E. (Eds.). (1993). Chartboook on health data on older Americans: United States (1992). *Vital and health statistics, 29.*

Cohn, M. D., Smyer, M. A., & Horgas, A. L. (1994). *The ABCs of behavior change: Skills for working with behavior problems in nursing homes.* State College, PA: Venture.

Drossman, D. A. (1978). The problem patient: Evaluation and care of medical patients with psychosocial disturbances. *Annals of Internal Medicine, 88,* 366–72.

Erikson, E. (1982). *The life cycle completed.* New York: Norton.

Freedman, V. A., Berkman, L. F., Rapp, S. R., & Ostfeld, A. M. (1994). Family networks: Predictors of nursing home entry. *American Journal of Public Health, 84*(5), 843–845.

Frederiksen, K., Tariot, P., & DeJonghe, E. (1996). Minimum Data Set Plus (MDS+) scores compared with scores from five rating scales. *Journal of the American Geriatrics Society, 44,* 305–309.

German, P. S., Rovner, B. W., Burton, L. C., Brant, L. J., & Clark, R. (1992). The role of mental morbidity in the nursing home experience. *Gerontologist, 32,* 152–158.

Gerrard, T. J., & Riddell, J. D. (1988). Difficult patients: Black holes and secrets. *British Medical Journal, 297:*530–2.

Goffman, E. (1961). *Asylums.* Garden City, NY: Doubleday.

Groves, J. E. (1978). Taking care of the hateful patient. *New England Journal of Medicine, 298,* 883–887.

Gurland, B. J. (1980). The assessment of the mental health status of older adults. In J. E. Birren & R. B. Sloane (Eds.), *Handbook of mental health and aging* (pp. 671–700). Englewood Cliffs, NJ: Prentice-Hall.

Hawes, C., Morris, J. N., Phillips, C. D., Mor, V., Fries, B., & Nonemaker, S. (1995). Reliability estimates for the Minimum Data Set for nursing home resident assessment and care screening (MDS). *Gerontologist, 35,* 172–178.

Institute of Medicine. (1986). *Improving the quality of care in nursing homes.* Washington, DC: National Academy Press.

Kahana, R. J., & Bibring, G. L. (1964). Personality types in medical management. In N. E. Zinberg (Ed.), *Psychiatry and medical practice in a general hospital* (pp. 108–123). Madison, CT: International Universities Press.

Krauss, N. A., Freidman, M. P., Rhoades, J. A., Altman, B. M., Brown, Jr., E., & Potter, D.E.B. (1997). Characteristics of nursing home facilities and residents. *Medical Expenditure Panel Survey, July* (2), 1–3.

Lair, T., & Lefkowitz, D. (1990). Mental health and functional status of residents of nursing and personal care homes. In *National Medical Expenditure Survey Research Findings 7* (DHHS Publication No. PHS 90–3470). Rockville, MD: Public Health Service, Agency for Health Care Policy and Research.

Lin, H. B., Katon, W., Von Korff, M., Bush, T., Lipscomb, P., Russo, J., & Wagner, E. (1991). Frustrating patients: Physician and patient perspectives among distressed high users of medical services. *Journal of General Internal Medicine, 6,* 241–246.

Litwak, E. (1985). *Helping the elderly: The complementary roles of informal networks and formal systems.* New York: Guilford.

Morris, J. N., Hawes, C., Fries, B. E., Phillips, C. D., Mor, V., Katz, S., Murphy, K., Drugovich, M. L., & Friedlob, A. S. (1990). Designing the national resident assessment instrument for nursing homes. *Gerontologist, 30,* 293–307.

Rose, M. K., Soares, H. H., & Joseph, C. (1993). Frail elderly clients with personality disorders: A challenge for social work. *Journal of Gerontological Social Work, 19,* 153–165.

Rosowsky, E., Dougherty, L., Johnson, C., Gurian, B. (1997). Personality as an indicator of "goodness of fit" between the elderly individual and the health service system. *Clinical Gerontologist, 17*(3), 41–53.

Rosowsky, E., & Gurian, B. (1991). Borderline personality disorder in late life. *International Psychogeriatrics, 3,* 221–334.

Sadavoy, J. (1987). Character disorders in the elderly. In J. Sadavoy & M. Leszcz (Eds.), *Treating the elderly with psychotherapy: The scope for change in later life* (pp. 175–229). Madison, CT: International Universities Press.

Sadavoy, J. (1996). Personality disorder in old age: Symptom Expression. *Clinical Gerontologist, 16,* 19–36.

Schnelle, J. F., Ouslander, J. G., & Cruise, P. A. (1997). Policy without technology: A barrier to improving nursing home care. *Gerontologist, 37,* 527–532.

Shea, D. G. (1998). Economic and financial issues in mental health and aging. *The Public Policy and Aging Report, 9*(1), 7–11.

Shea, D. G., Smyer, M. A. & Streit, A. (1993). Mental health services for nursing home residents: What will it cost? *Journal of Mental Health Administration, 20,* 223–235.

Smyer, M. A. (1989). Nursing homes as a setting for psychological practice: Public policy perspectives. *American Psychologist, 44*(10), 1307–1314.

Smyer, M. A., Cohn, M. D., & Brannon, D., (1988). *Mental health consultation in nursing homes.* New York: New York University Press.

Spayd, C. S., & Smyer, M. A. (1996). Psychological interventions in nursing homes. In S. H. Zarit & B. G. Knight (Eds.), *A guide to psychotherapy and aging* (pp. 241–268). Washington, DC: American Psychological Association.

Spore, D. L., Smyer, M. A., & Cohn, M. D. (1991). Assessing nursing assistants' knowledge of behavioral approaches to mental health problems. *Gerontologist, 31,* 309–317.

Strahan, G. W. (1997). An overview of nursing homes and their current residents: Data from the 1995 National Nursing Home Survey. In *Advance Data from Vital and Health Statistics, No. 280.* Hyattsville, MD: National Center for Health Statistics.

Strahan, G. W., & Burns, B. J. (1991). Mental illness in nursing homes: United States, 1985. *Vital Health Statistics, 13*(105).

Tariot P. N., Podgorski, C. A., Blazina, L., & Leibovici, A. (1993). Mental disorders in the nursing home: Another perspective. *American Journal of Psychiatry, 150,* 1063–1069.

Trexler, J. C. (1996). Reformulation of deviance and labeling theory for nursing. *Journal of Nursing Scholarship, 28,* 131–135.

Zarit, S. (1996). Interventions with family caregivers. In S. H. Zarit & B. G. Knight (Eds.) *A guide to psychotherapy and aging* (pp. 139–149). Washington, DC: American Psychological Association.

CHAPTER 16

Ethical Issues in the Clinical Management of Older Adults With Personality Disorder

Victor Molinari, PhD
Houston Veterans Affairs Medical Center

The subject of ethical issues in older adults with personality disorder (PD) must be viewed within a bio–psycho–social developmental context. In older adults with PD, aging changes coalesce with chronic exaggerated interpersonal styles and lead to clinically challenging ethical concerns. Just as in their past, older patients with PD continue the same relational patterns that have produced conflict before. However, the interpersonal losses and medical problems associated with aging often exacerbate their behavior and further strain informal and formal support systems to the limit. Chronic aggravation can replace prior sporadic familial crisis intervention, and precipitate a caregiver's final break from the ungratefulness of some aged individuals with PD. Unfortunately, this estrangement may force them into involuntary contact with a health care system that does not respond judiciously, with problematic consequences.

Older adults with PD are therefore frequently the "difficult" patients that geriatricians must interact with under less than optimal therapeutic circumstances. They do not get along well with other patients or residents, necessitating frequent staff intercession. Despite constant demands to fulfill their pressing interpersonal needs, they do not reciprocate by following professional advice. Feedback seems futile. The health team can spend much time and energy "putting out fires," then become angry when they realize that they have made little difference, or worse that they have been manipulated. Case management of these patients clearly requires an enhanced attunement to the ethical principles of the mental health profession.

This chapter explores the interrelated social, psychological, and philosophical aspects of ethical matters in older patients with PD, particularly those with the more dramatic/emotional Cluster B PDs. Although this material is multi-disciplinary in scope and blurs professional boundaries, for conceptual purposes each section will accent different content areas. The social section focuses on ethical issues in relation to health care and living arrangements, the psychological section emphasizes assessment and treatment themes, and the philosophical section highlights the individualist versus collectivist debate and the theory of responsible decision making. Each of these sections considers the natural interface of their subject matter with the realities of weak social support networks, an overtaxed legal system, and society's ageism in its varied forms. The fourth section introduces two case vignettes, and the final section discusses these cases vis-à-vis the aforementioned social, psychological, and philosophical quandaries confronting health professionals in the care of such patients. In the evolving area of ethical inquiry, the questions asked outstrip the theoretical frameworks available to generate answers. Because there is virtually no controlled research on ethical issues in older adults with PD, the ideas expressed here have by necessity been gleaned from readings of related literature. Although linked with the pragmatics of clinical experience, they are purposively exploratory in nature and hopefully heuristic in value, but await empirical verification.

SOCIAL

Society's ageism compounds the interpersonal difficulties of those with PD yielding a variety of ethical considerations, particularly in relation to health care and living arrangements. With the ever-accelerating changes in technology woven into the very fabric of Western society, the skills of many older adults are often considered anachronistic. Positive roles for the elderly have been reduced with limited age-appropriate replacements, except perhaps as repositors of accumulated cultural experience. Unfortunately, aging individuals with PD typically do not progress or are not accepted into the prosocial stature of the wise old man or woman imparting valued knowledge to eager young listeners. As individuals with PD grow older, they are frequently condescendingly tolerated as the stereotypical caricatures of "crabby old ladies" or "dirty old men." The age-inappropriate impulsivity characteristic of Cluster B PDs may be viewed in bemused fashion, with this decline in societal respect particularly difficult for those with narcissistic traits. The stage is therefore set for more frequent clashes between the magnified needs of the PD individual and the offerings of society.

It may be asked why society should be concerned with those older adults who have not made positive contributions, or who have been in constant conflict with societal norms, as with some Borderline or Antisocial PDs. The question of society's obligation to these older adults becomes salient in any discussion of the rationing of health care. Those with PD clearly fall into a long-term care model because their long-standing interpersonal problems produce chronic disruption in health care delivery. The managed care industry may be loathe to spend excess resources on some patients with Cluster B PD who are notorious for noncompliance with treatment regimens and subsequent relapse. If viewed under a misguided acute care model, there is little doubt that many of the more troublesome patients with PD will "fall through the cracks" of the public health system, or be jettisoned from the rolls of private companies.

Care of the frail elderly with PD is complicated for those (typically, Clusters B and A PDs) who in the past have emotionally distanced themselves from family members and friends. For example, ambivalent next of kin to a terminally ill older person with PD may give too rapid assent to their presumed "right to die," perhaps for less than humanitarian motivation. Overwhelmed spouses are probably the most common perpetrators of elder abuse and neglect (Pillemer & Finkelhor, 1988). Other older patients with PD have no available family members or friends to assist with their care, and are therefore likely to be forced to rely on formal support systems. Kapp (1996), in an interesting discussion on the "unbefriended," addressed many ethical issues in the provision of their health care that mirror those relevant to individuals with PD (who probably make up the bulk of the "unbefriended"). Because those with PD frequently have few family members to advocate for their care, the absence of clearly defined decision-makers can paralyze health providers when medical emergencies develop. Advance directives or appointment of a durable power of attorney become irrelevant when there is no one who knows what the person would do in general health-related situations. Even when family members or friends are involved, ambivalent caregivers may be less likely to implement the stated wishes of the person with PD.

Rigid health-related beliefs and a poor interpersonal manner can create an adversarial situation between patient, family, and health care providers. This sets the stage for premature civil commitment, forced treatment, and/or competency evaluations. As Grisso (1986) noted, competent decision making requires a fit between a person's capacity and environmental demands. A strong support system can decrease the challenges that an older patient faces and thus reduce the chances of having the elder declared incompetent, because guardianship proceedings are typically awarded in favor of the petitioner because they are seldom contested by older persons (Bulcroft, Kielkopf, & Tripp, 1991). Unfortunately, when family negotiations fail and guardianship is granted, the public appointee is less likely to have knowledge of the person and therefore will be unable to cater to the patient's unique characterological needs. An impersonal surrogate decision-maker may allow the legal care team to become de facto decision-makers, who may compromise heath care (e.g., limit life sustaining therapy for the terminally ill when their wishes are unclear) under increasingly strict cost-cutting mandates. Placement in a secure nursing home facility as a means of controlling disagreeable behavior may increasingly be viewed as an attractive solution. If nursing home placement is prematurely instituted, then the PD patient will be less likely to have a consistent advocate for proper institutional care (Kapp, 1996). The philosophy of the least restrictive environment becomes an illusory ideal in these circumstances.

With increasing age and decreasing social support, choice of living options becomes more restricted for those with PD. Many older people with PD live on minimal fixed incomes due to erratic work histories and poor long-term financial planning. Long-suffering spouses or relatives who have tolerated their behavior for many years may develop their own medical problems. When health fails or capacity declines, for the first time in their adult lives, they may be compelled to consistently interact with paid caregivers at home or in institutional settings. It is at this juncture that their exaggerated behavior patterns may first be brought to the attention of mental health providers or the legal system. Unfortunately, in hospital, day care, or rehabilitation sites, poor interpersonal skills may lead to early release with serious psychological and physical health consequences. Rigid interactive styles and racial/gender/religious beliefs can wreak havoc in institutional environments where minorities and women frequently provide the bulk of care. The Compulsive PD may become more anxious or depressed because the institutional routine cannot be controlled, Schizoid and Avoidant PDs may have difficulty with enforced socialization, the Borderline and Narcissistic PDs may become more demanding of staff time, and the Histrionic PD may not receive adequate medical treatment because chronic somaticization causes staff to overlook true medical disease.

PSYCHOLOGICAL

Coping with the varied and cumulative stresses of the aging process is fraught with emotional peril for those with fragile personality organization, and leads to ethical challenges in psychological assessment and psychotherapeutic treatment. At times, the inflexibility of the personality structure of those with PD causes failure to negotiate late-life developmental challenges (Sadavoy, 1996). For example, Paranoid PDs may increase the use of projection as their hearing fails, or the bedridden Compulsive PD may be less able to use activity or achievement as a defense against anxiety. Dependent PDs may feel abandoned by the loss of a loved one and be unable to take advantage of the opportunity for increased independence and responsibility. The barebones support system of many individuals with PD may be overtaxed, triggering involuntary commitment proceedings by the few concerned others if they refuse psychiatric evaluation and treatment. At these times, the stress of being "picked up" by authorities and transported to a hospital will exaggerate further their distinctive PD characteristics and often create an antagonistic relationship between patient and "helper." Unfortunately, necessary crisis intervention strategies may not be implemented because obstreperous behavior in older adults is often erroneously attributed to cognitive impairment rather than acute stress.

Teasing out the social, psychological, psychiatric, and medical dimensions of the older person's clinical presentation can be a daunting task even for trained geriatric professionals. PD behavior can be misdiagnosed as frontal lobe dysfunction, and competency of the person immediately called into question. Psychotropic medication may be inappropriately administered to reduce PD behavior that has been exaggerated by commitment and hospitalization, and misascribed as solely due to psychosis. Or conversely, concomitant Axis I symptomatology may be overlooked because of acting-out behavior, and potentially beneficial psychotropic medication not prescribed.

In inpatient and outpatient psychiatric settings, it is clear that to provide maximum benefit for older psychiatric patients with PD an interpersonal element must be added to whatever other therapeutic regimens are instituted (Thompson, Gallagher, & Czirr, 1988). However, the mandate for optimal care is compromised by psychotherapists who avoid or clash with such difficult patients. Despite the need for corrective interpersonal feedback, PD patients may be inappropriately banned from group therapies because of the disruptive non-cohesive climate they can initially create. Although research has consistently indicated that older adults improve with psychiatric treatment just as much as younger adults (Smyer, Zarit, & Qualls, 1990), geriatric therapeutic nihilism is still pervasive and can be intensified when dealing with an older patient with co-morbid Axis I and Axis II psychopathology. The management of difficult interpersonal behavior is hampered by unresolved or unacknowledged ageist countertransference issues. For example, the necessary firm limit setting for those with PD of any age may be compromised by clinicians with paternalistic biases. Or, mental health professionals with parents who themselves have exaggerated personality traits may have a difficult time providing a "containing" environment for the dramatics of Cluster B PD patients. Improper discharges from the hospital or transfers to more restricted sites due to PD "acting-out" might better be handled through consistent staff behavior. Negotiating such complicated psychotherapeutic transactions requires training in working with psychiatric patients with PD as well as older adults, something that is unfortunately still lacking in many graduate mental health programs.

Education in the identification and management of geriatric psychiatric and personality problems is especially important for front-line nursing staff who are in close contact with older adults with PD in hospitals and nursing homes. Given the rapid turnover of institutional personnel, optimal care obligates nursing home administrators to regularly schedule inservices for all nursing home shifts to assure a standard approach with these patients. Long-term care staff also require emotional support to deal with disruptive behavior. Team meetings are mandatory to reduce the splitting that occurs particularly in those with Borderline PD. Nursing personnel need to be able to ventilate their frustrations and brainstorm treatment strategies to reduce the potential for staff and patient abuse. They must accommodate to the situation rather than expect that the person with PD will quickly modify overlearned behavior patterns. Meetings with other non-PD residents and their families to apprise them of the therapeutic plan may be necessary to reduce risk of disagreeable confrontation. With all this time and effort demanded of staff, psychologists may soon be routinely asked to become involved with preadmission nursing home screening of potential residents with PD. On the one hand, it is helpful for nursing home staff to understand the unique personality styles of their new residents so that they can tailor their care plan accordingly. But, if identification of abnormal personality traits leads to screening out PD patients, major ethical questions arise given the limited housing options typically available for older adults in general and this difficult group of patients in particular.

PHILOSOPHICAL

Issues in the clinical management of older adults with PD have triggered a host of philosophical concerns and legal debate in relation to the ethics of autonomous decision making and the rights of the individual versus those of society. Recent discussions from a variety of philosophical perspectives have focused on the dilemma of whether to emphasize respect for the autonomous rights of the older PD, or whether to highlight society's beneficent responsibility toward the patient's health and social welfare, particularly with regard to decision-making capacity. Jecker (1990) noted that many feminist thinkers object to abstract theories of autonomy that view individuals separate from the intimate relationships they are embedded in and that provide the context for true moral decision making. From a philosophical view, High (1991) commented that individual autonomy should not be equated with independence from family values, and proffered the idea of the individual within the family context as the proper unit of analysis in ethical decision making. Psychoanalytic psychotherapists treating patients across the life span now question whether the traditional single-minded goal of individuation has too often been accomplished at the major expense of the person's socialization into a supportive kinship system that acts as a consistent buffer. This shift in perspective stipulates an approach that demands less immediate gratification of one's own need for the sake of family and community (Jordan, 1989). In a discussion of the gerontological and ethical dimensions of end-of-life issues, Clark (1991) recommended an open dialogue on value ideologies, and contrasted the more autonomous outlook of Americans with the collectivist Canadian approach. The latter viewpoint is consistent with the less individualistic Eastern cultural concept of the "familial self" (Roland, 1988). Clark (1991) advocated for a comprehensive dialogue on how to appropriately allocate health care resources, and described a new ethic that integrates elements of individualism with "shared principles of justice" (p. 638). However, these recent theoretical formulations have not been applied in a psychiatric context to clinical management decisions for those people who lack trust and have formed few permanent ties. The overriding emphasis in the lives of many patients with Cluster B PD has been the satisfaction of their own needs, often to the serious detriment of family and friends. They have rejected reciprocity in favor of irresponsible self-indulgence. With the natural limitations attendant on aging, formal support systems must now buttress overburdened informal support systems.

Morreim (1993) argued that the traditional model of decision making overlooks the connection between decision making and accountability, and enjoins the clinician to help patients generate this accountability in creative ways. Unfortunately, many individuals with PD do not exhibit reversible problems with accountable decision making. Those with Cluster B PD have throughout their lives straddled the fence between behavior that can be labeled psychiatric versus criminal in nature, and the onset of even mild cognitive difficulties may quickly bring them to the attention of the legal system or health care professionals. Expanding Morreim's conceptualization, McCullough, Coverdale, Bayer, and Chervenak (1992) proposed that for a person's decision-making capacity to be respected, patients must at some meaningful level assert ownership of their decisions. It may not always be ethically obligatory to respect impulsive behavior, particularly because it can lead to social and legal sanctions that may ultimately reduce autonomy even more significantly (Workman et al., 1997). For example, if an individual with a Cluster B PD is allowed the choice of living alone (which in the past has led to noncompliance with medication precipitating manic and aggressive behavior toward relatives) rather than being supervised by beleaguered but currently willing relatives, social support may be so further strained that no one would be willing to proffer caregiving afterward, ultimately eventuating in nursing home placement. In cases of cognitively impaired PD patients who require supervision, an institution might need to adopt the role of a surrogate family whose decisions take into serious consideration not only the individual's desires but their impact on other residents as well. The ethical caveats, contradictions, and pitfalls of this type of coercive "shared" decision making (Kapp, 1991) must be further explored by legal scholars, ethicists, patient rights advocates, and mental health professionals.

Along the same lines, Chervenak and McCullough (1991) argued that there are limits to a patients' refusal to accept proper medical intervention. They observed that activation of the right of patients to refuse recommended treatment is frequently coupled by requests for alternative medical management, which may sometimes justifiably be deemed "patently unreasonable" medicine from the physician's point of view. The patients' autonomy to make their own decisions therefore must be balanced against the clinician's autonomy to practice "good medicine." For example, along with a rejection of a recommendation to live in a personal care home (which may have been made by staff because of

chronic nonadherence to a medication regimen), there might be the implicit belief that nonetheless patients will be admitted to the hospital if noncompliance
leads to medical complications. At such times, paternalistic beneficence may
override the autonomy principle, because the ethical integrity of medicine
could be compromised by requiring clinicians to implement an alternative that
could cause medical instability and is clearly not in the long-term interests of patients. Even if it is in their best short-term interests, overuse of medical resources due to chronic irresponsible behavior (e.g., drinking leading to falls and
medical emergencies) obviously must be weighed against the harm to others
that could occur as the result of this behavior (e.g., victims of drunk-driving ac-
cidents). However, it is important to note that such principles should apply
equally to young and old adults alike. Rather than age per se, it is the physical
and cognitive disabilities concomitant with age, and thus the greater potential
for an older person's decision-making capacities to be called into question in relation to overutilization of health care resources, that make these issues more
relevant to the older patient with PD.

CASE STUDIES

MR. Z

Mr. Z was an 82-year-old single male admitted for alcohol detoxification
and delusional thinking that the "Jews" were trying to convert him. He
had been drinking a fifth of whiskey and 6 to 12 beers every few days prior
to admission. He had an extensive history of alcohol dependence, which
began in his early 20s, and has led to numerous arrests for public intoxication. He reported experiencing blackouts on numerous occasions, and acknowledged an awareness in recent months of occasional memory deficits. He came to the hospital because he was unable to continue payment
on his downtown hotel room where he had been staying since his arrival
in this city 2 months ago. This was suspected to be his pattern whenever
he ran into financial or medical difficulties. The only possessions he
owned were the clothes on his back. A physical examination revealed facial deformities, blindness in his left eye, and deafness in his right ear.

   Mr. Z was the only child of college-educated teachers. He attended a
year of college before dropping out to work in numerous short-lived sales
jobs and eventually to join the army during World War II. He considers
himself to be a "loner," traveling throughout the country on freight trains
since the death of his parents in the mid-1970s. He was in many physical
altercations throughout his life, and served multiple prison terms for
botched robbery attempts. During the course of one of his prison terms,
he believed that the warden was trying to poison him and was psychiatri-
cally hospitalized for 1 year receiving 20 electro-shock treatments (ECTs).

During his current hospitalization, he obeyed all the rules of the hospital except for smoking on the unit. No one ever visited him during his 2-month stay. With antipsychotic medication, the structured milieu, and group therapy emphasizing reality testing, Mr. Z's psychotic thinking decreased in intensity. However, although he scored 28/30 on the Mini Mental State Examination on admission, the staff noted short-term memory problems, and psychological assessment was requested. Neuropsychological testing revealed variable cognitive abilities with decline in executive functions and short-term memory for meaningful material. Projective testing indicated a narcissistic, antisocial individual who identified with petty criminals and felt comfortable in a prison environment. It was noted that under minimal stress his thinking could become disorganized and psychotic. An assessment of living skills indicated that he had difficulty with handling money and dangerous situations. Despite incapacity in certain areas, it was still unclear whether the patient was competent to make decisions concerning where to live, so the staff decided to closely monitor whether he was independently able to execute discharge plans. He expressed a desire to live by himself because he said he always did things his own way, and refused referral to a personal care home. However, he was unable to contact his bank or to explain how he was going to locate an apartment, despite detailed instructions from the social worker. There was also concern about whether he had the short-term memory or the motivation to continue with the antipsychotic medication needed to maintain his improved mental status after discharge. Finally, when he told the staff that he was going to find a job at the zoo and live there, legal guardianship proceedings were instituted. Because it was believed that he would elope from a less structured setting, nursing home placement was pursued. He was discharged to a secured nursing home facility with diagnoses of Alcohol-related Dementia and Antisocial PD (with additional paranoid, narcissistic, and schizotypal traits). It has been reported that he is doing well in this environment, perhaps because of his lengthy experience with institutional living.

MR. J

Mr. J was a 69-year-old, White male transferred from a medical unit to a geropsychiatry inpatient unit after a suicide threat. He had been admitted to the hospital after he broke his wrist 7 months ago. He was treated, discharged, and then almost immediately readmitted because he developed an infection—probably due to his not following a prescribed medical regimen and living in squalid conditions. His family observed that his home was uninhabitable and that he would be constrained to live in a motel room until it was repaired. The plumbing was broken and had rotted out the floorboards of some of the rooms. The family disclosed that while cleaning they removed many bags of garbage, seven broken lawn movers, nine broken televisions, and numerous bottles of alcohol. They were concerned about the unkempt premises and Mr. J's ability to take care of himself under these conditions; he adamantly claimed that there was nothing wrong with his residence. He had initially agreed to live in a personal care home, but then reneged saying that he did not live well with other people and that he should not have to pay to live somewhere else when he had his own home. He had been hospitalized for 6 consecutive months on various medical services, but when the time came for him to be discharged from the medical unit, he rejected the family's plan and said he would kill himself. Numerous psychiatric consultations found no evidence of depressive symptomatology, and it was felt that the patient was manipulating to stay in the hospital. He agreed to the transfer to the geropsychiatric unit so that he could be treated for his "hyperactivity."

Mr. J served in the Navy in World War II, and on discharge was hospitalized for his first of many psychiatric admissions. He then reenlisted in the service where he remained for approximately 20 years until conflicts with commanding officers forced him to leave the service. He has never held a regular job due to constant difficulties getting along with peers and following orders from superiors. According to his brother, problems in relationships were apparent even in childhood. Mr. J never married and currently lives alone. He lived in a series of places before moving in with his mother, who died about 6 years ago, and continues to live in his mother's home. He is part owner of the house, along with his brother and sister-in-law. Due to previous overpayments that he failed to report, he is not currently receiving a government pension.

On the unit, he was at times verbally threatening toward some of the patients with dementia who were confused and wandered into his room. Neuropsychological testing revealed mild cognitive difficulties, but it was believed that he was capable of taking care of himself. A family meeting with his brother and two sisters-in-law was held to discuss his impending discharge. After 3 weeks on the geropsychiatry service, they had been finally able to finish fixing the house at a cost of $10,000. He agreed to be discharged at this time, with a request that the social worker make an application for a VA pension. He was discharged with the primary diagnosis of a Narcissistic PD.

CONCLUSIONS

These vignettes highlight some of the social, psychological, and philosophical aspects of the ethical issues involved in the clinical management of older adults with PDs. They touch on health care overutilization, restricted discharge options, assessment and treatment snafus, troublesome legal questions, and fundamental philosophical controversies concerning respect for individual autonomy versus the good of society. When Mr. Z was a younger man and got into trouble, he simply hitched a train ride and escaped. Now with declining cognition, resurgence of psychotic symptoms, and scarce savings due to poor long-term planning, he has no one to rely on in his time of need. If he had stronger support, then it may have been unnecessary to apply for guardianship, a decision that eventuated in his release to a very restricted environment. But a case could be made that even the futile endeavors to contact family members were unwise given his long period of alienation from them, and the possibility that if the family were to be found they would then be confronted with an unfair stressful predicament concerning whether they should take over his care. An argument can also be introduced that the treatment team was too quick to presume incompetence because Mr. Z's values differed from their own middle-class ones. Much of the time in his past when he was not in prison, Mr. Z voluntarily lived alone. Maybe more of an effort would have been made to heed his desires for continued independence, had he ever sincerely attempted to accommodate to the rules of society.

Contrary to Mr. Z, Mr. J had a long history of intense ambivalent interactions with his family. They were quite upset by his living situation, but put forth their best effort to resolve it. Despite the money, time, and effort that the family spent trying to assist him, Mr. J appeared singularly ungrateful in his behavior toward them. Instead of scheduled meetings with the family to discuss discharge plans, a more humane therapeutic approach might have been for the staff to counsel them to reduce their emotional investment and divest themselves of the "helper" role that enabled him to stay out of an institutional setting only at great psychological cost to themselves. Mr. J has been able to "work " his family and the health system to his advantage. But, as aging progressively interferes with his ability to function at home, there will be additional encounters between this patient's narcissistic needs, aging and overburdened siblings, and a changing health care system that can ill afford social admissions to expensive medical units. Mr. J's autonomy as an individual must be honored, but without sacrificing his essential moral relationship with relatives that provides a context for the giving and expending of finite family resources (Jecker, 1990). The autonomy of the treatment team to make medically sound decisions and prevent patient injury must also be respected.

What should society's position be toward Mr. Z and Mr. J? The government's traditional paternalistic stance is challenged by such patients. Is it ever ethical to say "enough is enough," and refuse admission to individuals in medical need but chronically noncompliant with their prescribed therapeutic regimen? Despite only limited cognitive impairment, does the irresponsible health-related behavior precipitating their hospital admissions represent prima facie evidence for incompetence to conduct medical affairs and dictate subsequent government interference? What weight should be given to these older patients' responsibility to society and their narcissistic use of scarce health resources that deprive others of better care? What about Mr. J's responsibility to his family members? If a guardian is appointed for Mr. J in the future, who should it be? Is the best choice a close family member who has been involved with his care, but who disagrees with him about his ability to function at home? Or, should it be a "neutral" court-appointed guardian with little knowledge of his personal history? Was it ethical to "force" Mr. Z to live in a communal residence that had never before been tolerated by him? What does this say about the principle of the least restrictive environment with regard to older PD patients? Are nursing home personnel equipped to handle the psychological needs of Mr. Z? Is it ethical for a nursing home to admit a patient with a long criminal history who has the potential to be aggressive toward staff or vulnerable residents? Is it legitimate to use psychoactive medication to limit Mr. J's physical capacity while in the hospital in order to protect other patients from his verbally abusive behavior? Or should the patients with dementia who wander be restrained to protect them from the possibility of Mr. J "acting out" against them? Are criminal sanctions the best solutions to the petty illegal behavior perpetrated by older adults with PDs, which are frequently the last vestiges of their independent activity (e.g., Mr. Z's smoking in nondesignated places)? These questions pertain to a wide range of ethical considerations and point to the need for a more systematic and comprehensive ethical framework to guide geriatric mental health professionals in clinical decision making.

With the aging population, health professionals will increasingly treat older adults with PDs in a variety of geriatric contexts, including acute psychiatric and medical inpatient units, outpatient clinics, rehabilitation programs, and nursing homes. The dilemmas created by the intersection of a patient with rigid personality characteristics, ambivalent caregivers, nongerontologically trained providers, a health care system in the process of reform, and an ageist society appear formidable. The response must be directed by sound gerontological and mental health knowledge, and a philosophy that weighs the much-vaunted rights of the individual with the dictates of society for responsible behavior.

ACKNOWLEDGMENTS

I would like to acknowledge the thought-provoking discussions on ethical issues in older psychiatric patients that took place at the Houston VAMC and were integral to the conceptualization of this chapter. Participants included Larry McCullough, Richard Workman, Wright Williams, Pam Rezabek, Mark Kunik, Devi Khalsa, and Sandhya Trivedi.

REFERENCES

Bulcroft, K., Kielkopf, M. R., & Tripp, K. (1991). Elderly wards and their legal guardians: Analysis of county probate records in Ohio and Washington. *Gerontologist, 31*(2), 156–164.

Chervenak, F. A., & McCullough, L. B. (1991). Justified limits on refusing intervention. *Hastings Center Report, 21*, 12–18.

Clark, P. G. (1991). Ethical dimensions of quality of life in aging: Autonomy vs. collectivism in the United States and Canada. *Gerontologist, 31*, 631–639.

Grisso, T. (1986). *Evaluating competencies*. New York: Plenum.

High, D. M. (1991). A new myth about families of older people. *Gerontologist, 31*, 611–618.

Jecker, N. S. (1990). The role of intimate others in medical decision-making. *Gerontologist, 31*(1), 65–71.

Jordan, J. V. (1989). Relational development: Therapeutic implications of empathy and shame. *Work in Progress, 39*, 1–13.

Kapp, M. B. (1991). Health care decision-making by the elderly: I get by with a little help from my family. *Gerontologist, 31*, 619–623.

Kapp, M. B. (1996, November). *Long term care for the unbefriended: Legal risks and repercussions*. Paper presented at the 49th annual meeting of the Gerontological Society of America, Washington, DC.

McCullough, L. B., Coverdale, J., Bayer, T., & Chervenak F. A. (1992). Ethically justified guidelines for family planning interventions to prevent pregnancy in female patients with chronic mental illness. *American Journal of Obstetrics and Gynecology, 167*, 19–25.

Morreim, E. H. (1993). Impairments and impediments in patients' decision-making: Reframing the competence question. *Journal of Clinical Ethics, 4*, 294–307.

Pillemer, K., & Finkelhor, D. (1988). The prevalence of elder abuse: A random sample survey. *Gerontologist, 28*(1), 51–56.

Roland, A. (1988). *In search of self in India and Japan: Toward a cross-cultural society*. Princeton, NJ: Princeton University Press.

Sadavoy, J. (1996). Personality disorder in old age: Symptom expression. *Clinical Gerontologist, 16*, 19–36.

Smyer, M., Zarit, S., & Qualls, S.H. (1990). Psychological intervention with the aging individual. In J. E. Birren & K.W. Schaie (Eds.), *Handbook of the psychology of aging* (pp. 375–403). San Diego: Academic Press.

Thompson, L.W., Gallagher, D., & Czirr, R. (1988). Personality disorder and outcome in the treatment of late-life depression. *Journal of Geriatric Psychiatry, 21*, 133–146.

Workman, R. H., Molinari, V., McCullough L. , Rezabek, P., Khalsa, D., Trivedi, S., & Kunik, M. (1997). An ethical framework for understanding patients with comorbid dementia and impulsive personality disorders: Diagnosing and managing disorders of autonomy. *Journal of Ethics, Law, and Aging, 3*(2), 79–90.

Personality Disorders in Late Life and Public Policy: Implications of the Contextual, Cohort-Based, Maturity, Specific Challenge Model

Bob G. Knight, PhD
University of Southern California

In order to highlight the ways in which personality disorders of late life become policy relevant, a brief summary of observations about the role of personality disorders in younger adults is useful. Under the *DSM* multiaxial diagnostic system, personality disorders fall on Axis II. This placement is intended to call attention to the role of personality disorders in complicating the presentation, diagnosis, and treatment of Axis I disorders. It can be thought of as analogous to the role of the medical disorders placed on Axis III, which cause or complicate the Axis I disorder. In some individuals, the Axis I disorder may be caused by, or an aspect of, the Axis II disorder.

This distinction can affect mental health treatment of younger adults in a variety of ways. In general, it is thought that the treatment of Axis II disorders takes longer than the treatment of Axis I disorders. For younger adult populations, Kopta, Howard, Lowry, and Butler (1994) found a median effective psychotherapeutic dose of more than 104 sessions for characteriological symptoms as compared to 5 sessions for acute distress symptoms and 14 for chronic distress symptoms. Treating Axis I disorders when an Axis II disorder is present is also thought to take longer, and this has been demonstrated in older adults (Thompson, Gallagher, & Czirr, 1988). In clinical discussion of cases, Axis II disorders most frequently arise as a topic when the therapist is experiencing difficulty with the client. Axis II disorder clients tend to evoke a range of emotions in therapists including anger, depression, and boredom.

An aspect of the move toward managed care and, in general, of the move toward regulating access to psychotherapy has been a general policy that third-party payers will reimburse for the acute, presenting Axis I disorder, but not for personality reorganization. This policy seems to cut across private insurance and public insurers (Medicare, Medicaid). One policy issue for all ages in mental health care is whether there should be longer allotments of therapy visits for persons with Axis II diagnoses for the treatment of depression than for those without Axis II disorders.

ISSUES SPECIFIC TO LATE LIFE

For the past several years, I have used the framework of the contextual, cohort-based, maturity, specific challenge model (CCMSC) to consider the need to adapt psychotherapy for work with older clients (Knight, 1996). The model is also useful to raise questions about the potentially specific issues of personality disorders in later life.

Context

As noted in both chapters in this section, the social context of older adults poses challenges for persons with personality disorders and may render persons with strong traits dysfunctional for the first time in later life. As noted by Molinari, illness and resultant embeddedness in the health care system with its different set of rules and relationships is difficult for persons with Axis II diagnoses. In their turn, persons with Axis II diagnoses are challenging to health care professionals. In my clinical experience, a common reason for referral of older clients from physicians and from medical clinics has been excessive dependency and/or the hostile–dependent relationship characteristic of the Cluster B disorders.

This recognition, if general, forms another target group to consider when planning mental health services for older adults, especially in the blended medical-psychological context of managed care practices. That is, in addition to looking for persons with depressed mood, anxiety, and dementia, early identification of personality disorders of older adult patients with personality disorders would be an important early intervention strategy. By early identification and planning intervention strategies that take the personality disorder into account (e.g., letting psychotherapists rather than physicians manage the patient's dependency needs), unnecessary medical visits and unneeded staff frustration could be avoided. It would be an issue of considerable policy significance to determine how much "excess" medical utilization is due to Axis II disorders by older adults rather than Axis I. It seems plausible to hypothesize that the cost, and therefore potential cost savings, could be quite large.

The nursing home environment captures all of the same issues as acute care health services and intensifies them because, as Rosowsky and Smyer (chap. 15, this volume) note, the nursing home is home as well as health care facility. Difficult patients often have Axis II disorders or traits: demanding of staff time, eliciting anger, and playing "let's you and her fight." At present, the typical solution appears to be ejecting the offending patient from the facility. As noted by the authors, a more responsible approach is to intervene in order to effectively manage the patient. A key policy issue is how to distribute the costs of care for such difficult patients so that the inexpensive answer for individual nursing homes (patient discharge) does not become an expensive answer for the system of care and the third-party payer (e.g., Medicare or Medicaid). From the system perspective, such patients go through multiple admissions and discharges (with attendant assessments and other costs), often with time in acute medical or psychiatric facilities and intense case management costs with each move. However, for the individual units of the system, it becomes a game of "hot potato" with each nursing home or hospital "winning" by keeping the patient moving and not being last in line.

Cohort-Based Issues

Cohort differences are the differences between generational groups (e.g., GI Generation vs. The Boomers) that are often mistaken for developmental differences. For example, Abrams and Horowitz (chap. 4, this volume) cite a study by Eysenck (1987) on age differences in neuroticism and extroversion. Schaie (1995), using the sequential longitudinal designs of life-span developmental psychology, noted that cohorts from 1900 to WWII declined in extroversion, whereas cohorts since then have increased. In the same studies, he found that reactivity to threat, likely a facet of the personality factor neuroticism, has increased across cohorts since the beginning of the 20th century.

These findings about personality factors and facets suggest a possibility that has not, to my knowledge, been tested: Are there cohort differences in the prevalence of personality disorders? It seems plausible (to this author, anyway) that pre-Boomer generations were higher in obsessive-compulsive, avoidant, and paranoid disorders, whereas Boomers may be more prone to Cluster B disorders. Perhaps Generation X is shifting more toward Cluster C. Because individuals mature and develop adequate adjustment or personality disorders in specific socio-historical contexts that change over time, cohort-specific prevalence is possible. Only time and research can tell us if it is empirically true. (See Zweig and Hillman, chap. 3, this volume, for review of longitudinal personality research.)

This hypothesis has two implications. One is that ideas about changes in personality disorders with maturation through adulthood, based on cross sectional studies and cross-sectional clinical observations, confound age and cohort; theory may be misguided by this confound. The other is that planning for future mental health services for older adults would need to be cohort-based rather than age-based. Drawing from Abrams and Horowitz' (chap. 4, this volume) Table 4.2, if the effect is due to cohort differences, older clients of a decade or two hence will have higher rates of paranoid and narcissistic disorders. If it is due to age, then the current Boomers would move from narcissism to higher rates of schizoid and self-defeating personality disorders.

Maturity

The key theoretical issue is whether persons with personality disorders mature over the adult life span in the same ways that other adults are supposed to do. By definition, personality disorders should stay about the same throughout life, assuming that personality is fixed. Life-span developmental psychology has revealed some evidence for stability in personality and some evidence of possible change in coping styles. On one hand, it seems plausible that life experiences provide corrective re-education (e.g., through work experience, social experience, mental health treatment, prison experience) for persons with personality disorders, although if the term means anything at all, one would be forced to assume that they learn more slowly from experience than do persons with normal development in early adulthood. This is the type of argument advanced for the lower prevalence in late life (inconsistently found) of Cluster B disorders.

Of course, the absence of more dramatic symptoms described as typical in younger adults could be due to changing life circumstances and roles or to selective attrition of samples. The early adulthood years are characterized by a lot of firsts (marriage, children, jobs) and often by change and flux through these roles. It may be that even a person with a personality disorder thinks twice before quitting a job in anger at age 50, when he or she would not have at 25. Leaving one's third wife in the heat of an argument may send off warning bells at 55 that went unheeded when leaving one's first wife at 30. There may also be forms of selective attrition: Disorders that lead to high-risk lifestyles may decrease the likelihood of becoming old; antisocial personality disorder may make it more likely that a client will be in the correctional system at age 55 than in the mental health or medical systems.

If people do mature throughout adulthood, then the pessimism that attends working with Axis II clients who are younger needs to be ameliorated when working with older Axis II clients. In this scenario, working with an older Axis II is more hopeful because of the maturation, rather than less hopeful because of presumed "hardening of the personality." On the other hand, if the apparent changes are due to age-graded role changes, then we need to expand our clinical knowledge and our diagnostic categories so as not to miss important diagnostic distinctions because we expect clients in their 60s to show self-destructive behavior more appropriate to those in their 30s.

Specific Challenges

Older adults are more frequently coping with chronic illness, disability, and grief. Molinari notes that the illness dimension challenges older adults with personality disorders in more dramatic ways (even) than they do other older adults. His discussion of the ethics of end-of-life decision making with Axis II patients raises important clinical and ethical issues.

The interplay of dementia and personality disorder is important and understudied. More than 20 years ago, I visited a state hospital's geropsychiatric ward for older demented men who were violent. The director, a clinical social worker, pointed out to me case by case that these were men with histories of violence in their youth who had settled down in midlife and were violent again now that the dementia had loosened inhibitory control and erased learned control from memory. It is at least plausible that many difficult dementia patients are persons with personality disorder plus dementia. Note that using family members as sources for clinical history may not be helpful in this regard, insofar as people with personality disorders often deceive their families, or at least do not inform them of everything.

SUMMARY

Attention to personality disorders in later life have several implications for practice and policy. As at all ages, the decision not to pay for psychological interventions for personality disorders needs to be reexamined. Some adjustment of expectations for the time needed to treat Axis I disorders may be needed in the presence of some of the Axis II disorders. The effect of Axis II disorder patients on costs in the medical system and in long term care is unknown, but current knowledge would indicate that it could be quite large. The role of premorbid personality disorders in complicating medical treatment and long-term care of chronic illnesses and of the dementias is poorly understood at present, but is quite likely pervasive and profound. Understanding the prevalence of personality disorders in late life requires research to disentangle maturation effects and cohort differences, which have different and competing implications for future prevalence rates.

In short, the implications of understanding personality disorders in older adults for improved health and mental care are immense. The potential for cost savings in health and long-term care is excellent. The current knowledge base is limited, because the study of personality disorders in older adults is in its infancy.

REFERENCES

Eysenck, H. J. (1987). Personality and aging: an introductory analysis. *Journal of Social Behavior and Personality, 3,* 11–21.

Knight, B. (1996). *Psychotherapy with older adults* (2nd ed.). Thousand Oaks, CA: Sage.

Kopta, S. M., Howard, K. I., Lowry, J. L., & Butler, L. E. (1994). Patterns of symptomatic recovery in psychotherapy. *Journal of Consulting and Clinical Psychology, 62,* 1009–1016.

Schaie, K. W. (1995). *Intellectual development in adulthood: The Seattle Longitudinal Study.* New York: Cambridge University Press.

Thompson, L. W., Gallagher, D., & Czirr, R. (1988). Personality disorder and outcome in the treatment of late life depression. *Journal of Geriatric Psychiatry, 21,* 133–153.

Author Index

A

Aapro, N., 119, *132*
Abraham, K., 170, *171*
Abraham, M., 41, *50*, 57, *67*
Abrams, R. C., 10, *13*, 38, 46, 48, *49*, 55, 56, *57*, 59, 61, 62, 63, 64, 65, *66*, 69, 70, 71, 72, 73, 76, 77, 87, *91*, *93*, 101, *112*, 246, *251*
Adams, R. D., 200, *204*
Adker, G., 168, *171*
Agbayewa, M. O., 71, 72, 87, *91*
Agronin, M. E., 44, *49*, 217, 219, 225, 243, 250, *251*
Akiskal, H. S., *251*
Albanese, M., 243, *254*
Albert, M. S., 199, *204*
Alpert, J. E., 245, *252*
Alden, L. E., 81, *91, 92*
Alexander, F., 175, *186*
Alexopoulos, G. S., 48, *49*, 55, 56, 57, 59, 62, 64, 65, *66*, 69, 70, 72, 73, 76, 77, *91*, 101, *112*, 246, *251*
Allmon, D., 224, *226*
Allport, G., 97, 100, *112*
Alonso, A., 167, *172*
Alpert, J. E., 69, *92*, 245, *252*
Altman, B. M., 259, *273*
Alves, A. B., 247, *254*
Ambonetti, A., 43, *50*
Ames, A., 55, 57, 63, *66, 67*
Anderson, J., 239, *253*
Andreoli, A., 119, *132*
Andrews, G., 44, *49*, 130, *132*
Anstett, R., 261, *272*
Anstey, K. J., 223, *226*
Anthony, J. C., 56, *67*
Armstron, H. E., 224, *226*

Arndt, I. O., 241, *252*
Arntz, A., 80, *93*, 217, *226*
Artin, E., 96, *117*
Astill, J. L., 243, *252*
Aubuchon, P. G., 217, *225*
Ayd, F. J., 230, *252*

B

Baer, B. A., 36, *51*
Baiyewu, O., 260, *272*
Baker, L., 153, *173*
Baltes, P. B., 145, 146, *149*
Bandyopadhyay, D., 155, *172*
Bank, 144, *150*
Barber, J. P., 78, 79, 89, *92*
Barkham, M., 79, 80, *92*
Baron, R., M., 101, *112*
Barratt, E., S., 36, *49*
Bass, D. M., 104, *113*
Bates, K., 57, *68*
Bauer, H., 200, *202*
Bauer, J., 200, *202*
Baumeister, R., F., 109, *113*
Baumgard, C. H., 240, *252*
Bayer, T., 281, *287*
Bear, D., 190, 193, *203, 204*
Beardon, C., 38, 43, *49*, 78, *91*
Beats, B., 198, *203*
Beck, A. T., 72, 73, 82, 83, 84, *91, 92*, 216, 219, 221, 224, *225*
Becker, L. A., 99, *113*
Beckham, E., 43, *52*, 69, 78, 79, *94*
Beery, L., 104, 105, *116*
Bell, S. E., 43, *50*, 69, *92*, 240, *252*
Bem, D. J., 7, *14*, 98, 100, 112, *113*, 136, 137, *149*

Bender, M. 57, *68*, 102, *116*
Benedict, K. 84, *92*
Bengston, V., 45, *49*
Benjamin, L. S. 36, *51*, 82, *92*
Berg, L., 224, *254*
Beresford, T. P., 193, *203*
Bergmann, K., 46, *49*, 249, *252*
Berkman, L. F., 103, *113*, 258, *273*
Berlin, 58, *66*
Bibring, G. L., 153, 168, *172*, 176, *187*, 246, 247, 249, *253*, 261, *273*
Bierhals, A. J., 104, 105, *116*
Black, D. W., 43, *50*, 69, 81, *92*, 240, *252*
Blais, M., 84, *92*
Bland, R. C., 56, *66*
Blatt, S. J., 101, *113*
Blazer, D. G., 64, *66*, 240, *252*, 260, *272*
Blazina, L., 259, 260, *274*
Block, J., 8, *14*, 97, 98, *113*
Block, P., 102, *116*
Bloom, F. E., 200, *204*
Boiageo, B. A., 243, *253*
Boker, S. M., 140, *149*
Bonnefoi, B., 200, *203*
Bookwala, J., 103, 105, *113*, 117
Booth-Kewley, S., 102, *114*
Borchardt, L., 267, *272*
Bornstein, R., F., 101, *113*, 119, 128, *132*, 155, *171*
Borus, J. S., 69, *92*
Boswell, P., 71, 73, 74, 87, *92*
Bothwell, S., 36, *52*
Bouffides, E., 78, 79, 82, *92*
Bowers, W., 73, 81, *92*, *94*
Bowman, K., 104, *113*
Bowman, S. R., 103, 104, *113*, *115*
Bózzola, F. G., 234, *252*
Bradburn, N. M., 147, 148, *150*
Brandler, S., 240, *252*
Brannon, D., 258, 267, *272*, 274
Brant, 259, *273*
Breckenridge, J. S., 72, *94*
Brent, R., 64, *67*
Breslau, L., 177, *186*
Brim, O. G., Jr., 136, *149*
Brodaty, H., 223, *226*
Brody, J. A., 56, *68*
Bronfenbrenner, U., 100, *113*
Brouwers, P., 195, 196, *204*
Brown, A., 199, *203*
Brown, E., Jr., 259, *273*
Brown, R., 243, *253*

Bruss, G. S., 77, 78, 79, 80, *92*
Bryk, A. S., 140, *149*
Budman, S., 99, *117*, 157, *173*
Bulcroft, K., 277, *287*
Burns, B. J., 258, 259, *272*, 274
Burton, 259, *273*
Bush, T., 261, *273*
Butler, L. E., 289, *294*
Bulka, D., 45, *51*
Burke, J. D., Jr., 56, *67*, 240, *254*
Burns, E. M., 56, *66*
Burns, W., 59, *68*
Burvill, P. W., 102, *113*
Buss, A. H., 36, *50*
Buss, A. J., 10, *14*
Buie, D. H., 168, *171*
Buysse, D., 38, 43, *49*, 78, *91*

C

Cacioppo, J. T., 103, *117*
Caine, E. D., 65, *67*, 106, 109, *113*, *114*
Calabrese, J. R., 239, *253*
Campbell, J., 241, *253*
Cannell, C. F., 147, 148, *149*, *150*
Cappe, R. F., 81, *92*
Card, C., 55, 57, 62, 64, 65, *66*, 69, 70, 72, 73, 76, *91*, 101, *112*
Carmelli, D., 103, *117*
Carpenter, W. T., 242, *253*
Carstensen, L. L., 103, 104, *115*, 217, 218, 225, 226
Caserta, M. S.,104, 114
Casey, D. A., 57, *66*, 112, *113*
Casey, P. R., 40, *50*, 55, *66*
Caspi, A., 7, *14*, 98, 100, 104, 112, *113*, *116*, 136, 137, 149
Cath, F. H., 177, *186*
Chalmers, T. C., 58, *66*
Chambless, D., L., 80, *92*
Charney, D., 42, *50*
Chatterjee, A., 107, *113*, *117*
Chervenak, F. A., 281, *287*
Chin, S. J., 247, *254*
Chipuer, H., 8, *14*
Choca, J., 84, *92*
Christal, R. E., 121, *133*
Christensen, H., 58, *66*
Christenson, R., 64, *66*
Chrzanowski, G., 261, *272*
Clark, L. A., 35, 36, *50*
Clark, M., 103, *113*

Clark, P. G., 280, *287*
Clark, R., 259, *273*
Clark, S. J., 103, *113*
Clarkin, J. F., 6, *14*, 64, *67*, 82, *92*, 121, *133*
Class, C. A., 260, *272*
Clayton, P., 45, *52*
Cloninger, C. R., 10, *14*, 33, 35, *50*, 96, *113*, 234, *252*
Coccaro, E. F., 10, *14*, 202, *203*, 235, 243, *252*, 243, *253*, *254*
Cochrane, K., 235, *252*
Coffman, G. A., 57, *67*, 246, *253*
Cohen, B. J., 56, *66*, 156, 161, *172*, 202, *203*
Cohen, B. M., 242, *253*
Cohen, J., 75, *92*
Cohen, R. A., 259, *272*
Cohler, B. J., 96, 111, *113*
Cohn, M. D., 258, 267, 270, *272*, *274*
Colarusso, C. A., 164, *173*
Colling, G. H., 200, *204*
Collins, J. F., 43, *52*, 69, 78, 79, *94*
Commons, M. L., 145, *150*
Comstock, G. W., 104, *114*
Conger, J. J., 137, *149*
Contrada, R, J., 100, *113*
Conwell, Y., 65, *67*, 109, *113*, *114*
Cook, D. B., 121, *133*
Cook, M., 155, *172*
Coolidge, F. L., 56, 57, *66*, 99, *113*
Cooper, T. B., 235, *252*
Corenthal, C., 73, 75, *94*, 36, 43, *52*, *53*
Cornelius, J., 243, *254*
Coryell, W., 39, 40, 41, 42, 43, *51*, *52*, *53*, 75, *94*
Costa, P., 6, 7, *14*, 33, 34, 36, 45, *50*, 62, *66*, 71, *93*, 96, 98, 99, 102, 106, 109, *113*, *114*, *116*, 121, *132*, *133*, 138, 146, *149*, 156, *172*
Coverdale, J., 281, *287*
Cowdry, R. W., 195, 196, *204*, 243, 244, *252*
Cox, 65, *67*, 109, *113*
Coyne, J. C., 101, 112, *114*
Craighead, W. E., 78, 79, *93*
Crawford, F. S., 96, *117*
Cress, E., 12, *14*
Crique, M., 102, *114*
Crook, T. H., 202, *203*
Cross, C. K., 37, *50*
Cross, P. S., 55, 56, 62, *67*
Cross, S., 96, *114*
Cruise, P. A, 267, *273*

Cummings, J. L., 107, *116*, 200, *203*, 234, *253*
Curtis, G. C., 80, *92*
Czirr, R., 38, *52*, 57, 62, 65, *68*, 69, 71, 72, 73, 74, 75, 83, 90, *94*, 153, *173*, 217, 219, 227, 246, *254*, 279, *287*, 289, *294*

D

Dale, T. M., 241, *253*
Davies, R., 219, 220, *227*
Davis, J. M., 230, *252*
Davis, K. L., 10, *14*, 37, *52*, 195, *204*, 234, 235, *252*, *254*
Davis, R. D. & Associates, 82, 84, *93*
Dawson, D. V., 107, *117*
Day, N., 104, 105, *116*
DeJonghe, E., 266, *273*
Deltito, J. A., 247, *252*
Demby, 99, *117*, 157, *173*
Demopulos, C., 245, *252*
Depue, R. A., 10, *14*
Devanand, D. P. 57, *66*, 69, 72, *92*
DeVoe, M., 45, *51*
Dian, L., 200, *203*
Digman, J. M., 96, *114*, 121, *132*
Diguer, L., 78, 79, 89, *92*
DiMascio, A., 78, *93*
DiMond, M., 104, *114*
DiRito, D. C., 99, *113*
Dixon, R. A., 145, 146, *149*
Docherty, J. P.,40, 42, 43, *52*, 69, 78, 79, *94*
Donnelly, N. J., 243, *253*
Dormbrand, L. 218, *226*
Dorozynsky, L., 241, *252*
Dougherty, L., M., 119, 120, 121, 123, 126, *132*, *133*, 154, 160, 161, 170, *172*, *173*, 261, 263, *273*
Dowson, J. H., 159, *172*
Dressen, L., 217, *226*
Drossman, D. A., 261, *272*
Drugovich, M. L., 265, *273*
Drummond, D., 153, *173*
Duberstein, P. R., 109, 111, *113*, *114*
Duffy, M., 168, 169, *172*
Duggan, C., 44, *50*
Dunbar, F., 176, *186*
Dunham, R. L., 99, *113*
Durkee, A., 36, *50*

E

Edelstein, B. A., 124, *132*, 218, *226*
Elder, G. H., Jr., 100, *116*
Eliot, T. S., 19, *28*
Elkin, I., 43, *52*, 69, 78, 79, *93*, *94*
Ellason, J., 37, *50*
Elliot, F. A., 202, *203*
Emery, G., 72, 84, *91*
Emmerson, P., 102, *113*
Endicott, J., 73, 75, *92*, *94*
Engel, G. L., 176, *187*
Engels, M. L., 220, *226*
Erbaugh, J. 73, *92*
Erickson, E., 161, *172*, 263, *272*
Essa, M., 57, *67*
Eysenck, H. J., 62, *66*, 291, *293*

F

Faberow, N. L., 107, *114*
Fabrega, H., Jr., 57, *67*, 246, *253*
Fahlén, T., 247, *252*
Fallette, M., 161, 162, *173*
Faravelli, C., 43, *50*
Farmer, R., 34, *50*
Fava, M., 41, *50*, 57, *67*, 69, 78, 79, 82, *92*, 245, *252*
Fay, A., 216, *226*
Featherman, D. L., 140, *149*
Feske, U., 80, *92*
Fieve, R. R., 102, *116*
Finkelhor, D., 277, *287*
Finkelstein, S., 200, *203*
Finn, S., 7, *14*
Fiorot, M., 71, 73, 74, 87, *92*, 130, *133*
First, M. B., 75, *94*, 130, *132*
Flegenheimer, W., 81, *94*
Fleiss, J., 75, *92*
Florio, C. M., 98, *114*
Fogel, B. S., 46, *52*, 55, 57, 62, 65, *67*, 71, *92*, 111, *116*, 120, *133*, 136, 140, *150*, 156, *172*, 217, *226*
Fonagy, P., 37, *50*
Forbes, N. T., 109, *113*
Fowler, F. J., 147, 148, *149*
Frances, A. J., 34, 35, 36, *50*, *51*, *52*, 64, *67*, 121, *132*, 154, *172*, 239, *253*
Frank, E., 38, 40, 43, *49*, *50*, *51*, 56, 63, *67*, 69, 78, *91*, *93*
Frankenburg, F. R., 243, *252*

Frasure-Smith, N., 106, *115*
Frazier, L. D., 103, 105, *115*
Frederickson, B. L., 219, 223, 227
Frederiksen, K., 266, *273*
Freedman, V. A., 258, *273*
Freels, S., 234, *252*
Freeman, A., & Associates, 82, 83, *91*, 219, 221, 224, *225*
Freeman, C. P., 78, 79, 89, *92*
Freeman, D. H., 103, *116*
Freidel, R. O., 239, 243, *252*
Frenkel, J., 243, *254*
Freud, S., 169, *172*
Friedlob, A. S., 265, *273*
Friedman, H. S., 102, *114*, *117*
Friedman, M. P., 259, *273*
Friedman, R. S., 177, 180, *187*
Fries, B., 265, 266, *273*
Furner, S. E., 259, *272*
Futterman, A., 104, *117*

G

Gabel, J., 81, *92*
Gallagher-Thompson, D., 38, *52*, 57, 62, 65, *68*, 69, 70, 71, 72, 73, 74, 75, 83, 90, *94*, 104, 107, *114*, *117*, 153, *173*, 216, 217, 218, 219, 220, 221, 223, 225, *226*, 227, 246, *254*, 279, *287*, 289, *294*
Gantz, F., 70, 83, *94*
Gao, S., 260, *272*
Garb, H. N., 98, *114*
Gardner, D. L., 195, 196, *204*, 243, *252*, 243, 244, *252*
Garfein, A., J., 267, *272*
Gartner, A. F., 72, *93*
Gartner, J. D., 72, *93*
Gatz, M., 136, 146, *149*
George, A., 243, *254*
George, L. K., 155, *172*, 240, *252*, 260, *272*
German, P. S., 56, *67*, 259, *273*
Gerrard, T. J., 261, *273*
Gibbon, M., 75, *94*, 130, *132*, *133*
Gilewski, M., 104, 107, *114*, *117*
Gill, T., 12, *14*
Gilman, E. W., 96, *117*
Glass, D., R., 40, 42, *52*
Glavin, Y. F. W., 57, *67*, 246, *253*
Glisky, M. L., 96, *114*
Goffman, E., 262, *272*
Gognalons, M. Y., 119, *132*

Goldberg, E., L., 104, *114*
Goldberg, S. C., 239, 243, *252*
Goldsmith, S., 34, 35, *51*
Goldstein, A. J., 80, *92*
Goldstein, E. G., 243, 245, *252*
Goldstein, K., 198, *203*
Goldstein, R., D., 77, 78, 79, 80, *92*
Golomb, M., 41, *50*, 57, *67*
Gordon, C., 45, *49*
Gorelick, P. B., 234, *252*
Graham, J. R., 128, *132*
Gray, A., 202, *203*
Graziano, A. M., 124, *132*
Green, M. A., 80, *92*
Greenson, R., 157, 158, *172*
Gressot, G., 119, *132*
Griego, J. A., 57, *66*
Grisso, T., 277, *287*
Gross, M. E., 180, *187*
Grossman, S., 177, *187*
Grove, W. M., 98, *114*
Groves, J. F., 153, 167, *172*, 180, *187*, 261, *273*
Gruenberg, A. M., 77, 78, 79, 80, *92*
Gruenberg, E., 56, *67*, 240, *254*
Gunderson, J. G., 63, *67*, 242, 250, *253*, 242, *253*
Guralnik, J., 12, *14*
Gurian, B., 46, *52*, 56, 62, *67*, 70, *94*, 111, *116*, 119, 120, 125, *133*, 136, 144, *150*, 155, 156, 157, 170, *173*, 218, 226, 242, 243, *254*, 261, 263, *273*
Gurland, B. J., 12, *24*, 55, 56, 62, *67*, 247, *253*, 260, *273*
Gustafson, J. P., 21, *28*
Gutmann, D., 45, 47, *50*, 106, 112, *114*
Guze, S., 45, *52*

H

Habib, G., 200, *203*
Habib, M., 200, *203*
Hadzi-Pavlovic, D., 58, *66*
Hall, K. S., 260, *272*
Hall, W. D., 102, *113*
Hallmeyer, J., 39, 40, 41, *51*
Hamann, M. S., 80, *93*
Hambleton, R. K., 142, *149*
Hamburg, D. 180, *187*
Hamer, R. M., 239, 243, *252*
Hamilton, M., 73, *92*
Handen, B. L., 220, *226*

Hanser, S., 70, 83, *94*
Hardy, G. E., 79, 80, *92*
Harlow, S. D., 104, *114*
Harris, M. J., 101, *116*
Hart, R. P., 121, *133*
Hathaway, S. R., 127, 128, *132*
Hauser, P., 40, 42, *51*
Havens, L., 19, 26, *28*
Hawes, C., 265, 266, *273*
Hays, J. C., 104, *114*
Heard, H. L., 224, *226*
Hedges, L. V., 58, *67*
Helson, R., 45, 49, *50*, 106, 107, *114*, *117*
Helzer, J. E., 56, *67*, 240, *254*
Hendler, A., 159, *172*
Hendler, J., 128, *132*
Hendrie, H. C., 260, *272*
Henke, R., 243, *254*
Henry, G. W., 201, *203*
Herbert, J. A., 243, *252*
Herrmann, J., 109, *113*
Hersen, M., 70, *94*, 128, *133*
Hervig, L. K., 96, 103, *115*
Hertzig, J., 72, *93*
Hertzog, C., 145, 146, *150*
Heun, R., 39, 40, 41, *51*
Hicks, A., 159, *173*
High, D. M., 280, *287*
Hill, M. A., 107, *116*, 234, *253*
Hillman, J., 46, *50*
Himmelfarb, S., 104, *116*
Hinrichsen, G. A., 47, *53*, 69, 70, 71, 73, 76, *94*
Hinze, E., 164, 166, *172*
Hirschfield, R. M. A., 37, *50*, 101, *114*
Hirvenoja, R., 201, *204*
Hodel-Malinofsky, T., 190, *203*
Holland, P. W., 143, *149*
Hollander, E., 235, 243, 247, *254*
Holt, J. H., 56, *66*
Holt, R. R., 97, *115*
Holzer, C. E., III, 56, *68*
Hooker, K., 96, 103, 105, 111, *115*
Horgas, A. L., 270, *272*
Horowitz, L. M., 36, *51*
Horowitz, M., 72, *93*
Horowitz, S. V., 10, *13*, 56, 63, 64, 65, *66*, 70, 71, 87, *91*
House, J. S., 103, *115*
Howard, K. I., 289, *294*
Howard, R., 155, *172*
Hoyt, R., 239, *253*

Hudson, J. I., 242, *253*
Hulbert, J., 43, *50*, 69, *92*
Hunt, C., 44, *49*, 130, *132*
Hurt, S. W., 64, *67*
Huston, A. C., 137, *149*
Hutchinson, C., 105, *115*
Hyler, S. E., 36, *51*, 64, *67*, 128, *132*, 159, *172*
Hymowitz, P., 179, *187*, 239, *253*

I

Ilardi, S. S., 78, 79, *93*
Irwin, D., 243, *253*
Islam, M. N., 243, *254*

J

Jackson, A. N., 202, *203*
Jacob, M., 38, 43, *50*, 56, *67*
Jacobs, S. C., 104, 105, *114*, *116*
Jacobsberg, L. B., 34, 35, *51*, 239, *253*
Jacomb, P., 58, *66*
Jagger, C., 103, *113*
Janicak, P. G., 230, *252*
Jang, K., L., 96, *115*
Janitell, P. M., 57, *66*
Jansen, M., 80, *93*
Jarrett, D., 38, 43, *50*, 56, *67*
Jay, G. M., 267, *272*
Jecker, N. S., 280, 285, *287*
Jensen, H. V., 239, *253*
John, O. P., 96, *115*
Johnson, C., 119, *133*, *173*, 261, 263, *273*
Johnson, J. G., 119, 128, *132*
Jonas, J. M., 242, *253*
Jordon, J. V., 280, *287*
Jordon, K. G., 240, *252*, 260, *272*
Joseph, C., 264, *273*
Joshua, S., 159, *172*
Judd, P. H., 196, *203*
Judge, J. O., 12, *14*
Juolasmaa, A., 201, *204*

K

Kagan, J., 96, 97, 98, 111, *115*, 136, 137, 139, 144, *149*
Kahana, R. J., 153, 168, *172*, 176, *187*, 246, 247, 249, *253*, 261, *273*
Kaiser, R., 147, *149*

Kalish, K. D., 124, *132*
Kalton, G., 147, *150*
Kaltreider, N., 72, *93*
Kampman, R., 201, *204*
Kapp, M. B., 277, 278, 282, *287*
Karel, M. J., 136, 146, *149*
Karp, J. F., 38, 43, *49*, 78, *91*
Kasl, S. V., 104, 105, *114*, *116*
Kasl-Goldley, J. E., 136, 146, *149*
Kastrup, M., 56, *67*
Katon, W., 261, *273*
Katz, I. R., 106, *115*
Katz, S., 265, *273*
Kaus, C. R., 96, 111, *115*
Kavoussi, R. J., 243, *253*
Keith, V., 103, *115*
Keller, M. B., 37, *52*
Kellett, J., 81, *93*
Kemper, T. L., 199, *204*
Kenney, D. A., 101, *112*
Kernberg, O. F., 46, *51*, 156, *172*, 205, *214*
Kerr, T. A., 201, *203*
Kessler, R. C., 147, *149*
Kestenbaum, R., 81, *94*
Khalil, R., 200, *203*
Khalsa, D., 281, *287*
Khouzam, H. R., 243, *253*
Kiecolt-Glaser, J. K., 103, *117*
Kielcopf, M. R., 277, *287*
Kiersky, J. E., 57, *66*, 69, 72, *92*
Kihlstrom, J. F., 96, *114*
Kiloh, L., 44, *49*
King, D. A., 65, *67*, 106, *113*
King, P., 212, *214*
Kinlaw, M. M., 99, *113*
Klar, H. M., 10, *14*, 235, *252*
Klausner, E., 48, *49*
Klein, D. N., 250, *253*
Klein, M. H., 20, *28*, 34, 35, 36, 38, 40, 42, 44, *51*, *52*, 69, 71, 77, 79, 79, 80, 82, 89, *94*
Klerman, G. L., 78, *93*
Klingler, T., 39, 40, 41, *51*
Knapp, J. E., 103, *117*
Knight, B., 290, *294*
Koder, D. A., 223, *226*
Koerner, K., 217, *226*
Koestner, R., 96, 98, 111, *115*
Kohlenberg, R. J., 217, *226*
Kohut, H., 17, *28*
Kolb, B., 191, *203*
Kopta, S. M., 289, *294*

Korfine, L., 6, *14*
Kraepelin, E., 22, *28*
Kramer, M., 56, *67*
Kramlinger, K., 40, 42, *51*
Krantz, S. E., 219, 220, *227*
Krause, N., 103, *115*
Krauss, N. A., 259, *273*
Kroessler, D., 55, 62, *67*, 70, *93*, 119, 120, *132*, 154, *172*
Krupnick, J. L., 69, *93*
Kunik, M. E., 55, 56, 57, 62, 65, *67*, 70, 71, 72, 73, 76, *93*, 101, *115*, 154, *173*, 281, *287*
Kupfer, D. J., 38, 43, *50*, 56, *67*
Kusulas, J. W., 96, 103, *115*

L

LaBouvie-Vief, G., 45, *51*
Lair, T., 259, *273*
Laird, N. M., 58, *66*
Lakey, 103, *116*
Lambert, C., 81, *93*
Landerman, L. R., 259, *272*
Landerman, R., 240, *252*, 260, *272*
Landis, K. R., 103, *115*
Landry, J. A., 267, *272*
Lang, F. R., 103, 104, *115*
Larson, S. L., 129, *133*
Laster, L. J., 241, *253*
Lavelle, N., 38, 43, *49*, 78, *91*
Lazare, A., 167, *172*
Lazarus, A. A., 216, *226*
Lazarus, L. W., 216, 217, 223, 224, *226*
Leaf, P. J., 56, *68*
Lebert, F., 11, *14*
Lebovits, B., Z., 180, *187*
Lee, A., 44, *50*
Lefkowitz, D., 259, *273*
Leibovici, A., 259, 260, *274*
Leigh, T., 37, *50*
Lempa, M., 199, *203*
Lenzenweger, M. F., 6, *14*, 72, 82, *92*, *93*
Leon, A. C., 37, *52*
Leone, N., 243, *253*
Lesperance, F., 106, *115*
Leszcz, M., 45, *52*, 218, *226*
Leventhal, H., 100, *113*
Leverich, G., S., 40, 42, *51*
Levin, D. C., 201, *204*
Levin, S., 180, *187*
Levine, D. N., 200, *203*

Lewinsohn, P., 72, 84, *93*
Liang, J., 103, *115*
Lichtermann, D., 39, 40, 41, *51*
Liebowitz, M. R., 247, *254*
Lin, H. B., 261, *273*
Linehan, M. M., 81, *93*, 215, 217, 224, *226*
Lingjaerde, O., 78, 79, *94*
Links, P. S., 243, *253*
Lipscomb, P., 261, *273*
Lipsitt, D. R., 153, *172*, 177, *187*
Lishman, W. A., 190, 197, 198, 200, 201, *203*
Liskow, B. I., 241, *253*
Lister, P., 180, *187*
Litwak, E., 264, *273*
Liv, J., 243, *253*
Livesley, W. J., 13, *14*, 82, *93*, 96, *115*, 122, *132*, 153, *172*
Locke, B., 240, *252*, 260, *272*
Loebel, J. P., 65, *67*, 69, 72, *93*
Loehlin, J., 8, *14*
Looper, J., 243, *254*
Loranger, A. W., 6, 12, *14*, 36, *51*, 64, 65, *67*, 72, 77, *93*, 129, 130, *132*
Lord, F. M., 142, *149*
Lowry, J. L., 289, *294*
Luborsky, L., 78, 79, 89, *92*
Luccioni, R., 200, *203*
Lund, D. A., 104, *114*
Luria, A. R., 192, *203*
Luscher, K., 100, *116*
Luttels, C., 217, *226*
Lyness, J. M., 65, *67*, 106, *113*
Lyons, M., 128, *132*, 159, *172*
Lytton, H., 138, *149*

M

Magaziner, J., 259, *273*
Magnusson, D., 97, 100, *115*
Maier, W., 39, 40, 41, *51*
Maisto, S. A., 81, *94*
Malamud, W. I., 169, *172*
Malatesta, V. J., 217, *225*
Malone Beach, E., 267, *272*
Maltsberger, J. T., 167, *172*
Manheimer, E. D., 103, *116*
Manis, 96, 98, *117*
Manton, K. G., 240, *252*, 260, *272*
Markowitz, P. J., 239, 243, *253*
Markus, H., 96, *114*
Marmion, J., 57, *67*, 70, 73, 76, *93*

Marquis, D. H., 147, 148, *149*
Marshall, G. N., 96, 103, *115*
Marshall, W. L., 215, 217, *226*
Martindale, B., 165, 169, *172*
Marty, P. 176, *187*
Marzillier, J. S., 81, *93*
Masling, J., 96, 98, *115*
Masterson, J. F., 242, *253*
Maurer, G., 235, *252*
Mavissakalian, M., 80, *93*
May, P. C., 202, *203*
Mayman, M., 96, 98, *117*
Mayran, L., 37, *50*
McAdams, D. P., 96, 97, 98, 111, *115*
McCann, J., 84, *92*
McCarthy, M. K., 78, 79, 82, *92*
McClelland, D., 96, 98, 111, *115*
McConkey, K. M., 96, *114*
McCrae, R. R. , 6, 7, *14*, 34, 36, 45, *50*, 62, *66*, 71, *93*, 96, 98, 99, 102, 106, 109, *113*, 114, *116*, 121, *132, 133,* 138, 146, *149*, 156, *172*
McCullough, L. B., 81, *94*, 281, *287*
McCurry, S. M., 215, *227*
McEntee, W. J., 202, *203*
McGlashen, T. H., 238, 242, *253*
McGuire, R. J., 78, 79, 89, *93*
McHugh, P. R., 56, *66*, 156, 161, *172*, 202, *203*
McKinlay, J. B., 202, *203*
McKinley, J. C., 127, 128, *132*
McLean, N. E., 245, *252*
McLellan, A. T., 241, *252*
Meeks, S., 104, *116*
Mehlman, R. D., 177, *187*
Melges, F. T., 158, *172*
Mellman, T., A., 40, 42, *51*
Mellsop, G., 159, *173*
Meltzer, H. Y., 239, *253*
Melville, M., L., 240, *252*, 260, *272*
Mendelson, M., 73, *92*
Merry, J., 99, *117*, 157, *173*
Mersch, P., 80, *93*
Messner, E., 167, *173*
Mezzich, T. E., 57, *67*, 246, *253*
Milandre, L., 200, *203*
Miller, L., 196, *203*
Millers, A. L., 81, *93*
Millin, T., 4, *14*, 36, *51*, 70, 75, 82, 84 *93*, 124, *133*
Mitchell, V., 107, *114*
Mitropoulou, V., 235, *254*

Miyawaki, E., 243, *254*
Moane, G., 107, *114*
Mock, J., 73, *92*
Modell, J. G., 193, *203*
Moen, 100, *116*
Moffitt, T. E., 104, *116*
Mohs, R. C., 235, *252*
Molinari, V., 55, 57, 63, *66, 67,* 70, 73, 76, *93*, 167, *173*, 281, *287*
Monahan, D. J., 103. 105, *115*
Monahan, P., 81, *92*
Moore, J. T., 65, *67*
Mor, V., 265, 266, *273*
Morey, L. C., 36, *51*
Morgan, D. G., 202, *203*
Morikawa, T., 79, 80, *94*
Morreim, E. H., 281, *287*
Morris, J. C., 224, *254*
Morris, J. N., 265, 266, *273*
Morris, P. L. P., 106, *116*
Morrow, J., 219, 223, *227*
Moss, M. B., 199, *204*
Mountz, J. M., 193, *203*
Mouton, A., 84, *92*
Moyer, J., 69, *93*
Mroczek, D. K., 147, *149*
Mueller, T. I., 37, *52*
Mull, C. E., 56, *66*
Mullen, J. T., 104, *116*
Mulsant, B. H., 55, 56, 57, 62, 65, *67,* 70, 71, 72, 73, 76, *93*, 101, *115*, 154, *173*
Mundim, F. D., 247, *254*
Murphy, K., 265, *273*
Murray, E. J., 71, 73, 74, 87, *92*
Murray, H. A., 100, *116*
Murray, R., 44, *50*
Murrell, S. A., 104, *116*
Mussen, P. H., 137, *149*
M'Uzan, m. de, 176, *187*
Myers, J. K., 56, *68*
Myers, W. A., 205, 213, *214*

N

Nardi, A. E., 247, *254*
Nasrallah, A., 43, *50*, 69, *92*
Nathan, J. H., 56, *66*
Nathan, S., 243, *254*
Nduaguba, M., 39, 41, *51*, 56, 62, *67*, 243, *253*
Neff, C., 6, *14*

Neilson, M., 44, *49*
Nelson, J., 42, *50*
Nelson-Grey, R. O., 34, *50*
Nemiroff, R. A., 164, *173*
Nesselroade, J. R., 140, *149*
Nestadt, G., 56, *66*, 156, 161, *172*, 202, *203*
Neugarten, B. L., 45, *51*, 106, *116*
Newman, D. L., 104, *116*
Newman, S. C., 56, *66*
Newsom, J. T., 104, 105, *116*
Nickel, E. J., 241, *253*
Nierenberg, A. A., 69, *92*, 245, *252*
Nietzel, M. T., 101, *116*
Noble, E., 241, *253*
Nobler, M. S., 57, *66*, 69, 72, *92*
Nonemaker, S., 266, *273*
Norman, D., 84, *92*
Northrop, L. E., 124, *132*
Nowlis, D., 243, *253*
Noyes, R., Jr., 247, *253*

O

O'Brien, C. P., 241, *252*
Oksenberg, L., 147, *150*
Oldham, J. M., 36, *51*64, 65, *67*, 72, 77, *93*, 130, *132*
O'Leary, A., 100, *113*
O'Leary, K. M., 195, 196, *204*
Olkin, I., 58, *67*
Orn, H., 56, *66*
Orr, W., 250, *251*
Orvaschel, H., 56, *67*, *68*, 240, *253*
Ostfeld, A. M., 258, *273*
Ouslander, J. G., 267, *273*
Outakoski, J., 201, *204*
Oxman, T. E., 103, *116*
Ozer, D. J., 147, *149*

P

Pallanti, S., 43, *50*
Pankratz, L., 153, *173*
Paris, J., 243, *253*
Parker, C. R., 217, *226*
Pasquier, F. 11, *14*
Pasternak, R., 55, 56, 57, 62, 65, *67*, 70, 71, 72, 73, 76, *93*, 101, *115*
Pasupathi, M., 107, *117*
Patience, D., A., 78, 79, 89, *93*
Patterson, G. R., 139, 144, *150*
Patterson, R. L., 220, 225, *226*

Patton, J. H., 36, *49*
Pava, J. A., 69, 78, 79, 82, *92*
Paykel, E. S., 78, *93*
Pazzagli, A., 43, *50*
Pease, R. W., Jr., 96, *117*
Penick, E. C., 241, *253*
Pennybacker, M., 240, *252*, 260, *272*
Perel, M. M., 243, *254*
Permutt, T., 259, *272*
Perry, J. C., 46, 47, *51*, 119, 133, 244, 246, 249, *254*
Perry, K. J., 80, *92*
Perry, S., 178, *187*
Peselow, E. D., 102, *116*
Peterson, J., 104, *117*
Petit, H., 11, *14*
Petry, S., 107, *116*, 200, *203*, 234, *253*
Pfohl, B., 36, 40, 42, 43, *51*, 52, 53, 69, 73, 75, *93*, *94*
Philbrick, P. B., 99, *113*
Phillips, C. D., 265, 266, *273*
Phillips, K. A., 250, *253*
Pierce, G. R., 103, *116*
Pilkonis, P. A., 31, 33, 34, 35, 38, 40, 42, 43, *49*, *51*, 52, 56, 63, *67*, 69, 78, 79, *93*, *94*
Pillemer, K., 277, *287*
Pinch, C. F., 202, *203*
Pincus, A., 146, *150*
Plomin, R., 8, 10, *14*
Podgorski, C. A., 259, 260, *274*
Pollack, J., 81, *94*
Poncet, M., 200, *203*
Pope, H. G., 242, *253*
Post, R. M., 40, 42, *51*
Potter, D. E. B., 259, *273*
Powell, B. J., 241, *253*
Powers, J. S., 153, *173*
Prigatano, G. P., 201, *204*
Prigerson, H. G., 104, 105, *116*
Prusoff, B., 78, *93*
Pryzbeck, T. R. , 10, *14*, 96, *113*, 234, *252*

Q

Qualls, S. H., 279, *287*
Qualmann, J., 200, *202*
Quinlan, D., 42, *50*

R

Rabins, P. V., 56, *66*, 156, 161, *172*, 202, *203*

Raphael, B., 104, *116*
Rapp, S. R., 258, *273*
Rathus, J. H., 81, *93*
Raudenbush, S. W., 140, *149*
Raulin, M., L., 124, *132*
Ray, M. W., 96, *117*
Reedy, M., 45, *49*
Rees, A., 79, 80, *92*
Regier, D. A., 39, 41, *52*, 56, *67*, 240, *253*
Reich, J., H., 39, 41, 42, 43, *51*, 56, 62, *67*, 243, 247, *253*
Reichborn-Kjennerud, T., 78, 79, *94*
Reider, R. O., 36, *51*, 128, *132*, 159, *172*
Reiss, B. F., 158, 165, 169, *173*
Renneberg, B., 80, *92*
Resnick, R. J., 239, 243, *252*
Retzlaff, P., 84, *92*
Reynolds, C. F., III, 104, 105, *116*
Reynolds, S., 79, 80, *92*
Rezabek, P., 281, *287*
Rhoades, J. A., 259, *273*
Riddell, J. D., 261, *273*
Rifai, A. H., 55, 56, *57*, 62, 66, *67*, 70, 71, 72, 73, 76, *93*, 101, *115*, 154, *173*
Robbins, M., 196, *204*
Robins, C. J., 102, *116*
Robins, E., 73, *94*
Robins, L. N. , 7, *14*, 39, 41, *52*, 56, *67*, 240, *253*, 254
Robinson, R. G., 106, *116*, 200, *204*
Rogers, H. J., 142, *149*
Roland, A., 280, *287*
Romanowski, A. J., 56, *66*, 156, 161, *172*, 202, *203*
Roose, S. P., 57, *66*, 69, 72, *92*
Rose, J., 74, *94*
Rose, M. K., 264, *273*
Rosen, J., 55, 56, 65, *67*, 70, 71, 72, 73, 76, *93*, 101, *115*
Rosenbaum, J. F., 41, *50*, 57, *67*, 69, 78, 79, 82, *92*, 245, *252*
Rosenberg, S. E., 36, *51*
Rosendahl, E., 55, 57, 62, 64, 65, *66*, 69, 70, 72, 73, 76, *91*101, *112*
Rosenfelt, R., 36, *51*
Rosowsky, E., 46, *51*, 52, 56, 62, *67*, 70, *94*, 111, *116*, 119, 120, 121, 123, 125, 126, *132*, *133*, 136, 144, *150*, 154, 155, 156, 157, 160, 161, 166, 170, *172*, *173*, 218, *226*, 242, 243, *254*, 261, 263, *273*
Ross, C., 37, *50*

Roth, L., 59, *68*, 70, *94*, 128, *133*
Roth, M., 201, *203*
Rotton, J., 102, *116*
Rovere, M. L., 200, *203*
Rovner, B. W., 259, *273*
Rubin, E. H., 224, *254*
Ruff, R. M., 196, *203*
Runyan, W. M., 97, *116*
Rush, J., 72, 84, *91*
Russakoff, L. M., 36, *51*, 64, 65, *67*, 72, 77, *93*, 130, *132*
Russo, J., 261, *273*

S

Sackeim, H. A., 57, *66*, 69, 72, *92*
Sacks, H. S., 58, *66*
Sadavoy, J., 45, 46, *52*, 111, *116*, 120, *133*, 136, 140, *150*, 153, 157, 161, *173*, 178, *187*, 216, 217, 219, 220, 223, 224, *226*, 261, 262, 266, *273*, 278, *287*
Sainton, K., 37, *50*
Sakado, K., 79, 80, *94*
Sallaerts, S., 217, *226*
Salzman, C., 243, *254*
Samuels, J. F., 56, *66*, 156, 161, *172*, 202, *203*
Sanderson, C., 121, *133*
Sanderson, W. C., 81, *93*
Sandler, A. M., 205, *214*
Sanfilipo, M. P., 102, *116*
Sarason, B. R., 103, *116*
Sarason, I. G., 103, *116*
Sato, S., 79, 80, *94*
Sato, T., 79, 80, *94*
Schaeffer, N. C., 143, *150*
Schaie, K., W., 45, *52*, 145, 146, *150*, 291, *294*
Schamess, G., 157, *173*
Schatzberg, A., 243, *254*
Schectman, K., 12, *14*
Scheier, M., 103, *117*
Schneider, L. S., 57, *68*, 102, *116*
Schneier, F. R., 247, *254*
Schnelle, J. F., 267, *273*
Schroder, P. I., 165, *173*
Schrodt, C. J., 57, *66*, 112, *113*
Schteingart, D. E., 202, *204*
Schulz, P. M., 239, 243, *252*
Schulz, R., 105, *113*, 103, *117*
Schulz, S. C., 239, 243, *252*, 253, *254*

Schut, A., 243, *252*
Schwartz, J., 102, *114*, 243, *254*
Schwartz, M., 74, *94*
Scott, A. I., 78, 79, 89, *93*
Searle, J. R., 27, *28*
Seeman, T., 12, *14*
Segal, D. L., 59, *68*, 70, *94*, 128, *133*, 159, 160, *173*
Seivewright, H., 156, *173*
Serin, R., 215, 217, *226*
Shamoian, C. A., 77, *91*
Shapira, J., 107, *116*, 200, *203*, 234, *253*
Shapiro, D. A., 79, 80, *92*
Shaw, B., 72, 84, *91*
Shea, D. G., 271, *274*
Shea, M. T., 34, 36, 37, 40, 42, 43, 44, *52*, 69, 71, 77, 78, 79, 80, 81, 82, 89, *94*, 101, *114*
Shear, M. K., 104, 105, *116*
Shearin, E. N., 103, *116*
Shedler, J., 96, 98, *117*
Shifren, K., 103, 105, *115*
Sickles, M., 239, *253*
Siegler, I. C., 104, 107, *117*
Siever, L. J., 10, *14*, 37, *52*, 195, *204*, 234, 235, *252*, *254*
Sifneos, P. E., 176, *187*
Silberman, C. S., 59, *68*, 70, *94*, 128, *133*
Silva, P., 104, *116*
Simeon, D., 243, *254*
Simmons, S., 69, *93*
Singer, T., 57, *66*, 69, 72
Skinner, E. A., 56, *67*
Sloane, B. R., 57, *68*, 102, *116*
Smyer, M. A., 258, 259, 265, 267, 270, 271, 272, *274*, 279, *287*
Smyth, K. A, 107, *113*
Soares, H. H., 264, *273*
Sobel, E. F., 169, *173*
Soldz, S., 99, *117*, 157, *173*
Soloff, P. H., 235, 243, *254*
Solomon, D. A., 37, *52*
Solomon, J. D., 161, 162, *173*
Solomon, K., 46, *52*, 237, 238, 240, 244, 249, *254*
Sotsky, S. M., 43, *52*, 69, 78, 79, *93*, *94*
Spayd, C. S., 265, *274*
Speer, D. C., 57, *68*
Sperry, L., 217, 219, *226*
Spielman, L., 48, *49*
Spiro, A., III, 147, *149*

Spitzer, R. L., 8, *15*, 73, 75, 92, *94*, 122, 128, 130, 131, *132*, *133*, 159, *172*, 217, 226
Spore, D. L., 267, *274*
Sprung, G. M., 169, *173*
Staats, N., 123, *132*
Stadtmuller, G., 200, *202*
Stam, M., 247, *252*
Stampfer, H. G., 102, *113*
Stangl, D., 36, 40, 42, 43, *51*, *52*, *53*, 69, 73, *93*, *94*
Starker, S., 153, *173*
Starkman, M. N., 202, *204*
Staudinger, U. M., 103, 104, *115*
Steele, H., 37, *50*
Steele, M., 37, *50*
Steffen, A., 74, *94*, 216, 218, 219, 220, 223, 225, *226*, 227
Stein, D. J., 235, 243, *254*
Steiner, M., 243, *253*
Steingard, R. J., 78, 79, 82, *92*
Steingart, A. B., 70, 71, 73, 75, 87, *94*
Stevens, S., 161, 162, *173*
Stevens-Long, J., 145, *150*
Stewart, G., 44, *49*
Stiles, W. B., 79, 80, *92*
Stolorow, R. D., 164, *173*
Stone, M. H., 4, *15*, 154, 159, 165, *173*
Strack, S., 84, *92*
Strahan, G. W., 258, 264, 266, *274*
Strain, J., 177, *187*
Straker, M., 237, *254*
Strauss, J. S., 242, *252*
Strauss, M. E., 107, *113*, *117*
Streit, A., 271, *274*
Striker, G., 46, *50*
Stroebe, M. W., 104, *117*
Stroebe, W., 104, *117*
Strupp, H., 33, *49*, *52*
Suarez, A., 224, *226*
Sudman, S., 147, 148, *150*
Susman, V. L. , 36, *51*, 64, 65, *67*, 72, 77, *93*, 130, *132*
Svasz, S., 175, *186*
Svrakic, D. M., 10, *14*, 96, *113*, 234, *252*
Swaminathan, H., 142, *149*
Swan, G. E., 103, *117*
Swartz, M. S., 158, *172*
Sweet, R. A., 55, 56, 57, 62, 65, *67*, 70, 71, 72, 73, 76, *93*, 101, *115*
Szetela, B., 200, *204*

T

Takemoto-Chock, N. K., 121, *132*
Takkunen, I., 201, *204*
Tariot, P. N., 259, 260, 266, 273, *274*
Tataryn, D. J., 96, *114*
Taube, J. E., 259, *272*
Tellegen, A., 96, *117*
Teri, L., 215, 220, *226, 227*
Thase, M. E., 217, *227*
Thoits, P. A., 103, *117*
Thomas, H. M., 241, *253*
Thompson, L. W., 38, *52*, 57, 62, 65, *68*, 69,
 70, 71, 72, 73, 74, 75, 83, 90, *94*,
 104, 107, *114*, *117*, 153, *173*, 216,
 217, 218, 219, 220, 221, 223, 225,
 227, 246, *254*, 279, 287, 289, *294*
Tiernari, P., 201, *204*
Tischler, G. L., 56, *68*
Tobias, B. A., 96, *114*
Tomlinson-Keasey, C., 102, *114*
Törestad, B., 97, *115*
Trestman, R. L., 235, *254*
Trexler, J. C., 261, 262, 264, *274*
Tricot, L., 119, *132*
Tripp, K., 277, *287*
Trivedi, S., 281, *287*
Trujillo, M., 81, *94*
Trull, T. J., 99, *117*, 121, 129, *133*, 146, *150*
Tucker, J. S., 102, *114*, *117*
Tucker, R. C., 121, *133*
Tupes, E. C., 121, *133*
Turkat, I. D., 81, *94*
Turret, N., 57, *66*, 69, 72, *92*
Tyrer, P., 40, 46, *50*, *52*, 62, *68*, 156, *173*

U

Uchino, B. N., 103, *117*
Uhde, T. W., 40, 42, *51*
Ulrich, R. F., 243, *254*
Umberson, D., 103, *115*
Unverzagt, F. W., 260, *272*
Ureno, G., 36, *51*

V

Vaillant, G. E., 244, 246, 249, *254*
Van Denburg, E., 84, *92*
Van Hasselt, V. B., 70, *94*, 128, *133*
Van Norstrand, J. F., 259, *272*

Varghese, F., 159, *173*
Vasile, R. G., 42, *51*
Vernon, P. A , 96, *115*
Versiani, M., 247, *254*
Vickers, R. R., Jr., 96, 103, *115*
Victor, M., 200, *204*
Viederman, M., 176, 178, 179, 180, *187*
Villasenor, V., S., 36, *51*
Vine, R. G., 70, 71, 73, 75, 87, *94*
Visotsky, H. M., 180, *187*
Von Dras, D. D., 104, *117*
Von Korff, M., 56, *67*, 261, 273
Vuchinich, S., 144, *150*

W

Wade, J. B., 121, *133*
Wagner, E., 261, *273*
Wagner, R., 259, *272*
Wagner, S. C., 243, *253*
Wainer, H., 143, *149*
Walker, J., 104, *116*
Walls, C., 267, *272*
Ward, C., 73, *92*
Warshaw, M. G., 37, *52*
Watkins, J., 40, 42, *52*, 69, *93*
Watt, D. F., 196, *204*
Weinberger, J., 96, 98, 111, *115*
Weiss, J. A. M., 240, *254*
Weissman, M. M., 6, *15*, 34, 36, 37, 39, 40,
 41, 48, *52*, 56, *67*, *68*, 78, *93*, 240,
 254
Welch, L., 193, *204*
Welsh, K. A., 107, *117*

Wesner, R., 81, *92*
Westen, D., 36, *52*, 157, 168, *174*
Westlake, R., 55, 57, 62, 65, *67*, 71, *92*, 156,
 172
Wetzler, C., 123, 129, *133*
Wetzler, S., 81, *93*
Whiffen, V., 101, 112, *114*
Whitbourne, S. K., 109, *117*
Whitehouse, P. I., 107, *113*
Widiger, T. A., 7, *15*, 33, 34, 35, 36, 40, 42,
 44, *50*, *51*, *52*, 69, 71, 77, 79, 80,
 82, 89, *94*, 99, *114*, *117*, 121, *132*,
 133, 146, *150*
Wiggins, J., 146, *150*
Wilcox, J. A., 243, *254*
Williams, J. B. W., 75, *94*, 122, 128, 130,
 132, 133, 159, *172*

Williamson, G. M., 103, *117*
Willis, S. L. , 45, *52*, 145, 146, *150*
Wingard, D., 102, *114*
Wink, P., 45, 49, *50*, 107, *117*
Winnicott, D. W., 17, *28*
Winston, A., 81, *94*
Wishaw, I. Q., 191, *203*
Wisocki, P. A., 215, 216, 218, *227*
Wolfe, R., 219, 223, *227*
Wolfson, A. N., 243, *254*
Woodbury, M., 240, *252*, 260, *272*
Woodruff, D., 45, *52*
Woody, G. E., 241, *252*
Woolf, H. B., 96, *117*
Workman, R. H., 281, *287*
Wortman, C. B., 96, *103*, *115*
Wright, E., 201, *204*
Wylie, H., 161, *174*
Wylie, M., 161, *174*

Y

Yates, W., 39, 41, *51*, 56, 62, *67*, 243, 247, *253*

Young, J. E., 218, 219, 220, 224, *227*
Young, L., 159, *172*
Young, R. C., 56, 57, 59, 64, 65, *66*, 70, 72, 77, *91*, *93*, 246, *251*

Z

Zammit, G. K., 72, *93*
Zanarini, M. C., 243, *252*
Zarit, J. M., 218, 221, *227*
Zarit, S. H., 218, 221, *227*, 260, *274*, *279*, *287*
Zeiss, A. M., 216, 218, 219, 220, 223, 225, *227*
Zemansky, M. F., 57, *68*, 102, *116*
Zimmerman, M., 36, 39, 40, 41, 42, 43, *51*, *52*, *53*, *69*, 73, *93*, *94*
Zinn, W. M., 166, *174*
Zubenko, G. S., 55, 56, 57, 62, 65, *67*, 70, 71, 72, 73, 76, *93*, *94*, 101, *115*
Zuroff, D., 101, *113*
Zweig, R. A., 46, 47, *50*, *53*, 69, 70, 71, 73, 76, *94*

Subject Index

A

Age, 41, 55–65, 119
  of onset, 70–72
Ageism, 276
Aging, 12, 44–47, 212–214
  and normal personality development, 45
  and personality disorders, 44–46
  process of, 180
  recognition of, 212–214
Alcohol, 200–201
Alzheimer's Disease, 107, 197–200, 234
Antianxiety, *see* pharmacologic treatment
Antidepressant medications, *see* Pharmacologic treatment
Antisocial Personality Disorder, *see* Personality disorders (specific)
Anxiety, 80–81
Assessment, 33–34, 63–65, 119–120, 124–126, 129–131
  clinician, 64, 72, 129–130
  interview, 63, 74–76, 130
  Personality Disorder Examination, 72, 130
  psychometric models, 141–144
  self-report, 35, 127
  Structured Interview for DSM–III–R PDs (SCID–II), 130–131
Avoidant Personality Disorder, *see* Personality disorders (specific)

B

Borderline Personality Disorder, *see* Personality disorders (specific)

C

Caregiving, 105
Cognition, 10–12
Cognitive Behavioral Therapy (CBT), 83–85, 215–221, 223–225
  characteristics of, 216
  treatment efficacy, 223–225
Compliance, 237–238, 241
Countertransference, *see also* Psychotherapy, 165–170, 270

D

Defenses, 161
Dementia, *see also* Alzheimer's Disease, 182–183, 197–200
  Alzheimer's type dementia, 197–198
  frontal lobe dementia, 198–199
  vascular dementia, 199–200
Demographic factors, 41–42
Dependent Personality Disorder, *see* Personality disorders (specific)
Depression, 43–44, 65, 70, 72–80, 101–102, 220
  and personality, 101–102
  major depression, 10, 43, 65, 219
  treatment outcome, 70, 72, 80
Depressive Personality Disorder, *see* Personality disorders (specific)
Difficult patient, the, 258, 261–262, 275
Diagnosis (DSM), 4–13, 31–35, 61–62, 75, 138, 189–190, 217, 224
  Axis I, 36–39, 42, 47–48, 69, 77, 83, 119, 225, 233–235, 271–272, 289–290, 293

Axis II, 4–6, 9–10, 36, 64, 123, 225, 271–272, 289–293
    models of personality diagnosis, 34–35, 121
    personality disorders, 4–13
Dying, *see* Life transitions

E

Epidemiology of personality disorder, 38–42
    association with demographic factors, 41–42
    prevalence of, 39–41, 56–59, 70–72
Ethical issues, 275–286
    philosophical, 280–282
    psychological, 278
    social, 276–278

F

Five-Factor Model (FFM), 96–99, 107–109, 121

G

Goodness of fit model, 263

H

Heart disease, 106
Hospital/hospitalization, 278–279

I

Inpatient psychiatric settings, 279–280
Interpersonal relationships, 231–232
Isolation, 103–104

L

Life events, *see* Life transitions
Life transitions, 37, 39–42, 104–106, 243–247
    bereavement, 104–105
    dying, 26–28, 102–103
    physical illness, 106, 175–186
Longitudinal research, 46, 101, 240
Long-term care, 279–280

M

Major depression, *see* Depression

Measurement issues, 33–36, 123–126, 130–131, 136–147
    appearance or disappearance of symptoms, 138–139
    changing relevance of symptoms, 138
    Differential Item Functioning (DIF), 143–144
    dynamic versus static variables, 140–141
    heterotypic continuity, 136–140, 144–145
    Item Response Theory (IRT), 141–144
    instrumentation, 126–127
    norms and standardized information, 125–126
    reliability, 121–125
    validity, 123–125
Meta-analysis, 56–58, 63–65, 70
Methodological issues, 120–123
Models of personality (and personality disorder), 34–35
    categorical, 34
    dimensional, 34–35
    prototypal, 34
Mood disorders, 42–44
    clinical presentation, 42
    treatment outcome, 43–44
Mortality, *see also* Dying, 102–103

N

Narcissistic Personality Disorder, *see* Personality disorders (specific)
Neuroanatomy/neuroanatomical, 190–194
    frontal lobe dementia, 11, 190, 198–199, 234
    hemispheric lateralization, 192
    parietal lobes, 192
    subcortical structures, 193–194
    temporal lobes, 191
    vascular dementia, 199
Neuropsychological components and personality disorder, 194
    attention, 194
    executive functions, 196–197
    memory, 196
    verbal mediation, 195–196
    visual perception, 195
Nursing Home Reform Act (NHRA), 259–260, 265–268
Minimum Data Set (MDS), 265–267

Resident Assessment Protocols
(RAPs), 265
Nursing home resident, difficult,
261–262, 264
Nursing homes, 257–272
assessment, 265–268
consultation, 268–270
policy affecting, 270–271
staff, 264
treatment in, 265–268

O

Obsessive Compulsive Disorder, *see* Personality disorders (specific)
Organic Personality Disorders, 61, 234

P

Paranoia, 185–186
Paranoid Personality Disorder, *see* Personality disorders (specific)
Personality, 175–186
disorder, 262–263
research, 4
style, 179–182, 262–263
Personality change, 100,106, 197–202
with dementia and related disorders,
197
with medical conditions, 201, 234
with stroke, 200
Personality disorder clusters, 5, 64,
71–75, 87–88, 156, 235–250,
276–280
Cluster A, 5, 75, 87–88, 156, 235–239
Cluster B, 5, 71, 75, 87–88, 156,
239–246, 276–279, 281
Cluster C, 5, 64, 71, 75, 87–88, 156,
246–250
Personality disorders (general), 69–91,
262–263
epidemiology/prevalence of, 6
methodological issues, 8–10, 13
symptoms, 217–218
theories, 45–46, 82–83
treatment, 217–221
treatment outcome, 43–44, 69–61,
81–82
versus style, 179–182, 262–263
Personality disorders (specific)
Antisocial Personality Disorder, 138,
239
Avoidant Personality Disorder,
246–248
Borderline Personality Disorder, 9, 47,
157, 167–168, 213–214,
217–218, 220, 241–244
Dependent Personality Disorder,
246–248
Depressive Personality Disorder,
250–251
Histrionic Personality Disorder,
244–245
Narcissistic Personality Disorder,
179–180, 183–184, 212–213,
220, 245–246
Obsessive Compulsive Disorder, 193,
218, 249–250
Organic Personality Disorder, 61, 234
Paranoid Personality Disorder,
235–238
Passive Aggressive Personality Disorder, 250–251
Schizoid Personality Disorder,
184–185, 238–239
Schizotpyal Personality Disorder,
238–239
Personality traits, 4–6, 34–36, 282–263
Pharmacologic treatment, 81–82, 230–251
antianxiety, 230
antidepressants, 43, 231–237, 243
antipsychotic, 230, 243
consultation, 243
Policy issues and Axis II disorders,
289–293
Psychometric issues, *see* Measurement issues
Psychotherapy (therapeutic), 157–171
alliance, 158–159,163
challenges of, 18–19, 165–170, 270
countertransference, 165–170, 270
developmental work at old age,
161–163
differential identification, 159–161
goals, 170–171
importance of, 18
patient–therapist relationship,
157–158, 161, 167–168
transference, 163–165

S

Schizoid Personality Disorder, *see* Personality disorders (specific)

Schizotypal Personality Disorder, *see* Per-
        sonality disorders (specific)
Self-rating of personality disorders, *see*
        also Assessment, 35, 127–129
    Million Clinical Multiaxial Inventory
        (MCMI), 75, 81, 85–87, 128
    Minnesota Multiphasic Personality
        Inventory (MMPI), 127–128,
        145
    NEO–PI & NEO–PI–R, 7–8, 107,
        109–110
    Personality Disorder Questionnaire
        (PDQ), 128
    self-report inventories, 35, 127–129
Senile dementia, *see* Alzheimer's Disease
Social support, *see* Isolation

Stroke, 200
Suicide, 109–112

T

Temperament, 4–10
Transference, 163–165
Treatment models, 72–80, 82, 212–214
    cognitive-behavioral, 218–225
    contextual, cohort-based, maturity,
        specific challenge model
        (CCMSC), 290–293
    psychoanalysis/psychoanalytic,
        175–176, 280
    psychobiologic models, 234–235
    psychodynamic therapy/treatment,
        205–214